KEY PEOPLE, PLACES, AND EVENTS

The
HISTORY BUFF'S GUIDE
to the
CIVIL WAR

THOMAS R. FLAGEL

CUMBERLAND HOUSE

NASHVILLE, TENNESSEE

THE HISTORY BUFF'S GUIDE TO THE CIVIL WAR
PUBLISHED BY CUMBERLAND HOUSE PUBLISHING, INC.
431 Harding Industrial Drive
Nashville, Tennessee 37211
www.cumberlandhouse.com

Cover design by Gore Studio Inc., Nashville, Tennessee

Library of Congress Cataloging-in-Publication Data

Flagel, Thomas R., 1966–
  The history buff's guide to the Civil War / Thomas R. Flagel.
     p.   cm.
  Includes bibliographical references and index.
  ISBN-13 978-1-58182-371-4
  ISBN-10 1-58182-371-1 (pbk. : alk. paper)
  1. United States—History—Civil War, 1861–1865. 2. United States—History—Civil War, 1861–1865—Miscellanea. I. Title.
  E468.F57 2003
  973.7—dc21

                                                                      2003011445

Printed in Canada

4 5 6 7 8 9 10—10 09 08

For Mom, Dad, and Theresa

Contents

Prologue

WHILE COMPOSING THIS WORK, I had the pleasure of visiting numerous museums, archives, libraries, and battle sites. Amid them all, one stop stands out in my memory. At a battlefield park, while walking toward a row of cannon, I happened upon a family taking in the surroundings. Their young son, not more than ten years of age, scanned the particulars of the engagement from a bronze plaque. After reading a calculation of dead and wounded, the youth said out loud to himself, "Well, at least we got as many of them as they got of us."

Of all unions, one is indissoluble: the bond between present and past. We hold this truth to be self-evident in the case of the United States and its Civil War. More has been written about this conflict than any other event in the country's history. Debates continue over battlefield preservation and reparations to descendants of slaves. In the national capital, the Lincoln Memorial receives ten times the number of visitors than either the Jefferson Memorial or the Washington Monument. Although with malice toward none, a small boy can read of Americans fighting Americans and mentally picture it as "us versus them." Like the CSS *Hunley* and the turret of the USS *Monitor,* the war resurfaces and resides everlasting within the public culture.

Concerning my own connections, my great-great-great grandfather, Andrew Jackson Cook, served as a private during William Tecumseh Sherman's legendary March to the Sea. A distant uncle of mine died at the head of his regiment at the 1862 battle of Corinth, Mississippi. When my great uncle was a boy, he knew a handful of aged veterans, one of whom spoke infrequently and unhappily about his experiences in the infantry, and those stories were passed on to me.

Personally, I focused my early academic attentions on the history of modern Europe, primarily diplomatic and ethnic relations. Over the years, however, I began to delve deeper into the specter of the War

Between the States. Along with my increasing involvement, I was struck by the sincere desire from pupils and the general public to learn more about the subject. In spite of their curiosity, many communicated a frustration with the sheer volume of available material. Indeed, there are more than fifty thousand texts on the war alone, plus countless articles and dissertations.

I could at least advise not to begin with the popular treatment of the topic. In novels, films, and prevailing assumptions, the Civil War is often portrayed as a nationwide demonstration of unmatchable courage and honor, where all involved were ultimately victorious. Although noble, such sentiments hinder perspective. Field generals become faultless icons. Battles take on reputations far beyond their actual effect. From statesmen to widows, everyday people seem capable of nothing but grandiose acts of pure valor.

Concurrently, the mountains of literature can be just as muddling. Works are often too light and trivial to be of substance, or they are too narrow in scope or presentation to provide a solid sense of the big picture. The war appears simultaneously as a historical crossroads and a confounding tangle of cross-connections. The overriding question emerges: Where in the world to begin?

To clear the powder smoke, I sought to create a work of substantive launching points for new Civil War readers that would also furnish usable information and conversation fodder for aficionados. I found that one of the best ways to achieve these ends was to describe the people, places, and events of the war through lists. After three years of research, confirmations, consultations, and analysis, the end result is this bound volume.

Every list overtures with background information and criteria for the respective topic. Where appropriate, names and words appear in SMALL CAPS to indicate a subject appearing in another list. This collection is by no means a total account, since the number of potential lists is as infinite as the breadth of the war itself. Topics have been chosen for their respective capacity to illustrate the war's fundamental aspects in the most succinct way practicable. Some lists appear in chronological sequence to demonstrate progression. Others are ranked according to quality and quantity, placing the more renowned aspects of the war in their proper context.

The ultimate aim of the text is to furnish perspective on topics often maligned, misunderstood, or overlooked. This book is not intended to be the last word on the Civil War. Hopefully, it is an inaugural word, an accepted invitation to further explore one of the most pivotal and enduring chapters in American history.

This work never would have come to fruition without the better angels of my nature. Among this legion of the exceedingly tolerant and supportive are mentors Dr. Gladys Daly of Mount Mercy College and Dr. Marion "Buddy" Gray of Western Michigan University and my family and friends. Chief creative consultants are Michael Bryant of the U.S. Department of Education, Dr. Glenn Janus of Coe College, and the Prairiewoods Writer's Group of Cedar Rapids, Iowa. Karl Green of Cedar Rapids deserves the title of morale officer as well as editor. Much of my perspective on national parks and veterans issues comes from the wisdom of Edward Portz of Andrew, Iowa. The direction and professionalism of Ron Pitkin and Ed Curtis of Cumberland House Publishing in Nashville, Tennessee, have been most helpful. Ann and Tom Winner of Las Vegas, Nevada, provided considerable legal instruction; Frank Safranek of Omaha, Nebraska, assisted in archival work; and Mary Elworth of Chicago, Illinois, issued much-needed lessons in marketing. I am dependent on many archives and libraries for their assistance, particularly the Iowa State Historical Society, the University of Texas, the University of Iowa, Coe College, and the Durham Western Heritage Museum of Omaha. Lastly, my eternal gratitude goes to the history departments of Loras College and Kansas State University for guiding me in the discipline.

ANTEBELLUM

TOP TEN CAUSES OF THE CIVIL WAR

There was no single cause of the American Civil War. The initiation of armed hostility between groups required a complex networking of physical and intangible conditions, none of which the brightest minds in anthropology, political science, psychology, or any other discipline have been able to measure. Perhaps the best that can be done is to examine underlying differences between the warring parties and to look for possible sources and substances of those differences.

The following are ten key circumstances contributing to the division of the United States. A few were centuries in the making; others were relatively new phenomena. All progressively changed a relatively homogenous country into two distinct and confrontational sections, where "e pluribus unum" devolved into "us versus them."[1]

1. NORTHERN INDUSTRIALIZATION

At the beginning of the nineteenth century, considerable parity existed between North and South in terms of industry. In general, very little industrialization existed, and most manufacturing was done in homes or in small shops. When steam was harnessed, however, the production process migrated from farmhouses to factories. Inventions came from names such as Morse, Colt, Goodyear, McCormick, Fulton, and Singer, as did investment capital from families such as Rothschild and Vanderbilt.

Yet most of this industrialization took place in Northern states, and by 1860 the resulting disparity was striking. For every engineer in the South, there were six in the North. For every ship constructed in a Southern port, the North made ten. Free states milled seventeen times as much cotton, mined twenty times the amount of pig iron, produced thirty times the number of boots and shoes, and manufactured thirty-two times the amount of firearms as slave states. Indiana had more than two thousand miles of railroad track while Arkansas had thirty-eight.[2]

In the Deep South the wise investment was cotton, feeding the hungry mills of New and Old England with the most profitable crop in the United States. As a consequence, much of the North's capital went into factories, while most of the South's money went into the fields. In terms of wealth, investment, production, and labor, the country was dividing into two distinct entities.[3]

In 1860 Massachusetts produced more manufactured goods than the entire Deep South.

2. DISPARITY IN POPULATION

Paralleling industry, the distribution of the national population between sections was relatively equitable in the first years of the United States. Then high birth rates and immigration expanded the numbers quickly. In 1800 the national population stood at 5.3 million. By 1830 it had reached nearly 13 million. By 1860 the country climbed to 32 million people. Yet the sectional balance in the House of Representatives was long gone.

More than 22 million Americans lived in free states. Fewer than 10 million lived in slave states, and 4 million of those were the slaves themselves. Even with the constitutional measure of a slave as three-fifths of a person, Pennsylvania and New York had more seats in Congress than Alabama, Arkansas, Florida, Georgia, Louisiana, Mississippi, North Carolina, South Carolina, and Texas put together. Early on, Southern lawmakers realized that to be as effective in national politics as they had been in earlier days, they would have to rely on concessions over consensus.[4]

In 1860 the largest city in the United States was New York with nearly one million inhabitants. The twenty-seventh largest city was Richmond, Virginia, with thirty-seven thousand.

3. THE MORAL DEBATE OVER SLAVERY

For more than two hundred years whites generally treated slavery in North America as an uncomfortable predicament, a "peculiar institution" to be tolerated. A change of course came in 1831 when abolitionist WILLIAM LLOYD GARRISON dispensed with the civil dialectic and publicly repudiated slave owners as barbaric tyrants. Inducing a more direct reaction was the literate preacher, carpenter, and slave Nat Turner, who in the same year led the bloodiest slave uprising in Southern history. Both men prompted a pro-slavery backlash. Slavery's defenders proclaimed the peculiar institution as the only peaceful means of racial coexistence.[5]

In a decade, the "moral good" of slavery became a frequent theme among Southern lawmakers such as Sen. JOHN C. CALHOUN and newspaper editor ROBERT BARNWELL RHETT. Periodicals, including the CHARLESTON MERCURY and New Orleans trade magazine *De Bow's Review,* presented articles and editorials describing the virtuous role of slave ownership. Countering this, more than 250,000 Northerners joined antislavery societies by 1840.[6]

In print, politics, and the pulpit, both sides used ethics, biology, the Bible, economics, and the Declaration of Independence to defend their respective position. Always in the minority and often at odds internally, the two camps gave an impression of conspiratorial unity to their opposition. Slavery advocates appeared as a cohesive "Slavocracy," controlling not only four million slaves but also the nation as a whole. Likewise, many viewed abolitionists as wild-eyed radicals willing to break the law and incite riots whenever and wherever they could. This mutual suspicion only worsened with an 1857 Supreme Court Dred Scott decision and the 1859 arsenal raid at Harpers Ferry involving JOHN BROWN.[7]

In 1837 Presbyterians split into two sects over slavery, as did the Methodists in 1844 and the Baptists in 1845.

---

4. THE GROWTH OF SOUTHERN NATIONALISM THROUGH "STATES' RIGHTS"

Effective movements have effective rallying cries. All-encompassing slogans such as "Solidarity," "Lebensraum," and "Rule Britannia" have united disparate groups into powerful political entities. Such was the case with "states' rights" in the antebellum South.

In existence since the Federalist versus Antifederalist contest over the U.S. Constitution, the term achieved widespread popularity in 1828 and 1832 when Congress issued excessively high import tariffs against the wishes of several Southern states. Thereafter, the states' rights card became a popular Southern response to any unpopular national policy.

In reality, the federal government in 1860 was still a political runt. The country had no national bank, no national currency, no income tax, a minuscule army, the lowest import tariffs in fifty years, and an annual budget of a humble $70 million. Concurrently, states' rights advocates, such as Jefferson Davis of Mississippi, were very selective in application of the mantra. They demanded local supremacy over tariffs, slavery, and control of territories but called for a strong national government to enforce the Fugitive Slave Law, annex Texas, engage in a war with Mexico, and push for annexation of Cuba.[8]

More of a catch phrase than a policy, states' rights unified an otherwise divisive South. Landed gentry and the landless, bankers and the impoverished, slave owners and sharecroppers developed a cohesive lobby, a "David versus Goliath" platform against growing Northern influence.[9]

But now when Northern treachery attempts our rights to mar,
we hoist on high the bonnie blue flag that bears a single star.
                    —Lyrics to "Bonnie Blue Flag" (1861)

---

5. INTRUSION OF SLAVERY INTO FREE STATES

In 1858 when accepting his party's nomination for the U.S. Senate, Abraham Lincoln delivered his now famous "House Divided" speech, in which he warned: "I believe this government cannot endure permanently half slave and half free. . . . It will become all one thing or all the other." His comments stemmed from two incidents in particular: the 1850 Fugitive Slave Law and the 1857 Dred Scott decision.[10]

The former was one of five bills within the Compromise of 1850, a set of measures intended to offer concessions to both slave and free-soil advocates. A similar law had been in effect since the adoption of the Constitution, which required federal participation in capturing runaway slaves. The 1850 version stipulated that any black in a free state could be accused of being a fugitive slave. U.S. marshals were obligated to assist in searching for the accused, as were any citizens the marshals deputized. Expenses for capturing and returning slaves were borne by the U.S. Treasury. The accused could not testify on his own behalf nor could he call or question witnesses. Anyone aiding the accused was subject to prosecution. Any state law protecting the personal liberties of African Americans was null and void in fugitive cases.[11]

Allowed to remove "property" *from* free states by way of the Fugitive Slave Law, slave owners were also able to bring their "property" *into* free states after the Dred Scott decision. Scott was a slave whose owner had taken him into a free state and free territory, and the slave sued for his freedom. In a majority ruling, the Supreme Court dismissed his suit on a technicality, claiming Scott was not a citizen and therefore could not bring a case to federal court.

Rather than leave the decision as it was, Chief Justice Roger Taney stated African Americans were "so far inferior, that they had no rights which the white man was bound to respect." In other words, a person of African heritage, free or slave, was not a citizen. Further, the Court declared, the 1820 Missouri Compromise—which forbade slavery west of Missouri and north of 36° 30' latitude—was unconstitutional, as it restricted the right of property. In short, the Supreme Court denied citizenship to freedmen, curtailed free states' rights, and permitted slave owners to take their slaves anywhere they wished. Many Northerners began to suspect states' rights only meant "slave states' rights."[12]

> On March 4, 1861, Abraham Lincoln was inaugurated the sixteenth president of the United States. He was sworn in by the man who rendered the Dred Scott decision, Chief Justice Roger Taney—Southerner, former slave owner, and defender of Southern states' rights.

6. THE GROWTH OF NORTHERN NATIONALISM THROUGH "UNION"

Frustrated by the disproportionate political leverage of the less populated, less wealthy Southern states, many in the North began to romanticize regional differences. As with states' rights in the South, a mythical ideal of "Union" began to emerge in the North. The Union represented free labor, public education, and federal funding for public works such as canals and railroads. If the South could celebrate a world of aristocracy and agriculture (supported by slavery), the North could brag about populism and progress (supported by seventy-hour workweeks and child labor).

Central to the ideology of the Union was the underlying principle of democracy: the right of the majority. To repeatedly concede to the minority on issues, especially concerning free labor and free soil, was wholly undemocratic. Pointing to the Constitution's preamble, many Northerners began to consider themselves as "We the People" pitted against a South that appeared unwilling to "form a more perfect Union."[13]

In 1864 Lincoln officially ran for the presidency as a member of the Union Party, a coalition party of Republicans and War Democrats.

---

7. TERRITORIAL EXPANSION

By 1820 it was well established which states would be free or slave. Territories, however, were open for debate, and there would be much to fight over. Less than a million square miles in 1800, the United States nearly doubled with the Louisiana Purchase (1803) and almost doubled again after the war with Mexico (1846–48).

Armed with the popular ideology of "Manifest Destiny," many citizens North and South considered the continent, if not the hemisphere, the divine right of the United States. This aggressive foreign policy against Spanish, British, French, and Native American holdings fed the ravenous appetite of an expanding population and economy. It also created a showdown of "winner take all" between slavery and free-soil sections.[14]

The contrived war with Mexico was a thinly veiled attempt by Southern statesmen to secure more slave states. In the same light, Northerners pushed for homestead bills to virtually pay people to settle the Midwest and cried "54-40 or Fight" in demanding all of the vast Oregon Territory from Britain.

The greed turned to warfare with the 1854 Kansas-Nebraska Act. The U.S Constitution was not specific on whether the states or the federal government controlled the territories. With disputes escalating for and against either position, Illinois Sen. Stephen A. Douglas proposed a compromise: The residents of the territory in question would decide. Calling it "popular sovereignty," Douglas and many of the congressmen who passed the bill assumed antislavery settlers would choose Nebraska and pro-slavery settlers would move into Kansas.

Kansas, however, was north of the traditional 36° 30' line between free and slave soil. In a prequel to the larger version in 1861, the area devolved into civil war. In 1855 pro-slavery "Bushwackers" and antislavery "Jayhawkers" swarmed into the territory. Voter fraud turned into armed threats then open warfare. For five years, and well into the Civil War, the territory became aptly known as "Bleeding Kansas."[15]

On a national level, the conflict destroyed the Whig Party, cracked the dominant Democrats into North and South factions, and inspired a new party that would rise to the presidency in six years.[16]

During the presidency of James K. Polk, the United States acquired more than five hundred thousand square miles of territory—more than the land area of France, Italy, and Germany combined.

---

8. POOR LEADERSHIP

In 1858 future Secretary of State William H. Seward referred to the sectional crisis as an "irrepressible conflict." In so many words, Seward considered armed hostility as inevitable between slave and nonslave regions—a position shared by many contemporary observers. No party, no person, no movement was capable of diffusing any of the growing differences between the sections because the differences were too great. The Civil War was inevitable, so the argument went.

Countering this "inevitability" view is a distinct fact: The most prominent politicians of the time exaggerated rather than pacified differences. Antislavery, pro-slavery, Unionist, and states' rights spokesmen opted for confrontation over cooperation. Ultimately, the shortsighted tactic cost many of these hard-liners their authority, property, and lives.[17]

In the middle, advocates of compromise often lacked the ingenuity to offer anything but a set of offsetting offenses, as in the case of the Kansas-Nebraska Act. Perhaps the best example of poor statesmanship was the Executive Mansion itself. Between 1836 and the start of the war, all occupants were one-term presidents. Unable or unwilling to fully address the growing differences between North and South, incumbents lost reelection and, in some cases, failed to be renominated.

There was arguably one exception to this pattern. In 1848 Zachary Taylor won the presidency. Hero of the Mexican War, he had no political baggage. He in fact had never held elected office before. Born in Virginia, hailing from Louisiana, Taylor owned slaves, but he pledged to halt the extension of slavery and encouraged the admission of New Mexico and California as free states. When Southerners threatened secession, Taylor countered with the threat of military action, vowing to catch and hang anyone who dared oppose the laws of the nation. As a result, the Union held together. Yet in 1850, after only eighteen months in office, Taylor experienced a sudden digestive ailment and died.

> While a colonel in the U.S. Army, Zachary Taylor initially forbade his daughter to marry one of his officers, a lieutenant by the name of Jefferson Davis.

9. THE ASCENDANCY OF A SECTIONAL PARTY

Historically, major political parties in the United States were not exclusive to regions. In 1854, however, a new party emerged. Dedicated to internal improvements, protective tariffs, and the containment of slavery, the Republican Party grew from an idea to a political power in two

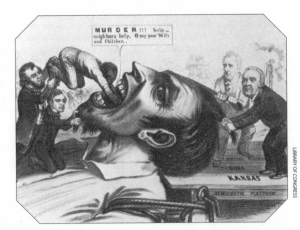

An 1856 Republican cartoon depicts its opposition to the popular-sovereignty issue in Kansas. Although the party made little inroads politically in the elections that year, four years later a Republican won the White House.

years, winning a third of all congressional seats and a third of the popular vote for president. Yet the party existed almost exclusively in and catered to the North.[18]

If the Republicans were to win the presidency, many in the South feared the nation's direction on slavery and other issues would not be to their choosing. Southern newspapers and lawmakers threatened a wave of secession in 1856 if JOHN C. FRÉMONT, a Republican, were elected. Instead, bachelor Democrat James Buchanan won, and the crisis appeared to pass.

Yet after four years of ineptitude, Buchanan became persona non grata across the country and even within his own party. Democrats failed to agree on a replacement candidate and split their numbers between Kentucky's John Breckinridge and Illinois's Stephen A. Douglas. In the resulting fissure of the largest political party in the United States, the candidate from the second-largest party won the White House.

Four days after the Republican victory, the South Carolina legislature called for a convention to consider secession. By December 20 the Palmetto State left the Union. Six more states soon followed.[19]

Tennessee Democrat Andrew Johnson (later to be president after the death of Lincoln) lambasted the separatists, arguing, "Then what is the issue? It is because we have not got our man." The London *News* was even more adamant: "And what outrage roused the reluctant men of peace at last? What was the Stamp Act of the present occasion? It was the loss of an election, a Constitutional election conducted in a regular and orderly way." The Republicans, however, were not listed on a single ballot in any Deep South state. The party of the North won the necessary electoral votes with less than 40 percent of the popular vote.[20]

Ultimately, it was not a proviso, uprising, court case, or moral crusade that triggered actual secession. The catalyst was the lawful election of a candidate who opposed the expansion of slavery into any territory in which it did not presently exist. Yet slavery was an "institution" on which a portion of the country depended for political, economic, and in many minds, cultural survival.[21]

Before settling on the title Republicans, the founders of the fledgling party called themselves the Independent Party, the Anti-Nebraska Party, and the People's Party.

---

10. SOUTHERN DEPENDENCE ON SLAVERY

To mention slavery as a primary cause of the Civil War is to invite comments to the contrary. In academic environments and elsewhere such a stance is generally considered frivolous, misinformed, naive. The reaction is almost Pavlovian.

Incentives to resist the slavery theory are manifold, but the overlaying motivation may be to preserve a sense of—for lack of a better term—reunion. A characteristic outcome of many wars is an eventual desire for reconciliation, which in the case of a reunified country is almost a matter of necessity. To create an environment of cooperation requires a reconstruction of dignity for the vanquished and a reformation of the past for the victor.[22]

Concerning the American Civil War, armed conflict erupted when one section split away and the other resisted. The departing section left to protect, among other things, a third of its wealth, over half of its labor force, its primary vehicle for economic opportunity, and its fundamental definition of social structure—in other words, slavery.

When the Southern states seceded in 1860 and 1861, they did not leave in the order of their geographic location, economic standing, political qualities, or level of industrialization. They left in almost the exact order of their percentage of slaves.

True, just one in three families in the South owned slaves, but in the 1861 convention that formed the Confederacy, 98 percent of the delegates were slave owners. The constitution they formed mentioned slavery more than any other subject. Selected as the Confederacy's vice president, Alexander H. Stephens declared in a speech made soon after the convention: "African slavery as it exists among us—the proper status of the negro in our form of civilization. This was the immediate cause of the late rupture and the present revolution." Robert H. Smith of Alabama concurred, adding, "We have dissolved the late Union chiefly because of the negro quarrel."[23]

The United States in 1860:

   Total value of all capital investments in manufacturing = $1 billion in gold

   Total value of all capital investments in slaves = $2 billion in gold

---

TOP TEN STATES WITH THE HIGHEST
PERCENTAGE OF SLAVES

"The Migration or Importation of such Persons as any of the States now existing shall think proper to admit, shall not be prohibited by the Congress prior to the Year one thousand eight hundred and eight."—Article 1, Section 9 of the U.S. Constitution

Historians estimate 550,000 Africans were imported for slavery into North America between the development of Jamestown, Virginia, in 1619 and the constitutional halt to the importation of slaves in 1808. As many as 50,000 were brought in illegally afterward. These 600,000 constituted approximately 8 percent of all individuals sold out of sub-Saharan Africa to the Americas, North Africa, Europe, and South Asia.[24]

Globally, slave populations did not sustain themselves. Combining exhaustive labor with poor food and shelter made for short lives. In the United States, however, the slave population rose steadily year after year, to where 600,000 Africans became 4 million African Americans by the eve of the war. Defenders of slavery attributed the growth to contented slaves and caring masters. Abolitionists credited the expansion to slave owners who bred their subjects. If asked, the slaves might have suggested the increase came from a natural desire to create families.

Principle causes were less preconceived. Most of the imported slaves were male. Over time, domestic slave births leveled the ratio of men to women. Tolerance to diseases in the Americas improved from generation to generation. Most significantly, a growing number of owners in the United States created an increase in the number of slave communities. All of these conditions offered opportunities for the enslaved to find companions, albeit in trying circumstances, and live long enough to bear children.[25]

Pre–Civil War accounts of slavery "dying out" came from those living in the oldest states in the Union, where indeed slavery was on the decline. In 1776 eleven of the thirteen original states held slaves. By 1800 the ratio was down to six of the thirteen. As Deep South crops of sugar, rice, and cotton became highly profitable ventures, many slave owners left their homes in Delaware, Virginia, Kentucky, and elsewhere in pursuit of new and open growing areas, bringing with them an insatiable demand and astounding supply of chattel labor.[26]

By 1860 most slaves lived in the Deep South. In 1860 dollars these four million (or one out of eight Americans) had an estimated worth of more than two billion dollars. In a matter of a century, slavery grew from a peculiar institution to the foundation of the Southern economy.

Along with the ten states listed here, five other states had significant proportions enslaved in 1860: Tennessee (25 percent—275,000 slaves), Kentucky (20 percent—225,000), Maryland (13 percent—87,200), Missouri (10 percent—115,000), and Delaware (2 percent—1,800). Slave numbers in these states were stable if not in decline. Nearly half of Maryland's 170,000 blacks were free. Delaware's capital city, Wilmington, had a total of 4 slaves. Still, slavery was widespread enough in these areas to create great divisions of loyalty among their respective citizenry.

Below are the states with the highest proportion of slaves to total population, according to the 1860 Census.

1. SOUTH CAROLINA (57.1%)

Home to some of the most committed Secessionists, a long-time vanguard to states' rights, first out of the Union, and the state that fired upon Fort Sumter, South Carolina also had the highest ratio of slaves to free people. For every three free citizens, there were four slaves. In some coastal areas, only one out of ten people were free. Of its growing population, 402,400 in South Carolina were slaves.

South Carolina also ranked first in the country with the highest proportion of slave-owning families, with nearly half possessing one or more persons. The principle crops dependent on chattel labor were rice and indigo along the coastlines and cotton farther inland.[27]

Unlike newer states farther south and west, the Palmetto State had a long history with slavery. Enslaved Native Americans and indentured whites provided labor in the colony's early years. In 1690 traders and owners began importing African slaves.

Before the age of cotton, rice was a lucrative commodity. The plant grew well in the malarial marshlands of the Carolina coast, and plantation owners acquired scores of Africans to perform the arduous work. Before slave importation was abolished, Charleston was one of the chief ports of entry for African labor. At the constitutional convention, South Carolina and Georgia expressed no interest in ratifying any document

LIBRARY OF CONGRESS

This 1862 image preserves a rare instance in which five generations of a South
Carolina slave family remained together on the same plantation.

that prohibited the international slave trade—a harsh stance both states
later modified.[28]

> From 1834 to 1865, it was illegal under South Carolina law to brand slaves.
> It was also deemed illegal to teach slaves to read and write.

2. MISSISSIPPI (55.1%)

In 1860 two states contained more slaves than free people: Mississippi
and South Carolina. Eleven of twenty Mississippians were slaves, and in
two counties (Issaquena and Washington) the ratio was almost nineteen
of twenty. The majority of slaves worked cotton plantations along the Mississippi River Valley.

Like most states in the Deep South, Mississippi experienced a population explosion in the nineteenth century, helped considerably by a booming cotton market. From 1830 to 1840 the price of cotton increased fourfold. In turn, there were 70,000 people in 1830 Mississippi classified as property. By 1840 that number had tripled. By 1860 it had more than doubled again to 437,000. Nearly half of all white families in Mississippi owned slaves, second again only to South Carolina.[29]

Larger slave populations usually meant harsher slave codes, and the Mississippi legislature enacted some of the strictest slave laws in the South. In 1857 a revised state law forbade an owner from freeing a slave under any circumstances. Those persons already freed were required to leave the state. Despite an overall population of 791,300 in 1860, only 773 were free African Americans.[30]

On February 10, 1861, Mississippian Jefferson Davis learned by telegram that he had been selected as provisional president of the Confederacy. The messenger was one of his slaves.

---

3. GEORGIA (48.2%)

In 1776 there were 16,000 slaves in Georgia, about equivalent to the number of slaves in the state of New York at the time. Plantation crops were rice in the coastal areas and tobacco farther inland. In 1792, while traveling in Georgia, Northern-educated Eli Whitney fashioned a simple and easily duplicated cotton gin, or engine, which separated seed from cotton three hundred times faster than by hand. Within two years national cotton exports increased twelvefold. By the mid-nineteenth century, the mechanized looms of England were processing more than a million tons of cotton, and the once floundering and costly practice of slavery was fully entrenched in American commerce.[31]

Second to Texas in land area and second to Virginia in farm acreage, Georgia's slave population ballooned accordingly. In 1800 there were 60,000 slaves. Thirty years later there were 217,500. By 1860 the number had grown to 462,000, almost as many slaves as there were in all of Cuba.[32]

Of the original thirteen colonies, only Georgia initially forbade slavery—a stance it reversed in 1750.

---

4. LOUISIANA (46.8%)

To scare slaves into obedience, a slave owner in a Border State might threaten to sell them "down south." Many times the owner was referring to the sugar fields of Louisiana. Cultivating sugar was notoriously harsh work, due in no small part to the proximity of the work to pestilence. Prime growing areas were in the flood plains and bayous of the Louisiana Delta, where diseases prospered. Sugar also required large work forces, which were almost universally treated with less care than smaller slave holdings. Some of the largest plantations in the South were in Louisiana. The state ranked first in the number of owners with 100 or more slaves (547).[33]

Although producing most of the country's sugar, Louisiana dedicated the majority of its tilled acreage to cotton, which grew predominately in the northwest part of the state along the Red River Basin.[34]

Before he died at the Alamo, knife-wielding Jim Bowie owned, traded, and smuggled slaves in Louisiana.

5. ALABAMA (45.1%)

Alabama and its neighbor Mississippi were living proof that the "Old South" was in fact very new. When Alabama became a state in 1819 there were some 100,000 inhabitants within its newborn borders. In 1830 there were 300,000. By war's start, the population had reached 1 million, and nearly half were classified as property by the state constitution.

Big plantation owners ruled in Alabama. In 1860 a mere .3 percent of the white population owned 30 percent of the slaves, 30 percent of the land, and 28.1 percent of the wealth. Cotton dominated the state's commerce, and the state was master of cotton, producing nearly a quarter of the nation's total in 1860.[35]

The capital at Montgomery served as the first seat of the Confederacy, from March to July 1861, but the state as a whole was decidedly rural. Only 7 percent of its population resided in towns of 2,000 or more. Most of the state's inhabitants, including its 450,000 slaves, lived in the middle third and along the Tennessee border to the north.

"Alabama" is a Choctaw word meaning "vegetation gatherers."

6. FLORIDA (43.9%)

Entering the Union on March 3, 1845, Florida didn't stay long. Not yet reaching its sixteenth birthday, Florida was smallest in population among the Confederate States both in total numbers (140,000) and number of slaves (63,000). The distant and young state was still third in line to leave the Union, seceding in January 1861.

Most slaves lived in the middle of the panhandle around Tallahassee, where the soil was most conducive to growing cotton. By 1860 95 percent of Florida's white fiber production occurred in this relatively small area.[36]

In contrast, the Florida Peninsula had been a longtime haven for runaway slaves. In the Second Seminole War (1835–42) an estimated one thousand escaped slaves fought alongside the Seminoles against the U.S. Army, resisting deportation to west of the Mississippi. Some fifteen hundred American soldiers died in the bloodiest and most expensive war with Native Americans in U.S. history. Most of the Seminoles and former slaves were killed or forcibly removed to western territories.[37]

Slaves first set foot on the Florida Peninsula in 1513, accompanying Spanish explorer Juan Ponce de León.

---

7. NORTH CAROLINA (33.3%)

There were slaves within its territory as early as 1680, but North Carolina slavery grew slowly and in small pockets. Few slave owners lived in the mountainous areas, just as there were few owners in similarly hilly regions of northwest Virginia and eastern Tennessee. Yeoman farmers there had little practical capacity or incentive to collect slaves for their small lots.

Most holders throughout the remainder of North Carolina owned fewer than ten slaves. Those in the west primarily worked their slaves in mining, herding, and rail work. Holdings of larger sizes resided mostly within fifty miles of the coast and along the southeast border of Virginia, growing rice, tobacco, and cotton. There was enough demand in the state, however, to enslave a third of a million.

Although cotton was the number one crop in 1860, farming the fiber in North Carolina was a precarious venture. The comparatively cool climate, along with soil worn out by years of tobacco production, made for poor yields. Many slaveholding families in antebellum North Carolina headed south and southwest in search of better conditions.[38]

In 1805 a North Carolina slave woman was accused of poisoning several whites. For her alleged crime, she was burned at the stake.

---

8. VIRGINIA (30.9%)

The first African slaves brought to the American colonies arrived in 1619 on the soil of Virginia, a year before the landing of the *Mayflower* in New England. Over time tobacco became the key commodity to which their labors were tied. The massive plantations of fifty slaves or more (of which there were few) existed farther to the south. But Virginia, by far the most populous of what became the Confederate States, also ranked first in slave population in 1860 with 491,000.

Virginia was also a hub of the slave trade, and owners found they could make more money dealing rather than working slaves. In the thirty years before the war, more than a quarter million slaves were sold in the home state of George Washington and Thomas Jefferson.[39]

Almost no slavery existed in the northwestern counties of the state, where yeoman farmers constantly struggled with their wealthy slave-owning counterparts for political control. Tied geographically and commercially to the Northern states, these residents rejected the Confederate experiment altogether and created Union-loyal West Virginia in 1863.

In 1860 there were more free blacks in Virginia (58,042) than slaveholders (52,128).

---

9. TEXAS (30.2%)

The very origin of the Lone Star State came from a move to protect slavery. Mexico had won its independence from Spain in 1821. That same year, Mexico granted some of its northern lands to Americans who wished to settle the sparsely populated area. What began as a trickle of three hundred families in 1821 quickly became a flood. By 1835 approximately thirty thousand Americans established residence in the region known as Tejas, bringing with them thousands of slaves.

In an attempt to control the tide, the Mexican government charged duties, set up military outposts, and abolished slavery. All of this did not sit well with the new tenants. After several bloody fights, including the battle of the Alamo, an Anglicized Texas won independence from Mexico in 1836. In 1845 the ever-expanding United States annexed the young republic.[40]

Most new settlers came from Southern states enticed by opportunities to grow corn, herd cattle, and raise cotton on the cheap and fertile land of the state's eastern third. In a matter of years cotton dwarfed all other commodities, leading to an explosion of slave importation. In 1836 there were 5,000 slaves in Texas. By 1850 the number surpassed 48,000. A decade later there were 160,000 and growing. Fifteen years before the Civil War, bondsmen constituted 16 percent of the state's total population. When Texas seceded in February 1861, more than 30 percent of its people were slaves.[41]

In 1860 it cost on average twelve hundred dollars to buy a slave and six dollars to buy an acre of farmland in Texas.

---

10. ARKANSAS (26.0%)

Arkansas was very much an undeveloped entity in 1860. There were no large towns, a handful of sizable plantations, and only a few miles of rail lines. The overall population of 435,000 ranked twenty-fifth in the nation. Of the fifteen slave states, Arkansas ranked thirteenth in the number of slave owners (12,000).

Most of Arkansas's 110,000 slaves arrived between 1850 and 1860, brought in from states to the east. The majority labored in the southeast corner of the state, where cotton grew well. North and western reaches of Arkansas consisted of small farms, which were far less dependent on slave labor and consequently less adamant about secession. Arkansas seceded nonetheless, leaving the Union in May 1861 to become the ninth state in the Confederacy.

In 1860, among all the slave states, Arkansas was dead last in the number of free blacks living within its borders (411).

TOP TEN EVENTS OF SLAVE LIFE

Despite the enduring image of slaves working on grand plantations, actual working conditions truly covered the spectrum. While most slaves labored in fields of cotton, rice, sugar, and tobacco, thousands also worked in factories, households, stables, and mines. Many endured a year of work in a single set of ragged clothes, while others dressed in finery as a sign of their owner's opulence. Some bondsmen were treated as members of the owning family, while others endured as equals to draft animals. Slaves lived in cities and on small farms, along coastal waters and inland, working under a fellow slave's whip or alongside whites.

Hence, to speak of an "average" slave life is ambiguous at best. There were common milestones, however. Following are ten ordinary circumstances of the extraordinarily hard life of slaves in the United States during the mid-nineteenth century.[42]

1. BIRTH

In the 1800s pregnancy and birth were dangerous times for any mother and child. Hardest hit were the poor, and slaves were the poorest. In the critical first trimester, diets short on protein and vitamins compromised fetal development. Squalid living conditions and harsh workloads further complicated pregnancies. Miscarriages and stillbirths of the very poor occurred at almost twice the rate of the general population. Low birth weights were normal. Still, birthing children was exceptionally prevalent among slaves. Congress forbade the importation of slaves by 1808, yet the U.S. slave population nearly quadrupled between 1808 and 1860.[43]

Typically, slave women worked until near full term, sometimes right up to the point of contractions. When birth was imminent, family members or a midwife assisted in delivery. Births often went unrecorded, and many slaves spent their lives not knowing their actual birthday. An elderly female slave or attending midwife cared for the infant while the mother recuperated. Sometimes within a week, sometimes within a day, the mother returned to work. On average, the newborn had a 50 percent chance of surviving his or her first year.[44]

The great abolitionist and former slave FREDERICK DOUGLASS never knew his date of birth.

2. CHILDHOOD

After Congress outlawed slave importation to the United States, owners began to think of slave children less as burdens and more as long-term investments (healthy five-year-olds cost one hundred dollars compared to two thousand dollars for a stout adult male). In larger slave communities, care for the young usually fell to aged female slaves and older children. Mothers returned from work up to four times a day to nurse infants. In smaller communities the mother usually raised her own child.[45]

For the young, the day consisted of simple games, exploring what there was of the grounds, Bible stories, a few chores, and long periods of tedium. It was not uncommon for slave children to play alongside their owners' children until the latter attended school. Immediately afterward that relationship changed. Several former bondsmen testified they did not know they were slaves until this transition occurred.[46]

Children started working all day by age nine or ten. Owners commended themselves for permitting such a "late start," at least compared to factory owners in New England who employed children as young as seven. Despite the initially light workload, slave children experienced the same privations, diseases, fears, and terrors as their parents, learning early on about their limited roles and rights.[47]

Of the U.S. slave population in 1860, more than half were under the age of twenty.

---

3. EDUCATION

"Teaching" involved rudimentary lessons in discipline. The physical being was taught to work long hours and endure substantial stress. Some were trained in skilled and semiskilled trades such as carpentry, cooking, sewing, or metalworking.[48]

Most owners considered any education beyond job skills to be superfluous if not dangerous. Bookish pursuits might inspire thoughts of independence, a cognizance of self, and familiarity with principles of justice not exactly conducive with subjugation. Many state laws forbade even basic literacy, fearing it as an invaluable tool for orchestrating escapes or insurrections. Possession of printed material was enough to warrant physical reprimand in some regions. As a result, perhaps only one out of twenty slaves knew how to read and write.[49]

Predominate were the lessons of punishment and reward. By personal or public demonstration, chattel bondsmen learned the potentially high cost of disobedience. Forms and degrees of reprimand varied greatly from master to master, but pain was the eternal threat. Among the myriad of punishments for infractions real or perceived were beatings, wearing of irons and bells (for runaways), solitary confinement, and whippings. Alternately, many owners offered incentives for productive work, such as holidays, money, plots for gardening, and better food.[50]

> In the late 1840s a school in Louisville, Kentucky, permitted slaves to attend, provided they had signed permits from their masters.

4. WORK

It was the reason they were brought to North American and other continents, and according to the New Orleans trade magazine *De Bow's Review,* forced labor and Africans were made for each other. "There is no class of working people in the world better cared for than the Southern slave," declared *De Bow's,* adding an African was "much happier, during the hours of labor in the sunny fields, than when dozing in his native woods and jungles."[51]

Work and slaves were measured in "hands." If ten hands were required to harvest a cotton field, an overseer assigned any combination from ten full hands (healthy adult males) to forty quarter-hands (children, the aged, and disabled). Heavy labor—clearing trees and mining—were reserved for full hands. Lighter duties—serving the household or tending gardens—went to half- and quarter-hands.

Slaves generally conducted work by one of two systems. The task system charged a slave with completing a predetermined quantity of labor. Goals were measurable: ears of corn, pints of turpentine, pecks of beans, leaves of tobacco. Since the quota was the driver, most task work went unsupervised, and a proficient laborer might gain precious free time by the end of the day or week. The other approach was the gang system and its images often associated with slavery: teams of laborers, fields of cotton or rice, work lasting all hours of daylight, and overseers monitoring progress.[52]

Cotton was king in the South, made profitable by Eli Whitney's gin and the backbreaking labors of field hands who harvested the crop. The South was not the lone benefactor of the harvest, however. Northern mills reaped significant profits as well. This mutual boon played a large role in perpetuating slavery well into the nineteenth century.

LIBRARY OF CONGRESS

Slave owners maximized income by hiring out their slaves during down times. Idle hands were contracted to businesses, factories, or small farmers for a few hours to several months. Slave traders maximized their profits by listing at auction the work skills of each slave.

> During the Civil War, owners were typically paid thirty dollars a month for each slave they supplied the Confederate government, whereas a private in the Confederate army received thirteen dollars a month.

5. RELIGION

In the early years of slavery in North America, owners vehemently resisted efforts to convert their chattel to Christianity. To own a "heathen" was a paternal and rational act, but to enslave a fellow Christian was perceived as unmerciful. Plus many owners considered it imprudent to expose slaves to stories of the Exodus and concepts of equality.[53]

Such thinking changed in the 1730s with the coming of the Great Awakening, a nationwide evangelical movement of conversion and redemption. Owners coupled this movement with Christianity's message of obedience, self-control, and accountability. Paradoxically, Christianity also appealed to generations of slaves, with its offers of eternal freedom in the afterlife, an almighty judgment of the oppressive and sinful, and a savior figure protecting the defenseless, impoverished, and abused.[54]

What resulted for many slaves, especially those held in larger numbers, was a vibrant synthesis of western African and western European religious elements. There were formal church services, predominantly Baptist and Methodist. In some places, whites preached side by side with blacks. Yet sermons of patience, honesty, and servile duties outnumbered references to the meek inheriting the earth.

On larger estates, some slaves attended "arbor churches." In a forbidden practice, slaves gathered together in outdoor clearings to hear oral histories from their elders, to confess or be scrutinized for improprieties against one another, to dance, to sing, to summon incantations, and to speak of deliverance from earthly suffering.[55]

Learning of Nat Turner's Scripture-inspired slave uprising in 1831, slave owners throughout the South declared a moratorium on slaves attending religious services of any kind.

---

6. MARRIAGE

As with religion there was utility in marriage for both the owned and owner. For slaves, marriage provided a degree of belonging, purpose, and a modicum of hope. In turn, owners believed a slave with family ties was less likely to run away or cause trouble.

The wedding itself was usually a simple affair. A few words of congratulations and expectations from an owner, pastor, or esteemed slave, and two became one. A common tradition involved couples joining hands and stepping over a broom. Occasionally the phrase "Till death, distance, or master do you part" was added to emphasize the wedding had no legal bearing. Approximately one-fifth of those married were later sold or traded apart.[56]

Courting before the marriage was far more difficult than the wedding itself. There existed limited time, virtually no privacy, and minimal opportunity. Communities were generally small, as most owners possessed six or fewer slaves. Travel between estates was possible only if the owner allowed it. Yet slaves still managed to seek and make new families. Four out of five slaves who lived to adulthood eventually married.[57]

Unlike their white owners, slaves as a whole did not permit cousins to marry.

---

7. ILLNESS

Nearly as dominant as work in a slave's world was the lingering threat of sickness. Poor drinking water and lack of privies promoted cholera, typhoid, and dysentery. Inadequate shelter and clothing made slaves especially susceptible to pulmonary ailments, tuberculosis and pneumonia being prominent killers. Diets of pork and grains but sparing in fruits and vegetables left immune systems unable to fight off illness. Towns, farms, and plantations in marshy river valleys and coastal areas were breeding grounds for disease.[58]

Yet in respect to health, slaves and poor whites apparently suffered equally. Epidemics of yellow fever, malaria, measles, mumps, and typhoid struck entire communities regardless of race. Prevalence of mis-shapen red blood cells among African Americans spared many from some of the most virulent forms of cell-attacking malaria. Yet this same condition subjected many more to sickle cell anemia, a condition lethal among the very young.[59]

Whether for economic and/or sentimental reasons, most owners made a sincere effort to care for their ill slaves. Since doctors were so few and medical knowledge so limited at the time, both whites and blacks normally opted for home remedies and rest. By the time of the Civil War, bloodletting and purging had fallen out of favor, but uses of folk remedies and superstitions remained among the general populace.[60]

Popular culture blamed many illnesses on "miasmata," a transparent mist emanating from dead plants and animals.

---

8. BEING BOUGHT AND SOLD

An American slave could expect to be sold once. Rarely did owners sell their slaves as a means of punishment, although the threat to do so was prevalent. Slaves learned to grieve the death of an owner regardless, because the departure of a master meant his slaves would be distributed among his heirs and creditors. Most often the reason was economic. In the cash-poor South, the fastest way to settle large balances was to offer a number of slaves as payment.

Some instances involved selling, lending, or giving slaves to family, friends, or business associates. When an owner sought the highest possible price, however, he billed his chattel to an auction house. During an auction, slaves were sold in batches and individually. Pamphlets listed supposed age, health, temperament, and starting price. Often slaves appeared on auction posters alongside livestock and farm equipment.[61]

Before the bidding commenced, potential buyers examined a slave as they would a dog or a horse: poking muscles, feeling bones, prodding open mouths to better determine quality. Slaves were made to walk and jump to attest to the soundness of their limbs and spines. Highly skilled or strong males brought the highest bids. Many young women were also taken at high price, condemned to unthinkable lives in the hands of adulterous buyers.[62]

Former slaves recalled physical or verbal abuse during their lives as a matter of course, but being sold was almost universally portrayed as the most traumatic event they experienced.[63]

Notoriously bad with finances, presidents Thomas Jefferson and John Tyler both sold some of their slaves to cover personal debts.

---

9. ESCAPE

Despite the obvious incentives to escape, few slaves ever made the attempt. Even fewer were successful. Each year fewer than a thousand managed to reach freedom.[64]

A great blockage to flight was a simple matter of logistics. Slaves lived mostly in virtual isolation from extended connections. Communication and mobility between adjoining communities were diligently monitored. Travel, if allowed, involved carrying written passes. Patrols and bounty hunters policed the countryside. Most slaves lived in the Deep South, where the path to freedom was longest.

Besides having little or no money, and with few opportunities to contact potential sympathizers and supporters, slaves had the distinct disadvantage of skin color, which was readily suspected and easily detected among the general Caucasian population. Despite its fame then and now, the Underground Railroad actually rescued far fewer than those who rescued themselves.[65]

An estimated third of all runaways were not attempting to reach freedom but to reach other family members who had been sold away. Those trapped in the deepest South, several hundred miles from Mexico or the North, posed as freedmen or moved at night. Others finding neither family nor free soil simply hid out among small enclaves of other runaways. Sparsely populated southern Florida was a popular destination for fugitive slaves.[66]

Four out of five runaway slaves were male.

---

10. DEATH

They called it "going home." As Christian whites were buried facing the holy lands of the east, so too faced the slave—toward Africa. Most adult deaths came by disease. Few slaves had the opportunity to succumb to old age; just 2 percent reached the age of sixty. Other large contributors were accidents, suicide, and murder. On the last, owners resisted killing a slave, usually not on moral grounds, but on the realization that a dead slave could produce nothing and had no resale value.[67]

If and when someone passed on, the immediate family watched over the body until nightfall. Beads, pieces of glass, and broken pottery accompanied the body into a simple casket or burial cloth. The older the slave or the more revered by the owning family, the greater the pomp of the burial. To maximize work hours, however, owners normally mandated the deceased be buried at night. The procession to the grave site was by tradition slow and morbid, a reflection of the sadness of the living. Yet after interment came the celebration for the dead, with song, spirits, food, and recognition of a successful escape for the deceased.[68]

Slaves had a life expectancy of less than twenty-two years, whereas whites during the same period lived an average forty-two years.

TOP TEN ABOLITIONISTS

The debate continues whether radical emancipationists played a major or minuscule role in the national fight over sectional discord. Some historians consider them naive and ineffectual, demanding changes for which the country was not ready. Others credit abolitionists with forcing an unpopular problem to a decision point.

What is certain is this: Abolitionists were not homogenous. There were pacifists and cutthroats, the pious and the vile, the compromising and the confrontational, as demonstrated by the following list. Presented here are the most prominent and effective spokespeople for the immediate, uncompensated, and total removal of human servitude from antebellum America. If they possessed any similarity, it may have been a collective repugnance for those conciliatory toward slave holders while claiming to loathe slavery, figures such as Henry Clay, Daniel Webster, and Abraham Lincoln.

Note the scarcity of women. By many accounts the heart and soul of the movement, the efforts of matriarchs such as Sojourner Truth, Angelina Grimké, and Julia Ward Howe were often compromised by a country only half slave but heavily chauvinist.

1. JOHN BROWN (1800–1859, CONNECTICUT)

An ardent oversimplifier with freakish stamina, John Brown failed at everything save breeding children and agitation. Father of at least twenty, he began his personal crusade against slavery late in life by assisting with the Underground Railroad in Ohio. Restless for more results, he aspired to liberate all rather than a few. Brown also believed no words matched the work of a good sword.

Heading to Kansas, Brown helped establish its "Bleeding" moniker of the 1850s with raids, skirmishes, and killings, targeting anyone inclined to bring slavery to the sunburned plains. No act defined his zeal more vividly than the Pottawatomie massacre. On May 24, 1856, Brown and several of his sons pulled five unarmed pro-slavery men from their homes and slaughtered them.[69]

After spilling more blood in Kansas and Missouri, Brown conducted his grand finale in the east. In October 1859, accompanied by three sons,

HISTORIC PHOTO COLLECTION, HARPERS FERRY, NHP

John Brown's 1859 insurrection began and ended at the Harpers Ferry arsenal.

fifteen followers, and financial backing from six prominent abolitionists, Brown captured the federal arsenal and armory at Harpers Ferry, Virginia. The plan was to arm and liberate the nearby slaves then lead them in Spartacus fashion into the Appalachians. From his new rogue state, Brown hoped to launch future raids southward to free all the slaves.

Although Brown succeeded in taking the arsenal, no slaves accepted his invitation. Instead, hundreds of angry townspeople descended upon Brown's men, killing several, and trapping the rest in a small brick building. By the time a detachment of marines arrived, led by Col. ROBERT E. LEE, the fight was essentially over.

Brown was tried and convicted of treason, not against the United States but against the state of Virginia. Hanged days before the beginning of the Thirty-sixth Congress, his fresh grave was apparently not deep enough. Legislators uniformly denounced Brown's tactics, but his aim was the real issue. Representatives and senators previously capable of walking a tightrope now had to publicly declare whether Brown's goal of freeing the enslaved was villainous or valid. Slavery remained on terra firma, but Brown destroyed the middle ground.

Although he condemned the cruelty of slavery, John Brown was known to be physically abusive to many of his children.

2. WENDELL PHILLIPS (1811–84, MASSACHUSETTS)

A handsome, successful, persuasive Harvard man, Wendell Phillips managed to make bitter extremism almost palatable. For decades he delivered the message of immediate and complete emancipation to the Northern states. From his pen came articles, pamphlets, and the popular books of *The Unconstitutionality of Slavery* (1845) and *The Philosophy of the Abolitionist Movement* (1854). With his voice, the "Golden Trumpet" leveled dramatic expositions upon large and receptive audiences.[70]

Phillips contended that compromise on slavery was tantamount to endorsement, and he turned his persuasive means against anything and anyone who opposed him. He declared the U.S. Constitution and its permission of slavery "a covenant with death and an agreement with hell." Against Lincoln he was particularly abusive, labeling him "the Slave Hound from Illinois" and a feeble man of "slow mind."[71]

Unlike many New England abolitionists, Phillips was not an elitist. He believed everyone had the right to life, liberty, and the pursuit of property, so long as said property did not include other humans. A sincere progressive, he championed women's rights and the rights of Native Americans, prison reform, labor reform, and prohibition. He gave away a fortune to the needy, all the while being what most abolitionists were not: approachable, understandable, and popular.[72]

His résumé included no defining breakthrough, no climactic showdown, just a long, steady construction of popular appeal against an institution he hated.

Phillips became a radical abolitionist when he married one. Yet Ann Greene eventually spent much of her adult life as a bedridden invalid.

3. WILLIAM LLOYD GARRISON (1805–79, MASSACHUSETTS)

Bald, bespectacled, bellicose William Lloyd Garrison was the model of inflexibility. Before him, abolitionism was a quiet affair led by Quakers and limited to modest goals. After his adoption of the cause in 1831 it became an open assault against the Constitution and the country.

Abandoned by his father at age three, largely self-educated, Garrison was working for a temperance journal in his twenties when a friend encouraged him to consider writing about slavery. Garrison became inspired.[73]

On New Year's Day 1831 he published his first issue of the *Liberator*, in which he proclaimed "let all the enemies of the persecuted blacks tremble." Two years later he cofounded the American Anti-Slavery Society and became a father figure to thousands of budding abolitionists. In his writing, lectures, and leadership, he mythologized the South as a land consisting mostly of plantations, mansions, heartless owners, beaten chattel, aristocrats, and adultery. Of slaveholders, Garrison said, "We do not acknowledge them to be within the pale of Christianity, of republicanism, of humanity."[74]

Yet Garrison blamed the North for allowing slavery to exist. Almost twenty years before the war, he promoted the idea of disunion. Let the South try to survive unprotected, he argued, and slavery would die on the vine.[75]

Garrison was the stereotypical abolitionist: righteous, unbending, accusatory. He refused to use violence, politics, even civil disobedience to initiate change, fearing such methods would only justify a backlash. His only tool was a constant, uncompromising moral argument. Over time this inflexible approach won him few new friends and cost him most of his old ones, including Frederick Douglass and Wendell Phillips. In the decade before the war, Garrison may have been increasingly famous, but his leverage on his own creation was slipping away.[76]

In 1831 the state of Georgia offered five thousand dollars for the capture and conviction of William Lloyd Garrison.

---

4. FREDERICK DOUGLASS (1817–95, MARYLAND)

By the time of the war Douglass was the most famous African American in the country. In his youth he was a slave who did not know who his father was, other than it was a white man.

Born Frederick Bailey, he escaped northward at the age of twenty-one and changed his name to avoid capture. After years of working as a laborer, he attended an Anti-Slavery Society meeting and was invited to speak. Thus began his lifelong career as the voice of the voiceless.[77]

He spoke throughout the North and England, started an abolitionist weekly in 1847 called the *North Star*, and stirred people to despise or cherish him. The latter group soon included William Lloyd Garrison, Wendell Phillips, and John Brown.[78]

Douglass's mass appeal stemmed from a passionate faith in democracy. The institution was, in his sincerest estimation, the liberator of human potential. When civil war loomed, he declared, "All that I have and am are bound up with the destiny of this country. When she is successful, I rejoice . . . and when she is afflicted, I mourn with her."[79]

Despite Douglass's growing fame, he was hardly a leader of his race, and he knew it. His periodical had five times the number of white subscribers as black. The apparent indifference of freedmen toward slavery perplexed him. He also became frustrated with his white audiences, including Lincoln, with whom he visited on several occasions. Repeatedly people praised his call for the immediate abolition of slavery, but few were motivated to action.[80]

In short, it was difficult for people to identify with Douglass. As a slave he lived in a large city (Baltimore), was exceedingly literate, and worked as a ship's carpenter. As a fugitive he had throngs of listeners, several patrons, and a mind brilliant enough to be intimidating.[81]

In 1845 FREDERICK DOUGLASS began an eighteen-month speaking tour of England, moving thousands with his orations of slave life. A group of admirers was so impressed, they gave him six hundred dollars so he could purchase his freedom.

---

5. GERRIT SMITH (1797–1874, NEW YORK)

Others brought ideals. Gerrit Smith brought money and paid dearly. In his quest to be an abolitionist, the New York businessman and philanthropist went from being a reformer to a radical to a recluse.

Moderate at first, Smith supported change through nonviolence. He donated thousands of dollars for the resettlement of freedmen to Liberia, gave twenty thousand acres to Oberlin College (one of the first schools in the nation to accept African Americans), and was president of the New York Antislavery Society.[82]

Smith was an oddity among the white abolitionists in that he worked with and listened to African Americans. In 1838, impatient for progress, he began to ask fellow society members to help fugitive slaves and offered his own home as a refuge. In 1846 he acquired 120,000 acres in the Adirondacks and gave freedmen plots of land so they could escape menial urban jobs. A friend and mentor of Frederick Douglass, Smith financed the *North Star* and other abolitionist newspapers. Perpetually flirting with bankruptcy, he spent a small fortune purchasing the freedom of slaves.[83]

While serving in the House of Representatives, Smith's methods became extreme. He resigned in protest of the 1854 Kansas-Nebraska Act, bought rifles for Kansas Free-Soilers, and called for an all-out war against pro-slavery Missourians. Then, in 1859, news came of John Brown's raid at Harpers Ferry.

When Smith heard of the insurrection and the loss of seventeen lives, he became withdrawn. Brown was an acquaintance, and rumors surfaced that Smith helped fund the plot—accusations Smith vehemently denied. The allegations, however, were true. Days after Brown was hanged, Smith suffered a nervous breakdown, began to hallucinate, and became suicidal. After nearly two months in an insane asylum, he started to recover.[84]

It was clear that Smith had changed. He openly criticized blacks and spoke of a "natural separation" of the races. When hearing of the plan to allow African Americans into the Union armed forces, Smith said it would be "a great favor to the old rascal to make him serve a good cause once in his life."[85]

After the war, alienated from the abolitionist movement, Gerrit Smith signed a bail bond to release Jefferson Davis from prison.

---

6. HARRIET BEECHER STOWE (1811–96, CONNECTICUT)

Measured by commitment, Harriet Beecher Stowe would not rate well among abolitionists. Measured by effect, Stowe stands among the elite.

In 1850 Congress passed a revised Fugitive Slave Law, itself an act of questionable legality. Incensed by its moral rather than legal ramifications, Stowe wrote a fictional account of slaves and masters entitled *Uncle Tom's Cabin,* or *Life Among the Lowly.* Appearing in 1851 as a series in the monthly *National Era,* the piece was verbose and excessively sentimental. It contained stories of heartbreaking slave auctions, harrowing escapes, callous beatings, and a Messiah figure in Uncle Tom. While it was no literary treasure, it did have mass appeal.[86]

Released as a book in 1852, when fugitive cases were becoming national news, Stowe's story sold three hundred thousand copies in just six months. In the next decade it appeared in sixteen languages and sold more than four and a half million copies. The book was in more American homes than any other work with the exception of the Bible.[87]

It spawned plays, poems, and waltzes. More significantly, it created widespread reaction. Queen Victoria was said to have wept over it. People who had never thought about slavery began to question the institution's morality and purpose. Pro-slavery voices called the book libelous and inflammatory.

For all intents and purposes, *Uncle Tom's Cabin* marked the beginning and end of Stowe's influence. None of her following works were as successful. Although she sent a son to war and made public demands for the immediate cessation of slavery, she discontinued her efforts after Lincoln's EMANCIPATION PROCLAMATION. Yet with one narrative, Stowe reached the indifferent and disconnected and did so with ingenious simplicity. Others employed logic, law, religion, racism, or economics to address the issue of slavery. Stowe used emotion.[88]

In the 1850s Harriet Beecher Stowe moved from Bowdoin, Maine, to Hartford, Connecticut. In the years after the war, one of her neighbors was a writer popularly known as Mark Twain.

---

7. ELIJAH PARISH LOVEJOY (1802–37, MAINE)

Presbyterian minister Elijah Lovejoy knew the risks of speaking out against slavery. Threats, beatings, loss of property, and loss of employment were all possible repercussions. No white person, though, had lost his or her life in defense of abolition.

Likelihood of harm by any measure was minimal within Lovejoy's first haunts of Maine and Pennsylvania. When he moved to St. Louis to manage the pro-emancipation *Observer,* a litany of threats convinced him to pull up stakes and head for friendlier territory. He started a new *Observer* in Alton, Illinois. Still, frontier Alton was a long way from cosmopolitan Philadelphia. Pro-slavery mobs destroyed his printing press on three separate occasions.

On November 7, 1837, news spread that Lovejoy had acquired another press. By nightfall a seething mob of two hundred, some of them armed, fell upon the building in which it was stored. Lovejoy and a handful of supporters were waiting for them, armed and ready to defend themselves.

The situation quickly deteriorated. Someone from inside the warehouse fired into the crowd. In retaliation, the mob attempted to set the building on fire. As Lovejoy rushed out to stop them, the pro-slavery crowd put five bullets in him. The following day they dragged his tattered body through the streets.

The first white martyr for the cause, Lovejoy's death was an infinitely stronger weapon than his life. Upon his demise, memberships in anti-slavery societies soared, an aimless John Brown pledged his life to the destruction of slavery, and Wendell Phillips declared, "The gun which was aimed as the breast of Lovejoy brought me to my feet."[89]

Elijah's younger brother Owen, himself an active abolitionist, helped organize the Illinois Republican Party and befriended a promising young lawyer named Lincoln.

---

8. THEODORE DWIGHT WELD (1803–95, CONNECTICUT)

He was intense, driven, self-critical. A friend considered him a person of "deep, wild gloom." William Lloyd Garrison called him "the lion-hearted, invincible Weld." He was a pioneer to his cause, yet his desire for anonymity kept him largely out of history's pages.[90]

Born in the east, Theodore Dwight Weld lived, taught, and lectured mostly in the Midwest, preferring schools and countrysides over cities and conventions. His lectures were like sermons; his writings resembled Scripture. His most influential work was *American Slavery As It Is: The Testimony of a Thousand Witnesses* (1839). The book was a blanket condemnation sewn from pro-slavery rags. Collecting more than twenty thousand discarded Southern newspapers from the New York Commercial Reading Room, Weld and his family extracted articles praising the "social order" of slavery, patrol parties, manhunts, physical coercion, and family auctions. The book sold one hundred thousand copies in a year and influenced later works from HARRIET BEECHER STOWE and Charles Dickens. His disciples included GERRIT SMITH, Edwin M. Stanton, Henry Ward Beecher, and his students from the Lane Seminary in Ohio, a school from which he was fired for his views.[91]

After twenty years of trying, Weld grew despondent. His attempt to convert the country seemed to furnish no lasting effect, and new abolitionists appeared to congratulate rather than sacrifice themselves for their mission. With his beloved wife, the fellow abolitionist Angelina Grimké, Weld settled into family life and continued his quiet commitment to education.[92]

In keeping with his contempt for fame and pride, Theodore Dwight Weld published *Slavery As It Is* anonymously.

---

9. THOMAS GARRETT (1789–1871, PENNSYLVANIA)

With resolute bravery, HARRIET TUBMAN rescued approximately 270 people from slavery through the Underground Railroad. Fellow conductor and Quaker Thomas Garrett helped 2,700. Tubman herself was among the stream of people to whom he offered money from his pocket, food from his kitchen, and shelter in his home.[93]

A member of the diminutive Pennsylvania Abolitionist Society, Garrett moved to Delaware, a slave state, in the 1820s and immediately began operations on the Underground Railroad. Authorities repeatedly threatened him with incarceration. Garrett repeatedly defied them, and with the help of freedmen in the Wilmington area, he was prolific.

In 1848, after more than two decades helping slaves escape through Delaware and Maryland, Garrett was apprehended and convicted (essentially of transporting stolen property). The ensuing fine of fifty-four hundred dollars financially ruined him.[94]

Quiet, grounded, defiant, Garrett is believed to be the model for the character Simeon Halliday in *Uncle Tom's Cabin*. Following the end of the Civil War and the repeal of slavery, African Americans of Delaware hailed the true-to-life emancipator as a hero and organized a parade in his honor.[95]

Like many abolitionists to follow, Thomas Garrett became a wanted man. For his capture, the state of Maryland offered a reward of ten thousand dollars—which was more than twenty times the average income of a Baltimore laborer.

---

10. GEORGE LUTHER STEARNS (1809–67, MASSACHUSETTS)

He amassed wealth in the lead pipe business, became infuriated by the Fugitive Slave Law and the Kansas-Nebraska Act, and began to invest in abolitionist futures. Clandestine he was not.

George Luther Stearns headed the Massachusetts Committee for Kansas, an arms-trafficking organization similar to the Kansas Immigration Society. He publicly raised credit and cash for the impoverished John Brown, including thousands from his own accounts, and became the militant's prime benefactor. From the New York State legislature he requested one hundred thousand dollars to arm and support Brown's free-soil crusade in Kansas, netting no money but much attention. Along with GERRIT SMITH, he was one of the Secret Six who funded the faulty raid on Harpers Ferry.[96]

Unlike many other activists, Stearns did not shy from his antislavery work after the EMANCIPATION PROCLAMATION. Under his initiative and in partnership with Frederick Douglass, the famed Fifty-fourth Massachusetts Regiment was formed as was the lesser-known Fifty-fifth Massachusetts. Stearns established schools for freedmen and their children, channeled funds to the families of African American veterans, and petitioned for the constitutional amendments ending slavery and establishing black male suffrage. A chief beneficiary of his labors was the War Department. Stearns recruited more than thirteen thousand African American troops in two years.[97]

John Brown carted two hundred Sharps rifles with him on his Harpers Ferry raid. These weapons of a would-be slave uprising were the personal property of George Luther Stearns.

TOP TEN FIRE-EATERS

The idea of secession was as old as the Union. At various times portions of states and territories threatened to separate from larger communities. Individuals who fostered such separatism were labeled fanatics, radicals, zealots—the Daniel Shays, the Nat Turners, the Chief Black Hawks.

The most ardent of Southern Secessionists were unceremoniously labeled "fire-eaters," a mocking devilment of their harsh words and deeds. Definitively in the minority, these men were hardly outsiders. A majority of them were self-made. Several were educated in the North. Although most owned slaves, nearly all were devout Unionists over much of their careers, changing their message when the process of compromise failed to establish lasting resolutions. Their reasons for secession were as varied as their personalities, but all stressed an impending loss of control.

Far from being discarded when separation took place, many provided considerable services to the Confederacy. The following are the most prominent fire-eaters listed in order of their intensity, ambition, and effectiveness in leading their respective states out of the Union in 1860–61.

1. ROBERT BARNWELL RHETT (1800–1876, SOUTH CAROLINA)

Several men were dubbed the "Father of Secession." None deserved it more than Robert Barnwell Rhett. Among the separatists, he was unsurpassed in longevity, conviction, and success.

A skilled speaker and lawyer, Rhett entered the South Carolina legislature in 1826, where he became a close associate of states rightist John C. Calhoun. As early as 1830 Rhett openly proclaimed secession as the only means to protect states from interstate tariffs, constriction of slavery, and other federal acts he considered tyrannical.

Serving in the U.S. House of Representatives from 1837 to 1849 and in the Senate from 1850 to 1852, he perpetually defended slaveholding interests and attempted to repeal the constitutional ban on international slave trading. When Congress refused to guarantee slavery in the territories acquired in the Mexican War, Rhett responded rather bitterly: "We are of the dominant Caucasian race, and will perform our part in civilizing the world, and bringing into beneficent subjection and cultivation its most productive regions of sun and beauty."[98]

In 1852 Rhett left the political arena to try his hand at the less restrictive avenue of journalism. Attaining ownership of the daily CHARLESTON MERCURY, he molded the publication into a national platform. As an owner of several plantations and hundreds of slaves, Rhett promoted a vision of a massive Southern empire reaching to California, Cuba, and perhaps as far as South America, where Southern agriculture, industry, and culture would grow to international prominence. His paper boasted, "We shall colonize Texas throughout, and the Chihuahua and a few more good Southern States. We shall have all the Gulf country when we have once shaken ourselves free of the puritans."[99]

In December 1860 the brash sixty-year-old was prominent among the delegates of the hurriedly assembled South Carolina secession convention. Pleased with the unanimous vote to leave the Union, Rhett proposed a convention for all slave states. He suggested centrally situated Montgomery, Alabama, and a February deadline before the recently elected Republican president could take office. When his advice bore fruit, Rhett was honored as one of South Carolina's eight delegates, contributing to the creation of the Confederate provisional congress and constitution.[100]

Hoping, even assuming to become the Confederacy's first president, Rhett lost the appointment to a more affable and moderate choice. Soon after the war began, Rhett became one of Jefferson Davis's harshest critics, accusing the president of the same charges he had leveled against the old Union. In 1862 Rhett resumed his duties at the *Mercury*, this time unleashing his fire upon the government in Richmond.[101]

Robert Barnwell Rhett studied law under Thomas Grimké, a fervent abolitionist.

---

2. WILLIAM LOWNDES YANCEY (1814–63, GEORGIA)

Born in Georgia, the future extremist with the musical voice spent much of his childhood in New York State, living with his strict abolitionist stepfather. Before turning thirty, Yancey settled into a law practice in South Carolina. The young man was a progressive. He supported public schools, prison and bank reforms, women's rights, and ran a Unionist paper called the *Greenville Mountaineer*.[102]

After marrying into a family with money and slaves, he moved to Alabama and promptly failed as a planter. Resuming his careers in law and editing, he gained a reputation as a pro-slavery Unionist. In 1844 Alabama Democrats selected him to fill a vacant seat in Congress, where Yancey underwent a change of heart. Nauseated by the eternal debate over slavery, he figured one of two things must happen: Either slavery had to be legally protected everywhere or the slave states had to leave.[103]

In the 1851 Slavery Convention in Montgomery, Alabama, he passionately lobbied for his state to secede and create a new country, yet he found few in agreement. Like ROBERT BARNWELL RHETT, Yancey stepped away from politics and practiced law until a better opportunity arose.

His shining moment came in the 1860 Democratic National Convention. He degraded the centrist candidate Stephen A. Douglas and demanded the party platform guarantee slavery in all U.S. territories. When the motion to protect slavery failed, Yancey led nearly every Southern delegate out of the convention. A split party, he reasoned, meant a Republican victory, and a Republican president meant secession for Alabama. Lincoln won, and Yancey led his adopted state out of the Union.[104]

As a senator in the Confederate Congress, however, the extremist did not enjoy much success. Ever for states' rights, Yancey fought Davis's attempts to centralize the government. Blatantly pro-slavery, Yancey failed miserably in a diplomatic mission to secure recognition from antislavery Britain and France. Returning to his senate seat in late 1861, he died in office in 1863, largely rejected by a country he helped create.[105]

When William Yancey was an infant, his birth father shared a law office with John C. Calhoun.

---

3. JOHN C. CALHOUN (1782–1850, SOUTH CAROLINA)

Secretary of war to James Monroe, vice president to John Quincy Adams and Andrew Jackson, a representative then a senator, the abstract, humorless, elitist John C. Calhoun was initially a staunch defender of central government. He advocated a strong military, a tariff on imports, and a national bank.[106]

By 1832 his convictions changed. A Northern-majority Congress passed a series of exceedingly high tariffs, adding as much as 50 percent to the cost of imports. Calhoun denounced these tariffs, first secretly then publicly, as unconstitutional. No government, he reasoned, could artificially inflate prices on all citizens to benefit a few, namely Northern manufacturers. Leaving his vice presidential post under Jackson to return to the Senate, Calhoun argued that a state could legally nullify any national law it did not directly endorse. South Carolina's attempt to nullify the tariff crumbled when Jackson threatened armed intervention, but Calhoun became the king of states' rights.[107]

In the years to follow, Calhoun emphasized any and all majority (read "Northern") threats against state sovereignty, especially in areas concerning slavery. A slave owner himself, Calhoun was more of a fire-breather than a fire-eater, as he had no real intention of seceding over any issue. For South Carolina to leave the Union, he said, was "the most fatal of all steps." Better to gain concessions by threat than to actually secede and lose all influence.[108]

In his dangerous tradition of brinkmanship, his final speech may have been his most destructive. Delivered by a fellow senator (Calhoun was too ill to deliver it himself), his text bewailed the loss of Southern safety and honor, accused the North of an assortment of tyrannies, and issued demands. He began and ended with a leading question: "How can the Union be saved? To this I answer . . . by adopting such measures as will satisfy the states belonging to the Southern section."

The requests were rather simple. To preserve the Union, the North had to amend the Constitution to perpetually guarantee slavery in all U.S. territories. It also had to provide new fugitive slave laws obligating the federal government to catch and return all escaped slaves hiding in free states. He also hinted that slave and free states should remain equal in number for all time. The North would do these things, reasoned Calhoun, "if she has half the love of the Union which she professes to have."[109]

In short, Calhoun issued rigid ultimatums that neither side could alter without losing face. He left little opportunity for rebuttal, however, dying just weeks after unleashing his bombastic rant.[110]

John C. Calhoun allegedly never told a joke in his life.

---

4. EDMUND RUFFIN (1794–1865, VIRGINIA)

Born to a family of wealth, Edmund Ruffin witnessed firsthand the relative decline of Virginia's once prosperous farmland, political leverage, and
national status. A brilliant agriculturist, Ruffin worked for years to promote farming improvements and commercial development in the South.
Although initially viewing slavery as evil, he gradually began to consider it
as the keystone to Southern economic survival.[111]

The fiery Virginian wrote, traveled, editorialized, and spoke for secession at every available opportunity. He viewed John Brown's raid on
Harpers Ferry as proof of what was to come if slave states did not secede
as a whole. To illustrate the abolitionist threat, he sent pikes from Brown's
raiding party to every state governor in the South. Later he gladly
attended Brown's trial and hanging.[112]

In 1861, by then one of the most prominent agitators, Ruffin
attended three state secession conventions and boasted a circle of associates that included fellow fire-eaters ROBERT BARNWELL RHETT, WILLIAM
LOWNDES YANCEY, JAMES D. B. DE BOW, and LAWRENCE KEITT. He zealously
advocated shelling Fort Sumter, hoping military action would pull his vacillating Virginia into an already established confederacy of seven states,
and he later had the privilege of being among the first to fire upon the
Charleston fort.[113]

Many claimed they would rather die than live in a country taken over
by the "Yankee race," but Ruffin meant it. A few months after ROBERT E.
LEE's surrender at Appomattox, Ruffin draped himself in a Confederate
flag and died from a self-inflicted gunshot wound to the head.[114]

It is said that before he reached age eleven, Edmund Ruffin had read all of
Shakespeare's plays.

---

5. LAWRENCE KEITT (1824–64, SOUTH CAROLINA)

King of violent Secessionist language, a brash Keitt was one of the
youngest and most vicious of the fire-eaters. Twice he attempted to brawl
in the House of Representatives. In May 1857 he accompanied Preston
Brooks in the bloody beating of Massachusetts Sen. Charles Sumner.
Resigning his seat thereafter, Keitt was promptly reelected, both symbolizing and glorifying the brutal convictions of slavery's defenders.[115]

Along with WILLIAM LOWNDES YANCEY and ROBERT BARNWELL RHETT, he was officially a Democrat yet knew the massive party would never exclusively serve the South. He consequently abandoned notions of ticket and national loyalty, writing in 1856, "I should rather my State should be the graveyard of martyred patriots than the slave of Northern abolitionists."[116]

A member of the South Carolina Secessionist Convention, Keitt successfully campaigned to have his state secede first. A delegate to the Montgomery Convention, he assisted in the creation of the Confederate Constitution.

When the convention ended, residents of Montgomery gathered amid band music and blaring fireworks to hear delegates speak of their new nation. Responding to shouts of his name, Keitt rose to announce: "The old Union is dead; its body has been carried to its last resting place; its honors and decorations have been laid upon the coffin." He would later punctuate his statement by spearheading the move to fire on Fort Sumter. Yet in three years, there would be a coffin for him. In May 1864 Brig. Gen. Lawrence Keitt was killed at COLD HARBOR.[117]

Plagued by a notoriously poor memory, Lawrence Keitt almost missed the Montgomery Convention because he forgot what day it convened.

---

6. LOUIS T. WIGFALL (1816–74, SOUTH CAROLINA)

Born of wealthy plantation owners, Wigfall matched LAWRENCE KEITT's affinity for violence. Wigfall was also partial to hard whiskey, fast women, and tall wagers, which cost him his ancestral home and most of his slaves. Avoiding creditors in 1846, he fled South Carolina and headed to Texas. He rediscovered successes and became a U.S. senator, largely due to his public opposition to Unionist governor Sam Houston. In the Senate he tirelessly defended Southern honor and slavery and threatened to splinter the Union "into more fragments than gunpowder would blow glass."[118]

At the height of the regional crisis in 1861, and while still holding his Senate seat, Wigfall personally encouraged Jefferson Davis to shell Fort Sumter. He later observed the bombardment in the company of commanding officer P. G. T. Beauregard.

Briefly serving as a brigadier general and then in the Senate, Wigfall worked in the committees for military affairs, foreign affairs, and territories. Yet he rarely displayed much talent beyond the ability to verbally abuse the United States, later turning his gift on Davis and staff.

When the Confederacy crumbled, Wigfall fled to England. Returning to Texas six years later, he never fully accepted the defeat of his cause and remained unreconstructed for the remainder of his years.[119]

Before the war, the temperamental Wigfall participated in several duels, registering one kill.

---

7. JAMES D. B. DE BOW (1820–67, SOUTH CAROLINA)

For James De Bow, the glorified portrait of the Old South, with its leisured gentlemen and mansion estates, was not only false, it was dangerous. Quiet, bookish, the son of a Northern businessman, De Bow knew the cotton states were experiencing unprecedented growth in industry, farmland, slaves, and slaveholders. Yet this prosperity was at risk because most of the nation's capital resided in the North.[120]

A passionate Secessionist, he argued that political separation would mean nothing until the South ended its long role as the North's economic vassal. To this end, he moved from South Carolina to New Orleans and set up the most successful and influential trade magazine in the antebellum South. *De Bow's Review* ran its first issue in 1846.

His pages spoke of Southern trade, industry, and universities rich and prospering. Articles described coal mines in Alabama, textile mills in Tennessee, business contacts in Brazil and Cuba, and rail lines in Virginia. Politicians, businessmen, doctors, and educators wrote for him, including fellow Secessionists LOUIS WIGFALL, WILLIAM PORCHER MILES, EDMUND RUFFIN, and LAWRENCE KEITT. In effect, De Bow preached fiscal secession.[121]

His work also defended slavery, saying that, for the South, the institution had become "country, life, death—everything." For the "inferior negro race" it was the path to safety and civilization. For the slaveholder it was the highest contribution to social order. For the nonslaveholder it was the best investment to "relieve his wife from the necessities of the kitchen and the laundry, and his children from the labors of the field."[122]

Putting his fiscal skills to the test, De Bow worked in the Confederate Treasury Department. Accepting military defeat in 1865, De Bow continued the fight on the social and economic plane, denouncing emancipation and fostering Southern businesses.

The motto of *De Bow's Review* was "Commerce Is King."

---

8. WILLIAM PORCHER MILES (1822–99, SOUTH CAROLINA)

Born on the Fourth of July, a friend of bully LAWRENCE KEITT and cerebral JAMES D. B. DE BOW, William Porcher Miles by nature resembled the latter. First in his class at the College of Charleston, assistant professor of mathematics at his alma mater, mayor of Charleston from 1855 to 1857, U.S. representative from 1857 to 1860, Miles was one of the brighter minds of the radical wing.[123]

A slave owner and constant proponent of a slave empire, Miles maneuvered in 1860 to take his state out of the Union, a task he helped to complete by the end of the year. To his constituents in the House of Representatives, he recommended they allow South Carolina to go in peace or else a war would come, a civil war "so bloody, so terrible that the parallel of it has never yet blotted the page of history."[124]

Like LOUIS WIGFALL, Miles served in all Confederate Congresses (provisional, first, and second), where he chaired the military affairs committee. Unlike many other fire-eaters, Miles was a staunch supporter of Jefferson Davis, at least until the war started to threaten South Carolina in 1864. Then Miles departed from his fire-eater past and called for arming the slaves to rescue the dying Confederacy.[125]

After the war Miles became president of the University of South Carolina.

---

9. THOMAS R. R. COBB (1823–62, GEORGIA)

Brother of Montgomery Convention chairman Howell Cobb, Thomas was the younger and more radical of the two. A prolific writer, one of his most popular books was *An Inquiry into the Law of Negro Slavery* (1858), a powerful defense of the institution as a moral and economic good. Commenting as a slave owner, he wrote: "The most desirable property for a remunerative income is slaves. The best property to leave his children, and from which they will part with greatest reluctance, is slaves."[126]

For Cobb the truest enemies were not abolitionist Northerners but Southerners who longed for compromise. Despite fierce opposition from Unionist Georgians such as Alexander H. Stephens, Cobb managed to lead Georgia out of the Union in January 1861. Afterward, his successes were few.

A delegate to the Montgomery Convention, he failed in a bid to reopen the international slave trade. His impassioned pleas to forbid free states from joining the Confederacy went ignored. The final straw came when the convention selected moderates Davis and Stephens to head the new government, a defeat that sent him into a depression.[127]

Completely disillusioned with the political environment, he turned to a military career. Serving in several campaigns in the eastern theater, Cobb was at the head of his brigade at MARYE'S HEIGHTS during the December 13, 1862, battle of FREDERICKSBURG. There a bullet shattered his thigh, and he bled to death.[128]

Thomas R. R. Cobb graduated first in his class at the University of Georgia.

---

10. JOHN S. PRESTON (1809–81, VIRGINIA)

Harvard-educated John Preston amassed his fortune through a sugar plantation in Louisiana. Moving to South Carolina while in his thirties, the successful slave owner, planter, and earnest art collector rose to the state senate in 1848, a post he maintained until 1856. A gifted speaker, Preston soon became the recognized "radical champion of states' rights," professing to his contemporaries, "The conflict between slavery and non-slavery is a conflict for life and death" and any state law was equal or superior to the federal constitution. Chairman of the South Carolina delegation at the 1860 Democratic National Convention, Preston followed WILLIAM LOWNDES YANCEY's lead and removed his state from the proceedings.[129]

During the war, Preston served as P. G. T. Beauregard's aide-de-camp at Fort Sumter and FIRST MANASSAS (First Bull Run). In 1862 he was commandant of a prison camp in South Carolina then reassigned in 1863 to head the Conscription Bureau, a thankless post he manned for the remainder of the war. Following the Confederacy's defeat, Preston fled to England but returned after three years.

In a postwar speech at the University of Virginia, the still famous Preston confessed to the student audience that he was, and would always remain, unreconstructed. "Glory, glory," he clucked, "glory to Massachusetts and her Hessian and Milesian mercenaries. . . . They cannot crush that immortal hope, which rises from the blood-soaked earth of Virginia."[130]

John Preston was a brother-in-law of Wade Hampton, who owned several plantations and more than one thousand slaves.

Politics

TOP TEN SIMILARITIES BETWEEN LINCOLN AND DAVIS

Legend clouds reality. Displayed as polar opposites in popular history, American presidents Abraham Lincoln and Jefferson Davis in fact shared several traits and experiences. Throughout their lives both men displayed exceptional intellect, uncommon kindness, resilience despite hardships, and an unbreakable commitment to principle. Arguably, the outcome of the Civil War helped make these and other attributes appear as strengths in one man and weaknesses in the other.

Unquestionably there were differences. Lincoln's formal schooling totaled less than one year at the primary level. By comparison, Davis attended prominent schools, including the U.S. Military Academy at West Point. Lincoln, a skeptic especially in his youth, never joined a church, although he would occasionally attend Presbyterian services with his wife. Davis was far more religious, a long-standing member of his church and a believer in an omnipotent and paternal deity. In opposition to the patient and earthy Lincoln, Davis possessed a lightning-quick temper and a preoccupation with honor. To achieve desired ends, Lincoln relied on timing and consensus, whereas Davis, the officer and slaveholder, was accustomed to being obeyed.[1]

Along with contrasts, there remain a number of fundamental similarities shaping and defining the two individuals who would lead their governments through a war neither wanted. The following are ten predominant similarities between Lincoln and Davis, shown in chronological order.

1. BOTH WERE BORN IN KENTUCKY

One hundred miles and less than a year separated the births of the two presidents. Just as legend states, Lincoln was born in a log cabin, but so was Davis.

In Kentucky's southwestern reaches, near present-day Fairview, Samuel and Jane Davis welcomed their new son on June 3, 1808. They named him Jefferson in tribute to the third president of the United States and gave him the middle name of Finis—Latin for *final,* perhaps hoping this tenth child would be their last. He was.

Two seasons later, on February 12, 1809, Abraham Lincoln entered the world just south of Hodgenville, Kentucky. Second child of Thomas and Nancy Lincoln, he was named after his paternal grandfather.

Both families moved out of state a few years after their sons were born, the Lincolns first to Indiana then Illinois, the Davises to Louisiana then Mississippi.[2]

Lincoln and Davis remain the only presidents born in Kentucky.

2. BOTH SERVED DURING THE BLACK HAWK WAR (1832)

Lieutenant Davis of the U.S. Army was posted in and around north-western Illinois when Chief Black Hawk led hundreds of Sac and Fox eastward to reclaim the area as their own. Missing out on actual combat, Davis later escorted the captured chief down the Mississippi to federal authorities in Missouri. Davis reportedly displayed much kindness to his prisoner.[3]

Perhaps in memory of his grandfather who was killed by a Native American, but definitely to escape his shopkeeping job in New Salem, Lincoln volunteered for the Illinois militia when the Black Hawk War broke out. He joined a company that consisted mostly of friends and neighbors. They elected him captain, a tribute he recalled later as one of his life's greatest moments.

Lincoln's days as an officer passed without incident, although he and his company were twice reprimanded for disobedience. After his thirty-day enlistment expired, he mustered for two more sessions as a private, but he saw no action save for "many bloody struggles with the mosquitoes."[4]

Among others who served in the Black Hawk War were Winfield Scott (later ranking Union general), Robert Anderson (Union commander at Fort

Sumter), Joseph E. Johnston (Confederate general), and Albert Sidney Johnston (Confederate general killed at SHILOH).

---

3. BOTH SUFFERED FROM DEPRESSION

It was called melancholia, depressions of the mind, and nostalgia, yet depression and other mental illnesses were beyond the understanding of early nineteenth-century medical science. Subsequently, diagnosis and treatment were often faulty, and the most severe cases were simply referred to as madness.

Lincoln displayed telltale signs of clinical depression early. Friends and associates recalled his long bouts of debilitating sadness, which led some to consider him shiftless and lazy. Much of the prose and poetry he wrote throughout his life contained unrelenting self-criticism, a focus on miseries, and a preoccupation with death.

As much as Lincoln was and is celebrated as a rugged individualist honed by the backwoods of the American frontier, he hated his childhood. One of his first recollections was the sound of animals feeding on prey. He grew up loathing the process of hunting and fishing, found little

Jefferson Davis was thirty-nine years old when he sought public office for the first time. He went on to become a champion of states' rights and the strict interpretation of the Constitution, especially in matters pertaining to slavery. When the war began, Davis was surprised he was elected to lead the new nation; he preferred a military appointment.

joy in working the rocky fields, and lost nearly everyone close to him. Before Lincoln turned ten, his younger brother and mom had died. Before he was twenty his only sister passed away.

Still, depression came to form much of Lincoln's behavior. To fight it, he employed his trademark wit, an iron commitment to privacy, and a historically underrecognized ambition that fueled his success.[5]

Davis's self-admitted struggle with depression emerged later in life. In his youth, little Jeff had a reputation as a dreamer and a prankster. At West Point, his fun-loving behavior cost him several demerits. Preferring to read classical literature rather than study the cold sciences of the curriculum, he graduated in the bottom half of his class.

After graduation, Davis's physical health deteriorated. He suffered bouts of malaria (which killed his first wife, Sarah), pneumonia, anemia, boils, dyspepsia, bronchitis, rheumatism, angina, ear infections, tooth decay, a bullet wound to the foot (from the Mexican War), and facial neuralgia. The last caused crippling headaches and rendered one eye nearly blind. His physical and emotional pain often left him bedridden for weeks. Under doctor's orders, he would sometimes take small doses of chloroform and opium to lessen the pain.[6]

Contemporaries of Lincoln and Davis who also suffered from enduring clinical depression included Mary Chesnut, Franklin Pierce, Samuel Clemens, William Tecumseh Sherman, Alexander H. Stephens, and Ulysses S. Grant.

---

4. BOTH LOST SONS BEFORE AND DURING THEIR PRESIDENCY

Even during their most strained and serious moods, Lincoln and Davis were partial to the company of children, especially their own. Such a heightened fondness intensified their grief when they lived to bury two sons each. Lincoln's second child, Edward, died of disease in 1850, just shy of a fourth birthday. Davis's firstborn, Samuel, succumbed to illness only days before turning two in 1854. Loss would strike each man again during the Civil War.

William Wallace Lincoln was a prodigy. As a young boy he was gifted with the pen, a voracious reader, and possessed an exceptional long-term memory. In early 1862 Willie came down with fever, probably typhoid.

After suffering for weeks, despite his parents' constant care, Willie died on February 20, 1862. He was eleven years old.[7]

On April 30, 1864, Davis and his wife, Varina, were sharing a basket lunch in the second floor of the Confederate White House while their children played outside. Shortly after 1 P.M., a servant came running for the president. Five-year-old Joseph had fallen from the balcony, landing headfirst on the brick pavement twenty feet below. He was still breathing when his parents reached him. Joseph lasted only a few more minutes.

Accounts indicate both men repeated a phrase to himself on the day of his loss. Davis spoke of divine will while Lincoln lamented his son was "too good for this earth." Each man allowed himself just one day of mourning before returning to work. Both men were visibly devastated for weeks and arguably scarred for life.[8]

Among others who lost children before or during the Civil War: Nathan Bedford Forrest, James Longstreet, Stonewall Jackson, Jeb Stuart, and William Tecumseh Sherman.

---

5. BOTH SERVED IN THE U.S. CONGRESS

Of the two, Davis's prepresidential résumé easily outweighed Lincoln's. Elected to the House of Representatives in 1846, Davis resigned his seat to serve in the war against Mexico. Afterward his congressional and military records made him a popular choice as Franklin Pierce's secretary of war. Elected to the nation's upper house in 1860, Senator Davis resigned his seat once again, returning to seceding Mississippi in 1861. In a farewell address to his colleagues, he spoke of sincere hopes that his and the other seceding states could leave the Union in peace.[9]

Lincoln served a single term in Congress, a member of the U.S. House of Representatives from 1847 to 1849. He spent much of his congressional energies attacking James K. Polk's war with Mexico on the grounds that it was an unprovoked scheme to usurp land. Most of his fellow Whigs felt the same way. Lincoln and his constituents nevertheless approved the budget for the war's continuation.[10]

In 1860 Jefferson Davis turned down an offer to run for president of the United States.

---

6. NEITHER REGARDED AFRICAN AMERICANS AS EQUAL TO WHITES

Owning as many as one hundred slaves, the son of a slave owner, and hailing from a state where half of its inhabitants were in bondage, Davis espoused the "moral good" of the institution. In Congress he called for the expansion of slavery into new territories and suggested Cuba, with its half-million slaves, was prime for acquisition.[11]

To the last, Lincoln was antislavery, not pro-slave. In one of the seven debates with political opponent Stephen A. Douglas, he continued to criticize slavery as a degradation of democracy and free labor. He added, however, "I am not, nor ever have been in favor of bringing about in any way the social and political equality of the white and black races." He vehemently opposed interracial marriages and African Americans holding public office, and he was skeptical of allowing minorities the right to vote or to sit on juries. Both publicly and privately, in the same vein as Thomas Jefferson, Lincoln called for the right to life, liberty, and the pursuit of happiness for blacks as well as whites. Yet he also believed there existed unbridgeable differences between the two groups that would prevent them from ever living on the same social plane. In August 1862, a month before he announced his EMANCIPATION PROCLAMATION, he spoke with a group of free black leaders. Recolonizing outside the United States was the only path to peace for both races, he told them. "It is better for both of us," he said, "to be separated."[12]

In the 1870 elections, the man voted into Jefferson Davis's vacated senatorial seat was Hiram R. Revels, the first African American senator in U.S. history.

---

7. NEITHER ASKED TO BE NOMINATED FOR PRESIDENT

In the first century of American politics it was considered poor form to campaign for oneself. Appointments to public office were decided not by the individual but by his political constituency.

Before their party convention in 1860, Republicans at all levels began to take notice as a gathering host of newspapers promoted a coy but compelling stump speaker from Illinois. This fellow, many observed, possessed none of the abolitionist extremism, personal vices, nor prominent enemies of other potential candidates such as New Yorker William Seward or Pennsylvanian Simon Cameron. Lincoln did not request to be considered. His aspirations were for the Senate.[13]

As it was, the Republican National Convention was held in Chicago. With brilliant internal maneuvering, advocates and agents of Lincoln rode a wave of favorite son sentiment to win nomination on the third ballot.[14]

Like Lincoln, Davis did not attend the convention that chose him, but he stayed clear for very different reasons. In the spring of 1861 delegates assembled in Montgomery, Alabama, to select a provisional president for the new Confederacy. Meanwhile, Davis was at his Brierfield plantation in Mississippi, retired from politics with no ambition to return. He was, however, willing to organize Mississippi volunteers for military service should the need arise. Ironically, Davis's display of patriotism and aversion to political gain impressed the convention considerably. They unanimously selected him as president. Although grateful, Davis later confessed that he was bitterly disappointed to have lost his chance to serve the Confederacy on the field of battle.[15]

> Neither man chose his vice president. Lincoln had never met Maine's Hannibal Hamlin before they were selected as running mates. Davis and Georgia's Alexander H. Stephens were not allies before selected to serve together, and their differences intensified to hatred when the war went badly.

8. BOTH CONDEMNED JOHN BROWN'S RAID

Nearly all whites in the South feared the possibility of a slave revolt. Nat Turner's bloody 1831 uprising in Virginia, a rapidly expanding slave population, stories of slave riots in Brazil and Cuba, and the rise of radical abolitionism intensified the anxiety. In October 1859, when JOHN BROWN and a group of armed followers raided the Harpers Ferry arsenal, fear turned into outrage.

Initially, Davis joined the fury. From the Senate floor, he proclaimed the event "a murderous raid," "a conspiracy," and "a rebellion against the constitutional government of a State." Had he been an extremist, Davis might have used the raid as a rallying point for Secessionists. After assisting in a senatorial investigation, he downplayed the incident. He noted there was no slave uprising. He also found no evidence of conspiracy. Davis concluded the raid was simply "an act of lawless ruffians, under the sanction of no public or political authority."[16]

Lincoln, on the campaign trail for the Republican Party, attempted to depoliticize the event. Many Southern newspapers interpreted the raid as a product of Northern radicalism if not a failed full-fledged conspiracy headed by "Black Republicans." Partial to the sanctity of law, Lincoln disapproved of Brown's methods. Lincoln, however, knew he would lose much of his support base if he denounced Brown's goal to end slavery. To save face, he attacked the man rather than the mission, publicly reiterating a hatred for slavery while dismissing Brown's raid as an act of "violence, bloodshed, and treason."[17]

> John Brown asked Harriet Tubman and Frederick Douglass to assist in the raid. Tubman accepted the invitation then declined due to illness.

9. BOTH WERE POLITICAL MODERATES

It is one of the great ironies of American history. In a time of political, economic, and social breakdown, while passions and problems were their most intense since the Revolution, moderates led the opposing sides.

After the Democrats split into Northern and Southern factions before the 1860 presidential elections, Davis attempted to reunite the party, going so far as to ask the presidential nominees from both sections to withdrawal from the race. A compromise candidate, such as New York governor Horatio Seymour, Davis insisted, would be the only way to defeat the Republicans and maintain the Union.[18]

While his contemporaries warmed to the idea of secession, Davis opposed it. Much like his mentor JOHN C. CALHOUN, Davis threatened secession several times in Congress. He also knew, as Calhoun did, that leaving the Union meant losing Southern leverage within it. A separate South would have no say on tariffs, no chance to retrieve fugitive slaves in the North, and no share of the Union's growing economic power.[19]

After the Union fell apart, Davis took no part in the Confederate Convention. When the convention chose him to be the provisional president, they did so on the grounds that Davis had effectively distanced himself from fire-eaters and other political extremists. Even as the new country worked to select a new flag and create a new Confederate Constitution, Davis suggested that the old flag and constitution would work just fine.[20]

Lincoln functioned on the principle that a radical stand left him no room to maneuver. He consistently placed himself in the center of divergent groups, a fact most prevalent during his presidency. His cabinet consisted of several political opponents. In military appointments, he granted lofty positions to ardent Democrats as well as Republicans. Historically viewed as the Great Emancipator, he refused to court the idea of ending slavery during the first year of the war. When political and military circumstances encouraged him to issue his EMANCIPATION PROCLAMATION, he made no attempt to abolish slavery within the four slave states still loyal to the Union. Before the 1864 election he changed the name of the Republicans to the National Union Party and selected as his running mate Andrew Johnson, a lifelong Democrat from Tennessee.[21]

Reportedly, Lincoln never referred to the Confederacy as "the enemy."

---

10. BOTH WERE ACCUSED OF WEARING DRESSES

A president can make an easy target for accusations, especially in times of uncertainty. Both the Federal and Confederate Constitutions guaranteed freedom of speech and press. Journalism in the mid-1800s was not the most ethical or precise medium. As a result, it was nothing less than open season on Davis and Lincoln during the war. Several newspapers portrayed both men as incompetent, dictatorial, vacillating, corrupt, and slow. Sometimes criticism stepped beyond abuse into the bizarre.

In February 1861 president-elect Lincoln traveled from Springfield to Washington by rail. To reach the capital meant passing through slave state Maryland, which had given its eight electoral votes to Southern Democrat John C. Breckenridge and was a hotbed of secession in its southeastern counties. Lincoln had received dozens of assassination threats before and during the trek, and several sources suggested an attempt would be made on his life when he changed trains in Baltimore.[22]

Rather than risk altercation, Lincoln chose to pass through in the middle of the night. To conceal himself further, he wore a loose overcoat and soft wool cap. His stealthy entry into Washington only strengthened criticism, however, and some portions of a hostile press interpreted the

The erroneous report that Davis had been captured disguised as a woman provided ample fodder for many newspapers.

coat to be a woman's frock. Lincoln was accustomed to opposition, but accusations of cross-dressing were rather new.

At the other end of the war, Jefferson Davis had become a convenient scapegoat. Just before Richmond fell to the Army of the Potomac, Davis and a small contingent of staff and associates sped southward by horse and wagon. Labeled a coward, Davis intended to link up with any remaining Confederate forces to continue the fight for as long as possible.

On May 10, 1865, Davis, his wife, and two others encountered Federal troops near Irwinville, Georgia. Hearing the approaching cavalry, Davis accidentally put on his wife's sleeveless overcoat, one very much like his own, and wore it underneath a shawl as he attempted to reach his horse. The Federals caught him soon after, overcoat and all. A vilifying rumor mill tailored the story into one involving a full-fledged dress.[23]

In 1861 a wool dress cost ten Confederate dollars. By 1865 rampant inflation pushed the price up to eight hundred Confederate dollars.

TOP TEN DIFFERENCES BETWEEN THE CONFEDERATE AND U.S. CONSTITUTIONS

March 11, 1861—Members of the Montgomery Convention, having assembled the previous month to declare the formation of a new country, rose one by one to give their final vote on the Constitution of the Confederate States of America. Represented were six states: Alabama, Florida, Georgia, Louisiana, Mississippi, and South Carolina. Also present were delegates from newcomer Texas, which had finalized secession just ten days earlier.

Together there were fifty delegates. All were male, white, formally educated, middle-aged, and experienced in civil service. Many were still fond of the old Union, notable exceptions being fire-eaters ROBERT BARNWELL RHETT of South Carolina, THOMAS R. R. COBB of Georgia, and LOUIS T. WIGFALL of Texas.[24]

Starting with an ad hoc provisional constitution, the convention worked to create a permanent version, first by a committee of twelve and then through debate from the assembly as a whole. Several delegates were encouraged if not ordered by their state conventions to adhere closely to the Federal Constitution. To roam far from the original, they feared, would give the impression that this new movement was seditious and fanatical. Also there was no time or need to reinvent something that had served them so well. Only Northern manipulation of the original Constitution, argued the Secessionists, had caused so much consternation. In what should have been seen as foreshadowing, no one seriously considered returning to the Articles of Confederation of 1777, a political experiment that floundered from disunity.[25]

Despite fueling angry exchanges between the delegates, the final draft received resounding approval. The convention, it appears, wished to present to the country and the world a united front. The end tally was unanimous; all fifty delegates voted to adopt the new constitution. From beginning to end it took them thirty days, less than half the time required for the creation of the one it replaced.[26]

Following are the top ten most significant areas in which the Confederate Constitution differed from its Federal counterpart in terms of the degree of departure and its eventual consequences on the operations of the Confederate political enterprise.[27]

The Confederate Constitution of 1861 . . .

1. . . . EXPRESSLY DEFENDED THE RIGHT OF SLAVERY,

Slavery nearly derailed the Constitution of 1787. Slave and free states could not agree on the inclusion or exclusion of slavery for the country as a whole. Eventually, the Philadelphia Convention used the ambiguous term "persons" rather than "slaves" and delayed final decision on the institution's fate, hoping future generations could peacefully resolve the issue.

Montgomery was not Philadelphia. Of the fifty-five members of the Philadelphia convention, 25 percent owned slaves. Of the fifty members of the Confederate convention, 98 percent were slave owners (although less than 30 percent of white males in the South owned slaves in 1861). Forty-eight of the fifty men were born in slave states, and thirty-three stated their profession to be "planter." Guarantees they had requested time and again from the old Union could now be attained without opposition.

When determining the number of representatives to be apportioned per each state's population, the Confederate version altered the infamous "three-fifths of all other Persons" clause to read "three-fifths of all slaves."

The Confederate Constitution also retained the ban on international slave trade, much to the disappointment of ROBERT BARNWELL RHETT and a handful of others. The convention knew that to repeal the clause would eliminate any chance of international recognition from antislavery Great Britain and France, and yet the convention replaced the word "Persons" with "negroes of the African race."[28]

In protecting a citizen's rights from state to state, the Confederate version added "the right of transit and sojourn in any State of this Confederacy, with their slaves and other property; and the right of property in said slaves shall not be thereby impaired." There also emerged a strengthened fugitive slave law, pledging the return of slaves "escaping or unlawfully carried" into another state or territory back "to whom such service or labor may be due."[29]

Concerning the future acquisition of any new territories (conceivably from Mexico, Cuba, or parts of Central and South America), the Confederate Constitution stated, "In all such territory the institution of negro slavery, . . . shall be recognized and protected by Congress," a provision powered by memories of Bleeding Kansas and the split of the Democratic Party over popular sovereignty.

Slavery was to be legal, protected, and enforced everywhere and in every state and territory to come. An irony existed that some may have seen but no one argued: In a movement founded on states' rights, the right of any state to infringe upon these federal regulations did not exist.

Absent from the U.S. Constitution, the terms "slaves" or "slavery" appeared in the Confederate Constitution ten times.

---

2. . . . OUTLAWED NEARLY ALL INTERNAL IMPROVEMENTS,

The concept of internal improvements vexed many nineteenth-century citizens, as it still does today. How was it right and just to take funds raised in one portion of the country and use it to finance projects in another? Young politicians from the developing West like Abraham Lincoln supported the policy. Most Southern politicians hated the idea. Rural and agrarian, the South simply did not have the fiscal appetite or the infrastructure requirements of the more urban and industrialized states to the North.[30]

In the old Union there wasn't much the Southern states could do. Much like decisions concerning slavery, decisions on appropriations were destined to be predominantly unfavorable to the South if done on a national level, because the South simply did not have the votes. In 1820 slave states had lost a majority in the House of Representatives. By 1850 parity in the Senate was gone, with no indication of equaling again.

For their decades of fighting against internal improvements, the delegates still could not eliminate the practice from their new constitution. Article 1, Section 8, Paragraph 3 stated the Confederate Congress could not "appropriate money for any internal improvement intended to facilitate commerce; except for the purpose of furnishing lights, beacons, and buoys, and other aids of navigation upon the coasts, and the improvements of harbors."

In 1853 the U.S. Government bought a tract of land from Mexico for $10 million in order to build a transcontinental railroad. The orchestrator of the Gadsden Purchase was Secretary of War Jefferson Davis.

---

3. . . . DELETED THE TERM "GENERAL WELFARE,"

From the preamble the Confederate committee of twelve omitted "provide for the common defense" and "promote the general Welfare." The term "general Welfare" was also stricken from Article 1. The old preamble, reasoned the delegates, invited the central government to override the best judgments, interests, and inherent responsibilities of the states.

Intentionally provincial in their rationale, the omissions were also anti-egalitarian in principle. The Southern "way of life," so often celebrated in Secessionist arguments, revolved around a kind of benevolent paternalism, where supposedly no one but wise men of education and property knew how to serve and provide for the remainder of the population. In an effort to dilute concepts of equality still further, there were motions to strike the words "We the People" from the document, a stance that was summarily dismissed as too extreme.[31]

How strong were "the People" in the new Confederacy? Unlike the Federal version, the Confederate Constitution had "people" typeset in lower case.

---

4. . . . OUTLAWED PROTECTIVE TARIFFS,

Of all the perceived threats upon Southern economic integrity and political honor, the most real was arguably the federal use of tariffs—the artificial increase of prices on foreign goods to protect domestic manufacturing. Many Southerners considered tariffs pointless, because the agrarian South had no great manufacturing interests to protect. More important, the South's cash-poor economy could ill afford to pay higher prices for imported items. Nearly every yard of cloth, section of rail, plowshare, pill, pistol, and locomotive in the South came from somewhere else.[32]

Tariffs also stunted Southern industrial growth as they increased the costs of drills, belts, boilers, bearings, and other basics required for transition from manual to mechanized production. The Confederacy would have none of that. In creating free trade, the convention hoped that the South would have an open and relatively inexpensive lifeline to Britain and France.

Unfortunately, as the Confederacy eventually learned, ceasing protective tariffs also liberated the Confederate government from the beefy revenues that came with them. During the war years the Union raked in more than $300 million from protective tariffs. Strangled by the blockade and unable to tariff much of anything, Confederate customhouses raised less than $4 million.[33]

In 1832 South Carolina threatened to secede from the United States, not over slavery, but over the federal imposition of high import tariffs.

5. . . . ADDED A LINE-ITEM VETO,

In 1861 one Northern state and one Southern state had line-item vetoes available to their governors. The Confederate Constitution adopted the policy, empowering the presidency to reject any portion of a prospective bill the executive deemed unwarranted.

The ease with which this provision gained acceptance reflected a fiscal skepticism among the delegates. Of the fifty members, forty-five had experience in state legislatures and twenty-three had served in the U.S. Congress. Many had witnessed pork-barrel issues and questionable rider projects attached parasitically to legitimate legislation.

Veto is Latin for "I forbid."

6. . . . DICTATED A SINGLE TERM FOR THE PRESIDENT,

George Washington declined to run for a third term, setting protocol for a self-imposed term limit for chief executives. No legal foundation existed, however, for a president to stop at two. With a collective suspicion of centralized power, the Confederate Convention imposed, "He and the Vice President shall hold their offices for the term of six years; but the President shall not be re-eligible."

History hardly justified much concern. A majority of presidents before Lincoln hailed from the South, eight owned slaves during their presidency, and most were sympathetic to Southern interests. Longevity was not an issue, as the last eight presidents all served four years or less, due in no small part to their respective inability to calm the rough waters of sectionalism.

Yet all seven states in the convention seceded from the Union because a section of the country elected a president they did not want. This was not a group ready to take a chance on any president ruling for long.[34]

The issue of duration was eventually invalidated by fortunes of war. Apparently, the Union army and navy were also interested in limiting the Confederate presidency to a single term.

The Twenty-second Amendment added a presidential term limit to the U.S. Constitution—ninety years after the Confederate Constitution stipulated such.

---

7. . . . OVERTLY MENTIONED GOD,

The phrase appeared in the Confederacy's provisional constitution, "invoking the favor and guidance of Almighty God." The wording survived without opposition through committee and convention to appear in the preamble of the final document.

Spiritual language was nothing new in American politics. The Declaration of Independence referred to "Nature's God," the "Supreme Judge of the World," and "a firm reliance on the protection of Divine Providence." In the fight over slavery, defenders quoted Bible passages and opponents spoke of a law higher than the U.S. Constitution. Each session of the U.S. Congress began with an official prayer (as it still does).

Yet to include a reference to "Almighty God" into the supreme law of the land was something the original Founding Fathers refused to do. The men of the Philadelphia Convention recounted medieval Rome, Bourbon France, a certain King George III, and other tyrannical regimes that claimed power by divine right. From the quills of James Madison and Thomas Jefferson came eloquent pleas for religious tolerance and an enduring separation of church from government.[35]

By comparison, the men of the Montgomery Convention wished to appear more evangelical in their sentiments, enjoining deity with deed. The image desired was that of a system still based on the mechanical logic of checks and balances but standing firm and righteous against a secular and heartless enemy.[36]

The national motto of the Confederacy was *Deo Vindice*—"God will avenge."

---

8. ... EASED THE PROCESS OF AMENDMENTS,

Changes can be proposed to the U.S. Constitution by a two-thirds approval from the House and the Senate, or by two-thirds of the states calling for a convention. Passage requires ratification by at least three-fourths of all states.

In a compromise between the hard-line states' rights faction and the conservative element, the Confederate Constitution allowed an amendment to be considered if only three separate state conventions called for it. To prevent a flood of amendments but still facilitate change, the three-fourths' provision for ratification was reduced to two-thirds.

All twelve amendments then existing in the U.S. Constitution were incorporated into Article 1 of the Confederate Constitution.

---

9. ... STIPULATED A SELF-SUFFICIENT POST OFFICE,

Article 1, Section 8, Paragraph 7 dictated "the expenses of the Post office department, after the 1st day of March in the year of our Lord eighteen hundred and sixty-three, shall be paid out of its own revenues." The establishment of post offices also existed in the U.S. Constitution, but there was no accompanying stipulation to operate in the black. Robert Toombs of Georgia introduced the idea in committee, and WILLIAM PORCHER MILES of South Carolina added the two-year time limit in convention.

The postal clause came from a political body fully aware that money and time were two luxuries it did not possess. Revenues were expected to be scarce. There was no national income tax. The convention omitted protective tariffs, cutting off a certainly unpopular but financially helpful source of capital. The Southern Confederacy had been born from a comprehensive distaste for fiscal intrusions, yet such intrusions were sorely missed once the financial costs of warfare began to accumulate.

A self-sufficient Confederate post office was in fact achieved in less than two years, but in the effort to keep costs down, the service became notoriously unreliable.

---

10. . . . AND DECLARED SUPREMACY OF STATE OVER CENTRAL GOVERNMENT.

From the 1830s onward the resounding chime of states' rights rang warm in the hearts of an increasing number in the South. It long stood as a popular expression, a default response to any unfavorable decision made by the federal government. By 1860, after bloody fights over territories, national elections, and fugitive slaves, the appeal had reached much of the Southern free population.[37]

Moved to maintain this sanctified message of states first, the convention began the defining document with "We the people of the Confederate States, each State acting in its sovereign and independent character."

For all the hope and glory of state supremacy, the means were largely absent from the Confederate Constitution. The president remained commander in chief of the army, navy, and state militias. Also, the president could attain the right to suspend habeas corpus (a right the Congress granted Davis early in the war). As stated above, the executive held the power of a line-item veto. Although never implemented, Article 1, Section 7 permitted members of the president's cabinet to hold seats within either of the congressional houses, a clause designed to offer leverage for defense of executive measures. Minting coins, forming treaties, regulating weights and measures, naturalizing citizens, plus setting and collecting levies were still in the hands of the central government and not the states.

The Confederate Constitution also replaced the idealistic phrase, "a more perfect Union," with the pragmatic assertion, "a permanent federal government." This suggested a centralizing rather than a confederating theme. By some interpretations the change also implied that the right to secede was an option in the Union but not in the Confederacy.[38]

For all the supposed clarifications and favorable alterations to this new Constitution, reality had its own purposes. Out of the frying pan and into the fire, the seceded states soon squabbled over the same issues of rights and sovereignty within the Confederacy as they had within the Union.[39]

There was a modicum of discussion within the convention to name the new country something other than the Confederate States. Suggestions included Chicora, Columbia, the Federal Republic of America, the Southern United States, the Gulf States of the Confederacy, Alleghenia, and Washington.

TOP TEN ACTS OF GOVERNMENT

It can be said that none benefited more from secession than the Republican Party. A division of the country also divided the Democrats, who usually held the presidency and dominated the House and Senate by large margins. Over the span of the war, Republican bills passed that would have never seen the light of day had the Southern balance remained.

Alternately, the Confederate Congress struggled tremendously. The growing pains of governance, the crippling lack of revenue, and the destabilizing force of an invading enemy created a need for a powerful centralized government—the very situation Secessionists claimed they were leaving behind. To make matters worse, if the Confederacy were to fail, Southerners in and out of politics knew what was in store. They would reenter a Union far more centralized and Republican than the one they had left.

In addition to the Internal Revenue Act, Legal Tender Act, and Conscription Acts (listed in FIRSTS, pp. 192–95), the following were the most significant acts of government in domestic politics. These ten have been selected for their effect on the direction of the war and their lasting influence on the country as a whole. They are listed in chronological order of implementation.

1. SUSPENSION OF THE WRIT OF HABEAS CORPUS (U.S., APRIL 27, 1861)

"To produce the body," the writ of habeas corpus is a long-standing pillar of English common law. Without it, citizens could be incarcerated without charges, evidence, or trial. Both the U.S. and Confederate Constitutions permit suspension of the writ in times of "Rebellion or Invasion."

Lincoln suspended the writ immediately. With his capital resting south of the Mason-Dixon Line and bordered by Confederate Virginia and slave state Maryland, he ordered a suspension for the Philadelphia and Washington areas. In 1862 he issued another abeyance for all arrests conducted by the military. In 1863 Congress authorized the suspension for the whole of the Union.

In February 1862 the Confederate Congress granted Davis similar powers. Denying an extension in 1863, legislators gave a limited renewal of Davis's authority in February 1864.[40]

Under the suspension, government officials could and did seize citizens suspected of espionage, draft evasion, inciting insurrection, desertion, trading with the enemy, and guerrilla activities, with and without evidence. Of the two sides, the Union suspended the writ with greater impunity, making an estimated fourteen thousand arrests over four years, mostly within the Border States.[41]

Throughout the war both presidents endured a steady stream of criticism for suspending the writ, accusing them of power mongering, abusing civil liberties, and vying for permanent dictatorship. Yet Lincoln and Davis actually discouraged suspension of the writ in cases of speech, press, and assembly.[42]

When Chief Justice Roger Taney protested the suspension of the writ of habeas corpus, Lincoln briefly considered arresting the chief justice.

---

2. CONFISCATION ACT (U.S., AUGUST 6, 1861)

Between his election and inauguration, a span of just four months, Abraham Lincoln watched seven states leave the Union. After the surrender of Fort Sumter, four more departed: Virginia in April, Arkansas and North Carolina in May, and Tennessee in June. July brought a military beating along the banks of Bull Run. Four slave states still remained, and Lincoln was willing to do almost anything to keep them from joining the Confederacy. This included upholding the Fugitive Slave Law, which mandated federal cooperation in returning runaways to their owners. His adherence to the law incensed abolitionists and militarists alike. In an effort to appease the nonseceded Border States, critics argued, Lincoln coddled slavery, over half the labor force of the rebellion.[43]

Forcing the issue were the slaves themselves, escaping to Union lines by the hundreds. If he instructed officers to hold on to them, Lincoln risked losing the last four slave states in the Union. If he handed the slaves back, he could surrender his base of support among free states and possibly Europe.

Republican-led Congress offered a compromise. Slaves used by the Confederate army—for example, in the construction of forts—could be confiscated as property used against the Union. All other escapees would be returned.

Congress passed a second confiscation act on July 17, 1862. Along with authorizing the seizure of land and resources of those supporting armed insurrection, the act also granted freedom to slaves escaping from inside Confederate-held areas, unless their owners were loyal to the Union. Five days after the bill passed, Lincoln began a rough draft of a proclamation to emancipate all slaves in enemy territory.[44]

Of the 179,000 African Americans who served in the Union army, more than half came from the slave states of Kentucky, Louisiana, Mississippi, and Tennessee.

3. HOMESTEAD ACT (U.S., MAY 20, 1862)

Although a bill had been in the works for decades, legislation to provide government land to settlers was extremely unpopular among Southerners and, understandably, Native Americans. President James Buchanan vetoed a version in 1860, suggesting it was unwise to give away land at no cost. Yet Republicans included the idea in their party platform.

Effective opposition left with secession, and the U.S. Congress passed the Homestead Act in 1862, restricting entitlement to those who had "never borne arms against the United States Government or given aid and comfort to its enemies." Citizens could gain ownership of designated public land up to 160 acres, provided they live on and "improve" that land for five years and pay a ten-dollar fee for the paperwork.[45]

The act was an early form of welfare and simultaneously garnered votes and fueled rapid expansion into the Dakotas, Michigan, Minnesota, and Missouri. By 1864, with the law not yet two years old, more than one million acres had been claimed by settlers.

Through the Homestead Act eventually a half million settlers received eighty million acres, an area of land more than twice the size of New York State.

4. PACIFIC RAILWAY ACT (U.S., JULY 1, 1862)

For a dozen years the federal government surveyed, debated, and coveted plans for the creation of a rail line from the East to the land, ports, and gold of California. Agreeing on the destination, Congress naturally had a division over the point of origination, and each region had valid points for arguing why it should be the eastern terminus. The North possessed a majority of the people, money, and industries, including a virtual monopoly on the production of rail iron and steam engines. The South owned the dual monarchy of King Cotton (the most lucrative U.S. crop) and the River Queen (New Orleans as the largest city west of the eastern seaboard). Of course this competition ceased with the outbreak of war.

Begun in 1862 and completed by 1869, construction of the Pacific Railway cemented Northern domination of commercial traffic, facilitated the reduction of bison herds from millions to one thousand, and made hinterland California a prominent and populous state in a matter of years. Along with these and many other dramatic changes, Section 2 of the act foreshadowed the continuation of a known pattern: "The United States shall extinguish as rapidly as may be the Indian titles to all lands falling under the operation of this act."[46]

In a show of patriotism, the corporation formed to lay down this track was named the "Union Pacific Railroad Company."

---

5. LAND-GRANT ACT (U.S., JULY 2, 1862)

Prior to the Civil War the best engineering colleges in the country were military schools. Students sought entry to the U.S. Military Academy at West Point and the Virginia Military Institute more for a degree in applied science than for a chance at a career in the army, which lacked luster on the basis of frontier duty, meager pay, and little chance for promotion. Opportunities for enrollment into these schools, however, were extremely limited.

The 1862 Land-Grant Act (introduced by Congressman Justin Morrill of Vermont) offered a fundamental change in the access and application of higher learning. For every senator and representative a state possessed, a state would receive thirty thousand acres of public land. States were to use or sell this land to establish and maintain schools of industrial, agricultural, and mechanical engineering. Most of the property was in the West, whereas most of the people were in the East. Thus the act was a lopsided arrangement indeed, but it eventually proved beneficial to the whole country, including the states temporarily detached from the Union.

Of limited effect during the war, the Morrill Act eventually made higher education available to the lower economic strata. Places such as Cornell and Ohio were joined after the war by Mississippi State and Texas A&M. Nearly 150 years later, more than 100 schools are commonly referred to as land-grant colleges.[47]

The 1862 Land-Grant Act stipulated the inclusion of classes in military tactics and strategy. These campus courses evolved into what is now known as ROTC.

6. EMANCIPATION PROCLAMATION (U.S., JANUARY 1, 1863)

Motivated by a growing public antagonism toward slaveholding, and seeking a way to reduce international sympathy with the Confederates, Lincoln wrote a preliminary emancipation proclamation in July 1862. Members of his cabinet suggested he wait until a Union military victory allowed him to present the proclamation from a position of strength.

Lincoln began work on the Emancipation Proclamation during the summer of 1862. He shared it with his cabinet in late July, and the members advised that he not publish it until the Union army had won a substantial battle.

LIBRARY OF CONGRESS

When the Army of the Potomac scored a close win at the battle of ANTIETAM, Lincoln made his declaration public.[48]

Observers in the South and Europe regarded the edict as an attempt to incite slave uprisings. Jefferson Davis labeled it "the most execrable measure in the history of guilty man." The LONDON *TIMES* was a little more vivid in its rebuke: "When blood begins to flow and shrieks come piercing through the darkness, Mr. Lincoln will wait until the rising flames tell that all is consummated, and then he will rub his hands and think that revenge is sweet."[49]

Perhaps half of the Union supported the proclamation, a fourth were against, and another fourth were in between. Meanwhile, soldiers witnessed firsthand the conditions of slavery, and the public sought ways to ennoble a costly war. Public backing gradually increased.[50]

The proclamation did not free a single slave, referring only to slaves in "states and parts of states wherein the people thereof, respectively, are this day in rebellion." To help bring these areas back into the Union, the proclamation included a passage declaring freed blacks "will be received into the armed service of the United States to garrison forts, positions, stations, and other places, and to man vessels of all sorts in said service."[51]

For slaves not in areas of rebellion, Lincoln was less generous. In December 1862 he advised Congress to create a constitutional amendment abolishing slavery in the loyal states by the year 1900.

---

7. TAX-IN-KIND MEASURE (C.S., APRIL 24, 1863)

Hesitant to tax their constituency, the Confederate Congress eventually found the government chronically short of funds and withering under inflation. To make up ground, the legislature enacted a comprehensive tax plan in 1863, hoping to put Richmond and the war effort back on stable economic footing.

The plan was rather abrupt, taxing alcohol, flour, rice, sugar, tobacco, and wool. Citizens were subject to income taxes and sales taxes up to 10 percent. Taxes were also to be levied on a myriad of professional licenses. Worst of the lot was a tax-in-kind measure, authorizing the government to seize 10 percent of all farm products.[52]

Designed to resolve food and supply shortages, the tax-in-kind levy worsened it. An army of three thousand government collection agents scoured the countryside, arbitrarily determining what constituted 10 percent of a family's animals and crops. In response, farmers hid their harvests or sold them on the black market. Much of what was confiscated never made it to the intended recipients. Storing and transporting acquired goods proved to be excessively complicated, leaving untold tons of bacon, corn, peas, and beef to rot in depots.[53]

For their title and tactics, Confederate tax-in-kind agents were unceremoniously referred to as "TIK men."

---

8. THE THIRTEENTH AMENDMENT (U.S., JANUARY 31, 1865)

The House and Senate passed a Thirteenth Amendment to the Constitution in February 1861. Had it been ratified, it would have prohibited any federal obstruction of slavery within the states. Nearly four years later a very different Thirteenth Amendment entered the House and Senate for consideration.

Introduced by Republican leaders in 1864, the brief clause stated: "Neither slavery nor involuntary servitude . . . shall exist within the United States, or any place subject to their jurisdiction." Passing easily in the Republican-dominated Senate, heavy Democratic opposition in the House left it well short of the required two-thirds majority.

In the November elections Lincoln retained his office, and his party made huge congressional gains. With impending dominance over government contracts and civil service opportunities, Lincoln and his associates convinced lame-duck Democrats that it was in their best interest to support the measure. On January 31, 1865, the Thirteenth Amendment passed with three votes to spare. Thunderous applause swelled throughout the chambers and lasted unbroken for several minutes. The recently finished Capitol dome shuddered as nearby batteries fired a hundred-gun salute.[54]

By December 1865 the required three-fourths of all states (including eight of eleven former Confederate states) ratified the amendment, removing slavery from the Constitution and the country.[55]

The war lasted forty-eight months. The Thirteenth Amendment consists of forty-eight words.

---

9. NEGRO SOLDIER BILL (C.S., MARCH 1865)

African Americans were serving in the Union navy by September 1862. Through the EMANCIPATION PROCLAMATION and other measures, recruitment into the army was in full swing by early 1863, although freedmen had tried to volunteer since Fort Sumter.[56]

A complicated affair for the North, arming blacks was a nonissue for the South, until attrition depleted Confederate ranks to the breaking point. As early as January 1864, Gen. PATRICK CLEBURNE openly endorsed the idea of turning slaves into soldiers. Jefferson Davis rejected the proposal without hesitation. But by November 1864, speaking before the Confederate Congress, Davis himself reluctantly suggested discussion on the matter. In Congress, among the press, and from slave owners, opposition was overwhelming.[57]

In the following months, support for a Negro Soldier Bill grew steadily, including an endorsement from a long silent ROBERT E. LEE. Still, the measure died in the Confederate Senate by one vote. Only Virginia, acting on its own behalf, passed a bill authorizing the formation of slave regiments.[58]

In the end, the effect was minimal. Virginia managed to form only a few poorly armed companies. Richmond fell before they could be sent into action. Yet the debate over the Negro Soldier Bill was an unintentional compliment to the slaves themselves, suggesting the Confederacy could not survive war or peace without their help.

In February 1865 Jefferson Davis received petitions supporting the enlistment of slaves into the Confederate army. The petitions came from Confederate soldiers stationed in the trenches of Petersburg.

---

10. AMNESTY PROCLAMATION (U.S., DECEMBER 25, 1868)

There was no definitive end to the Civil War, no peace treaty, no Armistice Day to speak of. For all intents and purposes, the life of the Confederacy had reached its end with Lee's surrender at Appomattox on April 9, 1865. Joseph E. Johnston, however, did not officially surrender his emaciated Army of Tennessee until April 26. There was one last battle, on May 13 at Palmito Ranch, Texas—a Confederate victory.

Political milestones were just as inconclusive. Jefferson Davis was not captured until May 10, 1865. In 1870 Georgia was the last Confederate state readmitted into the Union. Federal occupation of the South did not end until 1877.

A frequently cited termination point is President Andrew Johnson's granting a general amnesty on Christmas Day 1868. Johnson's days in the White House were coming to an end. So as to go out in a favorable way, he would "hereby proclaim and declare unconditionally, and without reservation, to all and to every person who directly or indirectly participated in the late resurrection or rebellion, a pardon and amnesty for the offense of treason against the United States."[59]

For Radical Republicans taking a hard-line approach to reconstructing the South, this was one more instance where Johnson was "soft on sedition." A Democrat from Tennessee, he became Lincoln's running partner in 1864 when the Republicans hoped to widen their appeal. Loyal to the Union, Johnson had no affection for African Americans, a point he proved repeatedly during his presidency.

In 1866 Johnson vetoed civil rights measures and opposed the Fourteenth Amendment, which secured citizenship to African Americans. He worked diligently to return confiscated land to former slave owners, acreage initially intended for disbursement to former slaves.[60] Despite such policies, the Democrats refused to nominate him for the presidential election in 1868.

When eleven Confederate states seceded, all of their U.S. senators resigned their seats, with the exception of a Unionist from Tennessee, Andrew Johnson. He remained loyal to the Union throughout the war and was rewarded with the vice presidency.

TOP TEN EVENTS IN FOREIGN AFFAIRS

Although not a world power in the nineteenth century, the United States was a rising force. Having bettered the British Empire in the Revolution and the War of 1812, taken one-third of Mexico in 1848, and opened the ports of isolationist Japan in 1854, little seemed to stand in the country's way. Consequently, the potent newcomer surprised much of the world when it suddenly seemed to crumble apart.

Far from occurring in a vacuum, the war in the United States was very much a multinational affair. Many American farms, railroads, plantations, mills, and banks ran on international investment. Nearly a quarter of the continent was foreign born. The American Revolution succeeded largely because of foreign intervention. If the Civil War turned into a stalemate, international relations could decide the outcome.

In chronological order, the following were the most significant transnational episodes of the war. Not surprisingly, these events involved the usual modes of international intrigue: smuggling, coercion, begging, and threats.

1. THE CONFEDERATE QUEST FOR DIPLOMATIC RECOGNITION (APRIL 1861–MARCH 1865)

Jefferson Davis and much of the South assumed that, sooner or later, France and Britain would officially sanction the Confederacy. The European powers encouraged this assumption by declaring the Confederacy a belligerent—a de facto government engaged in a war that was not illegal. Such a declaration was one step shy of granting de jure status—complete and diplomatic recognition of the government as sovereign and independent.[61]

Brimming with confidence, Davis was somewhat careless in selecting his diplomats. First to head the Richmond delegation was temperamental, uncouth, slave-owning, fire-eating WILLIAM LOWNDES YANCEY. Surprised by his inability to court European approval, Yancey vexed, "The antislavery sentiment is universal. *Uncle Tom's Cabin* has been read and believed." In September 1861 he resigned and headed home.[62]

His replacements, John Slidell and James Mason, fared little better. Reluctant participants in the *TRENT* AFFAIR, the two diplomats did not possess either the charisma or the diplomatic ingenuity required to sway their hosts. In all fairness, factors of greater significance worked against them.

Napoleon III of France was nearly indifferent to the American problem, and he would make no move to recognize the Confederacy unless Britain moved first. No fans of the United States, British prime minister Lord Henry Palmerston and foreign minister Lord John Russell were nonetheless lifelong veterans of public service. Despite bouts of nationalist rhetoric and saber rattling, the two were committed to "wait and see."

What they saw was a British public remarkably pro-Union. As much as the LONDON TIMES promoted the Confederacy, the London *Economist*, Edinburgh *Review*, and others were less than pro-South. British bankers and businessmen held interests in Union shipping, railways, and factories. The working poor had little sympathy for "Slaveownia." For all Britons, there was an empire to concern them with no need to invite the wrath of the Americans once again.[63]

The biggest block to recognition was the intermittent success of the Union army. Palmerston and Russell were close to mediating an end to the war when the Army of the Potomac edged the Confederates in the battle of ANTIETAM. Lincoln's following EMANCIPATION PROCLAMATION brought slavery to the forefront of the conflict; it was an institution Britain disdained even more than the Union. In the summer of 1863 mediation again came under consideration until the Union appeared destined for eventual success after victories at GETTYSBURG and VICKSBURG. That August the Confederate Secretary of State JUDAH P. BENJAMIN all but gave up on foreign recognition.[64]

Reportedly, only one nation ever diplomatically recognized the Confederacy: the German Duchy of Saxe-Coburg-Gotha.

---

2. THE BLOCKADE (APRIL 1861–APRIL 1865)

In April 1861 Lincoln declared a "blockade" of Southern ports. His verbiage surprised foreign merchants and public officials. Under international law, a country *blockades* another country, it *closes* its own ports. For a man normally careful with his declarations, Lincoln had, in so many words, recognized the Confederacy as an independent nation state.[65]

CSS *Virginia* was designed first and foremost to break the Union blockade.

International law also considers a blockade legal only when it is effective, that is to say, when "might makes right." At the time of Lincoln's statement, the Union navy consisted of only a few dozen functioning ships, many of them stationed in far-off waters. The Confederacy had thirty-five hundred miles of coastline, ten major ports, and hundreds of inlets, sounds, and bays. For months private vessels both foreign and domestic continued to pierce the Union's quarantine. Lincoln appeared to be losing both a military and legal battle.[66]

Yet armed with a superior industry and led by industrious Secretary of the Navy Gideon Welles, the Union began to achieve success on the waters. By late 1862 the Union had more than four hundred ships and twenty-eight thousand men monitoring Southern shores. In opposition the Confederacy mustered just thirty armed vessels and a few thousand sailors.[67]

For adventurous merchants, blockade running turned from a sport to a pitfall. In 1861 only one of ten runs failed. By 1865 the U.S. Navy caught half of all departures, convincing foreign navies to shy away from intervention. In the end, might did make right.[68]

Among the Confederate blockade-runners was a lightning-quick sailing ship called *America,* winner and namesake of the first cup race in 1851.

3. BRITISH MANUFACTURE OF CONFEDERATE CRUISERS
(JUNE 1861–SEPTEMBER 1864)

By the end of June 1861 France, Britain, and Spain declared neutrality toward the Civil War. This declaration permitted the selling of arms and ships to belligerents under international law. Immediately the Confederacy contracted British shipbuilders to construct seafaring cruisers.

British law, though, forbade selling armed ships to belligerents. Builders sidestepped the restriction by constructing unarmed cruisers, taking them out on "test runs" in open waters, then equipping them with weaponry in the Azores or the Bahamas. The Confederacy received some eighteen cruisers in this fashion.[69]

Designed to seek and destroy Union merchant vessels, three of these seagoing raiders were conspicuously lethal. The CSS *Florida* captured or sank thirty-six commercial ships, the CSS *Shenandoah* another forty, and the CSS *Alabama* an astounding sixty-six before being cornered and sunk near Cherbourg, France.[70]

U.S. citizens lost millions of dollars in ships and cargo. Insurance rates and import prices rocketed. Shipping companies refused service or sailed under foreign flags. Under the definition of "high seas," "belligerents," and "warfare" in international law, the Confederate raids were all above board.

Despite fervent efforts from its navy, the Union failed to stop the Confederate raiders. Nevertheless, the government did sue Britain for damages. In a landmark case, arbitrators finally settled the *Alabama* Claims in 1872, awarding the U.S. government $15,500,000 in British gold.

> While raiding ships in the Pacific, the crew of the CSS *Shenandoah* did not hear of its country's defeat until August 1865—four months after the fact. The crew surrendered the vessel in Liverpool, England, on November 6, 1865.

4. THE COTTON EMBARGO (SEPTEMBER 1861–APRIL 1865)

The plan seemed simple enough. Much of Britain's industry and exports involved processed cotton, and more than 70 percent of its raw cotton came from the southern United States. If Britain lost access to its white fiber, reasoned many Southern lawmakers, the British Empire would have to intervene on behalf of the South or face economic implosion.[71]

To speed up the process, Richmond discouraged farmers from growing cotton. Planters converted their fields to other crops. Some state and local governments made it illegal to grow or sell the staple altogether.

Ultimately, a multitude of conditions torpedoed the plan. First, the 1860 harvest was one of the best ever, and British warehouses were filled with the surplus. Even as stocks dwindled and factories shut down, the laboring poor of England backed the Union cause, blaming the shortage on the aristocratic Confederacy. By 1863 new supplies came in from Egypt, India, and Brazil as well as several tons smuggled out of the South. Last but not least, much of Britain saw the self-imposed embargo as blackmail, a tactic they found less than palatable.[72] Historian Charles Hubbard poignantly observed that, in the end, no one was more dependent on cotton than the South.[73]

In 1860 the number one U.S. export was cotton. By 1862 cotton exports were at 2 percent of prewar levels.

---

5. THE *TRENT* AFFAIR (NOVEMBER 1861–JANUARY 1862)

On November 8, 1861, Capt. Charles Wilkes of the USS *San Jacinto* captured and detained two men from the mail steamer *Trent* off the coast of Cuba. Neither pirates nor sailors, the men Wilkes seized were former U.S. Sens. John Slidell of Louisiana and James Mason of Virginia—two Confederate envoys on their way to seek diplomatic recognition from Britain and France.[74]

The Northern public celebrated the great catch, Congress gave Wilkes its official thanks, but Lincoln worried. Forcibly removing passengers from an unarmed ship in international waters was a blatant disregard for international law. The United States went to war with Britain in 1812 over high-seas impressment.[75]

Lincoln's fears proved warranted. When the British government heard of the capture and the ensuing celebrations in the North, an already volatile anti-American lobby in Britain called for war.[76]

The British cabinet under Lord Henry Palmerston demanded the immediate release of the prisoners, payment of reparations, and a formal apology. More than eleven thousand British troops were dispatched to Canada. Likewise, hawkish members of the U.S. Congress spoke of invading the northern provinces. Money markets crumbled. The American sectional crisis appeared to be at the threshold of a world war.

Measuring the situation, Lincoln saw little hope. To give in to British demands would make him appear weak and malleable. To resist would invite a two-front war. In typical fashion, he chose a middle path. Lincoln and Secretary of State William H. Seward quietly released Mason and Slidell, and Britain received a sum of money. Yet there would be no apology, as Wilkes had captured the men without orders. Congress angrily tolerated the decision, but Lincoln's critics had a field day.[77]

When news of the compromise reached war-fearing London, the reaction was somewhat different. Church bells rang out, people cheered in the streets, and crowds sang to peace and the monarchy.[78]

There was no functioning transatlantic telegraph cable until 1866, a device many believed would have diffused hostilities over the *Trent* Affair in minutes rather than months.

---

6. FRANCE IN MEXICO (DECEMBER 1861–MAY 1867)

Although the United States was not politically stable, its neighbor Mexico was fairing even worse. A series of civil wars had left Mexico fragmented and indebted. On December 8, 1861, more than six thousand Spanish troops landed at the gulf city of Veracruz, followed soon after by smaller contingents from Britain and France. They seized the customhouse intent on recouping the millions owed their governments and citizens.[79]

Over time the Confederate and Union governments noticed something peculiar: The French were not leaving. On the contrary, a few hundred French soldiers became a few thousand then tens of thousands. Napoleon III, emperor of France, had long harbored dreams of creating a foothold in Central America. With the United States distracted, he soon took control of half of Mexico.[80]

Instead of being praised for bringing order to the area, Napoleon was soon on the receiving end of open hostility. Mexican president Benito Juárez attempted to save the country by armed resistance. The Lincoln government also threatened military intervention after the conclusion of its own war. The Confederacy initially offered to assist the French in exchange for diplomatic recognition, but when the deal faltered, Paris envoy John Slidell warned of a combined Union and Confederate invasion force sweeping the French from the Western Hemisphere.[81]

Fearing reprisals both in Mexico and in Europe, the French began a gradual withdrawal in 1866. Their puppet emperor, Austrian Archduke Ferdinand Maximilian, stayed behind, much to his misfortune. In May 1867 Juárez and his soldiers captured Maximilian, tried and convicted him, and executed him by firing squad.[82]

> In May 1862, at the city of Puebla, the liberal Mexican government scored an unlikely victory against the French army. Although the one-day engagement did not drive the foreigners out, it did serve as a rallying point for future success. Mexico still celebrates that battle, fought and won on Cinco de Mayo.

7. THE U.S.-RUSSIAN ALLIANCE (1862–65)

Both Confederate and U.S. diplomats struggled to find allies during the war, but no major power appeared willing to choose sides. Then the Union found support from a most unlikely source.[83]

Lincoln had been a long-time critic of the Romanov dynasty. Before his presidency, when lamenting the anti-immigrant movement in the United States, he wrote, "I should prefer emigrating to some country where they make no pretense of loving liberty—to Russia, for instance, where despotism can be taken pure."[84]

In 1862 Russia was still a Romanov dominion, but surprisingly Czar Alexander II unilaterally pledged his support to the Lincoln administration. If France or Britain entered the war against the Union, vowed Alexander, Russia's position would be made clear in a "decisive manner."[85]

In the autumn of 1863 Alexander gave credence to his words when the Russian Imperial Navy staged simultaneous visits to the harbors of San Francisco and New York. The act was far from altruistic. During the Crimean War (1853–56), France and Britain had bottled the czar's fleet in the Baltic. Expecting another fight, Alexander sent his warships to America, simultaneously sparing his ships and flaunting a newfound partner.

LIBRARY OF CONGRESS

Russian ships visited New York and San Francisco in 1863 as a show of support
for the Lincoln administration.

Regardless of the motivation, the effect solidified Union prestige and
morale. If Britain and France were not going to join the North, they were
certainly less likely to oppose it hereafter. For seven months the Russian
navy remained, and its thankful hosts treated the crews with overt hospital-
ity. Few were more pleased with the imperial presence than U.S. Navy Secretary Gideon Welles, who wrote in his diary, "God bless the Russians."[86]

> Lincoln did not send his best men to St. Petersburg. His first ambassador
> was Kentucky abolitionist Cassius M. Clay, who became fond of street
> fighting with the Russian locals. Next was Simon Cameron, Lincoln's inept
> and corrupt first secretary of war, who quit promptly after meeting the czar.
> Cameron's replacement? Cassius Clay.

8. THE CATHOLIC QUESTION (NOVEMBER 1863–JANUARY 1864)

By 1863 the contest had clearly become one of attrition, which did not
bode well for the South. The Union outpopulated the Confederacy more

than two to one. In terms of white males of military age, the ratio was almost four to one.

Immigration was the major reason for the disparity. Nearly 30 percent of the North was foreign born, compared to just 9 percent in the South. Despite the outbreak of war, the trend continued. Hundreds of thousands still sailed into the harbors of New York, Boston, and elsewhere each year, replenishing the North with fresh workers and soldiers.[87]

Then, in the summer of 1863, Pope Pius IX wrote his cardinals in New York and New Orleans and called for peace. The news came as a ray of hope for the Confederacy. The majority of the huddled masses coming into the Union were from Catholic regions of Europe—Belgium, France, southern Germany, Ireland, and Italy. Jefferson Davis immediately sent a diplomat to Rome.

Envoy Ambrose D. Mann reached the pope in November 1863. In his hand was a letter from Davis, describing the unspeakable slaughter of Catholics in the New World. The Confederate president implored the pontiff to discourage Catholics from coming to America, or at least to deter them from volunteering to fight. He added: "We have offered up at the footstool of our Father who is in Heaven prayers inspired by the same feelings which animate your Holiness."[88]

The pope was visibly moved and offered to write a letter in response for the world to see. Mann was ecstatic. Rome had "all but recognized" the Confederacy.

The dream, however, ended with the pope's response. Although addressed to the "Illustrious and Honorable Jefferson Davis, President of the Confederate States of America," there was no mention of official recognition, no request to stop Catholic immigration, and no restriction on Catholics serving in the Union armed forces. The letter contained nothing except a repeated request to end the war.[89]

Over the course of the war there were more foreign-born Catholics in blue than there were Virginians in gray.

---

9. CANADA AND CONFEDERATE RAIDERS (JANUARY 1862–NOVEMBER 1864)

Of the possible escalations of the war, a border war between the North and British North America was the most likely. From the Revolutionary

War to President James Polk's threat of "54-40 or Fight," the American-Canadian boundary had been an arena of international hostility.[90]

High-ranking Confederates were hoping to foment this hostility into open warfare. Others, including Jefferson Davis, wanted to respect Canadian neutrality and still use the provinces as a staging area for raids. To this end, Davis sent several well-funded operatives to Toronto and other points north.[91]

Rumors foretold of inevitable sabotage in Buffalo, a Confederate legion of five thousand men headed for Maine, an army of thirty thousand from Poland bound for Nova Scotia, but nothing happened. Some of the more substantive threats—such as a plot to rescue prisoners of war from Johnson Island in Lake Erie and an attempt to start riots in Chicago during the 1864 election—were real. Cracked codes and Canadian detectives, however, uncovered schemes before they could take form, at least until autumn 1864.[92]

On October 20 a party of twenty or so Confederate raiders left Montreal and sifted into St. Albans, Vermont. Once there, they robbed three banks of two hundred thousand dollars, stole horses, murdered a civilian, and attempted to set the town on fire. A posse chased them into Canada, and it looked as if the South would get its two-front war.

Nothing of the sort transpired. Canadian sympathy for the South faded fast, and the provinces clamped down on subversive behavior. Even the most anti-Union citizens of British North America did not want to support guerrilla warfare, especially at the risk of facing a Union army of a half million.[93]

Before the war there were at least twenty thousand Southerners living in Canada. Nearly all of them were former slaves.

---

10. THE KENNER EXPEDITION (MARCH 1865)

In December 1864 Jefferson Davis sent Louisiana congressman Duncan F. Kenner on a secret diplomatic mission to Europe. Kenner was to offer the emancipation of Confederate slaves in exchange for recognition.

Kenner's assignment illustrated the grave condition of the Confederacy. Davis knew that under his constitution, only the individual states could grant emancipation, not the executive branch. Making matters worse, Davis never consulted the states over the plan. It is unknown what he would have done had either London or Paris agreed to the offer.

As it turned out, Davis had no decision to make. With all Southern ports blockaded, Kenner had to travel north incognito and sail out of New York Harbor, losing valuable time. He did not reach Paris until March 1865. Once there, Kenner listened to a reluctant Napoleon III defer to Lord Palmerston. With the Confederacy on its last legs, Kenner rushed to London and the prime minister. After hearing the offer of quid pro quo, Palmerston offered a snide retort, suggesting the Confederacy never proved itself in control of its alleged borders. Palmerston's cynicism became fact when Richmond fell two weeks later.[94]

Confederate congressman Duncan Kenner was one of the largest slave holders in the South, possessing more than four hundred persons at the start of the war.

Military Life

TOP TEN WEAPONS

In subtle macabre, history is marked in "ages" by the materials used in weapons of war: stone, bronze, iron. Combat in all those periods occurred at ranges from zero to fifty yards. On paper the Civil War appeared to maintain this primitive and personal link between enemies. Weapons of old remained. Swords, knives, and bayonets were considered as fundamental to equipping an army as haversacks and blankets.

Yet this war was different from its predecessors. Most wounds on Civil War battlefields occurred at ranges from two hundred to four hundred yards, practically nullifying the crude hacking weapons of the past. While still using materials of bronze, iron, even stone (at SECOND MANASSAS, THOMAS J. "STONEWALL" JACKSON's troops threw rocks when their ammunition ran out), the Civil War marked the dawn of warfare's Age of Distance.[1]

Credit goes to a single innovation introduced in 1849. Soldiers called it the "minee ball," although it's namesake was French Capt. Claude Minié (min-nee-Ay), and it was not a sphere but a conical cylinder with a hollow base. By 1855 the U.S. and British armies adopted the minié bullet as the standard for rifled muskets. Rifling had been in use for centuries, but to catch the spiraled grooves, lead bullets had to be slightly larger than the bore of the gun, slowing down loading time and causing a fair amount of jamming. When fired, the smaller minié bullet caught the rifling by expanding its base. Twenty years before the Civil War, soldiers marching upon a position could expect two or three musket volleys. The men in blue and gray encountered a rate of fire at least three times greater, starting at distances four times farther away.[2]

Quantity and quality of rifles and other weapons favored the Union. The Southern war machine lacked sufficient industrial equipment, engineers, and raw materials to keep pace, and small-scale domestic fabrication and international purchases smuggled though the blockade did not make up the difference. Fortunately for the South, an excellent source of weaponry was the Union army. After victories at FIRST MANASSAS, CHANCELLORSVILLE, CHICKAMAUGA, and elsewhere, Confederates seized tens of thousands of arms, paying far greater attention to gleaning the field than their comparatively well-stocked and considerably more wasteful opponents. In spite of all efforts at thrift, innovation, and capture, the Confederate supply of weaponry never equaled its demand.[3]

Below are the top ten weapons of the war, ranked by their respective volumes available to servicemen North and South.

1. RIFLED FIREARMS (3.5 MILLION)

The most numerous and deadliest of weapons in the Civil War cost around sixteen dollars and weighed less than ten pounds. At the war's beginning there were a total of fifty thousand muzzle-loaded rifled weapons in U.S. and Confederate-seized arsenals. By 1862 there were more rifled muskets in North America than there were Native Americans.

Appearing (and departing) early were seven hundred thousand rifles from Austria, Belgium, France, Prussia, and elsewhere, nearly all of aged and substandard design, dumped on the voracious American market in the first two years of the war. These pieces were of such varying caliber and poor quality that soldiers and ordnance officials on both sides despised them wholeheartedly. Of better repute was the first general-issue rifle in the U.S. Army: the Model 1841 (often called the "Mississippi Rifle" after 1847 when it was issued to Col. Jefferson Davis's First Mississippi Infantry during the Mexican War). Originally a .54 caliber, many thousands were later bored to .58 to accept minié bullets. Also prevalent in the Civil War were versions of the Model 1855 modified to fire with percussion caps. In all there were more than one hundred U.S. government–approved versions of rifled muskets, with many more independent and unique rifled firearms in use.[4]

The Springfield Rifle—a.k.a. U.S. Rifle Musket Model 1861 or Model 1863—was the most widely made by far, with more than seven hundred thousand produced at its home armory in Massachusetts and another nine hundred thousand created elsewhere to exacting standards. Second most common in the Union army and first in the Confederacy was the slightly lighter English-made 1855 Model Enfield, with eight hundred thousand copies in the war. The highly regarded .577-caliber Enfield could take the same minié bullet as the .58-caliber Springfield yet fire with almost twice the accuracy. Effective up to six hundred yards, the Enfield could kill from nearly a mile away.[5]

After the war Union soldiers could (and often did) buy their rifle from the U.S. government for six dollars.

---

2. BAYONETS (1.5 MILLION)

A soldier would beg, buy, or steal a good shoulder arm, even carving his name (against regulations) on the stock for insurance and sentiment. His bayonet, however, he ditched as soon as the opportunity arose.

The great majority of bayonets were triangular steel-tipped spikes of iron; others ranged from well-made knives to primitive sharpened rods. They made their impression visually more than physically. The mere sight of approaching spiked columns enticed the opposition to fire or flee long before contact was made. In the unusual event of hand-to-hand fighting, instead of jabbing with their bayonet as they were trained to do, soldiers habitually grabbed their musket by the muzzle and swung it like a club.

Less than one in one thousand wounds came from the tip of a bayonet, and these were usually by accident or camp quarrel. Bayonets were dangerous in close formation, plus they made the process of working a muzzle-loading gun all the more cumbersome. Soldiers found them useful as cooking implements, digging tools, can openers, candlesticks, and back-scratchers. Otherwise, men on the march commonly stabbed them into the soil or tossed them into the shrubs, moving on two pounds lighter, much to the frustration of officers and supply sergeants alike.[6]

There were a few incidents in which bayonets alone carried a position. In the October 3, 1862, battle of Corinth the Seventeenth Wisconsin swept a whole brigade from the field. In the dead of the night,

November 7, 1863, the Sixth Maine and Fifth Wisconsin stormed and captured almost an entire Louisiana regiment near Kelly's Ford, Virginia. At GETTYSBURG the immortal Twentieth Maine saved Little Round Top by charging downhill, bayonets forward, straight into two Alabama regiments.[7]

Infantry soldiers were sometimes referred to as "bayonets."

---

3. SWORDS (700,000)

Rifles and cannon of the Civil War relegated a once deadly weapon to more of a symbol of authority, better suited to impress and direct soldiers than to slice them apart. Civil War collectors prize swords far more than many of their original owners. Required to carry them, many officers and infantry sergeants found swords to be cumbersome and impractical. THOMAS J. "STONEWALL" JACKSON drew his sword so rarely it rusted in its scabbard.

Sabers and cutlasses did see limited application in the cavalry. Skilled horsemen used them with great effect as an offensive weapon, mostly in scare tactics. The tide turned at FIRST MANASSAS when Confederate cavalry brandished swirling sabers against inexperienced Union infantry. The North issued more than four hundred thousand to their horsemen over the course of the war, and many used the weapons with brutal effect in the 1863 clash of cavalries at Brandy Station.[8]

From old heirlooms to recent standard issue, manufactured by private firms domestically and in Europe, the number and types of swords in the war may never be accurately calculated.

While leading his brigade in Pickett's Charge, Gen. Richard Brooke Garnett came within a few paces of the Federal lines and then vanished in the smoke. His body was never found. Years later someone discovered his sword in a Baltimore pawnshop.

---

4. PISTOLS (650,000)

Handguns were as varied as rifles. Ranging from antique flintlocks to new revolvers, holding from one to nine shots, hundreds of variations saw use.

Most came from the foundries of Samuel Colt. The hefty Colt .44-caliber six-shooter became the official U.S. Army Model 1860 revolver, with more than one hundred thousand ordered by the government. Thousands more were acquired by soldiers out of their own pocket. The lighter and shorter Colt .36-caliber Navy revolver had two hundred thousand made from its 1851 introduction to 1865 and was the chief design for nearly all ten thousand Confederate-made pistols. Union purchases also included more than one hundred thousand Remington .44s, tens of thousands of Starr handguns, and dozens more makes and models. As with shoulder arms, most pistols fired cartridges made of cloth or paper or were loaded with loose powder and the bullet separately. Reloading was not a quick process.[9]

At first many new volunteers considered revolvers an essential piece of defense. Photograph portraits captured such fondness as many new recruits went to the studio to document their departure to the field with fire in their belly and pistols in hand. As the war progressed, officers and the cavalry tended to keep their revolvers while most enlisted men did not. Short range, heavy weight, and difficulty in care usually caused pistols to be sent home or traded away within the first few months of service.[10]

A popular pistol among Confederate generals was the double-barreled Le Mat, which held eight shots in its revolver chamber and a single load of buckshot in a lower barrel. A physician invented it.

---

5. SMOOTHBORE MUSKETS (600,000)

These shoulder arms differed from their rifled counterparts in that smoothbores were older, cheaper, and couldn't hit the side of a barn. They were also more readily available at the war's commencement. At the time of Fort Sumter, U.S. armed forces possessed three hundred thousand usable smoothbore muskets. The young Confederacy acquired almost a third of these from raided federal government stores. Militia, volunteers, and foreign sources brought in thousands more.[11]

Principal among these unrifled weapons was the U.S. Percussion Musket Model 1842, the last smoothbore and the first percussion-cap shoulder arm issued by the U.S. Army. Preceding this and in smaller numbers was the Model 1822. Virtually a Revolutionary War–era design, the Model 1822 used flint rather than a percussion cap to detonate its charge. Because of its ancient priming setup, the model misfired 15 percent of the time and was almost useless in the rain. If a Model 1822 did survive to see service in 1861, it was often retooled to fire with a percussion cap.[12]

Shooting a spherical lead ball, smoothbores had an effective range of less than one hundred yards. For closer targets, soldiers loaded "buck and ball," a large lead sphere resting on three smaller pellets.

Initially, these arms easily outnumbered rifled weapons on the battlefield. Losing their plurality by early 1862, smoothbores were all but gone in the North by 1863. Some Confederates, especially in the western theater, had to settle for smoothbores for the duration of the war.

Stonewall Jackson's wounds came from Confederate smoothbore muskets.

---

6. BREECHLOADING CARBINES (230,000)

A soldier had to stand or kneel to quickly load a musket, a serious drawback when in the line of fire and a considerable challenge when mounted on a horse. An alternative was the short and light breechloading carbine.

Early breechloaders suffered from deficiencies, namely the loss of pressure at the barrel's base when fired, eventually compromising the structural integrity of the weapon and the physical safety of its user. The perfection of copper cartridges and stronger breech integrity resolved most mechanical problems by the late 1850s. The high cost of producing these carbines (nearly four times as expensive as a standard rifled musket) made them unattractive to the U.S. Ordnance Bureau and financially out of reach for the Confederacy. There was also great concern that with faster-loading rifles, soldiers were prone to waste valuable ammunition.

Of the numerous types of carbines introduced, three were most prominent. The Sharps carbine (more than ninety thousand in action) shot a paper or linen .52-caliber cartridge. Rate of fire for a muzzleloading musket was three shots per minute at best, but the breechloading Sharps fired ten rounds per minute. Also popular was a perfected version of the Burnside carbine (fifty-five thousand in use), which was designed by the otherwise bumbling and luckless Union Gen. AMBROSE E. BURN-

SIDE. Also common and most impressive was the Spencer repeating carbine that fired a magazine of seven .52-caliber metal cartridges. Confederates lamented that a Union man armed with a repeating rifle could
"load up on Sunday and shoot all the rest of the week." By late 1864 the
Spencer was the standard U.S. cavalry firearm. Confederates lucky enough
to capture one could rarely find or purchase the cartridges with which to
load it. By 1865 the U.S. government secured more than seventy-seven
thousand repeating Spencers, eventually distributing several thousand to
infantry regiments.[13]

One of the greatest advocates of repeating rifles was Abraham Lincoln, who
personally tested several prototypes.

7. GRENADES (150,000)

The U.S. government ordered some ninety thousand Ketchum grenades,
conical devices with short-finned tails that ranged from one to five
pounds in weight. The rare Adams Excelsior (five thousand purchased by
the U.S. government) had multiple impact fuses peppered around its
spherical casing. Many hand grenades were of the impromptu or home-
made variety. In a pinch, men from both sides lit fuses on six-pound
artillery shells and threw or rolled them where needed. Soldiers also fashioned grenades by inserting a fuse and charge of gunpowder in a tin can
or discarded bottle and packing the remaining space with nails, broken
glass, and/or buckshot.[14]

Impressive totals mislead on this item. One-shot weapons with very
short range, grenades enjoyed extremely limited application, except as
defensive weapons from well-protected positions, such as at VICKSBURG,
Port Hudson, Battery Wagner, and Fort Sanders. Virtually of no use in
covert operations, as they announced a user's presence, grenades were
equally risky in large engagements due to the close proximity to one's
comrades. Detrimental also was the primitive art of detonation. Either
these small bombs failed to go off or they discharged at the slightest
prompting.[15]

Hand-held explosives were nothing new to warfare, having been used as
early as the fifteenth century.

8. ARTILLERY (15,000)

Only 4 percent of Civil War battlefield casualties came from the muzzle of a cannon, yet considering their tiny proportion to all other arms (0.3 percent), its easy to understand why columns and commanders were hesitant to advance on artillery.

Cannon fell into three main groups. Guns had a flat trajectory, mortars produced a slow, arching fire, and howitzers functioned as a hybrid of the two. From massive siege and coastal guns to miniature mortars, the variety and overlapping qualities of Civil War cannon are staggering. Pug pig-iron mortars, such as the Coehorn mortar, lobbed small explosives from trench to trench whereas Rodman Columbiads could fire a shell the weight of three men nearly four miles.[16]

Suffice to say the principal smoothbore was the Napoleon, a muzzle-loading gun or howitzer most commonly made of bronze. Versatile, mobile, capable of firing almost anything that fit in its 4.62-inch barrel, Napoleons accounted for more kills than most all other cannon types combined.[17]

This Union battery was photographed during the 1862 Peninsula campaign.

The chief rifled cannon was the 3-inch Ordnance Rifle, designed in 1863 by the U.S. Ordnance Department and sometimes referred to as a Rodman Rifle. Its range was greater than two miles.

Of the six hundred sizes and varieties of artillery ammunition seeing service, all fell into four basic types: canister (a container of hundreds of small fragments), grapeshot (usually nine golf ball–sized spheres suspended together), shells (fragmenting or solid), and cannonballs (fragmenting or solid). For attacks on ships and fortifications, shells and cannonballs were called for. Canister and grapeshot were used in short-range situations to shred men and horses.

Numerically, the Union enjoyed a consistent five-to-three artillery advantage over the Confederacy. The latter, even when it could procure fine field guns, suffered from the want of quality gunpowder. Distance, timing fuses, even successful firing were elusive for Confederate batteries. Yet as with small arms, artillery could always be "borrowed" from the enemy. In 1861 and 1862 the South attained more cannon by capture than by importation and manufacturing combined.[18]

Approximately five thousand artillery rounds were fired to and from Fort Sumter on April 12, 1861, without a single human fatality.

---

9. PIKES AND LANCES (10,000)

As the North American continent moved steadily into the Industrial Age, there occurred a newfound faith in an ancient weapon. Whether by blind optimism or extreme desperation, field commanders on both sides asked for and received thousands of pikes and lances.

At the outset of the war the Union's Sixth Pennsylvania, also known as Rush's Lancers, were outfitted with lances along with their firearms. In early 1862 THOMAS J. "STONEWALL" JACKSON requested new companies to be outfitted with pikes, and ROBERT E. LEE enthusiastically concurred. Eccentric and independent Georgia governor Joe Brown ordered thousands more for his state militia, proclaiming the crude weapons would be effective against invading cavalry.[19]

Although several individual examples survive in museums, these spearing devices were quickly discarded or never issued.[20]

There is one confirmed instance where lances were used in the war. During the February 21, 1862, battle of Valverde, New Mexico, a group of lance-wielding Texans charged the Federal lines with little effect.

10. MINES, A.K.A. TORPEDOES (10,000)

Covered or submersed explosives were relative newcomers in warfare. Soldiers referred to them interchangeably as mines and torpedoes. Nearly everyone considered them "unsporting" if not inhumane. Yet this did not prevent either side from using and perfecting these hidden explosives for use once it was apparent even the threat of a torpedo or mine could scare a regiment or ship into caution.

Land mines appeared initially at Yorktown, Virginia, in May 1862. Confederates buried Columbiad artillery shells just below ground level, where the weight of trampling Union feet detonated them. Later accounts told of similar devices at Fort Wagner in South Carolina, Fort McAllister in Georgia, and the battle of Blakely, Alabama.[21]

The more common water mines were in use from the beginning of the war. Torpedoes as such were not the propeller-driven cigar-shaped missiles of the twentieth century but were barrels, boxes, or casks of explosives, either suspended by tethers or attached to long poles. These crude new weapons were surprisingly lethal, sinking or severely damaging more than forty Union vessels, including seven ironclads.[22]

Sunk by a mine in the Yazoo River in late 1862, the gunboat *Cairo* was raised more than a century later and is now on display in Vicksburg, Mississippi.

A cache of shells after the war included an assortment of naval "torpedoes," now known as antiship mines.

LIBRARY OF CONGRESS

TOP TEN ITEMS IN A SOLDIER'S DIET

Soldiers fought for weeks without shelter, months without pay, and in some cases, years without new equipment, but hunger often destroyed their strength and morale in a matter of days. Thus feeding the ranks was a perpetual and monumental responsibility for each government. In essence, armies were large mobile cities. By March 1863 the eighty thousand men of the Army of Northern Virginia easily outpopulated Richmond. That same month there were more privates in the Army of Tennessee than there were people in Memphis. In July the blue and gray converging upon GETTYSBURG outnumbered the townspeople more than sixty to one.

Storage and preservation were problematic. Barrels, boxes, sacks, and cans were few and rarely water- or airtight. To aid longevity, meats were salted, cured, or smoked, and fruits and vegetables were dried and pressed, yet spoilage still claimed large amounts.

When rations proved inadequate, as they frequently did, soldiers supplemented their diet via trade, services, money, care packages, camp peddlers, enemy supplies, and even the haversacks of the fallen. Common was the ugly task of foraging, where homes and farms were picked clean by friend and foe alike.

Confederate armies and civilians exposed to battle zones suffered from want almost continually. Said one Union officer of his Confederate opponents: "Their faces were thin and cadaverous as though they had been starved to death. It is of course possible that this is the natural look of the race, but it appeared mightily to me like the result of short fare."[23]

Yet the South produced enough food for its entire population throughout the war. As with contemporary famines, shortages during the war were primarily a matter of distribution, and the Confederate transportation system was simply inadequate. Damaged rail lines and engines were difficult to repair or replace. There were different gauges and unconnected lines. Troops, munitions, and the wounded had rail priority over food. On the road, draft animals and wagons were requisitioned to haul guns rather than butter. Vital rivers and ports quickly fell into Federal hands. It was not unusual to see huge supplies of rations rotting in Confederate depots for lack of transportation.[24]

Yet even in the leanest times, famine turned to feast once a supply train arrived, a farm could be raided, or a depot could be captured. Below are the most prominent staples for the average Civil War soldier, ranked by the amount consumed.

1. WATER

Its supply was precarious and its source was often putrid. A soldier got his water from wells, rivers, streams, and even puddles. Along with filling his canteen, a soldier's water also served as the primary ingredient to the rest of his intake—coffee, soup, stew, dough, rare tea, and many odd recipes.

Ironically, water was also the source of many soldier deaths. Dysentery, cholera, typhoid, and other diseases came from ingesting contaminated water. In an attempt to combat the problem, the Union provided a convoluted variety of "purifying" strainers. Seen as just one more thing to carry, most men discarded the strainers and used a cloth or simply drank water straight.[25]

Water received little comment in letters unless men wrote of the wounded on the battlefield. The dying screamed for three things: home, help, and water—and not in that order. In describing ANTIETAM, Lt. John Burnham of the Sixteenth Connecticut wrote to his mother: "It was very hot weather, but fortunately there was a heavy rain on Thursday night and they managed to catch a canteen or two full of water by holding up the corners of their rubber blankets. One of our men, who was unable to get off the field, managed to pull off one of his boots and caught water in that and drank it." At SHILOH wounded men and horses gulped from a pool of water near the Hornets' Nest. Blood and bodies turned the water a murky crimson, in a place known after as Bloody Pond.[26]

Despite their need, the vast majority of soldiers probably spent most of the war in a state of manageable dehydration, where symptoms of headache and fatigue were considered a natural part of soldiering.[27]

> In October 1862 Federals and Confederates collided during a search for water. The ensuing battle of Perryville resulted in more than seventy-six hundred casualties.

2. BREAD

In a well-managed hospital or camp, a soldier might be fortunate enough to get fresh-baked wheat bread. In the field his bread ration was usually less inviting.[28]

U.S. ARMY MILITARY HISTORY INSTITUTE

Poor cooking could incapacitate soldiers as well as the enemy could. Some first-time cooks tended to fry everything they touched.

For the Union soldier it was usually "Army bread," also known as hardtack. Three inches square and a half-inch thick, unleavened, light, transportable, the crackerlike substance consisted of white flour, water, and a modicum of salt and was as hard as a rock. A daily ration was a pound, or about a dozen cakes. Men hated it and sang ungrateful songs about it, but they survived on it.[29]

Along with precious calories, hardtack often contained maggots, weevils, and larvae to the point that soldiers called the crackers "worm castles." A dusting of mold was par for the course. Still, smashed with a rifle or rock, the otherwise flavorless bread fortified soups, stews, and made a good mush when mixed with grease. The crackers were also baked, eaten with a spread of molasses or lard or gnawed plain.[30]

Bread for Johnny Reb was coarse, flavorless corn bread. Sometimes his cornmeal came in a small loaf, which was usually stale and hard. More often than not, he received his ration in meal form and baked it into small cakes or balled up on the end of a ramrod or used it in soups. If he was lucky, his meal consisted of milled wheat. If wheat or corn were not available, sometimes the men consumed ground rice or peas.

As much as the boys in blue disliked hardtack, Confederates made it a point to capture as many crates of the Union bread as possible. Outside of Atlanta in 1864, a division of Confederates advanced upon a Union supply depot and its million rations of hardtack. Asked to surrender "to avoid the needless effusion of blood," the Union commander responded, "We are prepared for the 'needless effusion of blood' whenever it is agreeable to you." He held on to save the depot and its rations.[31]

During the siege of Petersburg, ovens at the Union base in City Point, Virginia, churned out 123,000 loaves of soft bread every twenty-four hours.

---

3. SALT PORK

Bluish, foul smelling, saltier than salt, often containing hair, hide, dirt, and questionable pig parts, salt pork was the major source of meat and protein for the soldier in the field. A few veterans boasted as having developed a taste for it.[32]

Easier to produce and slower to rot than SALT BEEF, "sowbelly" was also a key source of fat, a primary recipe ingredient. Soldiers cooked their ration on a half canteen or skillet, then used the collected grease with cornmeal to make "cush," rice flour to bake "secession bread," and hardtack and water for "skillygallee." Bits of salt pork also served as the principle guest in stews and soups.[33]

A daily ration was a little less than a pound, and a Union soldier received his full ration more often than his foe. When salt pork was not available, smoked bacon was a frequent substitute.[34]

Before a march began, foot soldiers were instructed to pack three days' rations including salt pork, which they habitually ate in one sitting. This wolfing was sometimes a matter of weak willpower but usually an act of practicality. Stuffed in a haversack or in pockets, sowbelly oozed grease, gathered lint and dust, jumbled with the other contents, and rotted quickly. Better to eat it all, figured most soldiers, and take one's chances with foraging or resupply than to wait a few days and watch the rations become even more repulsive than they already were.[35]

The political term "pork barrel" comes from the Civil War era. Salt pork was shipped in barrels with gallons of fat used as packing material.

---

4. CORN

An omnipresent staple, corn was an accurate barometer of how the war was going. Corn bread was available when things were stable and safe. On campaign, corn came in the husk to be shucked and roasted over a campfire. On quick maneuvers, soldiers sometimes plucked corn straight from the fields and ate it green.

In autumn 1862 the men on BRAXTON BRAGG's march into Kentucky and ROBERT E. LEE's march into Maryland subsisted almost entirely on green corn and apples. During lighter moments, soldiers used kernels as currency in games of chance, but in times of desperation, men sifted around old animal troughs for a few pieces. In prisons such as ANDERSONVILLE and ELMIRA, a handful of grain was occasionally a man's ration for two days.[36]

In 1860 cotton was king, but the second largest crop in the South was corn.

---

5. BEANS

When meat was altogether absent, beans were the major protein alternative. They were definitely camp fare. Difficult to keep from spilling out of haversacks and requiring long cooking times, beans were rarely given out when the armies were on the move. If eaten undercooked, they produced a bellyache comparable to a knife wound, but in the hands of a skilled cook and mixed with a little grease and pork, beans ranked as high as good beef or fresh eggs in the hearts of hungry soldiers.[37]

Beans were immortalized quite often in songs. Soldiers concocted and crooned clever ditties on everything from the specter of death to the nuisance of lice, but the bean showed up in food-related lyrics more often than any other staple, including hardtack. One tune included the lines:

> There's a spot that the soldiers all love
> The mess tent's the place that we mean
> And the dish we like to see there
> Is the old fashioned, white Army Bean.[38]

Company cooks were often called "bean boilers."

---

6. FRESH MEAT

The highest quality meats came from foraging, when soldiers liberated farms and fields of cattle, sheep, and hogs. By no means was the collection limited to domesticated meats. Wild hogs, wild game, and jackrabbits made appearances on the plate, as did raccoons, squirrels, fish, and the occasional snake-kabob.

Otherwise, most armies brought along their own (the Army of the Potomac had a herd of beef cattle numbering in the thousands). Such drafted livestock tended to be of poor yield though, having marched as far and fast and suffering from the same lack of grain as the soldiers. Officers and the quartermaster corps frequently took the choicest cuts for themselves, leaving enlisted men with tough and gristled servings. Nevertheless, with no refrigeration available, the men had to consume the meat quickly.[39]

In more desperate times, unpleasant alternatives emerged. First to be slaughtered were draft animals: oxen, mules, horses. In some areas, wandering dogs had short life spans. When no other meat was available, the catching and consumption of rats devolved from a sport to a necessity, as was the case in besieged VICKSBURG, Port Hudson, Petersburg, and in nearly half of all prisons North and South.[40]

Commissary officers referred to cattle as "beef on hoof."

Herds of cattle accompanied the armies on the march. The animals were butchered as needed. Here two beef quarters cure under cover.

U.S. ARMY MILITARY HISTORY INSTITUTE

7. COFFEE

Nothing, including alcohol, ranked as high as coffee for the Civil War soldier. Men drank it before, during, after, and in lieu of meals. Many wrote of it in letters home, praising the soothing qualities of a pistol-hot cup of grind. Union soldiers rarely experienced shortages, although they surely would have consumed far more than their allotment. Some Yankees managed to secure a little sugar or milk, but most drank it black.

With the Union blockade cutting off supplies, Confederates swapped most anything for coffee. When it could not be bought, traded, smuggled, or stolen, men in gray made do by roasting and boiling nearly any alternative, including acorns, peanuts, corn, apples, peas, potatoes, and rye.[41]

> Some Union rations included a new and simple invention: a paste of
> grounds, sugar, and powdered milk they called "instant coffee."

8. PEAS

ROBERT E. LEE referred to peas as the Confederacy's "best friend," as peas were generally ample enough to keep an army going. For preservation, the vegetable usually came dried but was also confiscated from fields and gardens during the summer and autumn months. Desperate Confederate commissaries lacking wheat or corn occasionally ground peas and passed it off as meal. Similar in form and taste was the "goober," a flavorless, mealy peanut consumed in large quantity by soldiers in the tidewater region.[42]

When peas were not available, the alternatives were potatoes (sweet and Irish) or rice. On the Union side, there was the less common though much despised "dessicated vegetables," or as the men called it, "desecrated vegetables." A mishmash of beets, carrots, potatoes, and such, dried and compressed into sheets or bricks, this invention often contained stalks, tops, and all. One soldier, when examining the rehydrated vegetables lurking in soup, described it as "a dirty brook with all the dead leaves floating around promiscuously."[43]

> Dependent on their native staple of peanuts, soldiers from North Carolina
> and Georgia were sometimes referred to as "goober grabbers."

9. SALT BEEF

A full ration was a pound, which for many soldiers was a pound too much. "Salt horse," "mule," or "junk" fluctuated in availability but was consistent in its poor reputation. Men who could stomach SALT PORK were driven to profanity when describing salt beef. Meat packers maximized output by including as much of the steer as possible: neck, shanks, and a few organs. Especially susceptible to rot, whose telltale signs were a yellowish-green hue and overwhelming smell, salt beef was dissected for edible bits, roasted beyond recognition, readily traded, or rejected outright. Necessity became the mother of toleration in many situations, and hungry soldiers, especially the boys in gray, learned to force it down.[44]

> Tired of the preservative, soldiers referred to supper time as "eating salt."

10. FRESH FRUIT

Scurvy is a particularly nasty disease that can result in night blindness, receding gums, tooth loss, and in extreme cases, the rotting of lips, cheeks, and jawbones. It can also incite internal hemorrhaging. Unlike most ailments at the time of the Civil War, scurvy had a generally known cause, that is, the absence of fresh fruits and vegetables. Men and officers made certain to attain fruit as often as possible, usually by gleaning an orchard or paying a camp sutler's exorbitant prices for a few pieces. Prisoners and seaborne navies did not have such luxury, thus succumbing more readily to scurvy's caustic demonstrations.

Most frequently consumed were apples, followed by pears, berries, watermelons, strawberries, and peaches. Many claimed to have lived off green apples for days. An unfortunate side effect was the intestinal discomfort of downing fruit too early or too late in maturity. One soldier did not spare the details in a letter: "I ate a mush melon yesterday . . . and last night it made me sick. I went and threw it up and felt better after that."[45]

> Much has been written of THOMAS J. "STONEWALL" JACKSON's tendency to suck on lemons, but he habitually consumed a variety of fruit. Some theorize he did so to fight off scurvy; others note his hypochondriacal disposition and earlier bouts with dyspepsia that led him to adopt a low-fat, high-fiber diet.

TOP TEN MILITARY ORGANIZATIONAL UNITS

Understanding all variations of military field units can be one of the more difficult tasks for an aspiring Civil War enthusiast. Rest assured, Federals and Confederates struggled as well. Mammoth armies were decidedly alien to the American experience. George Washington's Continental Army fluctuated between four thousand to nineteen thousand. The United States deployed fifteen thousand men in the Mexican War. In 1860 the entire U.S. Army numbered just sixteen thousand, and the U.S. Navy added a mere nine thousand more.[46]

By 1864 the Confederate army topped a half million, and the Union army neared one million. As if huge numbers were not perplexing enough, there was a baffling tangle of reorganization made frequent by shifting assignments and intense attrition. Over four years of war, the Union Army of the Cumberland went through three name changes and six commanding generals. Either by promotion or transfer, an officer could expect to have at least four different commands should he survive. An enlisted man normally remained with the first regiment he joined, but that regiment could be shuffled in and out of larger units with unsettling frequency.[47]

Stated here are the ten prominent operational organizations used to keep it all straight, from largest to smallest. Some designations were as old as war itself; some were relatively new innovations. All existed to enable efficiency in command under circumstances where any delay, indecision, or disunity could be and often was catastrophic.

1. ARMY

The largest unit within each army was in fact an "army," ranging in size from 7,000 to 160,000 men, with totals tending to diminish the farther west they operated. The North created sixteen. The South, fragmented as it was by defending multiple points, formed twenty-three.

The North named its armies as it named its battles—after the rivers near their place of origin, such as the Armies of the Potomac, James, Tennessee, Cumberland, Ohio, and Mississippi. In a show of antifederalist thinking, the South titled most of its armies after states; immortal among these were the Armies of Tennessee, Mississippi, and Northern Virginia.

Major generals commanded armies in the Union. Major generals, lieutenant generals, or full generals led them in the Confederacy.

With casualties, furloughs, desertions, stragglers, and incoming recruits, the effective strength of an army was always difficult to ascertain. Estimating the size of one's own army, let alone the enemy's, was an educated guess at best.

Each side lost one commander of an army in battle: Confederate Gen. Albert Sidney Johnston (SHILOH) and Union Gen. James Birdseye McPherson (Atlanta).

---

2. CORPS

Created in France in the late 1700s and perfected by Napoleon Bonaparte, the corps system encapsulated the divisions of an army. Initially, groupings of two or three divisions were referred to as a command, wing, or grand division. By late 1862 both sides began to group divisions into corps.

The North designated each corps by number. In 1863, to aid organization and boost morale, Union corps were assigned badges. Worn on caps, on the breast, and sometimes appearing on tents and wagons, these insignia can still be seen today on monuments and historical markers. They included the three-leaf clover of the Second Corps, the Maltese cross of the Fifth, and the crescent moon of the Eleventh. Con-

Union Gen. Philip Kearny was the first to order his corps to bear an identifying mark. He had mistakenly reprimanded officers not of his command and vowed to never embarrass himself again. Other units favored the notion and chose emblems of their own. During Joseph Hooker's tenure as commander of the Army of the Potomac, he ordered corps badges be assigned officially. By 1864 more than two-thirds of the Federal troops in the front lines wore corps badges.

NATIONAL ARCHIVES

federates preferred to name several corps as well as divisions and brigades after their respective commanders. This method created not a little confusion when these commanders were transferred, promoted, demoted, or killed.[48]

Ranging in size from five thousand to twenty-six thousand men, led by a major general or lower, a corps could contain twenty-five cannon, fifty ambulances, and two hundred supply wagons. Some historians designate corps by Roman numerals, but clerks and officers during the war used digits.[49]

From head to tail, a marching corps could occupy over fifteen miles of road.

3. DIVISION

On the average, Union divisions contained six thousand men. At the beginning of the war, each Federal infantry division came appended with small artillery and cavalry units, consisting of one to four cannon and one hundred or so mounted soldiers. Intended to assist the large body of infantry, these supporting units proved too small to be effective. Eventually the North adopted the general practice of the opposition, allowing the big guns and the quick steeds to function as larger independent units.

Early on, Confederate divisions approached nine thousand strong. This numerical superiority provided simplicity and subsequent successes for the South, an advantage lost when supplies and manpower lessened as the war dragged on. Arguably the most famous division of the war was George E. Pickett's division, which was slaughtered on the last day of GETTYSBURG.

Like the corps, the division was a French creation.

4. BRIGADE

A Union division contained two or more brigades, whereas a Southern division had four brigades or more. Brigades usually had a brigadier general at the head of affairs, but it was not unusual to see colonels or even majors in charge during periods of heavy turnover. Brigades also had their own commissary and quartermaster officers.[50]

In the course of battle, a soldier had a perspective only of his immediate surroundings. In the best of conditions, he would have an idea how his brigade was fairing in the fight. Only afterward, when more information could be collected from other units, prisoners, and commanders could a soldier realize how his army had performed.

Among the many storied units was the Union's Iron Brigade, also known as the the Western Brigade and the Black Hat Brigade, which lost most of its eighteen hundred men on the first day of Gettysburg. The Union's Irish Brigade, marching with green regimental flags alongside the Stars and Stripes, lost more men during the course of the war (four thousand) than they ever had in the brigade at any one time. No brigade, however, was more famous than the Confederacy's Stonewall Brigade. Consisting of Virginia regiments and originally led by THOMAS J. "STONEWALL" JACKSON, this fierce and efficient military unit sustained heavy losses in several engagements until it was almost completely destroyed at the Bloody Angle in the 1864 battle of SPOTSYLVANIA.

There were seven different commanders of the Stonewall Brigade. Three died and one was captured while leading the brigade. Jackson and another were wounded after leaving it.

---

5. REGIMENT

A soldier identified first and foremost with his regiment. Ideally, regiments contained one thousand men, but attrition whittled most down to a few hundred. Veterans often resisted replenishment of their ranks with young recruits who were viewed as dangerously inexperienced. Yet more devastating was the consolidation of several depleted regiments into a new one. On several occasions, soldiers deserted rather than accept reassignment.[51]

Each volunteer regiment contained ten infantry companies or twelve cavalry companies called troops. Usually, a colonel or lieutenant colonel commanded. Infantry and cavalry regiments functioned separately, although Northern tactics tended to treat the cavalry as a unit assigned to a division, especially during the first half of the war.

By spring of 1864 "Colored" regiments constituted approximately 12 percent of Union forces, eventually numbering 120 infantry, 12 artillery,

Individual regiments and companies were comprised of men generally from the same way of life, city, town, or background. This was particularly true of the units formed of Northern immigrants, such as the German Americans of the Forty-first New York pictured here. Many newly arrived foreigners enlisted in the Union army because service would be rewarded with citizenship.

and 7 cavalry units. In total, there were 179,000 African American volunteers in blue.[52]

The Twenty-sixth North Carolina Infantry suffered the worst regimental losses in a single battle: 708 of 800 killed, wounded, or missing at Gettysburg.

---

6. BATTALION

The smallest self-sustaining military body was the battalion. Strictly speaking, the prewar U.S. Army considered a battalion as eight companies, totaling eight hundred men, led by a lieutenant colonel or major. During the war the term was far less precise. Teams of companies given assignments away from their divisions were often called battalions. These detached units performed specific tasks, such as foraging, sharpshooting, or pioneering (clearing trees and brush). Many of these battalions consisted of just two companies of a few hundred men.[53]

A collection of artillery batteries was often referred to as a battalion.

---

7. COMPANY/TROOP/BATTERY

If asked what unit he was from, a soldier responded with the name of his regiment then his company. A company was designed to have a captain at the head, aided by a first lieutenant, a second lieutenant, a first sergeant, four sergeants, eight corporals, two musicians, and from sixty-four to eighty-two enlisted men. As with other units, actual population and ranks varied greatly.

Companies on both sides were designated by letters A through K. Infantry companies A and B were usually the largest and best armed. Consequently, they were usually assigned the most critical role during combat, acting as the left and right flank of the regiment. Companies C through K normally manned the middle.[54]

The cavalry equivalent to a company was a troop, numbering one hundred riders each, with a dozen troops per regiment. The artillery version was a battery. Federal batteries usually consisted of six guns; the Confederate counterpart normally had four guns of similar caliber. Infantry companies could thin to a few dozen men before being replenished or redeployed. Because each man in a battery had a specific task, artillery companies were usually fully staffed at around ninety men.

Some of the best unit names in the Civil War came from the company level. The Baldwin Blues, Cherokee Lincoln Killers, Cumberland Plough Boys, Raccoon Roughs, Rutherford Rifles, etc. Companies also provided some of the most tragic stories. For convenience and camaraderie, recruits from the same town or county were often placed within the same company, troop, or battery. A tragic consequence of this practice was the collective effect upon that hometown, hamlet, or borough if the unit got caught in a deadly part of a battle and lost most of its soldiers.

Although each company was designated by a letter, the U.S. Army never had a J Company, as it looked too much like an I.

---

8. PLATOON

To facilitate communication during combat, a company divided into two platoons. Each platoon had two sections. Each section contained two squads. Each squad consisted of ten men.[55]

The dissemination of command was supposed to function along these lines: a company leader, nominally a captain, directed two platoons by way of his lieutenants. The first and second lieutenants kept their respective platoon in order and communicated commands through their sergeants. Each sergeant was responsible for his section of twenty men. Each section's two corporals assisted their own squad of ten privates. The final effect was to be a fast, effective chain of command from top to bottom.

In reality, few instances existed where all officers and men were present for duty, and when the shooting started, things only became worse. Noise, smoke, terrain, marching, shifting, and reforming tended to jumble squads together. Enemy rifle volleys and artillery shells sliced away big pieces of a once cohesive platoon. The chain of command was a misnomer at the platoon level. Instead, a platoon's subunits and multiple leaders worked more like a system of intentional redundancy, capable of fighting on when portions of it were broken or missing.[56]

> In battle, designated file-closers marched a few steps behind the platoons. These armed men were responsible for shooting anyone who attempted to run away from the fighting.

9. MESS

Although not an official unit, a mess gave a measure of stability to a soldier's day-to-day existence. Inspired by utility more than anything else, men naturally gathered in small groups to share equipment, duties, and talents. One or two men cooked while others scavenged or traded for food. A few might take on laundry if others would address the all-too-often sewing needs. During long marches the chore of hauling the heavy mess griddle passed from man to man.

For a soldier in a prison camp, joining a good mess would take on another dimension, as it would often be his only means of survival. Each member acted as scout, forager, bodyguard, and doctor. If one should die,

the only way for his family to learn his fate was for members of his mess to pass on the tragic news.[57]

If a soldier mentioned another individual when writing home, it was often someone in his mess.

10. SOLDIER

The smallest military unit was the private. The average soldier was five feet eight inches tall, weighed 143 pounds, and was twenty-three years old.

An example of how a soldier fit into the grand scheme can be seen in the October 3–4, 1862, battle of Corinth, Mississippi: Union Maj. Gen. William S. Rosecrans led the Army of the Mississippi and the Army of West Tennessee. Having too few divisions to form any corps, Rosecrans's five division commanders reported directly to him. One of these was Brig. Gen. Thomas A. Davies of the Second Division of the Army of West Tennessee. In Davies's division were three brigades and four artillery batteries. Leading his First Brigade of a thousand men was Brig. Gen. Pleasant Hackleman. Hackleman's brigade contained seven regiments, including the 346 men and officers of the Second Iowa, commanded by Col. James Baker. In charge of Company B of the Second Iowa was 1st Lt. John Huntington, and among his men was Pvt. Bavil Seymour.

Of the 21,000 Federals and 22,000 Confederates at the battle of Corinth, 8,762 were killed, wounded, or went missing. Of the 6 men mentioned above, only Rosecrans and Davies survived.[58]

Cleverly disguised, an estimated four hundred soldiers in the Civil War were women.

TOP TEN SURGICAL TOOLS AND MEDICINES

Unlike a contemporary medical practitioner who spends seven years and beyond in schooling and internship, a doctor of the mid-nineteenth century received perhaps two years of schooling, little of which was formal. It is fair to say the lack of training was in direct proportion to the lack of knowledge. There existed no comprehension of microbiotics. Diagnostics and treatment were little more than guesswork. Even the association of cleanliness and health was not generally understood within the profession.[59]

For the most part, Civil War doctors performed as best they could under ludicrous circumstances. Armies on both sides allocated just one surgeon and one or two assistant surgeons per regiment. There were shortages of support staff, equipment, and medicines, especially during and immediately after major battles. By necessity, doctors performed surgeries hastily and in schoolrooms, warehouses, barns, and open fields. Even before the war, the South was at a disadvantage, having fewer medical schools, pharmaceutical laboratories, and physicians per capita than the North.[60]

The tools and medicines below, in order of frequency used, illustrate vividly the Civil War surgeon's limitations. Notably, disease more than injury concerned doctors. Not every soldier was wounded, but nearly all fell ill at one time or another. Thus most of a doctor's medicines and tools were geared toward treating or preventing sickness.[61]

1. MERCURY

The cure-all was calomel, also known as blue mass, blue powder, or mercurous chloride. It consisted of chalk and honey and sometimes licorice that was mixed with mercury. Wards and doctors prescribed it for everything from headaches to syphilis. Mostly it was used as a flushing agent for bowel ailments. Unbeknownst at the time, the medicine was poisonous.[62]

Calomel was the most common of many metal-based toxins used. Among others were iodide of mercury, red oxide of mercury, mercury ointment, persulfate of iron, nitrate of silver, copper sulfate, sugar of lead, and acetate of lead. In liquid or powdered form, the medicine was mixed with water and taken orally. These concoctions did little beyond add to the misery of their recipients. Often, if a patient did not respond well to initial treatment, doctors assumed the dosage was too small and administered more.[63]

In 1863, realizing that mercury-based medicines were causing dehydration, severe salivation, tooth loss, destruction of the jawbone, and grave digestive damage, the surgeon general of the Union army, William Hammond, demanded calomel be removed from the army medical supply table. Fellow surgeons and the general public summarily dubbed him a quack, and he was dismissed from his post months later.[64]

Mercury was often used in the construction of hats. Long-term exposure to the mercury caused cerebral damage, inspiring the term "mad as a hatter."

2. ALCOHOLIC BEVERAGES

First and foremost was whiskey followed by brandy, wine, and other spirits in a doctor's repertoire of tinctures. Like mercury, alcohol was viewed as a medicine for the full spectrum of maladies. The wounded received doses, sometimes large ones, to ward off shock or to rally them for surgery. The sick received administrations for headache, weakness, fever, diarrhea, or loss of appetite. In reality, alcohol was of little benefit beyond temporarily quenching a thirst, yet its depressant qualities reduced a patient's perception or display of pain, thus making alcohol appear to heal him.[65]

As with other medicines of the period, alcohol did more harm than good, as it fatigued and dehydrated already weak patients. Whiskey did have the attribute of making bitter powders more palatable, especially quinine, which required a daily dose to keep malaria at bay.[66]

By 1862 the Confederate Medical Department had its own distilleries.

3. PLANTS

With more than half the soldiers on both sides having farm backgrounds, there was considerable faith in indigenous remedies. Familiarity and availability prompted the use of roots, oils, herbs, and barks. Shortages of more modern medicines forced Southern medics to use plants more often than their Northern peers.[67]

To the contemporary ear the medicinal lists of Civil War doctors may sound like witch's brew: juniper, dogwood, horsemint, ginseng, blood-wort, butterwort, snakeroot, wormseed, oil of cloves, oil of peppermint, oil of cinnamon, extract of dandelion, extract of rhubarb, and extract of sarsaparilla.

Prominent and effective in the treatment of malaria was quinine, which was made from the bark of the South American Cinchona tree. The North had ample supplies of quinine whereas the South suffered considerably from shortages as the war progressed. By 1864 quinine was selling for hundreds of Confederate dollars an ounce. In a desperate and unsuccessful attempt to replace it, Southerners tried extracts from the bark of willow, dogwood, and poplar trees.[68]

Doctors issued opium, usually as a liquid called laudanum, to treat extreme cases of pain, agitation, and dysentery. Confederate Gen. JOHN BELL HOOD, twice severely wounded, took it for pain. Diarist Mary Chesnut used it to fight depression. Where quinine saved thousands of lives, opiates compromised thousands more. Opium inspired the phrase "Old Soldier's Disease" for the legions who were still addicted to it decades after their service.[69]

In 1863 Confederate Dr. Francis Porcher released his *Resources of Southern Fields and Forests,* a work covering available natural medicines. It was six hundred pages long.

---

4. BANDAGES

Fine lint, gauze, adhesive plasters, and sometimes nothing more than cloth rags were used for hospital bandages. At the battle of ANTIETAM, medics on both sides exhausted nearly everything they had, and CLARA BARTON witnessed Union surgeons using corn husks. Bandaging was one area in which the South had an advantage. Lack of cloth forced Southern hospitals to use raw cotton, which tended to be less septic than other materials.

Whatever the medium, bandages were never sterile. Doctors made them worse by insisting they be kept moist, which may have comforted the wounded for a short time but provided an ideal environment for bacteria. Worse were times of shortage, when dressings were removed from the deceased, given a rudimentary rinse, and placed on the next injured man.[70]

When bandaging ran out altogether, maggots often collected in open wounds. To the amazement of observant attendants, the fly larvae ate the gangrenous flesh and left living tissue untouched, effectively cleaning the wound.[71]

To "decontaminate" wounds before bandaging, medics sometimes used carbolic acid, bromine, or turpentine.

---

5. SCALPEL

The surgeon's knife was a jack of all trades. It incised skin, cut bandages, scraped bone, sliced muscle, and lanced boils. It was also a vehicle for bacteria. In a lethal display of hygienic ignorance, surgeons went from patient to patient with the same scalpel, "cleaning" it with little more than a wipe across their aprons. This practice was most dangerous when dealing with older wounds, after infections had set in.[72]

Along with the standard straight knife, most surgeons had curved and blunted scalpels. Curved instruments could maneuver around tendons and bones and into sinuses. Blunted ends prevented the puncturing of nearby organs and arteries.[73]

As the war progressed, scalpels and other metal instruments became scarce in the South. Confederate foundries manufactured munitions rather than medical equipment, thus Confederate doctors made do with very little, sometimes depending on paring and kitchen knives to do their cutting. Confederate surgeon general Samuel Preston Moore scoured the South for spare scalpels and other instruments. He managed to procure a few instruments from retired doctors and from the families of deceased doctors, but the shortage was never resolved.[74]

There are reports of a Union soldier in a Confederate prison who amputated his own gangrenous feet with just a pocketknife.

---

6. SUTURE THREAD

Initially, both sides used silk or catgut to stitch up cuts, holes, and stumps. Over time, shortages forced Southern attendants to use cotton thread.

After the necessary surgeries, the wounded were usually placed under trees for the relative comfort the shade offered.

Rejoining skin and closing smashed arteries, ligatures also posed a great danger for the wounded. To thread their sewing needles, doctors either moistened the thread with saliva or rolled the ends between their unclean fingers. Stitched into the flesh, the contaminated material came in direct contact with bloodstreams and fragile tissue, promoting infections of the worst kind. There were many cases of amputation stumps rotting at the sutures. The infected area weakened and gave way, and the stump burst, necessitating an amputation higher up the limb.[75]

Effective suturing required time, an amenity field surgeons rarely had. Peter Alexander of the *Mobile Register* described what happened when doctors rushed the job of closing fresh amputations: "I have known of cases of amputation where the lapping part of the flesh was sewed together over the bone so stupidly that the thread would disengage itself and the bone [would] be exposed in less than twenty-four hours."[76]

When cotton sutures ran out, Confederate doctors were known to use horsehair.

Taken captive during the Seven Days' battles, these surgeons had to work in the open.

7. PROBES

To search out and remove bullets, shell fragments, bone slivers, and other unwanted foreign matter, Civil War surgeons used a wide assortment of skewers, hooks, and tweezers. Like scalpels and needles, probes were a major contributor to the spread of infection. Contaminated probes passed bacteria and pus from one part of the body to another, from one man to the next, from ward to ward.

The apparent indifference of some practitioners to the pain of the wounded was most acute when a probe was in use. Amputations, red and swollen with infection, received an awl poke or tweezers pull for a check on progress. To examine gashes, lacerations, and bullet holes, doctors jabbed and pulled with their instruments, sometimes asking the patient to help out by holding the flesh open with a free hand.[77]

> In April 1865, when examining Abraham Lincoln's head wound immediately after the shooting, attending doctors probed the bullet hole with their fingers—a common practice.

8. TOURNIQUET

Every standard medical satchel included straps for cutting off blood to limbs. These were usually employed on one of three occasions. Tourniquets were common at dressing stations, the first stop for the wounded, to slow arterial bleeding and enable soldiers to survive the trip to the field hospital. On the operating table, straps cinched the limb to prevent arterial flow, allowing surgery or stitching to commence. Lastly, a tourniquet would be called for after a limb artery disintegrated and burst from infection. In this last circumstance, mortality reached more than 60 percent, and tourniquets served to simply delay the inevitable.

In a pinch, a belt or a horse's bridle sufficed to staunch bleeding. There are several accounts where nurses simply held an artery closed with their fingers, sometimes for hours, until a surgeon could address the bleeding with forceps and suturing.[78]

Some doctors discouraged tourniquet use for fear of cutting off blood to healthy areas.

9. BONE SAW

There were sixty thousand partial or complete surgical removals of limbs during the war, and most were necessary due to the irreparable damage caused by soft lead projectiles. Those doctors who were willing and ready to use a bone saw, which looked remarkably like a hacksaw, were titled "butchers," "sawbones," and other choice names. What many soldiers may not have known was that the removal of an appendage within twenty-four hours of catastrophic damage gave the body an 80 percent chance of survival. After forty-eight hours, the survival rate dipped to 40 percent.[79]

There were two basic methods of amputation: circular and flap. A circular amputation involved slicing the skin in a perpendicular manner just below where the bone was to be pruned. The surgeon then cut away an inverted cone of muscles and tendons. An assistant pulled the flesh up along the bone, and the doctor sawed through the bone. A single-flap amputation used a diagonal cut across the limb. After cutting the bone and closing blood vessels, the doctor pulled the flesh over the bone to create a cleaner, more uniform closure than that of the circular pattern. A double-flap amputation required a V-shaped cut of skin and flesh up into the limb. The assistant peeled the two flaps back, allowing for a high cut of the bone.[80]

For all the criticism heaped upon army surgeons, three of four amputees survived the procedure, and most would not have lived long without it.[81]

Of all field surgeries conducted, 75 percent were amputations.

---

10. ANESTHETICS

In one of the greatest leaps in medicine before or since, ether and chloroform were discovered in the 1840s. Chloroform was more widely used. Patients were finally spared the pain of invasive surgery, and doctors could work on a stationary subject. The anesthetic was poured onto a cloth and held over a patient's nose and mouth. As soon as the patient went limp, the operation commenced. Anesthetics also proved helpful when cleaning and redressing deep wounds or burns.[82]

It is a myth that Civil War operations occurred without anesthetics. The screaming, writhing patient, however, is based on truth. Amputations were usually performed in open areas. To speed processing, patients were placed in queue, often within sight of the table. For those who were not already near madness from the agony of their severe wound, the news of impending surgery and the sight of the limbs, blood, and instruments of an operating area sent them into violent hysteria.[83]

Chloroform was widely available North and South, but there are accounts where even alternatives such as ether, alcohol, and opium were not available, and the patient underwent treatment fully awake. As witnessed before the age of anesthetics, patients consequently suffered lasting mental trauma more often than not. A considerable percentage succumbed to cardiac arrest during the procedure and expired.[84]

Stonewall Jackson received chloroform for the removal of his left arm. On his deathbed, Jackson described being anesthetized as "the most delightful physical sensation I ever experienced."

TOP TEN MODES OF COMMUNICATION

The Civil War straddled epochs in medicine, weaponry, and human rights. It also marked a communications revolution. In 1850 it took ten weeks to send information from St. Louis to San Francisco. In 1860 the Pony Express cut the time to ten days. By 1862 the telegraph accomplished the task in ten minutes. When the rockets' red glare flashed over Fort McHenry in 1814, less than 70 percent of adult white males could read and write. By the time artillery pounded Fort Sumter in similar fashion, the literacy rate had surpassed 90 percent. Not since the invention of movable-type printing presses had the Western world experienced such leaps in the speed and accessibility of information.[85]

Yet innovations were in their infancy, and war was not a good caretaker. Telegraph lines hundreds of miles long were silenced with axes and wire cutters. WILLIAM TECUMSEH SHERMAN noted that it only took one man and a match to break a rail line. Shortages left many Confederate printers and soldiers without paper and ink. Despite the dawn of progress, much of Civil War communications remained in the Dark Ages.

The following are the ten most common means of communication during military operations, from the rifle pits to regimental command, from camps to the capitals and beyond.

1. SPOKEN WORDS

As simple as it was, speech was the single most important communication medium of the war. News, orders, gossip, instructions, warnings, passwords, and taunts came chiefly by word of mouth.

Officers and sergeants on both sides worked around a shortage of manuals, maps, time, paper, and in some cases, literate soldiers. The enlisted spent interminable hours in drill, learning to perform a number of actions from simple verbal cues: move at the quick step, wheel right, charge bayonets, etc.

There were drawbacks of course. Without written instructions, detailed orders were easily forgotten, misinterpreted, or refuted. During the battle of Fair Oaks, for example, the otherwise dependable JAMES LONGSTREET either forgot or misunderstood verbal orders and marched his troops down the wrong road in the wrong direction.

Verbal communication in combat was also rather costly to the officer class. The method of massing infantry in close quarters was less a matter of obsolete tactics as it was a reflection of limited communication capabilities. By necessity, the best officers routinely conducted field operations in person, issuing commands directly to their troops. Evidence of this practice comes from the mortality rates of soldiers in the war. Around 6 percent of all enlisted men were killed in action or died of their wounds, whereas the same fate claimed more than 12 percent of the generals.[86]

For the enlisted, conversation was the principal pastime. Soldiers complained of officers, food, the weather, and supplies. They also chatted about home, politics, past and impending battles, and everything else from the lofty to the mundane. Troops in opposing trenches commonly exchanged words, from jibes of "Why don't you come on over, Billy Yank?" to offers of tobacco for coffee. In many instances, men on picket duty were kind enough to warn each other of imminent attack, giving a few precious seconds to abandon their forward position before it was too late.[87]

Perhaps no other battlefield manifestation of the spoken word was as unique and outstanding as the Rebel Yell, an inspired Confederate weapon used from FIRST MANASSAS onward to instill resolve in its authors and fear among its targets. Historian Bell Irvin Wiley described it as "a mixture of fright, pent-up nervousness, exultation, hatred and a pinch of pure deviltry." Union veterans recalled being terrified by the discord, but there are no verified accounts of a Federal unit running simply because they heard it.[88]

Apparently it took the excitement of battle to inspire a Rebel Yell. By the time the phonograph was invented (1877), no Confederate veteran could sincerely muster one, and thus an authentic Rebel Yell was never recorded.

---

2. WRITTEN REPORTS AND DISPATCHES

The war transpired before science and technology developed typewriters, copy machines, and even carbon paper, yet the military machines of both sides managed to produce enough paperwork to fill archives beyond capacity in a few short years. By 1865 written materials from the Union adjutant general's office were so voluminous they occupied a third of the floor space of the War Department. The Confederate military retained far less paperwork due to a smaller administrative network, shortages of writing and printing equipment, and the destruction of much of their documents during the last month of the war. And yet whole warehouses in and around Washington were filled with captured or copied Confederate documents by 1866.

A considerable amount of the volume came from the necessary red tape of conducting a continental war. Requisitions required at least three copies, and muster sheets required five. For every immortal quote on any major battlefield, there were thousands of pages of maneuver orders, promotions and reassignments, muster rolls, quartermaster reports, medical reports, correspondences, and responses that kept the machine running.

> Perpetually struggling with his limited ability to read and write, Confederate Gen. Nathan Bedford Forrest had almost all of his messages written by fellow officers.

3. DRUMS AND BUGLES

Union regulations called for a minimum of two musicians in each regiment—a drummer and a bugler. On the field, verbal communications traveled only so far, especially during the howl of battle. Visual communications were just as limited by weather, powder smoke, terrain, and cover of woods. Skins and horns however, could relay instructions to a thousand men in seconds.

Each brigade North and South had between fifteen and forty different bugle and drum calls. There were the basics, such as reveille or the similar assembly, the officers call, or the much-anticipated dinner call. In camp, men knew when to fall in for drill, water their horses, prepare to march, assemble for roll call, and extinguish campfires by way of snare rattles and bickering brass. Posted closely to commanding officers, drummer boys and buglers also relayed commands under combat conditions.

From sun-up to lights out, from saddle up to march forward, bugles and drums directed the concert. The tradition lingers today. Reveille and Taps, the latter call originating during the war, are both played every day in the U.S. Army.[89]

> One drummer boy achieved considerable fame. John Clem, a.k.a. Johnny Shiloh, joined the Union army at the age of nine, lost his drum to artillery

fire at SHILOH, was wounded at least once, reportedly shot a Confederate at CHICKAMAUGA, and retired a major general in the U.S. Army fifty years later.

4. TELEGRAPHY

In the 1830s the "magnetic telegraph" became the first tangible, functional device in the modern era of electronic information. A telegraph basically consisted of a sending and receiving device, a battery, and a length of copper wire strung along poles and through trees. Set at regular intervals, additional receivers and batteries amplified and forwarded electronic signals. Although there were still a number of signaling systems and languages available, the sturdy and simple system developed by Samuel Morse and Alfred Vail were widely accepted by the time of the war, connecting capitals with headquarters and headquarters with divisions.[90]

Under the jurisdiction of the adjutant general's department, the Southern military wire service was also responsible for secret service and flag signaling. The U.S. Military Telegraph Corps worked in conjunction with the Signal Corps until competition for control and resources led to a complete separation of the two in August 1864. All Union telegraphy was under the control of the War Department and not the generals in the field, much to the frustration of the latter (U.S. Secretary of War Edwin M. Stanton was in fact a former director of the Atlantic and Ohio Telegraph Company).[91]

More than any other form of communication, the Union dominated telegraphy. The South employed approximately fifteen hundred telegraphers, whereas the North had more than twelve thousand—a number larger than most Confederate armies. Both sides depended heavily on private corporations for hardware and operation, but the South had nothing that could rival the size or wealth of Northern-based companies such as Western Union or American Telegraph. As the war dragged on, the Confederacy lacked or lost vital wire and equipment, never having more than five hundred miles of telegraph in operation. In contrast, the Union eventually laid down fifteen thousand miles of wire, enough to span the continent five times. With limited means and engineers, Confederate telegraphy was often intercepted and deciphered. Reportedly, no Union code was ever compromised during the war.[92]

Lincoln ended each working day by visiting the telegraph office in the War Department. He usually made the trip from the White House on foot and unescorted.

5. SIGNAL CORPS

In 1859 Army surgeon A. J. Myer and West Point instructor Edward Porter Alexander experimented with a new long-distance communication system called wigwag. With the use of flags or torches, Myer and Alexander could send and receive visual messages miles away from each other. In two short years the system proved its worth under fire.[93]

Signalmen made use of any elevation they could find. In some instances they erected their own , such as this man-made station near Sharpsburg, Maryland.

Perched on hilltops and in tree roosts, in fort towers and on sailing vessels, both Union and Confederate Signal Corps maintained lines of communication, day and night, from FIRST MANASSAS to Appomattox. The method proved most valuable when other means, such as telegraphs and couriers, were cut off altogether. Some relays stretched as far as thirty miles. In the field, each brigade or division had a crew of three to five men. The team perpetually manned a telescope, awaiting incoming messages. In sending, a single flag or torch "wigwagged" numeric signals. A wave right to left signified a 1, a wave only from the right meant 2, and a dip forward showed 3.[94]

There were disadvantages. As was feared, transmission from open positions made messages susceptible to interception. Commanding the high ground at GETTYSBURG, for example, Union forces were able to catch a number of Confederate directives on troop movements. Both sides minimized risk by coding, encrypting, and abbreviating messages as often as possible. The job itself was a relatively dangerous one. Flagmen were prone to heavy concentrations of enemy fire. On both sides, one out of every twelve in the Signal Corps was a casualty.[95]

The success of the wigwag system came largely from the direction and initiative of its inventors. Myer went on to become the U.S. Army's first signal officer. Alexander, a Georgian, served as the Confederate chief of signal service at First Manassas. He later became an artillery officer under JAMES LONGSTREET, directing murderous fire at the battles of FRED-ERICKSBURG, GETTYSBURG, and COLD HARBOR.[96]

After examining the wigwag system in 1859, a military board approved the medium for use in the U.S. Army. Heading the board was a lieutenant colonel by the name of ROBERT E. LEE.

---

6. MAIL

The most prevalent and lasting link between the military and civilian populations came by way of personal mail. Surviving letters have also given later generations the most accurate glimpse of a soldier's everyday life. On every kind of paper under all imaginable conditions, men wrote or dictated millions of letters, expressing their fears, desires, frustrations, assumptions, and experiences. In turn, the men read of the same from home.

For the impoverished enlisted man, the mail functioned as a physical lifeline as much as an emotional one. Troops asked for clothes, food, medicines, an illicit nip of whiskey or whatnot. Friends and family obliged as best they could, as did the postal services. In fact, there were accounts of deliveries speedy enough to transport cooked meats and jarred fruits to their addressees in fine order.[97]

More than anything else, the men simply asked their friends and family to write back and possibly send paper, ink, and stamps if they could spare some. Unfortunately, enemy activity, mobile armies, and the low priority of mail bags on supply trains meant that soldiers wrote far more letters than they received. In many instances, soldiers resorted to begging, even shaming loved ones to write, not realizing the fragile nature of the postal line. One officer wrote, "I am sure that you havent entirely forgotten that you have a husband in the army." An enlisted man was even less subtle, writing "when you come to reflect that you have seen me for perhaps the last time on earth I feel as though I ought to hear from home at least once a week."[98]

Mail service was not exactly dependable. One Confederate soldier recalled getting a letter from his wife ten months after she sent it.

---

7. ARTILLERY AND SMALL-ARMS FIRE

Weaponry had its own language. Distant rifle pops were the work of snipers. A sudden crackling usually came from a skirmish line under assault. Steady rumbles told of a large-scale engagement. Sporadic booms signified artillery fire intent on harassment while shuddering earth and crashing trees meant field guns were hammering a position in concert. In combat, no other form of communication moved as quickly as news from the mouth of a weapon.

Commanders miles away from the fighting often depended on the sounds of battle to know when and where to move. It is said that NATHAN BEDFORD FORREST fought his battles almost literally "by ear." At ANTIE-TAM, ROBERT E. LEE calculated when and where he should shift his outnumbered troops by listening to the changing sounds of rifle fire. Returning on horseback from a conference in Washington, Union commander PHILIP H. SHERIDAN overheard distant artillery fire too intense to be considered routine. He galloped to his army and found them in full retreat from Confederate attack, rallied them, and reversed the outcome of the battle of Cedar Creek. The war itself began with a solitary artillery blast. A battery from nearby Fort Johnson signaled the commencement of the shelling of Fort Sumter.

Civilians also learned of nearby battles from the noise of gunfire. Baltimore residents claimed they could hear the growl of the last day of GETTYSBURG. The reverberation of Grant's early morning assault at COLD HARBOR was so tremendous that it rattled windowpanes in Richmond, twelve miles away.[99]

Sometimes there was no noise. In this and other wars, an eerie phenomenon occurred known as "acoustic shadows" or "silent battles." Soldiers within a few miles of an active engagement heard nothing, while others farther away clearly detected the thunder of arms. Attributed to wind direction, topography, and varying air densities, these pockets of utter stillness could and sometimes did keep detached units oblivious to changing tides of battle. Officers from both sides reported acoustic shadows at the battles of Seven Pines, Gaines's Mill, Perryville, STONES RIVER, and CHANCELLORSVILLE, among others.[100]

Gunfire occasionally saved lives. During the cold winter's night after the battle of Fredericksburg, many of the wounded, unable to crawl or walk out of no man's land, shot off their muskets to show where they were and that they needed rescuing.

---

8. BATTLE FLAGS

Whether symbolizing the company, regiment, or country, a battle flag in the Civil War was as instructional as it was inspirational. Lines could move, break, shift, and move again. Rumbling wagons, screaming animals, and thundering weapons drowned out voices and bugles. Throughout all the confusion, a soldier depended on his unit's banner to instantly show where his comrades were and where they were headed.

It was the highest honor and a considerable act of courage to be in the color guard, for not only did flag-bearers act as the nucleus for the unit, they were also destined to be a key target for the opposition. One Texas infantry regiment lost eight flag-bearers at ANTIETAM. A North

GEORGE CARPENTER, *HISTORY OF THE EIGHTH REGIMENT VERMONT VOLUNTEERS, 1861–1865* (1886)

Regimental colors usually marked a unit's position and the focal point of the fight.

Carolina unit lost fourteen at GETTYSBURG. There are several accounts where men held their standard aloft in battle despite missing parts of their bodies.[101]

Accordingly, capturing a battle flag was a most prestigious accomplishment. Such a prize testified that the opposition was rendered effectively headless during a fight. Nowhere was this better proven than at FIRST MANASSAS, where the general lack of battle flags contributed to the chaos of one of the ugliest and most disjointed contests of the war.[102]

One flag often sent the wrong signal. The first national flag of the Confederacy, with its three red and white horizontal bars and a canton of white stars on a blue field, looked much like the Union flag at a distance. To resolve the problem, a new version was adopted in March 1863, sporting a canton of the Confederate Battle Flag resting on a white field. In a calm wind, however, this second version resembled a flag of surrender. A final version contained a vertical red bar at the flag's right edge, but this came just months before the end of the war.

At Gettysburg the First Minnesota captured the battle flag of the Twenty-eighth Virginia. In 2001 the state of Virginia requested that Minnesota return it. As of 2003 Minnesota still possessed the banner.

9. NEWSPAPERS

As so often happens in times of war, a love-hate relationship persisted between the military and the press. With lines of communication short and tenuous, newsprint was commonly the only means by which soldiers and officers alike caught a glimpse of the big picture. On the other hand, a single page from a single issue could endanger an army. In 1862 HARPER'S WEEKLY printed an up-to-date map of the Army of the Potomac's Peninsula campaign, complete with the locations of Union trenches, supply lines, and GEORGE B. MCCLELLAN's headquarters. Alternately, newspapers could be lifesavers. JEB STUART and his cavalry lost contact with Lee's columns during the start of the Gettysburg campaign. A Northern newspaper, eager to inform the Pennsylvania public of the approaching danger, divulged Lee's path of approach. Stuart saw a copy and found his way back to his commander.[103]

As a rule, officers tended to give little away to correspondents. THOMAS J. "STONEWALL" JACKSON was known to be pleasant but silent to news hounds. P. G. T. Beauregard, JOSEPH E. JOHNSTON, and others excluded correspondents from their camps for months at a time. WILLIAM TECUMSEH SHERMAN, accused of being insane more than once by the press, deemed reporters cowards and spies. Some, such as publicity monger George Armstrong Custer, openly courted the attention of reporters. Yet all labored to get their hands on newspapers as often as possible in hopes of learning something new about the enemy.[104]

Comparatively, papers were more abundant in Union camps, a direct reflection of easier access, wider selection, and greater supply of paper and machinery. Confederates attained a considerable amount of this print via trade. One Virginia grayback wrote home: "The Yankees are still on this side of the river. The picket lines are within speaking distance of each other and we exchange newspapers with them every day."[105]

When enlisted men failed to get their hands on civilian newspapers, they wrote their own. Printing on nearby presses or on smaller ones "acquired" along the way, soldiers produced as many as 150 camp, garrison, and hospital papers during the war with names like the *Waltonville War Cry*, the *Rebel Banner*, and the *Haversack*. Union presses had at least three different papers named *Stars and Stripes*. Camp papers, selling for a nickel or more and numbering from a few to a few thousand, contained anything from details on proper dress and drill to camp regulations, fiction pieces, satire, overviews of past engagements, and ads from nearby sutlers and photographers.[106]

One Union hospital paper had a less than encouraging name. The editors entitled it the *Soldier's Casket*.

---

10. PHOTOGRAPHS

For many men in the middle 1800s the Civil War was the first, and for some the only, time they had their photograph taken. When circumstances allowed, soldiers ventured to nearby studios or traveling photographers, parted with a week's pay, and received a dozen copies of their "shadow." Friends and family saw their boy in his best uniform trim, posing proudly in these cartes de visite.[107]

Providing a greater communicative impact upon soldier and citizen, were group photos and landscapes. Through handheld viewers (most landscapes were stereo images), people saw parts of the country they had never been to and pictures of companies and companions they would never see again. Scenes from camps, forts, and hospitals delivered a nationwide sense of realism to the conflict. Shots of battlefields and the dead, taken from a few hours to several days after the fighting, brought much attention to the hearts and minds on the home front. In a foreshadowing of television's impact on later wars, some of the more ghastly scenes intensified popular movements for and against the war's continuation.[108]

A few insightful military men recognized photography's potential. The camera made an excellent copy machine for large and complex maps. Intelligence officers scoured over group photos to find spies. The Union navy photographed battle-damaged coastal forts to gauge the effects of naval bombardment. The Union army studied landscape shots, scrutinizing the topography for prime defense and depot positions.[109]

In spite of the newness, expense, and fragility of their medium, photographers produced more than ten thousand landscapes on tin, copper, or glass during the war. Of the cartes de visite taken of the humble soldier, there were perhaps a million.[110]

There are fewer than 150 known photographs of Abraham Lincoln.

TOP TEN CAUSES OF MILITARY DEATHS

For a soldier's mortality, the Civil War was a monument to bad timing. The Industrial Revolution facilitated the mass production of weaponry, but the medical revolution and its use of antiseptics was years away. Remington and Colt came long before Pasteur and Lister.

To replicate the Civil War, assemble hundreds of thousands of men, many with questionable health. Subject them to crowded camps and ship hulls, fatigue, terror, bad food, bad water, raw sewage, extremes in weather, and poor habits in hygiene. Position them against an enemy with similar traits. Arm both sides with millions of mid-nineteenth-century weapons, pit them against each other for four years, and you have a basic idea of how healthy the war was.

Included below are conservative death counts on each side for each cause. Accurate totals are impossible to ascertain, especially for the Confederacy. Incomplete or lost records, multiple causes, and misdiagnoses contribute to imprecision, but the estimates are nonetheless astounding. Not making the list but causing numerous fatalities were accident, bronchitis, cholera, drowning, execution, exposure, fire, heat stroke, murder, scurvy, suicide, and venereal disease.[111]

1. KILLED IN ACTION (C.S. 54,000; U.S. 67,100)

Old generalship and older tactics fared poorly against new technologies. Rifled weapons and minié bullets increased a soldier's effective firing range threefold, but traditional military methods still depended on massed infantry at close range. Consequently, whole companies could be gunned down in short order. Storming well-defended positions also increased body counts.[112]

The chief culprit was the bullet itself, which accounted for more than 90 percent of battle fatalities. A soft low-velocity bullet spread apart inside the body, causing excessive and often irreparable tissue damage. Amputations and their sickening frequency attested to its destructive talents on bones, but lead did its most lethal work on arteries and organs. On average, of every hundred fatalities on a battlefield, five died from limb wounds, twelve from punctures to the lower abdomen, fifteen from damage to the heart or liver, and more than fifty from lacerations to the head or neck. In all, one of every sixty-five Federals and one of every forty-five Confederates were killed in action.[113]

Nearly half of all Civil War battlefield graves are marked as unknown.

2. DYSENTERY AND DIARRHEA (C.S. 50,000; U.S. 45,000)

No disease claimed more lives than dysentery and diarrhea. Unaware that fecal contamination of food or water was the culprit, officers routinely set up latrines dangerously close to water supplies, soldiers relieved themselves just about anywhere, and food preparation was generally unsanitary. Soldiers called it the "quickstep," and nearly all contracted it at least once.

The major symptom was severe expulsion, as the body desperately tried to rid itself of intestinal contamination. Stool was bloody and sometimes laden with mucus. A person hit with the "fluxes" also experienced fluctuating fever, acute abdominal pain, brutal headaches, and vomiting. Within hours a fit soldier became nearly immobile from infection.[114]

Dysentery and diarrhea struck in every area of the country and during any season. Doctors treated it with oral doses of opium, copper sulfate, castor oil, lead acetate, or calomel (a mercury chloride powder), yet all known treatments had little or no success in curbing dysentery's potency or prevalence. About one in forty cases were fatal. Death came from dehydration, exhaustion, and/or the rupture of an intestinal wall.[115]

Unfortunately, dysentery and diarrhea were only part of the picture. Diseases altogether killed twice as many soldiers as did combat. Hardest hit were African American soldiers who lost fourteen times the number of men to illness as were lost on the battlefield.[116]

Diarrhea is from an ancient Greek word meaning "I flow away."

3. DIED OF WOUNDS (C.S. 40,000; U.S. 43,700)

Combat produces a ghastly mélange of fates upon flesh. One body gouged by artillery shrapnel might survive, while another nicked by a bullet might die instantly. Confederate Col. John B. Gordon was hit five times at the battle of ANTIETAM, including a bullet to the face, and lived to tell about it. On the first day of SHILOH, Confederate Gen. Albert Sidney Johnston was leading a charge atop his horse, enjoying his initial success, and totally oblivious to an arterial wound at the knee that soon killed him.[117]

For those who survived to reach field wards or hospital boats, the prognosis was far from rosy. With internal medicine still primitive, damage to vital organs was irreparable by human intervention. It was fatal to be "gut shot," that is, to receive any laceration of the small intestine, stomach, bladder, liver, or kidneys. Urine, blood, and/or fecal matter seeped into the abdominal cavity and accumulated, providing a painful, poisonous death within three days.[118]

If the body did not infect itself, there were plenty of outside sources. Bullets and shrapnel entering the body carried lead along with cloth from the victim's uniform, dirt, oils, and the like. In treating these wounds, doctors and nurses worked with dirty hands and fingers. Instruments wet with blood and pus were cleaned with a light rinse or a quick wipe. By necessity, many hospitals were stationed near transportation hubs, which meant dust-billowing roads and soot-belching trains.

The first photographs of battlefield casualties were at the Antietam battlefield.

LIBRARY OF CONGRESS

Consequently, nearly all wounds became septic. Pus in the blood, then known as pyemia, killed almost every victim, as did tetanus. There was also gangrene, a crawling death of unspeakable stench. The infection cellulitis, called erysipelas, appeared as warm, red swelling; it meant death more often than not. Formation of whitish "laudable pus" was thought to be a good sign, a flushing out of contaminates rather than an indication of massive infection.[119]

In Vietnam one in four hundred of the wounded perished. In the Korean War one of every fifty wounded American soldiers died of their injuries. In the Civil War one in seven wounded Federals and nearly one in five wounded Confederates died, sometimes within minutes, sometimes after months of suffering.

How did an officer die? Look at his statue. If his horse has both front feet kicking high above ground, he died in battle. One hoof raised means the rider died of wounds. A horse standing on all fours signifies the officer did

They were followed with images such as this one at Gettysburg.

not die of job-related maladies . . . or on the horse he rode. Horses and other draft animals had about a seven-month life expectancy in the war. As many as three hundred thousand horses died during the war.

4. TYPHOID (C.S. 30,000; U.S. 34,800)

Doctors called it "camp fever" or "continuous fever," and many believed "myasma" (putrid air) was the cause. In reality, typhoid bacteria entered through the mouth via contaminated water or food. Outbreaks occurred when waves of new recruits arrived, bringing the disease with them.[120]

An afflicted soldier first experienced what seemed to be the flu, with aches, sleeplessness, and headache. As the bacteria entered the bloodstream, the illness intensified. The tongue turned a brownish hue. High fever followed, along with complete weakness, vomiting, constipation or diarrhea, and a distended and tender abdomen. Rashes of pink spots appeared on the skin. Victims often slipped into mental delirium and convulsions.[121]

Many so-called treatments involved hourly teaspoons of turpentine, mercury-based or lead-based medicines, or other toxins. Some physicians administered powdered quinine, hoping it cured typhoid as it cured malaria.[122]

The men called it the "killing disease." Of every three cases, one was fatal. Death came either by complications, including meningitis, heart failure, and pneumonia, or by intestinal ulcers rupturing and flooding the body with bacteria. For those who survived the month-long ordeal of the disease, there was a long road to recovery, and relapses were common. Nearly a third of typhoid survivors remained carriers for years.[123]

Some units were so afflicted that men labeled them "typhoid regiments."

5. PRISON (C.S. 26,100; U.S. 31,200)

Take your pick of exits. With limited record-keeping in prisons, especially in the South, exact causes and number of deaths are unknown. The estimates above are conservative. Disease played a predominant role, with dysentery, diarrhea, typhoid, and pneumonia claiming the most victims.

The graves at Andersonville were not unlike the many burial grounds at other prison camps in the North and South—but there were so many.

Thousands more succumbed to starvation, dehydration, exposure, murder by guards, murder by fellow inmates, and suicide.

Rations were minuscule and raw sewage was abundant in the deadliest prisons, problems caused by the BREAKDOWN OF THE PRISONER EXCHANGE during the latter half of 1863. In the widespread overcrowding that followed, more American prisoners of war died in 1864 than in any other year in history.[124]

> Only one person was ever convicted of war crimes in the Civil War—
> Confederate Capt. Henry Wirz, commandant of ANDERSONVILLE.

6. PNEUMONIA (C.S. 17,000; U.S. 20,000)

An inflammation of the lungs, pneumonia preyed on soldiers weakened by wounds, hunger, and illness. A continuous presence in hospital wards and prison grounds, it flourished in the field during the coldest months, where damp ground, icy winds, and bone-chilling rains sapped the immune system. Pneumonia was commonly referred to as "pulmonary," and one in six sufferers died from it.

At first a soldier felt listless and cold, his chest began to hurt, and a fever erupted. This was followed by labored breathing and sleeplessness. Syrupy brown spit, agonizing headaches, and a fluctuating pulse were typical.

Treated today with antibiotics, there was no known cure in the mid-nineteenth century, and an observant doctor could usually tell when the end was near because he had seen it often enough. Breathing and heart rate slowed down, skin became drenched with sweat, and signs of delirium became pronounced. Death came from overwhelming infection, toxemia, meningitis, or heart failure.[125]

Perhaps the most famous case of fatal pneumonia was Thomas J. "Stonewall" Jackson. He succumbed to the disease after being weakened by the amputation of his left arm following his wounding during the battle of CHANCELLORSVILLE.

---

7. MALARIA (C.S. 20,000; U.S. 10,000)

Also called rubeola or "remittent fever," malaria caused chills, fluctuating fever, anemia, and swelling of the spleen. Conventional thinking at the time attributed malaria and many other illnesses to "bad air," which was common enough in marshy, swampy areas. Not until the beginning of the twentieth century did science realize malaria came from protozoa-carrying mosquitoes.[126]

Peak outbreaks occurred in late summer or early autumn, when mosquito populations hit their apex. Cases in Union armies increased as the men pushed farther south. Malaria did find a worthy foe in its human target, however. Prevention and treatment were known long before the cause. Areas of standing water were drained or avoided. Quinine was administered to the sick in heavy doses and daily to almost all soldiers as a preventative measure. At least three million cases existed in the armed forces alone, but most were not deadly. The South suffered more because of limited access to quinine supplies.

Death, if it did come, was not pretty. Convulsions, vomiting, delirium, and diarrhea set in, followed by a coma then death.[127]

Alexander the Great died of malaria.

---

8. SMALLPOX (C.S. 8,000; U.S. 7,000)

Like measles and chicken pox, smallpox is a one-time disease. Unfortunately for about 20 percent of the Civil War soldiers who contracted it, once was enough to be lethal.[128]

Medics often mistook smallpox for chicken pox, measles, or syphilis until telltale red pustules and crimson blotches formed. In one to two weeks the pustules scabbed over and remained for a month or more. For those who survived, scarring was common.

For smallpox—also known as "variola," the "prowling spotted beast," and "sledgehammer"—the preventative measure was vaccination. Cowpox injections had been in use for nearly seventy years, but most doctors used a cheaper method whereby the scab of an infected person was introduced into the skin of a healthy person via pinprick. Inexact, scab vaccinations were sometimes too heavy in dosage, resulting in a full-blown case of smallpox for the recipient. For the majority who did not become ill, there remained the concern of whether their vaccination had worked at all—a question answered when the next outbreak entered camp.[129]

Those most susceptible to smallpox were men from rural areas, African Americans, and Native Americans, who as children were rarely exposed to the disease. The mustering of African American troops in 1863 created a large outbreak among them, and hundreds of new recruits died.[130]

Smallpox has killed more humans than any other disease in history.

9. TUBERCULOSIS (C.S. 7,000; U.S. 7,000)

A bacterium passed by respiration, tuberculosis prospered in camp. Close quarters, fatigue, and poor diet increased susceptibility. Afflicted soldiers displayed signs of exhaustion, which rarely received sympathy from superiors. Then there were aches, enlargement of glands in the neck, and fever accompanied a pronounced, harsh cough.

Civil War vernacular referred to tuberculosis as "consumption," because it effectively devoured its victim. Bacteria attacked vital organs, especially the lungs, where coughing simply accentuated the damage. Gradually, fatigue and weight loss set in and accelerated. If a soldier began to cough blood, a doctor could be certain it was tuberculosis, but by then the lungs were too far gone for anything to be done.[131]

> Those who were afflicted in the lungs could, by coughing, disperse four billion tuberculosis bacilli in a single day.

10. MEASLES (C.S. 6,000; U.S. 5,200)

This was another camp disease spread by human contact. Epidemics broke out every time there was a surge in mustering: summer of 1861 on both sides, winter of 1863–64 among African American troops, and spring 1864 for Confederate draftees. Within these waves of green recruits were thousands who had never been exposed to the childhood disease.

Ten or so days after exposure, an infected soldier came down with a fever, cough, watery eyes, and runny nose, making it appear as if he had a severe cold. Days later the cough intensified and rashes formed around the hairline and neck as tiny red spots. Nostrils effused mucus constantly, then the rash spread. Fevers ran as high as 106 degrees. Dots on the skin turned to large blotches, running together and advancing. The afflicted complained of their skin being on fire. Visible symptoms lasted up to two weeks.

The disease swept quickly through a camp yet subsided within a month or so. Fatalities among the troops were rare, about one in twenty cases, and most deaths came from complications, predominantly pneumonia.[132]

> In the first summer of the war more than 14 percent of the Confederate army in northern Virginia had measles.

The Home Front

TOP TEN HARDSHIPS

Combined Confederate and Union forces did not exceed 1.5 million men at any one time. Outside the martial light stood 31 million noncombatants, enduring, feeding, and repairing whatever the war created.

Civilians grew the crops, rolled the bandages, worked the factories, made the wagons, and sewed shoes and shirts and wounds, albeit without the fanfare of military honors. Many died, consumed by fire and lead in places like Manassas, Fredericksburg, and Atlanta as well as Baltimore, Knoxville, and New York City. To survive, citizens turned to relief agencies, pension programs, and almshouses, but mostly to family, friends, and community.[1]

Without question, the Southern home front fared badly, sacrificing a greater proportion of men, money, and land to the war than did Northerners. Few had it worse than slaves who remained in bondage while undergoing the same privations as free Southerners.

Following are just a few of the hardships weathered on the home front. Set in no particular order, the magnitude of each experience varied greatly from home to home.

1. DEATH OF A FAMILY MEMBER IN THE SERVICE

The news came from a friend, an officer, a nurse, perhaps a newspaper. Sometimes the messengers were the dying themselves, since various untreatable illnesses and wounds worked slowly enough to permit a final letter home. All told, more than 630,000 soldiers died out of a population of 32 million, a ratio six times worse than the Second World War. A similar proportion of losses in the year 2000 would have meant 5.5 million Americans dead.[2]

With high infant mortality rates and life expectancies of less than fifty years, death was not infrequent in nineteenth-century America, but most people died at home and among family. Closure was elusive when a loved one perished far away on some battlefield or operating table. Adding to the pain was the knowledge that a life was cut short. The average age of a soldier North and South was twenty-three.[3]

With the exception of high-ranking officers, most Civil War dead were not returned home for interment. Many families went and retrieved the body, provided enough information was available. For tens of thousands of families, such information did not exist. Not until 1913 were dog tags standard issue. Before then, some men wrote their names on their clothes or on slips of paper should they die. Yet corpses decomposed quickly, especially in warm weather. Burial crews worked in haste and rarely had time to identify bodies, provided they could read the names to begin with. Grave detail often went to slaves, former slaves, and the unskilled, among whom illiteracy was common.[4]

Sometimes there was no body to bury. Many were ground into the earth by horse hooves and wagon wheels. Thousands drowned. Square hits from artillery shredded the living and the dead. After several battles soldiers recalled seeing bodies eaten by hogs.[5]

From 1861 to 1865 the number of orphans in the United States more than doubled.

---

2. CARING FOR THE WOUNDED

Soldiers typically feared mutilation over death. After four years of combat, much of that fear came true. Thousands of young men experienced blindness, deafness, muscle and bone injury, respiratory damage, organ damage, brain damage, and burns. Doctors performed more than sixty thousand amputations. The war caused some half million wounds.[6]

The federal government was willing to compensate such sacrifices with scaled pensions. For example, an enlisted man who lost both feet or

LIBRARY OF CONGRESS

The wounded were frequently tended in private homes, and these often included enemy soldiers as well.

one foot and one hand was eligible for a pension of twenty dollars a month. Loss of both hands or both eyes meant five dollars more.[7]

State, federal, and charitable institutions established a modicum of facilities for the disabled—veterans homes, lodges, temporary facilities, and the like. The majority of wounded were discharged to the care of their families. Conventional wisdom considered the home as the most able environment for rehabilitation. Pervasive faith in the "healing household" emanated from a cultural perception of women as caregivers.[8]

Mississippi set aside 20 percent of its 1866 budget for artificial limbs.

---

3. CARING FOR THE MENTALLY TRAUMATIZED

Relatives of soldiers recalled personality transformations. Many discharged servicemen displayed violent tendencies, underwent long periods of withdrawal, or suffered flashbacks and nightmares. Alcoholism and opiate addiction increased after the war, not only among veterans but also among relatives of servicemen. Immediately after the war, two out of three men sentenced to state prisons in the North were veterans.[9]

Known today as post-traumatic stress disorder, the ailment mystified doctors at the time. Some physicians hypothesized it was a problem with the heart, which had been damaged by lack of rest and excessive marching. Others considered abnormal behavior as a natural response to the upsetting experience of soldiering.[10]

Authorities reserved hospitalization in federal and state asylums for only the most overt cases of mental dysfunction, those diagnosed ignominiously as insane. Union doctors declared just 819 cases of insanity among the two million soldiers who served. As with the physically wounded, nearly all other cases were sent home.

Although families lacked formal training in caring for the traumatized, this may have been a plus. Doctors treated psychological cases with bromides, morphine, flushing agents, and radical diets. Some physicians actually tried to cure alcoholism with doses of whiskey. In a show of ignorance, the *Medical and Surgical History of the Union Army* placed insanity, nostalgia, and sunstroke all under the category of nervous diseases.[11]

Psychological anomalies probably contributed to marital strife. In the twenty years following the war, the national divorce rate increased 150 percent.

---

4. FOOD SHORTAGES

The war actually caused an increase of food production in the South. In trying to starve Europe of their cotton, planters and farmers switched crops from fibers to foodstuffs. Chronic shortages ensued nonetheless. In short, the people could not get to the food and vice versa.[12]

Federal conquests cut off major sources: Louisiana sugar by 1862, Texas beef and Tennessee pork in 1863, Georgia rice and Virginia corn by 1864. Nothing compared, however, to the loss of the South's principle trading partner—the North. Wheat, oats, milk cows, mutton, barley, and salt were Northern-dominated commodities. From 1861 to 1863 wheat prices tripled. Milk and butter costs quadrupled. Other than keeping the animal alive, the only way to preserve meat for extended periods was with salt, and salt prices exceeded their prewar levels by 2,000 percent. In scenes reminiscent of the French Revolution, citizens rioted in Richmond and other towns, crying for bread. Not a few welcomed the end of the war in spite of being vanquished. One young girl was heard to say: "The Yankees have come! And now we'll get something to eat."[13]

On the Northern home front, beef and sugar were not always as plentiful due to the war effort, but farmers produced bumper crops of wheat and corn. Pork production nearly doubled. While Confederates in besieged VICKSBURG were down to eating mule meat, Northerners were shipping surplus grain to Europe.[14]

By mid-1864 a pound of butter cost twenty Confederate dollars, or a month's wages for a private in the army.

---

5. GUERRILLA WARFARE

In theory, partisan rangers targeted vulnerable lines of enemy supply and communication. In practice, thugs North and South used the war as an excuse to destroy for the sake of gain, revenge, and sport. More often than not, the brunt of such paramilitary activity fell upon civilians.

From the Florida Peninsula to St. Albans, Vermont, guerrillas wrote some of the ugliest chapters of the war. Fighting was most prevalent where Unionist and Secessionist territory overlapped, and just as the war divided the country, it also divided states, communities, even families.[15]

HARPER'S WEEKLY

Guerrillas, or "irregular soldiers," were among the first to bring the war to the home front. They preyed on soldiers and civilians alike, especially in remote and less-populated areas.

One of the great inconsistencies of the war was that cavalry raids in the eastern theater were labeled *raids*. Similar operations in the western theater were condemned by Northern newspapers as the lawless acts of "highwaymen."

In October 1862 Confederate guerrillas hanged forty-four pro-Union citizens near Gainesville, Texas. Unionists attacked and murdered pro-Secessionists in turn, from the northern counties of Louisiana to the panhandle of Florida. On August 21, 1863, William C. Quantrill led 450 pro-South raiders into the valley of Lawrence, Kansas, burning much of the town and killing more than 150 unarmed men and boys. Arson, scalping, and lynching were so prevalent along the Missouri-Kansas border, Union officials evacuated the residents of entire counties for the duration of the war.[16]

If unconventional warfare was not enacting reprisals, it was provoking them. In 1864 Union officers justified slash-and-burn tactics against civilian property in the Shenandoah Valley and across Georgia as proper retaliation for Confederate guerrilla activities.[17]

During the war, as many as twenty-five thousand guerrilla fighters participated in "unconventional warfare."

6. COMBAT

For large portions of the country the home front was the battlefront. By 1865 the war destroyed most or all of Atlanta, Columbia, Petersburg, Port Hudson, Richmond, VICKSBURG, and countless other towns and hamlets. Two major battles rendered FREDERICKSBURG a ghost town. Winchester, Virginia, changed hands more than seventy times.

Union states hosted the war's bloodiest day (ANTIETAM), the bloodiest battle (GETTYSBURG), and hundreds of other engagements. Citizens of Virginia experienced the most fighting—more than twenty-one hundred events, ranging from minor skirmishes to major battles. Next was Tennessee with fourteen hundred. Missouri underwent eleven hundred. The rest of the Confederacy endured thousands more.[18]

For the families who could not or would not outrun a battle, the horrors are barely imaginable. The Chancellors of the eponymous Virginia crossroads emerged from their cellar to see their yard covered with bodies, limbs, and dead horses and their prized piano being used as an amputation table. Union doctors confiscated a farmhouse near Malvern Hill at the conclusion of the the SEVEN DAYS' BATTLES. Children cowering in the basement recalled seeing blood seep through the floorboards. After the battle of FRANKLIN, John McGavock's home filled with the dead and the dying. The bodies of four generals grew stiff in his gallery. Hundreds of dead and wounded covered his yard and filled his outbuildings.[19]

As armies moved on, civilians were left with the wreckage. For two months the town of Gettysburg was a sprawling Union hospital. By 1865 Louisiana's Red River Valley was one continuous wasteland. Years after the war, field plows in Maryland continued to find shallow graves as well as unexploded ordnance.

One of the first civilians to die in combat was eighty-four-year-old Judith Henry, killed when Union artillery fire crashed into her home during the battle of First Manassas.

---

7. REFUGEE LIFE

Survival often meant fight or flight. By necessity, untold thousands chose the latter. Leaving behind their homes and communities, those at risk trekked off with as many possessions as they could carry, seeking safety that many never found.

Migrating to towns in search of food, shelter, and work, refugees often worsened conditions that were already tenuous. After Memphis fell to Northern forces in 1862, Unionist refugees from Kentucky, Alabama, and Tennessee flooded the town. By 1863 Washington involuntarily hosted some ten thousand runaway slaves and perhaps a greater number of former Confederate citizens. By 1864 Richmond's population had tripled, its tenements and homes "full from cellar to roof." Schoolrooms throughout the capital were packed, not with pupils but with destitute families.[20]

For many the decision to leave homes and communities was not theirs to make. Slave owners, fearing the loss of their human property, left their farms and plantations for the relative safety of the Confederate interior or to Texas, their slaves of every age in tow. Citizens were forced out of New Orleans, Atlanta, and elsewhere by Union decree. Before waging battle there in 1862, AMBROSE E. BURNSIDE ordered the evacuation of Fredericksburg. Residents young and old walked out into the December cold with nowhere to go.[21]

Along with hunger, homelessness, and poverty, castaways white and black often had to contend with thieves and cutthroats. As a consequence, refugees often ran toward armies rather than away from them, seeking protection from the lawless.[22]

One of the first refugees of the war was Mary Custis Lee, wife of the famous Confederate general. Her ancestral home, confiscated by Federals early in the war, eventually became Arlington National Cemetery.

---

8. HAVING FAMILY MEMBERS IN THE SERVICE

Not every family sent a son or brother into the service. Age, disability, protected occupation, and evasion kept many males from the ranks. Not all who sent their fathers, uncles, or brothers off to war were saddened to see them go. For every brave heart there was a scoundrel to match. Many wives enjoyed a newfound independence with the departure of their spouses.[23]

Yet for many more, when a family member was away, dread and anxiety were constant companions. In the North, more than a third of all men of military age served in the war. For the South, it was nearly two-thirds. Bad news came too often for much optimism to take root. Major battles meant 15 percent casualties or higher. Disease killed twice as many as did bullets and shells. Some relatives could not keep their thoughts to themselves. One letter from a North Carolina woman was a fair representation. After years of supportive and patriotic notes to her son, she wrote, "If you all Stae theaire you all will bee kild I want you all to come home."[24]

Adding to the emotional duress were the physical demands of raising a family alone or with reduced help. Many women recalled working the family farm alone while raising several children. A brief furlough might bring a husband back to help for a few days, but his visit often brought another mouth to feed nine months later.[25]

Letters describing newborns, sickness, worry, and shortages proved to be too much for many soldiers North and South. Risking prison time, the lash, branding, even execution, men deserted their units to return to their families.[26]

Catherine Cooper of Tennessee had ten sons serve in the war. Five did not survive and four of the remaining five were wounded.

---

9. INFLATION

In terms of the household economy, the Civil War was not the popular image of plantation belles and senator wives lamenting the price of bonnets. Some homes did pass through the war without financial worry. For the rest, it was four years and more of shortages, speculation, graft, and poor economic planning.

In the 1850s federal expenditures were modest, averaging $70 million per year. After 1861 the Union government spent $500 million per year. The Confederacy spent $250 million yearly. To help cover these massive increases, both governments printed paper money unbacked by gold. Without specie or complete faith in military victory to shore up the paper money, inflation flourished.[27]

In the North, inflation rose 100 percent over four years. In the South, the rate neared 100 percent every year. In both regions, wages rose just 60 percent.[28]

Although devaluation of money hit the North hard, especially among the lower classes, it devastated the South. Family savings were wiped out. People hoarded gold and silver, which reduced bank supplies of specie further. As early as 1862 businesses began to refuse Confederate currency. People were unable to purchase basic necessities. By 1864 rents were up 300 percent. Cloth that sold for pennies a yard in 1860 came to cost $500 a yard. Food prices were up 1,000 percent from the time of secession.[29]

Immediately after Lee's surrender at Appomattox, it took twelve hundred Confederate dollars to buy one U.S. dollar.

---

10. HARDSHIPS OF UNSKILLED AND SEMISKILLED LABOR

Although few individuals if any welcomed war, free labor must have entertained some level of optimism. Competition for jobs marched off. Orders for military goods poured in. Surely a chance for better pay and treatment was at hand. Instead, workers North and South faced four years of disappointment.

In the North, wages remained low when manufacturers drew from a large pool of immigrants, women, and children. There were many instances of people working fourteen-hour days, six days a week for three dollars. In the South, labor suffered as it always had, from the under-mining institution of slavery. Unskilled and semiskilled workers lost jobs to hired-out slaves and whites desperate for work.[30]

The chief weapon of the working poor was the organized strike. In January 1862 construction of the desperately needed ironclad *Merrimack* crawled to a stop after a shipyard labor boycott. New York alone saw more than forty trade strikes in 1864. Most protests, however, failed from lack of numbers, from workers unable to survive long without pay, and at times, from submission to bayonets.[31]

Before the war the United States was not a picture of financial parity. North and South, 30 percent of the citizenry owned 95 percent of the wealth.

TOP TEN ACTS OF DISSENT

Union and Confederacy, each side fought itself as much as the other, contending perpetually with fissures old and new. Weakening both governments was their very basis of power. The U.S. and Confederate Constitutions guaranteed freedom of speech, press, and assembly, dangerous things to have when the fortunes of war did not go well. Victory, defeat, or standoff, the contest cost on average millions of dollars and more than four hundred lives each day. People who initially anticipated a brief fight wondered whether the struggle would ever end. As late as 1863 the Union was signing five-year volunteers.[32]

To counter discontent, governments appealed to patriotism and the ideals of their cause. On a more practical side, there was espionage, censorship, and the suspension of the writ of habeas corpus (jailing citizens for extended periods without charges or evidence). Likewise, the militaries used perks, patrols, and punishment to coerce citizen-soldiers into a modicum of obedience.

Then there was money. Washington pledged compensation to any Southerner who could prove he or she aided the North and shirked the Confederacy. By the 1870s the United States paid out $4.6 million to seven thousand successful claims. The Confederacy offered similar rewards, such as $100,000 for the sinking of the USS *Constitution*—a prize no one managed to claim.[33]

Below are the most common and widespread acts of dissent during the war, ranked by the number of participants. Estimates are just that, as some individuals dissented for brief periods while others committed themselves to insurgence for the duration. For the most part, dissenters were neither traitors nor martyrs. Most were simply trying to keep their own principles and bodies in one piece.

1. SLAVE INSUBORDINATION (3 MILLION)

The traditional pro-slavery image of the obedient and contented servant dissolved soon after the war started. Owners were infuriated if not terrified by the quick collapse of their institution as more and more slaves refused to cooperate.

Masters tried desperately to hold on to their property. Thousands took their slaves far from the front lines, willing to sacrifice homes and land before surrendering their chattel. Others resorted to scaring their property with stories of "damned Yankees" sending captured slaves to Cuba or lashing them to plows. Slave patrols were increased to watch for runaways. Some communities resorted to arresting scores of slaves suspected of plotting riots.[34]

The large slave uprisings never occurred. Instead, slaves resorted to less confrontational methods. Escape was the most conspicuous. Before the war, perhaps five thousand slaves attempted to run northward per year. After the war started, the number increased to five thousand or more per month. To retaliate against their owners, a few slaves committed theft and arson. Few actually assaulted their owners. The vast majority simply stopped laboring, especially when overseers and masters were absent or when Union forces were near.[35]

Recognizing a serious decline in productivity, the Confederate Congress passed the Twenty Negro Law in October 1862. Anyone who supervised twenty or more slaves was thereafter exempt from military service. The act did not have the desired effect, as only a few thousand planters and overseers opted out of the army, which was not enough to restore discipline among millions of slaves. Conversely, those without slaves (almost 90 percent of the Confederate enlisted) charged the Richmond government with favoring the rich, and morale in the ranks sank to new lows.[36]

In 1864 one slave set fire to his master's home then ran away, a scene repeated several times during the war. This case was unique because the owner was Jefferson Davis, and the building was the Confederate White House.

---

2. PEACE MOVEMENTS (1 MILLION)

Accused of sedition, treason, and sabotage, most armistice advocates simply believed the war created more problems than it resolved. In the North dissenters were primarily the Peace Democrats. In the South, having no political party to rally around, peace campaigners were lumped together as Reconstructionists or Tories. Regardless of their location, most called for a restoration of the Union with or without settlement on slavery, and their numbers grew whenever military fortunes faded.[37]

In the Confederacy there was the clandestine Order of Heroes of America, operating in North Carolina and eastern Tennessee, and the Peace and Constitutional Society around the Ozark Mountains. In the Union the anti-emancipation Knights of the Golden Circle worked in the Midwest, later changing its name to the Order of the Golden Knights and the Sons of Liberty. Both sides linked the growing power of eastern banks, contractors, and government with the rising number of armless men, fatherless children, drafts, deaths, and taxes.[38]

To counter these peace movements, Confederate press and politicians condemned them as tools of turncoats and Unionist sympathizers. In the North pro-war factions formed jingoist clubs with memberships in the thousands, such as the Union League in the Midwest, the Union Club in major eastern cities, and the Loyalists among the well-to-do's.[39]

The most ardent critics of the armistice lobby were the soldiers themselves. As tired of the war as anyone, men in uniform nonetheless loathed the thought of endangering their lives while folks back home undermined their sacrifices. A soldier from Wisconsin spoke for both gray and blue when he said of peace campaigners, "I would shoot my own father if he was one."[40]

By 1864 Gov. Joseph E. Brown of Georgia seriously considered making a separate peace between his state and the Union government.

HARPER'S WEEKLY

Southern sympathizers were dubbed "Copperheads," more as a reference to the snake and not the often-mentioned copper penny with which they allegedly identified themselves. *Harper's Weekly* depicted them as a threat to Liberty, a symbol of the Union.

3. DESERTION (320,000)

There were some 200,000 desertions from the Union side and more than 120,000 from Confederate ranks. ROBERT E. LEE estimated he lost at least 20,000 during the September 1862 march to ANTIETAM alone, with an equal or greater number on the return. The Army of the Potomac experienced an exodus of similar size after the December 1862 debacle of FREDERICKSBURG.[41]

The synonym for desertion—cowardice—manifested itself more often with men who stayed in the ranks. When battle was imminent, the less reputable feigned illness, straggled far behind their columns, or skulked in woods and ravines until the fighting was over. Those who left on a more permanent basis did so for a patchwork of reasons. Pay and provisions were poor or nonexistent. Incompetent generals, meager rations, harsh weather, and bad news from home convinced many to leave. For some the excitement of joining simply disappeared under the drudgery of actually serving.[42]

Home was a common destination. A large portion of Confederate truants went back to their families and farms to help harvest a crop or move to safer areas. Others collected in Unionist counties sympathetic to their situation or fled to Mexico. Union men often went home as well. Others fled to "safe-havens" for deserters in western Pennsylvania or beyond the Mississippi. An estimated eighty-five thousand Union men fled to Canada.[43]

Of the 76,000 Union deserters who were caught, almost all were returned to duty. Officially, 141 were executed.

---

4. DRAFT EVASION (250,000)

From a pool of more than one-half million on each side, drafts netted just 46,000 conscripts for the North and 180,000 for the South. For the rest who were called up, many volunteered. Others hired substitutes or were exempted for professional, physical, or psychological reasons. Well more than 100,000 on each side simply failed to report.[44]

Fraud was a popular ruse. In the South men claimed professions, illnesses, or injuries they did not have. In the North healthy men bribed surgeons for rejection slips, claimed they were single parents when they had no children, or in a few cases dressed as women.[45]

Many resisters, however, banded together and were as militant as crack soldiers. Armed, organized, supported by deserters and sympathetic locals, they outran or drove off conscription officers. In the South, Unionists collected in and controlled whole counties, mostly in the northern reaches of Alabama, Arkansas, Georgia, Mississippi, and Texas. The draft all but failed in east Tennessee. On several occasions recruiting officials were beaten or murdered.[46]

In the North belligerent opposition was more urban and even more explosive. Concentrations of working poor were the most resistant, fearing the loss of their jobs, possibly their lives, for the emancipation of the very group with whom they competed for employment. Outright draft riots erupted in Baltimore, Boston, Chicago, Cincinnati, Milwaukee, New York, St. Paul, and dozens of smaller communities.[47]

The worst draft riot erupted in New York City in July 1863. Soon after the CONSCRIPTION ACT went into effect, mobs began to storm New York draft offices. Sporadic violence turned into four days of full-scale chaos, led mostly by Irish laborers. Private homes were ransacked. Offices at the NEW YORK TRIBUNE were set on fire. Looting and arson destroyed whole city blocks. Order resumed only after soldiers from the Army of the Potomac, sent straight from their fight at GETTYSBURG, marched into the city and started shooting into the crowds. Through three days of violence, rioters lynched at least six African Americans, and the U.S. Army killed more than one hundred rioters.[48]

To fail medical examinations, several men on each side faked insanity or performed very real self-mutilation.

---

5. PACIFIST MOVEMENTS (200,000)

At the time pacifists were referred to as "non-resistants." Some conveniently turned pacifist once the war started; others were intellectual idealists who deemed nonviolence as the only viable avenue of resolution. The vast majority of pacifists refused to fight on religious grounds.

Religious commitment to nonviolence was nothing new to American history. Mennonites refused to fight in the French and Indian War. Shakers adamantly opposed the Revolutionary War. Ironically, many pacifist religions echoed militant Southern nationalists, denouncing national trends of urbanization, industrialization, and materialism.[49]

Such traditions were in direct conflict with a country at war. When the draft was introduced, the matter degraded to a stalemate. At first both governments permitted objectors to decline military service, provided each draftee send a substitute or pay hundreds of dollars in exemption fees. Some acquiesced and served and were summarily ousted from their communities. Others appeared in camp but declined to carry arms. Still more refused to participate at all, proclaiming faith in a higher law than that of civil government. Such a position often resulted in legal and physical persecution.[50]

Near the end of the war both governments permitted pacifists to serve in noncombat roles, such as working with the sick and injured or gathering provisions. The state of North Carolina assigned pacifists to work in salt mines. While many accepted, the majority did not, choosing instead to weather the consequences of their convictions.[51]

The war's bloodiest day transpired on pacifist land. The Dunker sect owned a humble church building outside the town of Sharpsburg, Maryland, near Antietam Creek.

---

6. SERVING WITH THE OPPOSITION (160,000)

Conflicting loyalties split communities, friendships, and families. Not all men stayed rooted in their own soil. Citizens from every Confederate state left to serve in blue. Florida, Louisiana, North Carolina, and Texas had more than a thousand citizens each in the Union ranks. More than 8,000 men from Arkansas and 31,000 from Tennessee signed up.[52]

The Border States in turn gave tens of thousands to Confederate service. Maryland provided more than 20,000 soldiers to the Confederacy as did initially neutral Kentucky. Missouri had 40,000 in gray, almost three times as many men as Florida.[53]

A hard blow to the folks at home were "galvanized" troops—prisoners of war who joined the opposition to secure their release. Some 6,000 former Confederates switched sides as did an untold portion of Union men. An even larger loss for the South was the number of former slaves who volunteered to fight for the Union. Of the 179,000 African Americans who wore the blue suit, more than 100,000 of them were runaway slaves.[54]

> The highest-ranking Confederate officer was adjutant general Samuel Cooper, a native of New Jersey.

7. THE SPLIT OF VIRGINIA (150,000)

Since its creation, Virginia was of two personalities. The Piedmont and tidewater region trafficked slaves and tobacco. Connected to the cotton states and Europe, its history was of landed gentry and power politics. West of the Alleghenies, however, slave numbers were low and state taxes high. Small farmers had little influence in Richmond let alone anywhere else, and merchants traded with Toledo and Pittsburgh before Mobile and London. Predictably, after eastern Virginia declared itself in the Confederacy, western Virginia petitioned the Union for financial and military help.[55]

By the autumn of 1861 Union forces under GEORGE B. MCCLELLAN pushed the Confederates, briefly led by ROBERT E. LEE, out of the region. Citizens established Wheeling as the capital for what they hoped would be a new state. A referendum in October 1861 approved the fracture of the original colony, and in June 1863 fifty counties of Virginia became the newest star on the Union standard. Lincoln's cabinet openly hoped the process would repeat itself in eastern Tennessee and elsewhere.[56]

> The state of West Virginia was originally to be named Kanawha.

8. BOUNTY JUMPING (20,000)

The monthly pay of a citizen-soldier amounted to a pittance. Real money came from the cash he received for volunteering, ranging from ten to fifty dollars in the South to three hundred dollars in the North. State and local bonuses increased the amount. Some of this money was paid up front, and the incentive to pocket it and immediately desert was too much for many.

Officially considered deserters, jumpers rarely made it to the front lines. They deserted at loading stations, literally jumping from trains and ships or walking off from their first day in camp. The more adventurous then traveled to a new town under a false name, signed up, and repeated the process. Bounties were much smaller in the Confederacy, and as such so was the number of Southerners who tried their luck. The problem was nothing short of chronic in the North.

The Union record for bounty jumping belonged to John O'Conner, who claimed to have jumped thirty-two times.[57] O'Conner received four years in jail. Others were given much harsher punishment for one offense. Fines, prison time, and hard labor deterred some. A number were shot while trying to escape from their newly formed unit. In 1864 outside of Indianapolis, one Union defector punished himself. Leaping from a speeding train, he bounced off an embankment, went under the cars, and was sliced to pieces.[58]

To discourage jumping, enlistment officials in Concord, New Hampshire, photographed every new recruit.

---

9. BREAD RIOTS (20,000)

Before the age of refrigeration, springtime was known as the "starving season," when stores of harvests were nearing depletion. In the Confederacy, the war exacerbated the problem.

General distress turned into full-fledged riots in the spring of 1863. In four Georgia cities mobs attacked warehouses and shops. Salisbury, North Carolina, witnessed the destruction of groceries and dry-goods stores as well as jewelry and clothing stores. Troubles continued through the summer. Protesters marched through the streets of Mobile, Alabama, chanting, "Bread or blood."[59]

The most infamous of these riots occurred in the Confederate capital in April 1863. Richmond's prewar population of forty thousand had swollen to one hundred thousand. Nearby farms were decimated from two years of fighting. When several hundred women marched on the state mansion to petition against exorbitant food prices, Gov. John Letcher provided no answers, so the crowd sought immediate redress. Growing to a few thousand by the time they reached the commercial district, a mob of women, men, and children laid waste to ten square blocks.

The governor, the mayor, and local militia could not restore order. Into the rioters ran Jefferson Davis, who forced his way onto a wagon bed. He begged the crowd to disperse, threw what money he had to them, and said they were welcome to whatever he possessed. The rioters refused to move. Davis then threatened to have them shot, and the militia began to load their rifles. Moments passed. As the detachment primed their weapons, the rioters began to walk away.[60]

Social unrest continued in the South, but mostly in localized incidents. Most realized that by 1864 unbearable prices were due less to a surplus of graft and more to an absence of food.

> During the Richmond bread riot, Jefferson Davis would have ridden his horse into the crowd, but it had been stolen the previous day.

10. TRADING WITH THE ENEMY (UNKNOWN)

Soldiers exchanged newspapers for a bit of food. Smugglers sold cotton for gold. Although illicit deals occurred everywhere, especially along border areas, there were two major portals for extralegal trade in the Civil War.

In 1862 Memphis and NEW ORLEANS fell to Union forces. In order to lure Confederate citizenry back, the occupying military created an economic union of sorts, permitting local trade to resume with the North. Washington soon realized it was unable to control what was being traded and by whom as bribes, kickbacks, and black markets were rather elusive.[61]

Cotton, tobacco, and sugar went north. Shoes, salt, food, medicine, stolen military equipment, cloth, and cash went south. Loyalists screamed betrayal. Confederates wanted to starve the Union of its cotton; Unionists wanted to starve the South of everything. In reality, illegal trade helped keep Northern businesses and Southern bodies alive.

Undoubtedly, the biggest winners were the smugglers. Hyperinflated prices from wartime embargoes drove prices as high as the risk to life and limb. When laborers and farmers made four hundred dollars a year, some traders made one hundred times that. In 1863 ULYSSES S. GRANT lamented, "No honest man has made money in West Tennessee in the last year, whilst many fortunes have been made there during that time." Unfortunately for Grant, some of the profiteers were men in Federal uniform.[62]

> The U.S. Congressional Committee on the Conduct of the War estimated that $30 million worth of Union goods reached the Confederacy through Memphis alone.

TOP TEN NEWSPAPERS

From 1835 to the start of the Civil War, the number of newspapers in the country went from eight hundred to twenty-five hundred. Advances in telegraphy, literacy, and rail transport enabled dailies and weeklies to become the principle source of national news.[63]

Yet journalism was a hobbled fledgling. War correspondents were a recent innovation (only six American reporters covered the Mexican War). Each reporter was in effect one pair of eyes and ears on the battlefront. Federal and Confederate militaries exercised priority over mail, telegraph, and rail lines. For all the technical advances of the age, most papers still printed on archaic presses, a few sheets of paper at a time. With war, famine, pestilence, and death, there was plenty of news to write about. The problem was collecting and distributing everything that was fit to print.[64]

To gather information, correspondents and editors gleaned every conceivable source: officers, enlisted men, public officials, prisoners, scouts, and other newspapers. With a hodgepodge of hearsay and unrelenting time pressures, journalists were notoriously susceptible to rumor. Reports from eyewitnesses and sources in good standing told of ROBERT E. LEE's capturing Washington in 1862, GEORGE B. MCCLELLAN's dying in action in 1863, Jefferson Davis's committing suicide in 1864, and France's granting diplomatic recognition to the Confederacy in 1865.[65]

While rumors were a constant, Northern newspapers grew, mostly from networking and large revenues. In contrast, most of the South's

Newspapers were readily available in most Northern camps in the eastern theater—and many found their way into Confederate camps as well.

LIBRARY OF CONGRESS

eight hundred papers withered and died. Pro-Confederacy presses either fell to invading armies, survived by becoming nomadic (the *Memphis Appeal* published on the run for three years), or simply stopped printing, since nearly all paper, ink, printing machinery, and telegraph equipment was manufactured in the North. Under siege in 1863, the *Vicksburg Citizen* began printing on wallpaper. By 1864 Southern telegraph and rail networks had disintegrated. By 1865 the major source of information in the South was newspapers smuggled from the North.[66]

The following represent the most prominent newspapers of the era. Note that eight of ten listed are eastern papers. At the time, the East Coast dominated communication hubs. Consequently, most newsprint covered eastern battles, leaders, and issues. Elsewhere, fewer reporters meant fewer reports (for example, no Southern newspaper had a correspondent at the 1861 battle of WILSON'S CREEK in Missouri). As a result, people were more familiar with names such as GETTYSBURG, *Monitor,* and Lee than they were with Corinth, *Cairo,* and Lyon—an imbalance that remains today.[67]

1. *NEW YORK HERALD* (EST. 1835)

The most popular daily on the continent was also one of the most raunchy. By printing a wide array of debauchery and deluge, love affairs, spectacular tenement fires, and suggestive personal ads, the *New York Herald* managed to sell an average of one hundred thousand copies a day (more than most dailies could sell in a month). Perhaps Abraham Lincoln was grateful when the *Herald* turned out to be one of his critics.[68]

Fueled by a public lust for the spectacular, the New York rag translated big revenues into a competitive edge. Most dailies had one or two war reporters. The *Herald* employed sixty correspondents plus telegraphers, stenographers, printers, and a score of engravers. The paper owned state-of-the-art printing machines, producing one hundred thousand copies in a few hours. Tents and wagons sporting the paper's banner were common fixtures at Union encampments, although they were not always welcome.[69]

With some of the most venomous anti-administration rhetoric outside Dixie, *Herald* editorials defended the Southern right to secede, proclaimed the virtues of slavery, criticized Lincoln incessantly, and portrayed Union Gen. WILLIAM TECUMSEH SHERMAN as insane. It shocked the North with embellished accounts of federal defeats, such as FIRST

MANASSAS (First Bull Run), where it described how Confederate victors had "severed the heads of our dead from their bodies, and amused themselves by kicking them as footballs."[70]

At war's end the paper rode the bandwagon praising the victors but maintained its sensationalist roots. In detailing the capture of Jefferson Davis, the *Herald* perpetuated the rumor that the Confederate president disguised himself as a woman to escape.[71]

During the 1863 Vicksburg campaign, William Tecumseh Sherman charged *Herald* correspondent Thomas W. Knox with espionage and had him court-martialed.

---

2. *NEW YORK TIMES* (EST. 1851)

Henry J. Raymond was a long-time employee of Horace Greeley at the *New York Tribune* until he could no longer take Greeley's preachy vacillations. Raymond pledged instead to make his new paper the vanguard of impartial accuracy. Although not always maintaining his avowed professional distance, Raymond did create a daily newspaper of international renown by its third year of operation.

The *Times* truly found its element once the war started. Its offices bustled with visiting politicians, military brass, and civil servants. Editors busily processed reams of incoming dispatches and correspondence. As readers struggled to make sense of the *Herald's* sensationalism and the *Tribune's* moralizing rants, the *Times* appeared as the most dependable and best informed of the metropolitan dailies.[72]

Unhampered by a political agenda, the *Times* called battles as it saw them, such as the 1862 Shenandoah fight at Cross Keys. Presented as a Union victory by many Northern papers, the *Times* correctly reported it as a bumbling loss. Several dailies prematurely reported the 1863 battle of CHANCELLORSVILLE a draw. *Times* writers collected and confirmed testimonials then revealed the extent of the Union's crushing defeat.[73]

As precise as it tried to be, the *Times* was just as susceptible to misinformation as any other. In various battles it occasionally reported Confederate casualties to be double their actual number. When ROBERT E. LEE marched toward GETTYSBURG with eighty thousand men, the *Times* guessed he had an unthinkable five hundred thousand.[74]

During the New York draft riots of 1863, angry mobs targeted African Americans and local papers. To protect the *Times* building, editor Henry Raymond and his employees procured and manned a pair of Gatling guns.

3. *NEW YORK TRIBUNE* (EST. 1841)

In constant battle with the seedy *Herald* was the morally righteous and radically Republican *Tribune,* a daily its editor Horace Greeley called "worthy of the virtuous and refined, and a welcome visitant at the family fireside."[75]

Of the *Tribune's* many objectives, the abolition of slavery was foremost. While most Northern papers shied away from the unpopular topic, the *Tribune* provided full coverage, chastising slavery as the nation's greatest impedance to economic, political, and moral growth.

Anyone willing to compromise on slavery received quick *Tribune* revenge. Upon centrist Sen. Stephen A. Douglas the *Tribune* showered headlines such as "The Doom of Douglas" and "Douglas Dumb." Soft-on-emancipation Maj. Gen. GEORGE B. MCCLELLAN was, according to Greeley's paper, "anxious for the preservation of Slavery." For Lincoln's initially distant stance on emancipation, the *Tribune* labeled him a coward.[76]

Although a major source of national and international news for readers across the country, the *Tribune* was best known for its ability to agitate. Its most famous wartime headline was undoubtedly "Forward to Richmond!" an overzealous catch phrase repeated in the summer of 1861. Impatient for a major attack against a Confederacy largely untested since the fall of Fort Sumter, the *Tribune* rallied much of the North around the war cry. Under tremendous public pressure, Lincoln sent an untested Union army forward to Richmond and defeat at FIRST MANASSAS.[77]

In August 1862 Greeley printed an open letter to Lincoln, which he headlined as a "Prayer of Twenty Millions" and all but accused Lincoln of being an instrument of slaveholders. A month later the *Tribune* praised Lincoln at length for issuing the EMANCIPATION PROCLAMATION.

Late in 1862 the *Tribune* predicted imminent Union victory, yet after CHANCELLORSVILLE in May 1863 it recommended an arranged peace. The paper quickly reverted to its nationalist fervor after the July 1863 Union wins at VICKSBURG and GETTYSBURG. Thus was the nature of one of the largest newspapers in the country: erratic, confrontational, seditious, and patriotic, often within the same issue.[78]

For its German-American readership, the *Tribune* employed a Vienna-based writer to provide news from the old country. Over time, its foreign correspondent's submissions became excessively dogmatic, and the newspaper was forced to part ways with Karl Marx.

4. *RICHMOND DAILY DISPATCH* (EST. 1850)

The first American penny paper south of Baltimore was a bedrock defender of the Confederate government. Fortunately for Jefferson Davis and his administration, the *Richmond Daily Dispatch* was also among the most widely read papers in the South. In March 1861 it had eighteen thousand subscribers, dwarfing the operations of the other four Richmond dailies put together. By the end of the war, the *Dispatch* had thirty-three thousand steady customers.[79]

As with sensationalist papers, the *Dispatch* practiced minimal allegiance with accuracy. Somehow, Lee's GETTYSBURG campaign was a resounding victory. Concerning BRAXTON BRAGG's frequent use of executions to instill discipline among his troops, the *Dispatch* praised his vigor, adding: "An example or two will have a fine effect." The 1864 battle of Winchester cost the Confederates the entire Shenandoah Valley, but the *Dispatch* reported the battle as a display of Confederate strength, "with the exception of the loss of ground."[80]

Even in the waning weeks of the war, the paper managed to retain its confident demeanor: "The *Dispatch* is published this morning on a half sheet only, because of the fact that all our employees—printers, reporters, and clerks—are members of military organizations, and were called out, yesterday by the Governor, to perform special services for a short time."

The duration was indeed short. Two weeks later, the Army of the Potomac overran Richmond's defenses. Fires erupted throughout the city, and the offices of the *Dispatch* burned to the ground.[81]

Along with the *Dispatch*, fires in Richmond destroyed the newspaper offices of the *Enquirer*, *Examiner*, and *Sentinel*. Only the *Richmond Whig* remained standing and later reopened "under new management."

5. *HARPER'S WEEKLY JOURNAL OF CIVILIZATION* (EST. 1857)

If one were to open the pages of a penny paper in 1860, there would be four to eight pages of narrow columns in small print but no pictures. Practical application of photos in newsprint was still four decades away. The London *Illustrated News, Frank Leslie's Illustrated Newspaper,* the *New York Illustrated News,* and others managed to oblige with the ages-old craft of woodcarvings. Dominating these picture weeklies was New York-based *Harper's Weekly Journal of Civilization.*[82]

In its first years, *Harper's* backed Democrats then swung Republican after Fort Sumter. Nearly sycophantic in its patriotism, it had its skeptics, and at times, the criticism was well founded. In an effort to display Union might during McClellan's 1862 Peninsula campaign, the paper published an informative map of the Federal army's disposition, including troop placements, division identifications, and the location of McClellan's headquarters. For its imprudent presentation, *Harper's* briefly closed its offices by order of the government. Later that summer *Harper's* excused John Pope's reversal at SECOND MANASSAS (Second Bull Run) by claiming he had just a "handful of men." Pope's numbers were closer to seventy-five thousand.

Yet later in 1862 it had the objectivity to call the Union failures at FREDERICKSBURG an act of "imbecility" and "treachery." With both healing and harsh words, punctuated by numerous ornate images, *Harper's* managed a circulation of 120,000 per issue.[83]

Due to a mixup of nearly identical source photos, *Harper's Weekly* accidentally presented the likeness of a man named William Grant as the face of Ulysses Grant throughout the war.

---

6. *CHARLESTON MERCURY* (EST. 1822)

ROBERT BARNWELL RHETT's *Charleston Mercury* was the voice of the fire-eaters. Despite a very small readership (circulation rarely hit five thousand), the paper was one of the most quoted periodicals prior to the war, reaching the most influential desks in the country.

Certainly the *Mercury* enjoyed its largest political influence before the war, acting as the most prominent Secessionist paper in the nation.

More editorial than informational, the daily retained a strict doctrine. It was for states' rights, namely Southern states' rights, and would defend them against any threat.[84]

This dogmatic loyalty superseded all else, including the Confederate war effort. The paper vehemently opposed Jefferson Davis's attempts to enforce a national draft, collect income tax, and dictate military operations over and above the wishes of the states. Its editorials called Davis "egotistical, arrogant and vindictive" and a man of "terrible incompetency and perversity." The anti-administration message held considerable appeal among governors and state legislators, who began to sense little difference between Washington, D.C., and Richmond.[85]

One wonders if there were personal motives directing the perpetual attacks upon the executive branch. In 1861 *Mercury* owner Rhett fervently believed he was to be the first president of the Confederate States of America. He was more than a little disappointed when a moderate from Mississippi was elected in his place.[86]

Before the war a number of Northerners subscribed to the *Charleston Mercury,* including a Springfield attorney named Abraham Lincoln.

---

7. *CHICAGO TIMES* (EST. 1854)

Chicago Times editor Wilbur F. Storey was a tall, white-haired die-hard Democrat and a bully of a man. Using sensationalist rhetoric to undermine the Union war effort, he became a major voice of the dissenting Copperhead movement.[87]

Pages were thick with the accounts of alleged testimonials from Federal soldiers lamenting the endless hardships of army life, corruption, disease, and bad generals. Editorials predicted an inevitable Confederate victory.[88]

The paper was particularly brutal against Lincoln. The president's Gettysburg Address was, according to the *Times,* a national embarrassment of "dishwatery utterances" and a "perversion of history." Lincoln's Second Inaugural fared little better. After hearing the president wish "malice toward none; with charity for all," the *Times* labeled the speech "slipshod" and "puerile."[89]

Proving any publicity is good publicity, the *Times* vaulted into the national spotlight when the U.S. military attempted to silence is presses. Union commander AMBROSE E. BURNSIDE, relocated to the Department of the Ohio after his failure at FREDERICKSBURG, ordered the *Times* closed for its "disloyal and incendiary sentiments." In the early hours of June 3, 1864, a company of blue coats surrounded the *Times,* stormed the building, and destroyed copies of the day's edition. Days later Lincoln rescinded Burnside's well-meaning but politically hazardous edict and allowed the *Times* to resume business. Yet the incident cemented the status of the *Times* as the voice of the opposition.[90]

Wilbur Storey earned a large readership and not a small number of enemies. As death threats poured into his office, he armed himself with pistols and grenades should anyone attempt to fulfill their promises.

---

8. *RICHMOND ENQUIRER* (EST. 1804)

A venerable standard of the Democratic Party prior to the war, the *Richmond Enquirer* had a reputation of prudence and objectivity, much in the same manner as the *New York Times.* In 1860 it opposed secession, as did most of Virginia. After Fort Sumter, however, the *Enquirer* became a fortress for Southern morale, and its traditional candor took a short hiatus.

When describing the Confederate repulse of the Army of the Potomac in the 1862 Peninsula campaign, the *Enquirer* marveled how the success came "in so short a time and with so small cost to the victors." Its editors failed to mention that the "small cost" was nearly twenty thousand Confederate dead and wounded in a week of fighting. The daily continued to present most battles, win or loss, in a favorable light. Somehow it translated Lee's defeat at the battle of ANTIETAM as "one of the most complete victories that has yet immortalized confederate arms."[91]

By late 1863 the paper kept up a brave front in spite of the tightening blockade and a string of Confederate defeats. If its writers refrained from bad news, the physical appearance of the paper itself reported otherwise. Printed with blurred and feeble ink, the daily came as a single sheet of ratty pulp, speaking volumes of the Confederacy's withering supplies.[92]

Over the course of 1864 the paper gradually returned to its roots of accurate reporting. Its columns began to acknowledge critical FOOD

SHORTAGES and INFLATION and criticized the Confederate Congress for lack of action. Yet it continued to recognize the resolution of citizens and soldiers and remained confident in "Lee's indomitable army" even as "the sullen sound of the distant gun" rattled the windows of its downtown Richmond office.[93]

In October 1864 the *Richmond Enquirer* publicly endorsed the arming of slaves. It was the first major newspaper in the South to do so.

---

9. *RICHMOND EXAMINER* (EST. 1847)

Self-educated, clever, judgmental, unrestrained John M. Daniel led his *Richmond Examiner* on a crusade of bitter enmity against just about everything. Borrowing a page from the *New York Tribune*, Daniel used controversy and intrigue to establish a readership reaching as far away as Texas.[94]

He spurred his readers with fabricated stories of universal graft, elaborate conspiracies, and extramarital escapades. No one was safe from the paper's wrath—not governors, not nurses, not prisoners. The rag described Confederate Gen. Braxton Bragg as having "an iron heart and [an] iron hand and a wooden head." Certainly the assessment of Bragg was closer to the truth than the paper's description of slaves, calling them a "totally distinct and inferior animal or species of animal from the Caucasian."[95]

Predictably, neither Davis nor Lincoln fared well in its editorials. The Confederate president was "an amalgam of malice and mediocrity" and "affable, kind, and subservient to his enemies." By January of the war's final year, the *Examiner* was calling for Davis's overthrow. Similarly, the Federal army was a "horde of thieves, robbers, and assassins in the pay of Abraham Lincoln," and Lincoln himself was a "Yankee monster of inhumanity and falsehood" and "an ugly and ferocious old Orang-Outang from the wilds of Illinois."[96]

Swinging from insightful wit to degenerate sarcasm, the *Examiner* spearheaded a fleet of skeptical papers in the South, including the *Raleigh Standard*, *Richmond Whig*, and *Charleston Mercury*. But neither its editor nor the paper would survive the war. Daniel died of illness just as the Union army stormed the city of Richmond.[97]

Before the Civil War, *Examiner* editor John Daniel threatened to duel with an uncooperative freelance writer named Edgar Allan Poe.

10. LONDON *TIMES* (EST. 1785)

The eminent international paper covering the Civil War was the London *Times*, a paper Lincoln called "one of the greatest powers in the world." Yet for Lincoln it was an ominous force. Aristocratic, nationalistic, and openly critical of American populist democracy, the *Times* offered hope and exposure for the Confederacy.[98]

In July 1863 the Union captured VICKSBURG and won decisively at GETTYSBURG. The *Times* saw things differently. The loss of the Mississippi River town, reported the daily, was probably a rumor. Meanwhile, GETTYS-BURG was nothing more than a raid, a draw at that, and ROBERT E. LEE was on the verge of another attack into Maryland. Furthermore, large portions of Indiana were under Confederate occupation, NEW ORLEANS was about to be retaken, and members of Lincoln's cabinet were debating whether to sue for peace and repeal the EMANCIPATION PROCLAMATION.[99]

The denial never abated. Sherman's March to the Sea was instead a desperate escape attempt by isolated bluecoats, sprinting for the coast in hopes of a naval rescue. By January 1865, in the Confederacy's painful twilight, the *Times* maintained, "The rebellion lives and thrives, and gathers force and increasing resolution day after day, and year after year."[100]

Finally acknowledging the remote possibility of a Union victory, the *Times* predicted at least five million white Confederates would first lay down their lives, followed by three million slaves "all as bitterly opposed to the Yankees as their masters."[101]

The *Times* ultimately proved incorrect on most of its predictions, but it did reflect a widely held European contempt toward the bloodshed of the Civil War. In 1914 American newspapers presented a similar attitude toward a European war of even greater carnage.

One of three London *Times* correspondents in the United States, Frank Lawley was a former member of Parliament. He requested the overseas assignment after he accrued massive debts from gambling and other questionable ventures.

TOP TEN ALTERNATE NAMES FOR THE WAR

Historically, wars bear multiple names. The First World War was not known as such until the Second World War erupted, before then being called the Great War, the Third Balkan War, the War of the Empires, etc.

For the American Civil War, scholars have found more than seventy different monikers, such as the War of Kindred Races, the Late Unpleasantness, and the War for Separation. A few are less than tasteful, but each reflects the conflict's ultimate meaning to the beholder. Most often, participants and observers referred to it simply as "this war," "this terrible war," or "this civil war."

Several names originated long after the fact. Only after 1865 was it referred to as *the* Civil War, an act of American bravado, overlooking as it does the prevalence of intranational wars around the globe. Listed below are the most common alternative names used in letters, speeches, diaries, articles, and conversations shared among those caught in its time.

1. THE REBELLION

Preceding the presidential elections of 1860, moderates spoke in tempered tones to potential separatists. Presiding President James Buchanan exercised considerable restraint over the next few weeks for fear of offending the slave states into reaction.

When South Carolina seceded in December 1860, followed soon after by six more states and four more after the fall of Fort Sumter, Unionist articles and speeches let loose with indictments of sedition, treason, and rebellion. Radical Republicans used the term *rebellion* frequently, intending to maximize patriotic fervor and justify harsh retribution during and after the war.

Quite a few Secessionists took to the title, accepting the nickname of Rebs and reveling in stories of soldiers unleashing the Rebel Yell. The RICHMOND DAILY DISPATCH described its pride through verse.

> Then call us Rebels, if you will,
> We glory in the name,
> For bending under unjust laws,
> And swearing faith to an unjust cause,
> We count as greater shame.

LIBRARY OF CONGRESS

Part of the ambiguity of the war is captured in this image of two boys in homespun uniforms staring down Union horsemen while their sisters play.

Ironically, Confederates described pro-Union regions within their borders, such as north Arkansas and east Tennessee, as areas "in a condition of rebellion."[102]

By 1861 colonized North America had experienced scores of rebellions in its short history, including Bacon's Rebellion (1676), Shay's Rebellion (1786), the Whiskey Rebellion (1794), plus several major slave revolts and wars with Native Americans.

2. THE REVOLUTION, THE SECOND REVOLUTION, WAR FOR SOUTHERN INDEPENDENCE

Many separatists in 1861 could not help but compare their plight to that of the Founding Fathers. Both "revolutions" were attempts to split away from a perceived repressive government. Both were led by a plantation-owning, slaveholding Southerner with a military background. Slavery was legally protected in eleven of the thirteen original colonies.

To a lesser extent, but just as sincerely, Unionists expressed a firm association with the Revolution. In 1861 as in 1776 artisans from Boston and Philadelphia and farmers from the Potomac and Merrimack River Valleys fought against an aristocracy determined to break the will of the country.[103]

Portraits of George Washington adorned the Confederate Convention in Montgomery as well as Lincoln's box at Ford's Theatre. Jefferson Davis strategically held his second inauguration on Washington's birthday, while to the North, Unionists (a.k.a. Yankees) sang "The Battle Cry of Freedom."

Over time, Southerners in the Second Revolution discovered they shared several undesirable qualities with colonists in the first. Both suffered from horrible inflation and shortages, could not pay their soldiers, and pleaded at length for European intervention. Yet, for the Confederacy, there would be no savior Lafayette.[104]

Just like the original colonies, there were thirteen Confederate states—in theory. Missouri and Kentucky had seats in the Confederate Congress and were represented on the Confederate flag, which had thirteen stars.

---

3. THE WAR BETWEEN THE STATES

Commonly used then and now, the War Between the States is one of the more accurate titles for the Civil War. A war between two regions, it was also very much eleven states against nineteen, with the Border States wedged between.

When the war started there was no national bank, federal income tax, or national currency on either side. State legislatures and governors shouldered most of the responsibility for recruiting, supplying, arming, transporting, and funding their troops. Volunteer regiments on both sides were named after the state in which they were created. When the Union enacted a draft in 1863, it established quotas by state. In the Confederacy, public assistance to families of soldiers came from state agencies.

As several historians have noted, the United States is treated as a singular term today, whereas citizens used it in the plural sense during the nineteenth century. After the war, an expanded federal government and a rewelded Union gradually changed the vernacular from "the United States are" to "the United States is," but one tradition remains intact. Monuments to soldiers North and South are almost always exclusive to a state.[105]

In the 1980s the Sons of Confederate Veterans ceased all use of the term "Civil War" and now only use "the War Between the States" in their official documents.

4. THE WAR FOR STATES' RIGHTS

A nostalgic return to the colonial period, a political manifestation of independence, the sanctity of the state over the central government was going to justify, inspire, and save the Confederacy from the oppression of the Union—or so hoped the proponents of states' rights.

In the harsh reality of civil war, this doctrine had a downside. At times, the War for States' Rights looked to have a dual meaning: the Union against the Confederacy and the Confederacy against itself. Governors such as Zebulon Vance of North Carolina and Joseph E. Brown of Georgia bitterly opposed efforts from the Confederate Congress to impose drafts and taxation. Many Southerners wondered why they should send their own food, supplies, and sons to defend other states. Alternately, citizens in areas of heavy fighting, such as Virginia and Tennessee, became disillusioned after years of collateral damage while watching other states go relatively untouched.

Private letters from both soldiers and citizens expressed fears of losing personal liberties, not to the Union, but to the government in Richmond. At first a rallying cry, the call for states' rights was beginning to look like the Confederacy's greatest problem.[106]

One of the six Confederate generals to die at the battle of Franklin was States Rights Gist of South Carolina.

5. THE WAR AGAINST NORTHERN AGGRESSION

In his First Inaugural address, Lincoln appealed to the South to avoid war: "In your hands, my dissatisfied countrymen, and not in mine is the momentous issue of civil war. . . . You have no conflict without yourselves being the aggressors."[107]

Lincoln's initial inaction against the Confederacy, consisting of seven states at the time of his swearing in, caused much consternation among his hawkish supporters. The president assured both friend and foe he intended no hostile action, but he would keep his pledge to "hold, occupy, and possess" that which belonged to the United States.

When the issue arose of surrendering or supplying a federal fort still under construction in Charleston Harbor, South Carolina, Lincoln chose to resupply. The South had its gesture of confirmed aggression. Yet once shells fell on the fort on April 12, 1861, Lincoln and the North had theirs.

For the Union to win the war, however, it had to attack. The Confederacy had the option of staying on the defensive. As a consequence, Johnny Reb could honestly tell Billy Yank, "I'm fightin' because you're down here."

By 1863 the Union had the largest army on earth.

---

6. THE BROTHERS' WAR

Wars of separation usually involve opposing ethnicities, religions, or language groups, where loyalties and boundaries are easily surmised. Such was not the case in 1861. Most people within the United States shared a common language and history. Religious denominations, business partnerships, and most political parties transcended geographic boundaries.

Figuratively and literally, the Civil War was a brothers' war, splitting families and friendships apart. There were Southerners fighting for the Union and Northern-born men siding with the Confederacy. The problem was most intense along the border regions. Missouri men squared off against each other at VICKSBURG, Irish regiments did the same at FREDERICKSBURG. Lincoln and Davis, the opposing presidents, were both from Kentucky. Sometimes the split reached down to the family level. Congressman Henry Clay had three grandsons fighting for the Union and four for the South.[108]

These ties made the war all the more emotional and sometimes all the more confusing for its participants. Yet these same connections made a degree of peaceful reconciliation possible, even desirable, after the most deadly American war to date.[109]

On September 20, 1863, Confederate Brig. Gen. Benjamin Hardin Helm was killed at the battle of Chickamauga. News of his death deeply saddened his close friend and brother-in-law, Abraham Lincoln.

---

7. THE WAR FOR CONSTITUTIONAL LIBERTY

Since 1789 the supreme law of the land had been the U.S. Constitution. As the document aged, so evolved situations demanding close and critical interpretation, especially when significant matters arose around issues not specifically addressed by the instrument.

In the case of slavery, however, the Constitution was clear. Slavery was permitted in individual states. When determining the number of congressional representatives due each state, Article 1 used the words "three fifths of all other Persons" meaning slaves as a separate classification. Article 4, the original fugitive slave law, mandated that "other Persons" escaping their owners into another state "shall be delivered up on Claim of the Party to whom such Service or Labour may be due."

No passage, however, implied a right to secede. Interestingly enough, the Confederate Constitution did not include one either. Nevertheless, secession was an implied constitutional right, or so argued its subscribers. Used by Confederates to defend their position, variations of the War for Constitutional Liberty emerged from Unionists as well. Along with proclaiming the Union as permanent and indissoluble, several pointed to Article 1, Section 8, which granted Congress the right to "provide for calling forth the Militia to execute the Laws of the Union, suppress Insurrections, and repel Invasions."

On questions of constitutionality, one of the most ardent defenders of slavery was the U.S. Supreme Court, dominated by Southerners and headed from 1836 to 1864 by Roger Taney, a former slave owner and ardent states' rights advocate.

---

8. MR. LINCOLN'S WAR

Citizens often named a war after its perceived prime instigator. An 1832 Sac and Fox insurrection in Illinois went down in history as the Black Hawk War. The war with Mexico (1846–48) was more often called Mr. Polk's War. The conflict of 1861 was initially called Mr. Greeley's War by a number of Americans, referring to the squeaky-voiced editor of the bombastically antislavery NEW YORK TRIBUNE.

To many in the South the chief cause and sponsor of the war was Abraham Lincoln. The Union was intact until Lincoln won the presidency. Rather than negotiate with the Confederacy after the fall of Fort Sumter, he chose force, a path from which he did not waver for four years. For a person claiming to be committed to the sanctity of the country, he appeared willing to demolish a good deal of it.

Over time the title Mr. Lincoln's War also became popular in the North. Democrats in support of a negotiated peace, anti-administration newspapers, pacifists, and others leveled their criticism upon the chief executive. Not a few cartoonists depicted the Springfield lawyer as fond of the power he had attained. SUSPENDING THE WRIT OF HABEAS CORPUS, expanding the national budget 400 percent, and making no effort for a diplomatic resolution, Lincoln was the most powerful president ever, and he was so during the largest war in American history. For many it all appeared to be of his choosing.

A common Southern designation for Union soldiers was "Lincolnites."

---

9. THE WAR TO FREE THE SLAVES

Ironically, fire-eating Southerners uttered the phrase War to Free the Slaves first, primarily to shock Southern Unionists and moderates into siding with the Confederacy. Since his election and well into his second year in office, Lincoln played down this possibility, insisting the war was for the preservation of the Union and nothing more. To prove his point, he reprimanded Maj. Gen. JOHN C. FRÉMONT in 1861 when "the Pathfinder" unilaterally announced slaves of Missouri Secessionists were free.[110]

On September 22, 1862, bolstered by a marginal Union victory at ANTIETAM, Lincoln issued his EMANCIPATION PROCLAMATION. Nevertheless, he maintained his original position that this and any move he made was for the preservation of the Union. Abolitionists and over time much of the Northern public asserted the moral high ground, proclaiming the war as a crusade for human liberation.[111]

In 1862 Lincoln calculated the U.S. government spent more money on the war in three months than it would take to purchase all five hundred thousand slaves in the Border States.

---

10. THE WAR OF THE BLUE AND THE GRAY

Employed sparingly during the conflict, usage of *blue* and *gray* did not become widespread until years later. Most Union men wore blue, once general standards and supply enabled uniformity by late 1861. Federal regiments still did what they could to maintain self-identity within regulations, preferring certain shades, tunics, or millinery over others.[112]

Plagued by shortages, Johnny Reb had a tougher time complying with his army regulations calling for cadet gray double-breasted coats and sky blue trousers. For much of the war, especially the first eighteen months, Confederate soldiers furnished their own clothes. In 1862, as supplies began to catch up with requisitions, the stereotypical gray uniforms became widely available. Yet as the blockade tightened and Richmond's finances worsened, an increasing number of soldiers went to

During the 1862 Peninsula campaign, George Armstrong Custer posed for two photographs taken with captured former West Point classmate James B. Washington, a great-great-grandnephew of George Washington and an aide to Joseph E. Johnston. Images were made with and without the child. Washington suggested the photographer title the image "Both Sides, [and] the Cause."

wearing homespun cloth dyed with walnut hulls and copperas. The tint-
ing gave a yellowish brown look of butternut, a prevalent hue in the war's
final year.[113]

For those far from the fighting, both in distance and time, the patchwork of shades was hidden from view. Color photography came seventy
years after Appomattox. For generations the only color images of the war
came from paintings and lithographs, which tended to glorify and tidy up
battle scenes. A perception emerged of finely fitted legions dressed in
immaculate blue and gray.

North and South, citizens often referred to Confederate soldiers as
butternuts.

In Retrospect

TOP TEN FIRSTS

Frequently granted the nebulous title "first modern war," the War Between the States is also credited with birthing a multitude of maiden events. Most of these distinctions are misplaced, as the war enhanced far more than it created.

The Crimean War (1853–56) witnessed the first use of railroads and telegraphy in military operations as well as the pioneering of organized nursing. Photographers made a handful of exposures during the Mexican War (1846–48). Free blacks and slaves fought in the American Revolution (1775–83). The French employed dog tags in the early 1800s and balloon reconnaissance in the early 1700s. Rifles, grenades, land mines, and multi-barreled "machine guns" had been around since the Middle Ages.[1]

Conversely, the Civil War was not the last of many things. Slavery remained for years in Cuba and Brazil and never ended in areas of Southeast Asia and sub-Saharan Africa. In the 1950s all eleven states of the former Confederacy maintained laws of segregation. In the later decades of the twentieth century, citizens of Kansas, California, and Hawaii contemplated seceding from the Union.

Yet the war was still a vanguard event in a few cases. The following were the first of their kind in American or world history. They are ranked chronologically, although their impact upon the war and the world is left to the reader's imagination.

1. FIRST NATIONAL INCOME TAX IN AMERICAN HISTORY (AUGUST 5, 1861)

It must have been a bitter pill for states' rights advocates. The price of secession included the creation of a first-ever national income tax, both for the United States and the Confederacy.[2]

The first siphoning came from the U.S. government, enacted four months into the war. It was a dream by today's standards. In order to increase revenue, Congress imposed a tax of 3 percent on all yearly income above eight hundred dollars, an amount well above the annual revenues for most farmers and laborers. In 1862 a new plan taxed cigarettes, liquor, stamps, inheritance, and a mountain of other items. It also expanded the income tax to 3 percent for earnings above six hundred dollars and 5 percent on the rare income above ten thousand dollars.[3]

Even less fond of taxation than Northerners, Confederates waited until 1862 to impose an income tax of 5 percent. By 1864 the levy was up to 10 percent. With much of its wealth in slaves and land, and a large portion of its population under occupation, the Confederacy had little to collect and no way to collect it. In the end the South financed most the war on the less invasive but highly speculative printing and borrowing of money.[4]

Rising prices rather than taxation was the true money burden on citizens. INFLATION neared 100 percent in the North and 9,000 percent in the seceded states by war's end.[5]

After the war, the U.S. government suspended the income tax for years but never closed the department created to enforce it. Ever since the Civil War, Americans have lived with the Internal Revenue Service.

---

2. FIRST PAPER CURRENCY AS LEGAL TENDER (FEBRUARY 25, 1862)

By Christmas 1861 the U.S. government was nearly bankrupt. Creating a self-fulfilling prophecy of economic collapse, citizens hoarded gold and silver. Tax revenues were not due for months. Daily federal expenditures reached millions of dollars. Lincoln lamented, "The bottom is out of the tub."[6]

To alleviate the immediate problem, Secretary of the Treasury Salmon P. Chase demanded the issue of a paper currency. Paper money existed, from state and city banks, even shops and railroads. The system worked because most transactions were local, but Americans from all regions historically distrusted federal control over money. The U.S. Constitution permitted the minting of coins, but it mentioned nothing of paper. For the Federal government to print money was unconstitutional, or at least an abuse of power, some argued.

Legal implications aside, lawmakers feared the public would reject a national scrip. As non-interest-bearing and unbacked by gold or silver, U.S. notes could become as worthless as the paper on which they were printed. Chase assured this money would be different.

Unlike existing paper money, or the notes the Confederate government, states, cities, and business were printing, the U.S. currency would be legal tender. With a few exceptions, citizens, businesses, and the government itself had to accept the money "for all debts public and private." Practicality won over suspicion, and Congress passed the Legal Tender Act of 1862. The U.S. Treasury issued $150 million in notes.[7]

The Confederate money guaranteed nothing, except to be redeemable in gold or silver two years after the *successful* conclusion of the war. In four years, the U.S. government issued $450 million in notes; which retained most of its value. The Confederacy printed $1.5 billion in notes, counterfeiters added millions more, all of which became little more than souvenirs with the fall of Richmond.[8]

Printed green on one side, U.S. national currency was nicknamed "greenbacks." Printed with low-quality ink that faded after brief use, Confederate money was sometimes called "graybacks," but the term was more often a pseudonym for lice.

---

3. FIRST BATTLE BETWEEN IRONCLADS (MARCH 9, 1862)

Neither the *Monitor* nor the *Merrimack* (rechristened the CSS *Virginia*) was the first iron-armored warship. France created the first seagoing ironclad in 1859, with Britain building two in 1860. Ironclad ships, however, had never faced one another in battle—until the Civil War.[9]

Intended to break the Union blockade, the CSS *Virginia* was almost as long as a football field and sported ten guns, four inches of armor, and a crew of 320. In her hull were five massive coal-burning boilers, capable of giving the "floating barn roof" a top speed of just a few knots. Launched from Norfolk, Virginia, on March 8, 1862, the slow ship quickly proved its mettle in action.

The lumbering ironclad headed for U.S.-held Hampton Roads, where three sailing ships and two steam frigates, all amply armed, blocked the mouth of the James River. Unimpressed, the *Virginia* rammed one ship, blasted another, and chased another aground. More than 240 U.S. sailors died that day. The *Virginia* took ninety-eight direct hits but experienced no damage.[10]

Word of the *Virginia*'s success sent Lincoln's cabinet into a panic. Secretary of War Edwin M. Stanton feared the indomitable ship would sail up the Potomac and shell the White House. It would be prudent, Stanton insisted, to evacuate the cities on the eastern seaboard.[11]

That same night, a recently finished Union ironclad was towed into Hampton Roads and moored next to the grounded Federal warship. More than 170 feet long, the "cheese box on a raft" floated level with the water, except for a turret sheathed in eight inches of layered iron and holding two cannon. Faster and more maneuverable than the *Virginia*, the USS *Monitor* was just as sturdy.

Next morning the two warships hammered each other in a four-hour battle. Solid shots (each weighing more than a person) clanged against cast iron and deflected in all directions. *Virginia* ran aground then freed herself. *Monitor* took a direct hit to its pilothouse. Each ship tried to ram the other. The battle ended in a draw. Both sides scrambled to make more armored ships. The days of sails and masts were numbered.[12]

The Confederacy spent $173,000 to build the *Virginia*. The Union spent $1.5 million just to review ironclad contractors and designs.

---

4. FIRST NATIONAL MILITARY DRAFT IN AMERICAN HISTORY (APRIL 16, 1862)

The year 1862 did not start well for the Confederacy. February defeats at FORTS HENRY AND DONELSON cost thirteen thousand men and exposed Tennessee to conquest. Failure at PEA RIDGE surrendered half of Arkansas. NEW ORLEANS, Kentucky, and northwest Virginia were all but back in the Union. New volunteers were few. ROBERT E. LEE, newly appointed military adviser to President Davis, recommended drastic measures.

In March Davis went before the Confederate Congress and proposed conscription for all able-bodied men between eighteen and forty-five. Those selected would serve three years or until the end of the war. One-year volunteers, most of them close to the end of their term, had to serve two additional years.

Legislators were furious. Not only did this violate the sanctity of states' rights over the central government, it also illustrated the failure of Richmond to manage the resources, patriotism, and lives pledged to it since Fort Sumter. Reluctantly, two-thirds of the Congress voted for the Conscription Act, mandating eligibility of men not older than thirty-five. Exempted from the draft were skilled workers deemed invaluable, such as telegraphers, mail carriers, train engineers, plus all Confederate and state government officials—the very men who enacted the draft law.[13]

Draftees were allowed to hire substitutes, but this sparked accusations of "rich man's war, poor man's fight." The slogan's intensity grew in the following draft, which exempted owners of twenty or more slaves.

The Union followed suit in March 1863. Sparking protests and riots, the draft netted only forty-six thousand of more than seven hundred thousand eligible. The rest paid a commutation fee of three hundred dollars, purchased substitutes, found exemption, or simply went into hiding. As with the Southern call up, the Union draft coerced thousands to volunteer. The promise of bounties and choice of regiment was more appealing than being thrown into the mix and labeled a conscript.[14]

Among those in the Union who hired substitutes—future president Grover Cleveland, J. P. Morgan, Andrew Carnegie, and Lincoln's personal secretary John Nicolay. Lincoln himself hired a substitute—John Summerfield Staple—for five hundred dollars.

5. FIRST PRODUCTION OF MACHINE-STITCHED SHOES (1862)

An enduring myth suggests that, out of necessity, the South was more inventive than the North. Creative though it was in finding alternatives, such as saving horsehair for sutures, sorghum for sugar, and dried acorns for coffee, the Confederacy never matched the Union's eruption of innovation. In four years the Confederate Patent Office granted 266 patents, whereas its Union counterpart granted more than 16,000.[15]

By mail and in person, the White House and War Department received a blizzard of conceptuals, prototypes, and blueprints. Some wavered between comical and tragic, such as exploding bullets, steam-powered flying machines, weather-predicting equipment, and chemical and biological weapons. A handful of others could not be ignored, including a pair of shoes brought to Secretary of War Edwin M. Stanton.[16]

There was nothing revolutionary about the footwear except for the way it was made. In 1858 inventor Lyman Blake patented a design for a specialized sewing machine. In 1862 Gordon McKay improved the design and began production with it. The machine stitched the soles of shoes to their uppers. Unexciting compared to the Gatling gun of the 1850s or the first use of chloroform in the 1840s, the invention was nonetheless a monumental achievement in that the process was previously done by hand.[17]

The McKay machine produced shoes cheaper, stronger, and one hundred times faster than before. Skilled shoemakers, in short supply during the war, were no longer required to fill huge army requisitions. Leased to subcontractors, McKay's contraptions produced more than two million shoes in a year. All the while, thousands in the Confederate army marched barefoot.[18]

In 1895 the United States produced 120 million pairs of shoes. More than half were made with McKay sewing machines.

---

6. FIRST U.S. MEDAL OF HONOR (MARCH 25, 1863)

Medals were not a standard part of the American military. Traditional thinking considered them undemocratic and unnecessary. Ideally, serving one's country was to be rewarding enough. For Union soldiers, this service often meant months of morale-sapping tedium wintering in camp, patrolling occupied areas, and waiting in siege lines. Even less eventful was blockade duty. In guarding thirty-five hundred miles of coastline with hundreds of other ships, a crew could go for months without making contact with a bona fide blockade-runner.[19]

To bolster morale, Congress authorized the president in late 1861 to award navy personnel a Medal of Honor in recognition of efficiency and gallantry in service. In the summer of 1862 the army Medal of Honor was introduced (an air force version was added in 1956).

The first recipients were members of the April 1862 Andrews Raid (also known as the Great Locomotive Chase), a party of twenty-one Ohio soldiers led by Kentucky spy James J. Andrews. Stealing a train engine at Kennesaw, Georgia, north of Atlanta, the band hoped to sabotage tracks and bridges but were soon captured near the Tennessee border. Eight were eventually hanged, eight escaped, and six were exchanged. On March 25, 1863, Secretary of War Stanton awarded the medal to six of the survivors. Eventually, all received the medal save for the civilian Andrews, who was one of the eight who were hanged.[20]

In all, 2,625 soldiers and sailors received the medal during the war. A reexamination of all awards in 1917 resulted in more than 900 revocations, but no other war neared the number of recipients as the War Between the States. Next closest was the Second World War, with 433 decorations. Over time, conditions for its issue became increasingly stringent, and now most honorees receive the award posthumously.[21]

For the Confederacy, no equivalent existed. The most a soldier could receive was a promotion or a favorable review in an official report.[22]

> The current navy Medal of Honor is almost identical to its original 1863 version, where the human figure of Discord cowers before Minerva (the Roman goddess of war), the two symbolizing the Confederacy and the Union respectively.

7. FIRST WOMAN SURGEON IN U.S. MILITARY HISTORY (SEPTEMBER 1863)

Before, during, and long after the war, American culture condemned women attempting to enter the medical profession in any capacity. Only a few medical schools accepted female students, and fewer communities allowed women doctors to practice.[23]

The military was no different. In 1861 medical practitioner and graduate of a Syracuse medical school Mary Edwards Walker applied for a surgeon's commission in the Union army. Officials rejected her outright.[24]

Between hounding Washington officials for reconsideration, she volunteered as a nurse. She also provided assistance to families visiting loved ones in camp hospitals. Early in 1864 she finally received an appointment as an assistant surgeon in the Army of the Cumberland, the first woman surgeon ever commissioned by the U.S. military.[25]

Evidence suggests her appointment may have been more for her capacities as a spy than as a doctor. In 1864, while crossing enemy lines to care for civilians, she was taken prisoner and convicted of espionage. The recipient of considerable ridicule, she served four months in a Richmond prison. Her jailers, however, acknowledged her commission and exchanged her, along with other Union surgeons, for seventeen Confederate medical personnel.[26]

In 1865 Mary Edwards Walker received the Medal of Honor. A review board repealed the decoration in 1917 because she was technically a civilian. In 1977 the award was reinstated, and Walker remains to date the only female recipient of the award.

---

8. FIRST TIME A SUBMARINE EVER SANK AN ENEMY SHIP (FEBRUARY 17, 1864)

Diving contraptions existed long before the Civil War. A fully encased one-man vessel of ingenious design tried to sink a British ship during the American Revolution by attaching a bomb to its hull. Robert Fulton experimented with below-water vessels before he began his work on steamships. Nevertheless, a submarine had never sunk a ship in wartime.[27]

In a fit of optimism, both Union and Confederate governments contracted for submarines. Launched in 1862, the four-man USS *Alligator* proved too unwieldy and never saw combat. The two-man CSS *Pioneer* was scuttled in New Orleans to avoid capture. The following CSS *American Diver* was lost while being towed out into Mobile Bay. Then there was the *H. L. Hunley*.[28]

Built in an Alabama machine shop and brought to South Carolina by rail, the *Hunley* was forty feet long and barely four feet wide. Engineers equipped it with two hefty hatches, tiny portals, ballast tanks, rudders, fins, and a faulty air shaft. Two of its test runs ended in disaster, drowning twelve men and its inventor in the process. Ultimately, the *Hunley* proved deadlier to its crew than to the enemy.[29]

On the night of February 17, 1864, a crew of eight crawled inside the converted boiler, an engineering wonder bobbing in the cold waters of Charleston Harbor. Huddled to one side, sitting in candlelight, the crew began to operate the drive shaft crank, and the pilot steered the submarine into the open water. From its bow projected a twenty-foot iron pole holding a ninety-pound keg of black powder, destined for the USS *Housatonic* out in the harbor of Charleston.

The crew of the *Housatonic* knew to be on watch. The *Hunley* and most other "secret weapons" were hardly unknown to either side. When a lookout spotted a suspicious rippling in the harbor waters, Union fears were confirmed.

Just as the alarm bells rang out, the *Hunley's* spar torpedo detonated. Fire, water, wood, and bodies flew skyward. The *Housatonic* rolled to port. Sailors scrambled for the mast riggings as the ship sank in shallow water.[30]

Damaged in the attack and equipped with primitive navigation equipment, the *Hunley* wandered seaward and sank, drowning all 8 hands. Only 5 of *Housatonic's* 155 perished, yet the *Hunley* had done something never before accomplished. Not until 1914 would a submarine sink another ship.[31]

After the war, circus mogul P. T. Barnum offered one hundred thousand dollars for the recovery of the *Hunley.* The immortal sub was eventually found and raised—136 years after it went down.

---

9. FIRST ASSASSINATION OF AN AMERICAN PRESIDENT (APRIL 14, 1865)

Lincoln knew full well that head of state was not a safe occupation. In his lifetime, attempts were made on the lives of Queen Victoria and Andrew Jackson, and assassins succeeded in ending the lives of two czars, an emperor of Mexico, a prime minister of England, and a king of Afghanistan. In 1862 alone, assassins murdered the presidents of Colombia and Honduras. After the fall of Richmond, Jefferson Davis seemed to be the next likely target, as thousands North and South blamed the Confederate president for the war and its consequences.

It was April 14, Good Friday. Just days before, ROBERT E. LEE had capitulated outside Appomattox. Similar news was expected from North Carolina, where WILLIAM TECUMSEH SHERMAN had JOSEPH E. JOHNSTON cornered. Washington, D.C., was in a festive mood.

News spread that Lincoln would be attending Ford's Theatre that night to see *Our American Cousin,* a mediocre play starring Laura Keene. Exhausted but feeling obligated to make an appearance, Lincoln went.

A single bullet reaped horrible consequences for the South after the war.

Assigned to guard the presidential box were a White House footman and a policeman, the typical arrangement. Except for public speeches and on travels, Lincoln rarely had anyone guarding him. Perhaps more guards would have been present had Lincoln's original guests accepted his invitation, but U. S. Grant and his wife had cordially declined.

As the play progressed, the policeman wandered from his post, and the footman thought nothing of allowing a famous stage actor to call on the president. Moments later, the actor put a large-caliber bullet into the back of the president's head.

Lincoln lived nine more hours, unconscious. Carried to a boarding house across the street, he slowly hemorrhaged to death in front of his cabinet, doctors, and his wife. At 7:22 A.M., April 15, 1865, his heart ceased.[32]

Three other U.S. presidents died by assassination: Civil War veterans James A. Garfield (1881) and William McKinley (1901) and veteran of the Second World War John F. Kennedy (1963).

Lincoln had long frequented the playhouses of the capital. On one visit to Ford's Theatre, he partook of a play entitled *The Marble Heart*, starring John Wilkes Booth.

10. FIRST WOMAN EXECUTED BY THE U.S. GOVERNMENT (JULY 17, 1865)

Conspiracy theories erupted after the slaying of Lincoln. The implicated included the papacy, Secretary of War Edwin M. Stanton, and the Confederate army. In flight from recently captured Richmond, Jefferson Davis was also a prime suspect. Yet there was no doubt about the hit man.

Several witnesses recognized the assassin immediately as he leapt from the president's box. A star of Ford's and many other theaters, John Wilkes Booth made no attempt to hide his face as he limped across the stage, brandished a dagger, and shouted, *"Sic semper tyranus"* ("Thus ever to tyrants," the state motto of Virginia).

The murder investigation quickly led to Mary Surratt's Washington boarding house, where Booth was a frequent visitor. After a few questions, police arrested the forty-two-year-old Surratt when she denied knowing Lewis Powell, alias Lewis Paine, a man who attempted to kill Secretary of State William Seward on the night of the assassination. Paine, along with several other members of Booth's inner circle, was one of Surratt's boarders.[33]

Surratt and seven men were tried in a military court. Evidence against her was speculative. Her son John was familiar with Booth. An associate of hers, John Lloyd, testified Mary spoke to him on the day of the shooting about acquiring some firearms. Otherwise, there was nothing to link her with the conspirators. A national desire for revenge, however, prompted the conviction of all eight defendants. Four were to be hanged, including Surratt.

Two days after sentencing, on a hot summer afternoon, Surratt, Powell, George Atzerodt (assigned to kill Vice President Andrew Johnson), and David Herold (who helped Booth escape from Washington) entered the courtyard of the Old Capitol Prison. Led to the gallows, their legs were bound. Hoods were placed over their heads. Powell begged for Surratt's life, proclaiming her innocent. Just before the stroke of 2 P.M., the platform upon which they were standing swung away. Officials let them hang for half an hour.[34]

John H. Surratt, Mary's son, fled the country and spent time in Rome. Nearly captured, he fled to Alexandria, Egypt, where he was eventually apprehended. Brought to trial in 1867, he was released for lack of evidence.

TOP TEN MOST SIGNIFICANT BATTLES

Images of charging horses, bursting cannon, and waving flags tend to inspire the imagination more easily than scenarios of financial balance sheets and cleverly worded legislation, but there is much discrepancy among historians as to the importance of battles in history. Traditionalists might condone the "great man theory" in which generals and presidents are the principle directors of fate, whereas social and economic historians often interpret battles as expressions rather than instigators of existing conditions.

Whatever the view, it is important to consider that in the case of the Civil War, large portions of the opposing sides opted for warfare to settle their differences. In turn, battles within the war played a noticeable role in determining political options, economic climate, and national morale. One Confederate soldier offered a poignant view of battles and their role: "If we don't get at each other some time, when will the war end?"[35]

Militarily speaking, cavalier strikes and spur-of-the-moment miracles did not decide the war as much as long, decimating struggles. Within those campaigns, there were battles of lasting effect, some of which are represented below. Listed here, in chronological order, are the military engagements marking the greatest change in the nature of the war in terms of military, economic, and political consequences.

1. FIRST MANASSAS (VIRGINIA, JULY 21, 1861)

In the relative quiet after Fort Sumter, impatient with the Confederate presence just miles from Washington, Horace Greeley's NEW YORK TRIB-UNE declared "Forward to Richmond!" Weeks later the newspaper recommended the North and South negotiate a peaceful settlement.

A close fight between green troops, First Manassas (First Bull Run) ended with a timely counterattack from the Confederates, who worked from the defensive for most of the action. Considering their inexperience, Union soldiers attacked much better than they withdrew. Rumor and roadblocks turned an otherwise orderly disengagement into a full-fledged panic, sending Confederate morale skyward.[36]

The popular view is to consider First Manassas a costly win for the South. Overconfidence from the win, so the theory goes, actually lulled

the Virginia theater, and the Confederacy as a whole, into a fatal compla-
cency, while the North mobilized for a long fight. This is an odd interpretation in light of the results.

The Union did not launch another offensive toward Richmond for
the rest of 1861 and several months into 1862. If the Washington area
prepared for war, so did Virginia. Safe from harassment, the Confederacy's most populous and industrialized state organized defenses and
gathered munitions. The "overconfidence" of Manassas would serve
the Virginia theater well, acting as the base for future victories at the
Seven Days' (June–July 1862), SECOND MANASSAS (August 1862), the
Shenandoah Valley (March–September 1862), and CHANCELLORSVILLE
(May 1863).

A late arrival to the battle, one of the many famous onlookers to First
Manassas was Confederate president Jefferson Davis, who briefly
considered leading a group of stragglers into combat.

---

2. FORTS HENRY AND DONELSON (TENNESSEE, FEBRUARY 6, 12–16, 1862)

It is easy to dismiss rivers when looking at a map. The twenty-first-century
traveler rarely thinks of waterways, as they are made almost irrelevant by
concrete roads and steel bridges. To a military tactician in the nineteenth
century, however, the cartographer's blue lines were formidable obstacles
and potential death traps. Rivers were also highways on which an army
could move deep into its opponent's territory.

There are only three major rivers leading from the North into what
was the Confederacy: the Mississippi, the Cumberland, and the Tennessee. Stemming from the Ohio River, the latter two enter northwest
Tennessee a dozen miles apart. Guarding the Tennessee was Fort Henry,
and holding the Cumberland was Fort Donelson.

In ten days, ULYSSES S. GRANT led a combined land and water assault
upon the forts and delivered the Union its greatest victories of the war to
that point. Of the two battles, Fort Donelson is by far the more famous.
Maintained today as a national battlefield park, it was the larger and latter
of the two contests and the site of a costly Confederate blunder. Winning
the Cumberland provided a water route along the Kentucky-Tennessee
border, which the Union used to take the vital rail link of Nashville.

Union victories at Forts Henry and Donelson were the first good news for the North and signaled the presence of Ulysses S. Grant.

Arguably, the Union triumph at Fort Henry was more significant. The Tennessee River cuts through the western third of its namesake, skirts the northwest corner of Mississippi, runs across north Alabama, approaches Georgia, then reenters the southeast edge of Tennessee. The Union used this river run to secure major victories at SHILOH (April 1862), Iuka (September 1862), Corinth (October 1862), and CHATTANOOGA (November 1863).

> Refusing terms of capitulation to his captives at Fort Donelson, U. S. Grant received the nickname "Unconditional Surrender" Grant.

3. NEW ORLEANS (LOUISIANA, APRIL 23–25, 1862)

It was by far the largest city in the South, holding more people in 1861 than Atlanta, Charleston, Montgomery, Nashville, and Richmond put together. The linchpin between the Father of Waters and the Seven Seas,

New Orleans trafficked more commerce than all other Southern ports combined. The Confederacy could not give it up, let alone give it away.[37]

Yet several factors doomed the Crescent City. In early 1862 a Union advance toward the railroad hub of Corinth, Mississippi, forced Confederate troops out of Louisiana and into the bloodbath of SHILOH. Left holding New Orleans proper were three thousand militia, supported downriver by several small ships, one functioning ironclad, and two masonry forts—all of which was little challenge to a Union fleet of forty-three gunboats and a land force of fifteen thousand. On April 24, 1862, after shelling the two river bastions into rubble, Union Rear Adm. David G. Farragut ran his ships upriver and captured New Orleans the next day, with Gen. BENJAMIN F. BUTLER's army close behind.

The fall of New Orleans was a crushing blow to the South, the rough equivalent to the Union losing New York City. The fact that New Orleans fell after minimal fighting made the news particularly bitter to loyal Confederates.[38]

In short order, the Union captured a metropolis of 180,000, gained inroads to the Confederate interior, seized the lower part of the Mississippi, and added a premium port to its blockade operations. For all of this, the Union lost 36 men killed and 135 wounded.[39]

The Union hero of New Orleans, Rear Adm. David Glasgow Farragut, was born in Tennessee and married a Virginian. His mother, who died when he was a child, was interred in New Orleans.

---

4. THE SEVEN DAYS' BATTLES (VIRGINIA, JUNE 25–JULY 1, 1862)

Despite the overwhelming caution of Union commander GEORGE B. MCCLELLAN during his Peninsula campaign, the Army of the Potomac had drawn within sight of the Confederate capital. HARPER'S WEEKLY predicted Richmond would fall in days if not hours. The combined armies numbered a fifth of a million men, but the Union held a two-to-one advantage.

Replacing a recently wounded JOSEPH E. JOHNSTON at the head the Confederate defenses, the heretofore unimpressive ROBERT E. LEE chose to attack. In six different battles within a week, Lee drove the Union forces back. Performing far better than their cautious leader, the Federals won most of the battles and induced twice as many casualties as they received. Consequently, many in blue were shocked to hear the command to retreat day after day.[40]

Eventually, McClellan abandoned hope plus tons of equipment—including thirty-one thousand rifles—citing he was facing overwhelming numbers. Lee fumed at not bagging the entire Union force. The effect on their respective countrymen was immeasurable. Southerners elevated Lee to mythical greatness. Many Northerners wanted to charge McClellan with treason. The effect on the troops could be calculated. The Union won four of six battles outright and retreated six times. The Confederates drove the Federals back nearly thirty miles and away from Richmond. Altogether, more than twenty-eight thousand men were killed or wounded. Taken collectively, the Seven Days' battles cost more lives than any other battle with the exception of GETTYSBURG.[41]

To hasten his army's retreat after the Seven Days, Union commander George B. McClellan contemplated leaving all of its supplies, weapons, and ammunition behind.

---

5. ANTIETAM (MARYLAND, SEPTEMBER 17, 1862)

After hearing of Robert E. Lee's impressive victory at SECOND MANASSAS, British foreign secretary John Russell wrote to Prime Minister Lord Palmerston: "The time is come for offering mediation to the United States Government, with a view to the recognition of the independence of the Confederates." The date on the letter was September 17, 1862.[42]

Ten days later news reached London of another battle "to the northwest of Washington," which had transpired the same day Russell had suggested a radical change in British policy. Details of the battle were not yet clear, but evidently the Union had prevailed, and Lee was falling back.

Militarily, the triumph was marginal. The Union victory near Sharpsburg broke a string of Confederate victories in the region, at a cost of twelve thousand Union dead and wounded. Loyal Northern newspapers initially called Antietam a smashing success then lashed out at the obvious negligence of the Federal command. A win, however, allowed Lincoln to announce his EMANCIPATION PROCLAMATION, bringing a new sense of purpose to his country and to the war.[43]

LIBRARY OF CONGRESS

The stalemate at Antietam allowed Lincoln to publish the Emancipation Proclamation. It also ended the command of George B. McClellan.

Lee would not attempt another sortie for ten months. Jefferson Davis fell into despair, as did many citizens and soldiers of his country who assumed Lee's successes would continue unabated. In ten hours the South lost more than eleven thousand killed and wounded, a number larger than many Confederate cities. It also meant the end of British plans to intervene.[44]

> At the time of the battle, there were around thirteen hundred residents of Sharpsburg, Maryland. After the battle, dead soldiers in the immediate area outnumbered them four to one.

6. CHANCELLORSVILLE (VIRGINIA, MAY 1–4, 1863)

When hearing of the Union defeat near Chancellorsville, a Northern newspaper editor could hardly believe the news. "My God! It is horrible—horrible, and think of it, 130,000 magnificent soldiers so cut to pieces by less than 60,000." Chancellorsville was one of the most unexpected, almost unimaginable achievements of the Confederate military.[45]

Facing a vastly larger army and about to be outflanked, Lee ignored nearly every military axiom and divided his forces three ways. With his left, he outflanked the flankers then crushed them between his left and his center. When his right came under attack, he gathered his divided army and defeated that advance as well.

Much of the victory was due to the blundering hesitation of the Union commanding officer Joseph Hooker and the brilliant leadership of the Confederate corps commanders, particularly THOMAS J. "STONEWALL" JACKSON. Regardless, the image of Lee was the beneficiary, and the Virginian looked as unstoppable as ever. Summing up the emotions of many fellow Unionists, Republican Sen. Charles Sumner cried, "Lost, all is lost."[46]

Yet the victory cost the life of Jackson and killed or maimed 22 percent of Lee's Army of Northern Virginia. Rather than GETTYSBURG, many see Chancellorsville as the high tide of the Confederacy, soon to ebb from the overconfidence Lee displayed in Pennsylvania two months later.[47]

During the battle of Chancellorsville, at least one Union soldier was the victim of corrupt government contractors. He discovered his rifle cartridges were filled with dirt rather than gunpowder.

---

7. GETTYSBURG (PENNSYLVANIA, JULY 1–3, 1863)

An abrupt fight with legendary tales of heroism, the largest and bloodiest battle ever fought in North America, Gettysburg captures the imagination unlike any other Civil War battle, especially when compared to the slow, extenuated grinds of the blockade, Vicksburg, or the siege of Petersburg.

Because of its size, northern location, and dramatic turns of battle, Gettysburg also invites a deluge of what-if scenarios or counterfactual history. Against countless variables, any hypotheses on different outcomes and effects are basically guesswork.[48]

What the battle did provide was a major surge in Union morale. Many soldiers in the Army of the Potomac felt as if the recent defeats at FREDERICKSBURG and CHANCELLORSVILLE were avenged. The army expelled Lee from the North as it had done at ANTIETAM.

Yet the Union president was less than pleased. George Gordon Meade failed to pursue his beaten opponent, allowing the Confederates to cross back into Virginia unopposed. "This is a dreadful reminiscence of McClellan," vented Lincoln, fuming over what he viewed as a lost chance to capture the Army of Northern Virginia in total. In a scathing rebuke to Meade, he wrote: "Your golden opportunity is gone, and I am distressed immeasurably because of it." To admonish a victorious general, however, would be to undermine the victory itself. Lincoln never sent the message.[49]

On the Confederate side, sympathetic journalists referred to Gettysburg as a "brief setback" if not a victory. It was in fact the deadliest battle of the war for the South. Nearly a third of the Confederacy's largest army was gone. Desertions accelerated rapidly. Lee remained on the defensive for the rest of 1863 and never invaded the North again. Yet the loss was not total. His army would live to fight another day—another 645 days, to be precise.[50]

Victor of the largest battle ever fought in North America, Union commander George Gordon Meade had been born in Spain.

Pickett's Charge at Gettysburg proved unsuccessful in routing the Union army. As a result, Lee retreated to Virginia and never again came north. In terms of the battle itself, many have emphasized it was lost by Lee rather than won by Meade.

LIBRARY OF CONGRESS

8. THE SURRENDER OF VICKSBURG (MISSISSIPPI, JULY 4, 1863)

On the afternoon of July 7, while working through his frustration over the limited victory at GETTYSBURG, Lincoln received a visit from a visibly ecstatic Gideon Welles. With telegram in hand, the navy secretary informed the president that Vicksburg had fallen to U. S. Grant and W. T. Sherman. Embracing the messenger and the good news, Lincoln beamed, "I cannot in words tell you of my joy over this result! It is great, Mr. Welles! It is great!"[51]

For months, the Union army had tried charging, digging, flanking, and shelling its way into the Mississippi town. After Grant's army surrounded the city and laid siege for forty-seven days, the Confederate stronghold capitulated on the Fourth of July. As specifics came in, Lincoln had even more reason to celebrate. Grant had taken 31,600 prisoners and more than 170 cannon, six times Meade's catch at GETTYSBURG. Nearby Port Hudson fell soon after, contributing 5,000 more prisoners and giving the Union control over the length of the Mississippi.[52]

The fall of Vicksburg gave the Union complete control of the Mississippi River and split the Confederacy in half.

LIBRARY OF CONGRESS

Paris and London heard the results of GETTYSBURG a few days before learning of Vicksburg, but it was the news of the latter that sent Confederate credit on a dive. Domestically, inflation in the South accelerated, as did its military desertions.

Losing the mighty river, the Confederacy also lost connection to Arkansas, much of Louisiana, and Texas, which held more cattle and horses than any other state. For the Union, the dollar surged in strength, and the growing Midwest could once again trade with the world. The end of the Vicksburg campaign also freed up men and materiel for operations eastward, namely in Virginia and Georgia, where Grant and Sherman would launch their final grand offensives of the war.[53]

The Confederate commander at Vicksburg was John Clifford Pemberton, a native of Pennsylvania.

---

9. THE WILDERNESS (VIRGINIA, MAY 5–6, 1864)

The names of Grant and Lee are frequently mentioned in the same breath, but the two generals faced each other for less than a quarter of the war. Their reintroduction (they had met briefly during the Mexican War) occurred in the thickets south of the Rappahannock River, in an area known simply as the Wilderness. The fighting was close to where Lee had achieved his greatest victory a year earlier at Chancellorsville.

For two days, in close and brutal fighting, 101,000 Federals and 61,000 Confederates slashed into each other. Lee had once again stemmed a Union advance, registering over 14,000 killed and wounded while losing 7,750 of his own.[54]

The Union had lost in Virginia again, but rather than retreat northward and recover, Grant moved south, determined to continue the engagement until he outflanked or broke through the Confederate line. The Wilderness signaled the beginning of almost continual engagement that would finally terminate the stalemate in the East.

Although Grant's plan would take eleven months to work, the immediate affect of the advance upon his troops was remarkable. Suffering yet another loss under yet another general, and losing more than twice the casualties as their opponent, the Federals were animated. One Union soldier commented, "We began to sing. . . . We were happy."[55]

·   In the battle of the Wilderness, Confederate Gen. James Longstreet was
    wounded by gunfire from his own troops. Stonewall Jackson had been
    wounded by his own troops at Chancellorsville, a little over a year before
    and a little over a mile away.

---

10. JONESBORO (GEORGIA, AUGUST 25–SEPTEMBER 1, 1864)

In August 1864 time was running out for the Lincoln government.
Grant's once aggressive Wilderness campaign had stalled on the outskirts of Petersburg; he had fifty thousand casualties to show for his
efforts. The Democratic Party gathered for its national convention and
declared the war a failure, a message heartily received by a growing
peace movement in the North. Lincoln's own Republican Party started
to turn on him, seeing him less of an incumbent and more of a burden.
He sulked, "It seems exceedingly probable that this administration will
not be re-elected."[56]

WILLIAM TECUMSEH SHERMAN and his three armies offered no
encouragement. Since May they had marched toward Atlanta from Chattanooga. On the way they lost twenty-five thousand casualties, including
the life of promising James B. McPherson at the head of the Army of the
Tennessee. Although under siege, Atlanta still stood.[57]

On August 25 Sherman instructed his forces to leave their trenches to
the west of the city and headed south. Confederate Gen. JOHN BELL HOOD
declared victory, believing Sherman was retreating. Sherman instead
headed to Jonesboro to cut the rail lines supplying Atlanta. After several
days of denial, Hood realized he was about to be trapped, set fire to his
supply depots, and retreated. On September 1 Union forces moved into
the city unopposed.[58]

At the time Atlanta was known as the "Gate City." It lived up to its
nickname for the Union. Its surrender opened the way for Sherman's
March to the Sea and a swath of devastation through Georgia and the
Carolinas. More important, the fall of Atlanta was a clear indication that
the war would soon end in favor of the Union. In the November elections,
Lincoln retained the presidency by a wide margin.[59]

Real estate development has all but eradicated the battlefield of Jonesboro.

TOP TEN BEST
COMMANDING GENERALS

Schools, streets, and newborns continue to be named after endeared commanders of the Brothers' War. Conversely, some generals are still vilified. For a nation traditionally indifferent to history, such peculiar and enduring sentiments are understandable. These American generals fought over American peach orchards and American wheat fields, contested the country's very definition of self-determination, and by their actions helped write seminal chapters of a national epoch.

Ranking the 1,008 generals of the Civil War depends on one's criteria. For soldier morale, JOSEPH E. JOHNSTON may stand highest. In ferocity, few can top Nathan Bedford Forrest. GEORGE B. MCCLELLAN is among the very finest in terms of supply and organization. The following are the best commanding generals based on their respective success in managing the primary variables of military operations, including tactics, logistics, communications, and overall strategy. Most important, they are measured for the magnitude of their contribution to the success of their side.[60]

1. THOMAS J. "STONEWALL" JACKSON (C.S., VIRGINIA, 1824–63)

He was never wasteful with his soldiers yet pushed them farther and faster than any other commander. He won on the offensive and defensive, led forces small and large with equal precision, and used terrain and timing to defeat his opponents. With limited means, he played a major role in nearly every Confederate victory in the eastern theater. Perhaps his early departure spared him from eventual defamation, but while alive, Thomas J. Jackson had no equal on either side.

Eccentric, superstitious, overtly pious, and hypochondriacal, Jackson differed little from many other Americans of the period, but in the military, he was a complete misfit. He was far from gallant, rode his horse in an ungainly fashion, acted aloof, humorless, awkward, and was often the target of ridicule from his unimpressed pupils at the Virginia Military Institute. Then the war started.[61]

To his troops he was best known as "Old Jack" or "Old Blue Light," the latter nickname coming from the way his sky blue eyes glared in the midst of battle. He earned the title "Stonewall" while standing his ground against harsh opposition at FIRST MANASSAS. Yet it was his 1862 Shenandoah Valley campaign that catapulted him into legend. From March to June 1862, with forces ranging from four thousand to seventeen thousand, far from rail and reserve support, vastly outnumbered, Jackson accomplished a military feat that remains a subject of international study. In three months he drove off three armies and held a fourth to the outskirts of Washington. His men captured thousands of men and millions of dollars in weapons and supplies, marched and countermarched hundreds of miles, and secured the upper Confederacy's primary source of grain and cattle for the remainder of the year.[62]

A harsh disciplinarian, but not without purpose, Jackson was quick to punish and even execute the disobedient. The rest he pushed to the limit. Before the battle of SECOND MANASSAS, Jackson marched an entire corps of twenty-four thousand to a Federal depot at Manassas Junction, consumed or destroyed the entire cache and disappeared, covering fifty miles in two days. Figuratively and literally, Jackson created a lean fighting force, a "foot cavalry" unburdened by excess baggage, spoils, or the sickly. Few of his soldiers were fond of their taskmaster, but they were proud of the wins they habitually achieved.[63]

ROBERT E. LEE prized Jackson, for it was Stonewall's men who held the field at Second Manassas, allowing Lee to move up reinforcements and win the day. In September 1862 outside Sharpsburg, Maryland, a vastly outnumbered Lee found his back to the Potomac and sixty thousand bluecoats advancing on his position. To Lee's assistance came Jackson, marching up from his recent conquest of Harpers Ferry with two divisions, arguably sparing the great general from annihilation along the banks of the ANTIETAM. While Lee jabbed at Joseph Hooker outside CHANCELLORSVILLE, Jackson delivered a crushing left hook, marching twenty-four thousand men undetected past the Army of the Potomac then slamming into its right flank. It was a pivotal achievement and his last.

Riding reconnaissance that night, Jackson was accidentally shot by his own men. Languishing on his deathbed, he received a letter from the grateful Lee: "I should have chosen for the good of the country to be disabled in your stead."[64]

Early in the war, Thomas J. Jackson thought one of his officers would do well leading mounted troops, so he reassigned Jeb Stuart from the infantry to the cavalry.

2. WILLIAM TECUMSEH SHERMAN (U.S., OHIO, 1820–91)

He had lived in the South for a dozen years, owned slave servants, and detested the rise of agitating abolitionists. As a result, William Tecumseh Sherman understood the Confederacy better than most any other general in blue.[65]

Approachable, unceremonious, internally intense, and highly intelligent, Sherman led his brigade ably at FIRST MANASSAS, one of the few Union officers to do so. Yet he fell into a depression soon after, frustrated by the escalation of the war and the carnage that was sure to come.

Transferred unwillingly to Kentucky, Sherman told the War Department it would take at least two hundred thousand troops to launch an offensive from the Bluegrass State. Word of his request leaked out, and several newspapers judged him insane. Sherman's estimations for success were not far off, but at the time, he was acting fatalistic and marginally paranoid, frequently claiming that much of Kentucky's civilian population were Confederate spies.[66]

Subsequently transferred, Sherman regained himself and his reputation after a solid performance as a division commander at SHILOH, receiving accolades from his immediate superior, ULYSSES S. GRANT. Thereafter, the two men were fast and loyal allies.

In many ways, Sherman was the antithesis of Grant. Better with organization and supply, excitable, racist, and frequently inflexible, Sherman was also a superior strategist. Grant smashed into armies; Sherman outmaneuvered them (with the exception of Kennesaw Mountain, where he lost 2,000 to the Confederates' 270). Although he lost several battles, he knew how to win campaigns. In 1863 he helped secure the Federal rear at VICKSBURG, assisted in lifting the Confederate siege of Union troops at CHATTANOOGA, and repeated the feat immediately at Knoxville. The next year, Sherman conquered Atlanta, largely by maneuver.[67]

The campaign for which he is most famous (and infamous) is his late 1864 March to the Sea. Often criticized, or at least depicted in inglorious terms as a harbinger of "total war" that included civilians, Sherman's strategy differed little from ROBERT E. LEE's 1863 campaign into Pennsylvania. Lee intended to take Harrisburg, and fortune willing, the city of Philadelphia; an original version of a march to the sea. Sherman succeeded where Lee failed, and in destroying property, Sherman broke the will of the opposition without forcing the body counts of a COLD HARBOR, a CHANCELLORSVILLE, or for that matter, a GETTYSBURG.[68]

Before the war, Sherman was superintendent of a school that later became Louisiana State University.

---

3. ROBERT E. LEE (C.S., VIRGINIA, 1807–70)

Feverish admirers hail Robert E. Lee as the patron saint of the Lost Cause, a knightly figure who rallied mortal disciples against heartless modernism. Critics note that he lost a third of his men and half of his battles.[69] Regardless of one's position, there are general truths that endure scrutiny. Lee's premier weapons were his corps commanders, an unsurpassed ability to anticipate his opponents' actions, and a willingness to depart from traditional tactics. His unflinching commitment, exemplary conduct, and personal bravery in the line of fire inspired his men, his people, and his president. With inferior materiel, scant food, and dwindling ranks, "Marse Robert" repeatedly fought off the largest and best-equipped army on earth.

It is safe to say he was not afraid to use his soldiers. To push back the Federal army from the gates of Richmond in 1862, Lee used up fifty thousand men in four months. For his brilliant 1863 win at CHANCELLORS-VILLE, he lost thirteen thousand in three days. The 1864 WILDERNESS campaign halted yet another Federal invasion but cost Lee sixty thousand casualties. He was effective but expensive.

The best and the worst that can be said of Lee is that he fought for Virginia first and last. While his departure from the U.S. armed forces after a quarter century of service is well known, many observers fail to appreciate something less obvious but just as authentic. Lee was not particularly loyal to the Confederacy either.

In 1862 Lee bolstered Richmond's defenses with troops he removed from South Carolina and Georgia. When Jefferson Davis asked him to send reinforcements to besieged Vicksburg in 1863, he instead launched an offensive into Pennsylvania to relieve pressure on Virginia. His president once asked him where the next line of defense should be if Richmond were lost. He responded that there would be no other line.[70]

Yet in his fixation, Lee indirectly provided the Confederacy a great service. In protecting his home, he also protected the Confederacy's most populous state (for both slave and free populations), its largest source of capital wealth and weapons, and a major source of its draft animals and grain. His presence forced the Union to commit a disproportionate amount of men and supplies for the protection of Washington, resources that otherwise would have been free to move upon other states. In defrocking one-time heroes like McClellan and "Fighting Joe" Hooker, outwitting John Pope and AMBROSE E. BURNSIDE, and keeping George G. Meade and U. S. GRANT at bay for nearly two years, the devout Virginian gave the South more hope and the North more despair than any other figure in the war.[71]

Lee's record in major engagements—eleven wins, twelve losses.

---

4. ULYSSES S. GRANT (U.S., OHIO, 1822–85)

 He was not particularly intelligent or inventive. Costly frontal assaults at VICKSBURG, the WILDERNESS, and COLD HARBOR demonstrated an inability to learn from previous failures. He let his men die on the field or in prisons before negotiating with the enemy. Yet this unassuming man from Galena, Illinois, proved to be the only Federal commander willing to use the strongest weapon available to the Union: attrition. Arguably, he was also the only general on either side to orchestrate a truly unified war effort.[72]

Defeat itself did not stop him. It stopped his fellow commanders often enough: John C. Frémont, Don Carlos Buell, Franz Sigel, and Nathaniel Banks in the West, Irvin McDowell, George B. McClellan, John Pope,

Ambrose E. Burnside, Joseph Hooker, and George G. Meade in the East. Through perseverance, Grant eventually triumphed in both theaters.

His unique trait of calm focus in the face of destruction was apparent in the Tennessee battles of FORT DONELSON and SHILOH. Both times, the Confederates opened offensives upon his lines. Both times, his men were not prepared. Both times, Grant himself was miles away, anticipating no imminent action. Yet both times he rode to the front and personally rallied his beaten troops, using a composed, calculating demeanor to reassure and reassess, turning defeats into hard-fought victories.[73]

His two great prizes, Vicksburg and Richmond, exemplified his effective use of abrasion. At first there were the preliminary rounds of reconnaissance and maneuver, followed by an exchange of fierce blows with tremendous loss of blood and no conclusive results. Rather than accept defeat in either affair, Grant resorted to strangulation by siege, letting time and superior numbers work in his favor.

After his appointment to general in chief of the Union armies in March 1864, he again accomplished something his predecessors and adversaries could not. He coordinated simultaneous assaults upon multiple theaters, eliminating the opposition's ability to concentrate its defenses. Grand attacks began in Louisiana, the Virginia coast, the Shenandoah Valley, northern Virginia, and Georgia. The latter three would propel Philip H. Sheridan, William Tecumseh Sherman, and Grant himself into international fame and wither the South into capitulation in a little over a year.

When Grant lost, he usually lost to Robert E. Lee, to whom he can credit nine of his eleven major combat defeats.

5. JAMES LONGSTREET (C.S., SOUTH CAROLINA, 1821–1904)

Fighting from FIRST MANASSAS to Appomattox, commander of the First Corps of the Army of Northern Virginia, careful, stalwart, dependable Longstreet innately comprehended the precious limit of Southern numbers, perhaps better than any Confederate general. His tool of choice was the counterattack, launching assaults only after weakening an opponent from the protection of a defensive stand.[74]

Blue-eyed, fair-skinned "Old Pete" was a man of clear kindness and few words. Good to his troops, his impressive height and sturdy build added to his image of a stolid and steady officer, an image that lasted through twenty-four years of military service: twenty for the United States and four with the Confederacy. A veteran of the SEVEN DAYS, ANTIETAM, GETTYSBURG, and the WILDERNESS, Longstreet's finest hours included his near-perfect infantry and artillery stand at MARYE'S HEIGHTS, his devastating counterattack against John Pope's massive army at Second Manassas, and his assault through the Federal lines at CHICKAMAUGA.[75]

Lee frequently consulted him for advice, gave him premier assignments in several battles, and referred to him endearingly as "my old war horse." Longstreet routinely performed orders with cohesive operation yet remained flexible and opportunistic once battles were in motion. Although not tremendously successful in independent command, Longstreet at the head of a corps proved to be the equal of Jackson.[76]

Longstreet's granite reputation eventually crumbled, although it happened after the war. In the late 1860s he joined the Republican Party and spoke of conciliation with the victors. Consequently, several prominent Confederate colleagues reassessed his war record and openly questioned his loyalty as a Southerner. They recalled his failed 1864 siege of Knoxville, Tennessee, where he sent hundreds of men to their deaths in the deep moats of Fort Sanders, and they pointed to his apparent lethargy with troop deployment on GETTYSBURG's second and third days.[77]

In response, Longstreet suggested the fault belonged to others, including his recently deceased mentor, ROBERT E. LEE. For this, Longstreet effectively erased his successes from Confederate lore.[78]

In 1848 Longstreet (fourth cousin to the bride) was best man at the wedding of Julia Dent and Ulysses S. Grant.

---

6. JAMES EWELL BROWN "JEB" STUART (C.S., VIRGINIA, 1833–64)

Critics and admirers alike label him cavalier, immature, cocky, reckless. Many dilute his achievements as acts of foolish youth, made possible by blind luck and an initially inferior enemy. Jeb Stuart indeed pushed luck and limits, but his methods were far from haphazard. He worked tirelessly to create and maintain an orderly and industrious staff, removed officers

he deemed ineffective, was skilled in governing artillery, infantry, as well as cavalry, and led forces from two hundred to twenty thousand to victory.[79]

Perhaps Stuart's greatest contributions happened before the great battles: gathering priceless information at minimal cost. Before attacking McClellan during the 1862 Peninsula campaign, Lee asked Stuart to run reconnaissance. To oblige, Stuart and his troops rode completely around McClellan's army, destroyed supplies, and captured soldiers. More important, he revealed just how cautious and stagnant the Army of the Potomac had become. The cost of this productive romp? Stuart lost only one of his one thousand men.[80]

The man called "Beauty" provided an encore before the battle of SECOND MANASSAS. Riding behind enemy lines, Stuart and fifteen hundred men destroyed supply wagons and took three hundred prisoners. They even captured Union commander John Pope's dress coat, personal baggage, and tens of thousands of dollars in gold and greenbacks. The greatest prize was Pope's own dispatch ledger, containing information on the Union army's strength and disposition.[81]

After ANTIETAM, Stuart again circled McClellan and one hundred thousand soldiers. Stuart's party of eighteen hundred left McClellan stunned albeit thirty hostages and twelve hundred horses lighter. Just two of Stuart's troops were missing after a raid of 125 miles.[82]

Hailed as a cavalry genius, the former infantry officer accomplished some of his most valuable work as a director of artillery and footmen. At FREDERICKSBURG, a Federal attack swept forward against THOMAS J. "STONEWALL" JACKSON and the Confederate right flank. Stuart repulsed the advance by unleashing his horse artillery upon the Union's left flank. At CHANCELLORSVILLE, Stuart took over the Second Corps of the wounded Jackson, using infantry and artillery to force Hooker into full retreat.[83]

There are two incidents where Stuart is heavily (and to a degree justly) criticized. In June 1863 near Brandy Station, Virginia, Stuart staged a mock cavalry battle for admiring citizenry. Days later a real battle fell upon him. More than ten thousand mounted bluecoats swarmed down upon Stuart's position. After attacks and counterattacks, with blasting pistols and swinging sabers, the Confederates held the field. Stuart declared it a great victory, where in reality he allowed the enemy deep within his territory and lost forever the image of cavalry superiority. Weeks later, during the Gettysburg campaign, Stuart set off on another encircling raid. He captured or destroyed supplies and wagons, but he also left Lee blind and deaf to the whereabouts of a fast-moving Army of the Potomac. Some historians blame Lee for giving Stuart vague orders. Others criticize Stuart for leaving Lee while behind enemy lines.[84]

In 1864, while the Army of Northern Virginia was fighting for survival at SPOTSYLVANIA, Stuart intercepted Union cavalry a dozen miles from Richmond. As Stuart directed his men on the front lines, a retreating Federal put a bullet in his abdomen. The following day Stuart was dead at age thirty-one of perotonitis. Upon hearing the news, Lee wept repeatedly.

Reflective of his youthful chides, Jeb Stuart nicknamed fellow officer William Hullihen "Honeybun."

---

7. GEORGE H. THOMAS (U.S., VIRGINIA, 1816–70)

The pinnacle of professionalism, George H. Thomas was unshakable, calculating, reserved, loyal to his men and his superiors, and probably the best defensive general on either side. He tolerated nothing but the most professional behavior from himself and others and habitually worked near the front lines. Thrice his troops saved the Union from devastating losses and twice nearly obliterated the Army of Tennessee. Yet, for being Virginia-born and hesitant to attack, he was also a target of suspicion from many in the Union, including ULYSSES S. GRANT.[85]

A veteran of the Seminole Wars and the Mexican War, a West Point instructor in cavalry and artillery, at six feet tall and two hundred pounds, Thomas had the look and reputation of stability. This stability was put to the test at the battle of STONES RIVER, where he was one of three corps commanders under William S. Rosecrans. On the first day Confederates forced portions of the Union line three miles backward. Federal casualties exceeded ten thousand. Union corps and divisions overlapped and melted, but Thomas exuded a calm tenacity, kept soldiers supplied with ammunition, and directed a unified withdrawal to safer ground. That night Rosecrans convened a council of his officers, and several advised withdrawal.

Thomas interjected and insisted: "This army does not retreat." The Army of the Cumberland remained, and two days later were victorious.[86]

Thomas repeated his performance on a much larger scale at the 1863 battle of CHICKAMAUGA, when three Confederate divisions came pouring through a breach in the Federal line. A third of the Union army broke and ran, including its commander, Rosecrans. Thomas, second in command, remained steadfast and managed to keep a majority of the Army of the Cumberland on the field. By Confederate Gen. JAMES LONGSTREET's count, there were twenty-five assaults upon the Union gap, but the Federals reformed and retreated yet did not break. What started as a rout became a withdrawal of cohesion. Known before as Old Tom, Slow Trot, and Pap, Thomas became nationally renowned as the Rock of Chickamauga. Lincoln said of Thomas's performance, "It is doubtful whether his heroism and skill . . . has ever been surpassed in the world."[87]

Thomas's finest moment came days before he was about to be removed from command. After the 1864 battle of FRANKLIN, where JOHN BELL HOOD's Army of Tennessee suffered horrid losses by attacking Union trenches, Hood moved toward the Tennessee capital, where Thomas and sixty thousand Federals were stationed. Hood dug in and waited, hoping Thomas would attack him.

Grant hounded Thomas to strike the weakened Confederates. Telegraph after telegraph threatened Thomas with dismissal if he did not move. The Rock apologized but informed Grant that a lack of horses and two successive ice storms jeopardized any assault. Days turned into weeks, and Grant feared Thomas had become another McClellan.[88]

When the sun came out in mid-December, the Virginian proved he was no Virginia Creeper. Just as Grant planned to go westward to relieve him personally, Thomas sent forth fifty-five thousand men, jabbing Hood's right flank then smashing into his left. In two days, with a supremely organized offensive, Thomas inflicted more than six thousand casualties (twice as many as he received) and pushed Hood out of Tennessee. The once great Confederate army of the west had fought its last major battle.[89]

In 1831 Nat Turner's Rebellion ravaged Southampton County, Virginia. The largest slave revolt in U.S. history killed more than sixty whites in two days. Some of the residents managed to escape in time, including fifteen-year-old George H. Thomas.

---

8. PHILIP H. SHERIDAN (U.S., NEW YORK, 1831–88)

 His detractors claimed his star only rose when the Confederacy was at its weakest. His admirers looked beyond his violent and destructive tendencies. With all his faults and advantages, Philip H. Sheridan possessed WILLIAM TECUMSEH SHERMAN's organizational efficiency, ULYSSES S. GRANT's willingness to attack armies, and GEORGE H. THOMAS's wisdom not to waste lives.[90]

At five foot five inches and 115 pounds, with stout legs, tight black hair, and eyes set in a permanent scowl, the West Pointer had the physique and look of kinetic intensity. Shy as a youngster, he grew into a nervous, judgmental, sometimes vicious adult who rarely offered any measure of forgiveness. In milder terms, Sheridan was a shrewd perfectionist. He began the war as a quartermaster and commissary officer. Precise and efficient, he was also very much a soldier's soldier. He worked relentlessly to provide enlisted men with the best weapons and rations available. A Sheridan trademark, he never shied away from a fight with fellow officers, even his superiors, if he thought they were neglecting their men.[91]

Achieving a field command in May 1862, Sheridan revealed a dichotomous nature. He became calm when people panicked and furious when others were complacent. On the first day of STONES RIVER, Confederate attacks sent two Federal divisions flying rearward. Sheridan's division resisted the onslaught. He lost all three of his brigade commanders and 40 percent of his men, the worst losses he would ever experience in the war. Yet his steady and belligerent withdrawal helped Union lines reform and eventually launch a successful counteroffensive.[92]

In contrast, his greatest victory and purest display of temper may have been at the October 1864 battle of Cedar Creek. Impressed by the proficient and ferocious Sheridan, Grant gave him command of the Army of the Potomac's cavalry and the responsibility of conquering the Shenandoah. The young Sheridan set in motion a scorched-earth policy, killing or confiscating livestock, burning grain, destroying barns. He even struck at the farmsteads of pacifist Quakers and Dunkers, reasoning that anything left could potentially benefit the enemy. While Sheridan was returning from a conference in Washington, some eighteen thousand Confederates under Jubal Early attacked and routed Sheridan's thirty thousand.

Sheridan arrived on the field to see his men dejected and resigned. Exploding into fury, swearing at the top of his lungs, he rode through his troops and fashioned a spirited counterattack. In an afternoon Sheridan's men recaptured all the ground they had lost and took most of Early's artillery, wagons, ambulances, and ammunition.[93]

Up to that point the Shenandoah had been where Union military careers, and thousands of Federal troops, had gone to die. In 1862 NATHANIEL BANKS, JOHN C. FRÉMONT, and Irvin McDowell failed to take it. In early 1864 Franz Sigel and David Hunter also faltered. Then, after months of ruthless destruction and a moment that became known as Sheridan's Ride, the Valley was effectively in Union hands for good.

Sheridan would go on to lead his horse soldiers in the pursuit and capture of the Army of Northern Virginia near Appomattox Court House.

Among the Union officers who personally witnessed Sheridan's Ride were future presidents Maj. William McKinley and Col. Rutherford B. Hayes.

---

9. PATRICK CLEBURNE (C.S., IRELAND, 1828–64)

Brave, beloved by his soldiers, and one of two men of foreign birth to rise to major general in the South, Patrick Cleburne remains a sentimental favorite among Civil War historians—and for good reason. He evolved from a complete incompetent to the most adept, farsighted, and fierce division leader of the Confederacy.[94]

As a youth in his native Ireland, the serious and reserved fellow showed little promise. Academics were not his strong point, the sciences especially. He served briefly in the British army with no distinction. He then immigrated to the United States in 1849 and joined the Confederate army when his adopted Arkansas seceded.

Leading a brigade at SHILOH, Cleburne's own performance was deplorable. Starting with twenty-seven hundred men, he ordered a series of attacks that made no impact upon strong defenses. The second day he was down to eight hundred, and he again attempted a reckless charge. By battle's end, all but fifty-eight of his men were captured, wounded, missing, or dead.[95]

Rather than blame his superiors, he reassessed everything he knew about warfare. Coordinating with his junior officers, he paid greater attention to organization and supply prior to a campaign. Before battle, he used sharpshooters to probe and reduce enemy positions. If an attack was ordered, he advanced using the protection of terrain and concentrated his firepower rather than simply launch a massed charge.[96]

Cleburne's revised methods brought success to BRAXTON BRAGG's otherwise dismal 1862 campaign into Kentucky. In a fight for Richmond, Kentucky, Cleburne's men captured hundreds of Federals. At Perryville, Cleburne again pushed into enemy lines with success, until Bragg ordered a retreat. As mule- and horse-drawn wagons struggled over the hilly escape route, Bragg ordered the wagons and twenty thousand rifles therein destroyed. Cleburne instead ordered teams of men to carry the load up the steep inclines. He and his men escaped with the cache intact.[97]

In the New Year's fight at STONES RIVER, Cleburne's division was the most successful in pushing back the Union line, only to be pulled back when attacks failed on other sections of the front. When Sherman's blue wave swept Bragg from Chattanooga in late 1863, it was Cleburne and his division who held on, refusing to budge from the north edge of Missionary Ridge. To clear this last obstacle, the Federals concentrated their forces upon him, and still Cleburne's outnumbered and outgunned men did not give way. Only when he learned of the demise of the rest of Bragg's army did Cleburne order a withdrawal, and while doing so fought vicious rear-guard actions against Federals three times his numbers.[98]

Hating the pomp and elitism often accompanying his grade, Cleburne was an odd mixture of practicality and ice-cold bravery. During standoffs in battle, he'd personally roam into no man's land to retrieve discarded weapons. In hopes of securing British and French diplomatic recognition and to strengthen the depleted army, he was the first Confederate general to propose liberating and arming slaves. Dubbed the Stonewall of the West, he received a fine compliment from a man normally averse to showering praise; ROBERT E. LEE called him "a meteor shining from a clouded sky."[99]

Able to succeed in spite of serving under the likes of Bragg and LEONIDAS POLK, the quiet but driven man from Ireland did not live to see the end of the war. Cleburne was one of six Confederate generals to die at the slaughterhouse of Franklin. He was within fifty yards of the Union lines when he was shot through the chest.[100]

At the battle of Richmond, Kentucky, a minié ball hit Cleburne in the side of the face, smashed two teeth, and exited past his lips. In a rare show of humor, he later joshed that he caught the Union bullet in his mouth and spat it right back.

---

10. NATHAN BEDFORD FORREST (C.S., TENNESSEE, 1821–77)

With no military experience and six months of formal education, this Tennessee plantation owner fused a talent for leadership with a penchant for violence and rose from a private to lieutenant general. Arch nemesis WILLIAM TECUMSEH SHERMAN called him "the most remarkable man our Civil War produced on either side."

Nathan Bedford Forrest was almost forty years old when he joined the Seventh Tennessee. Standing six feet two inches tall, the driven and imposing Forrest became impatient with lesser men. To rectify the situation he raised and equipped a mounted battalion with his own money. The battalion fittingly elected him their commanding officer.[101]

Ineloquent, barely literate, his lack of education embarrassed and frustrated him, yet it may have been one of his greatest strengths. Understanding only the basics of military tactics, he in turn communicated them in their most basic terms. As a result, his men knew quickly and exactly what to do. Common phrases included, "Get there first with the most" (attain the high ground with superior forces), "Bulge 'em" (conduct feinting attacks), "hit 'em on the end" (attack the enemy flank), or "mix with 'em" (establish close quarters and eliminate artillery opportunity).

A battle near Guntown, Mississippi, exemplified his tenets on combat. Learning that eight thousand Federals (including three thousand cavalry and eighteen guns) were coming from Memphis to subdue him and his thirty-five hundred men, Forrest assessed the situation. The area near Brice's Crossroads was heavily wooded, which could hide his inferior numbers. He could use feints to hold the advance column of Federal cavalry until his entire force moved into place. For the Union infantry to arrive in time, they would have to march quickly through narrow, muddy roads on a brutally hot and muggy day. The Northern boys would become exhausted, strung out, and therefore susceptible to flank attacks. With the enemy so deep in his territory, Forrest could follow up any success with unmerciful pursuit.

The engagement transpired almost precisely as he predicted. Forrest's men bagged all but two Federal cannon, nearly every wagon, plus food, weapons, horses, and more than sixteen hundred prisoners.[102]

In contrast, his most infamous act is undoubtedly the butchery at Fort Pillow, Tennessee. On April 12, 1864, Forrest and his men surrounded a Federal garrison stationed on the Mississippi near Memphis. After a short battle, the fort surrendered. Angered by the presence of three hundred African American soldiers among the garrison of nearly six hundred, the victorious Confederates began to kill prisoners, including the wounded. More than two hundred Federals perished plus another one hundred were seriously wounded. Forrest lost just fourteen killed. Excused by the Confederate government as a natural result of battle, and condemned in the Union as a massacre, evidence suggests the latter. Although not ordering the killing, Forrest expressed no remorse for the incident.[103]

Ingenious in limited operations, Forrest's tangible contribution to the Confederate effort was relatively small. A common observation about this otherwise brilliant tactician was that he played a large part in small battles and a small part in large battles.

In April and May 1863 Forrest pursued a long-range Union raid into Alabama led by Col. Abel D. Streight. On May 3 he cornered his prey, roughly fifteen hundred Federals, with only six hundred men. To mask his inferior numbers from Streight, Forrest shifted a single gun in and out of sight several times while negotiating surrender terms for the Federals. After capitulating and discovering the ruse, Streight protested. Forrest replied, "Ah, Colonel, all's fair in love and war."

TOP TEN WORST
COMMANDING GENERALS

Compared to other military conflicts, the American Civil War was not unique or particularly outstanding in its display of inept military leadership. If anything, the war's duration of four long years provided time for corrective measures. A number of underachieving generals resigned of their own accord while others progressed from mediocrity to varying degrees of competence. To monitor poor performers, Confederate officials created a Bureau of the War while the Federals constructed the sometimes helpful, sometimes libelous Committee on the Conduct of the War. Wounds, disease, and accidents pruned several more bad generals, but there remained a wide array of individuals worthy of harsh criticism.[104]

Perhaps hundreds of generals were less competent than the ten listed here. These ten, however, lost more ground, created more problems, squandered more time, and achieved fewer gains with more men than any other commanding officers in the war. Some failed through recklessness, others by receding. Some communicated too little while others said far too much. A few spent all of their time preparing while others prepared not at all. Each man won at least one battle. Not one indicated he knew how to win a war.

1. BRAXTON BRAGG (C.S., NORTH CAROLINA, 1817–76)

 With thatch brows, dark eyes, and thistle beard, Braxton Bragg's countenance was appropriately that of a cornered animal. To his subordinates, he was vindictive, contrary, and deceitful. In combat he committed horrible mistakes repetitiously. He ruled by fear and executed scores of his soldiers for slight infractions. Although few could question his bravery, Bragg often questioned everyone else's, yet he maintained the trust and devotion of a powerful army buddy, Confederate president Jefferson Davis.

The tragic play began in 1862 at SHILOH, where Bragg ordered several small, unsupported bayonet charges into well-defended artillery positions.

When his men were summarily slaughtered, he blamed their immediate officers. For his brazen aggressiveness, Bragg received a promotion.[105]

Later in 1862 Bragg initiated a campaign into Kentucky with no clear objectives. Encountering heavy opposition at Perryville, he again employed piecemeal attacks and again lost lives with no result, abandoning more than three thousand of his dead and wounded on the field. Bragg's tactics were so inept and baseless, fellow officer Henry Heth feared Bragg had "lost his mind."[106]

In overall command at STONES RIVER, Bragg finally attempted a unified attack—over terrain completely unsuitable for such an undertaking. Several regiments became easy targets as they advanced across open ground. Others had to sift through heavily wooded areas, losing contact with their support flanks. Miraculously, his men achieved early successes, but Bragg followed up with uncoordinated forays upon the best-defended section of the enemy line. Of the eighty-eight Confederate regiments at Stones River, twenty-three of them suffered 40 percent casualties or more. According to Bragg, victory evaded him because his officers displayed neither courage nor cooperation.[107]

His one major victory came at CHICKAMAUGA, due primarily to a well-timed attack by JAMES LONGSTREET. Still, the Federals slipped away when they might have been destroyed in full. For this Bragg again chastised his men. An exasperated Longstreet wrote, "I am convinced that nothing but the hand of God can save us or help us as long as we have our present commander."[108]

His last great fight and greatest failure occurred over the key rail junction of CHATTANOOGA. Bragg held the high ground of Missionary Ridge to the east and towering Lookout Mountain to the southwest, nearly surrounding a half-starved Union garrison trapped in the town below. His positions should have been impregnable. When ULYSSES S. GRANT and heavy Federal support rescued the garrison and routed Bragg, Grant wrote, "The victory of Chattanooga was won against great odds . . . and was accomplished more easily than was expected by reason of Bragg's making several grave mistakes." Once again, Bragg accused his junior officers for the failure.[109]

After Chattanooga, Jefferson Davis recalled Bragg to Richmond—to serve as his chief military adviser.

---

2. GEORGE B. McCLELLAN (U.S., PENNSYLVANIA, 1826–85)

When George B. McClellan took command in the East after the disaster at FIRST MANASSAS (First Bull Run), the Union's future suddenly looked brighter. Second in his class at West Point in 1846, a meritorious fighter in the Mexican War, published author on modern European warfare, and leader of the victorious Ohio volunteers in western Virginia, McClellan reorganized a ragged mob into the disciplined and confident Army of the Potomac. A brilliant organizer, McClellan was also narcissistic, uncooperative, racist, delusional, and openly hostile toward his superiors. The press dubbed him the Young Napoleon.

Perhaps the newspapers should have specified which Napoleon. During his first eight months at the head of the largest and best-equipped army on earth, McClellan did not mount a single major offensive. Once in command, he became cautious and borderline paranoid, constantly claiming his army of 110,000 was vastly outnumbered. In the spring of 1862 McClellan estimated there were 200,000 well-armed Rebels between Washington and Richmond. In fact there were fewer than 60,000. In his Peninsula campaign into Virginia, a force of just 13,000 stopped his 60,000 outside of Yorktown. At ANTIETAM, McClellan feared he was outnumbered more than two to one. The opposite was true, confirmed by captured enemy orders he had seen days before.[110]

Among the very worst in the art of communications, he gave vague orders and rarely if ever consulted his officers. Always nearby to receive the accolades of his troops during a grand review, he was conspicuously absent when the firing started. On occasion his lack of leadership was of great benefit. McClellan was safely aboard a gunboat on the James River when his troops threw back ROBERT E. LEE at the battle of Malvern Hill.[111]

An emotional man, McClellan was prone to sending contradictory if not accusatory messages, as was the case during the battle of Gaines's Mill. McClellan telegraphed Lincoln to report an imminent victory only to recant soon after with stories of impending ruin, adding: "If I save this army now, I tell you plainly that I owe no thanks to you or to any other persons in Washington. You have done your best to sacrifice this army."

Fortunately for McClellan, an officer at the War Department deleted this portion of the message.[112]

His worst trait may have been the ferocity with which he fought his allies. He quarreled with cabinet members and repeatedly referred to Lincoln as a baboon, an ape, and the "original gorilla." During the battle of SECOND MANASSAS, McClellan refused to send reinforcements to John Pope's short-lived Army of Virginia. For his uncoordinated and poorly timed attacks at Antietam, he blamed his friend AMBROSE E. BURNSIDE.

Relieved of command in October 1863, McClellan fought Lincoln one more time—as the Democratic nominee during the 1864 presidential election. Fittingly, thousands within the Confederacy viewed McClellan's potential election as their last great hope to win the war.[113]

McClellan's West Point classmates chose him Most Likely to Succeed.

---

3. AMBROSE E. BURNSIDE (U.S., INDIANA, 1824–81)

If Jefferson Davis can be condemned for letting senti-mental favorites remain as generals far too long, Ambrose E. Burnside is proof that Lincoln can be accused of the same.

Quiet, honest, personable, humble to a fault, Burnside drove himself relentlessly, often without sleep, to compensate for a lack of military talent few acknowledged more readily than himself. Yet Burn-side had a remarkable start. In early 1862 he led a series of combined land and naval operations along the North Carolina coast, bagging islands, ships, forts, seaports, railheads, and thousands of Confederates.[114]

After George B. McClellan's costly yet fruitless Peninsula campaign, Lincoln offered the Army of the Potomac to Burnside. Taken aback, the loyal friend of McClellan rejected the offer. Lincoln pocketed the proposal but noted the modest integrity of this different kind of general. After the egocentric John Pope failed at Second Manassas, Lincoln again asked Burnside to take the helm in the eastern theater, and again he refused. When McClellan stalled after the battle of ANTIETAM, Lincoln once more offered command of the Army of the Potomac to Burnside, in spite of the tragedy at BURNSIDE'S BRIDGE. Burnside reluctantly accepted.[115]

It did not take long for Burnside to give credence to his humility. Just weeks after taking command, he orchestrated the disaster at FRED-ERICKSBURG. As was his nature, he accepted full responsibility and tenured his resignation. It was now Lincoln's turn to reject the offer, and Burnside stayed in command. Burnside then took his army on the infamous Mud March, where he attempted to flank Lee by crossing the Rappahannock farther upstream. Just as he began, a rare January downpour, along with trudging feet and turning wheels, churned the dirt roads into a massive trap. Rather than stop, Burnside moved ahead. Wagons sank axle deep, soldiers fell exhausted, cannon were lost, and mules drowned. After three days Burnside finally called it off, and Lincoln transferred him to Ohio.[116]

For all his integrity and confessed limitations, Burnside cannot be reduced to a magnet of poor luck. He habitually gave ambiguous information and instructions, showed minimal attention to supply or discipline, and rarely planned further than his next move. These deficiencies could not have been better illustrated than his 1864 return to command of the Ninth Corps of the Army of the Potomac outside Petersburg, where he watched his scheme of THE CRATER end in bloody confusion.[117]

> Before the war, Burnside walked down the aisle with his Kentucky fiancée, who suddenly changed her mind at the altar and dumped him.

4. LEONIDAS POLK (C.S., NORTH CAROLINA, 1806–64)

One of three clergymen to become a Confederate general, tall, elegant Leonidas Polk had a battle résumé that read like a hit parade of Confederate failures: Kentucky, SHILOH, STONES RIVER, Atlanta.

Before the war he had befriended cadet Jefferson Davis at West Point, but he resigned from the army after graduation to join the ministry. Over a span of thirty-four years Polk became Episcopal bishop of Louisiana, attained a sprawling plantation and four hundred slaves, and served not a single day in the armed forces. When the war broke out, his old friend Davis made him a major general.[118]

For Davis and his cause, Polk created a string of disasters, primarily because of his persistent unwillingness to follow orders. First was his 1861 blunder at Columbus, Kentucky, followed in 1862 with BRAXTON BRAGG's invasion of the Bluegrass State, where Polk again played the shortsighted maverick. Under orders to attack the right flank of Don Carlos Buell outside of Perryville while Edmund Kirby Smith was to hit Buell's front, Polk decided it was too dangerous and retreated to safer ground. He neglected to inform his associates of this last-minute withdrawal, condemning Smith's men to defeat.

In the bloodbaths of SHILOH, STONES RIVER, and CHICKAMAUGA, Polk continued old habits: conducting independent actions without conferring with fellow officers, issuing nebulous orders, showing no talent for offensive or defensive tactics, and sporting none of the intelligence that friends assumed this tall, ivory-haired preacher possessed.

The incompetence ended outside Atlanta in June 1864. Gens. JOSEPH E. JOHNSTON, William Hardee, and Polk scaled a hill to observe enemy operations north of the city. Two incoming Federal artillery shells encouraged the party to take leave of their vantage, but when Polk turned back for a last look, a cannonball slammed through his chest, killing him instantly.[119]

Polk was apparently more proficient as a minister than as a general. During the war, he baptized Gens. Joseph E. Johnston and John Bell Hood, and performed the ceremony at John Hunt Morgan's wedding.

---

5. EARL VAN DORN (C.S., MISSISSIPPI, 1820–63)

Earl Van Dorn commanded Confederate forces in two pivotal battles in the West. He lost them both—badly.

Graduating from the U.S. Military Academy near the bottom of the Class of 1842, Van Dorn became a favorite of fellow Mississippian Jefferson Davis when they served together during the war with Mexico. His gentle face topped with thick, curly locks gave Van Dorn a somewhat effeminate appearance, yet in his service on the American frontier, the Second Seminole War, and the Mexican War, he displayed an almost psychotic affinity for combat.[120]

Given the rank of major general in 1861, he took command of the enormous Confederate Trans-Mississippi District. With bravado as mammoth as his jurisdiction, he pledged to push north, take St. Louis, and bring Border State Missouri into the Confederacy. In the ensuing March 7–8, 1862, battle of PEA RIDGE, Van Dorn's seventeen thousand troops easily outnumbered Samuel Curtis's eleven thousand Federals, but the cavalier Van Dorn was not prepared. He had long ignored the physical needs of his men, and he was about to pay a heavy price. Trudging through the mud and snow, his men were short on warm clothes and rations. Deprived of weapons and sufficient ammunition, hundreds of his soldiers went into battle armed with squirrel rifles and shotguns. Many in his three brigades of Native Americans opted for more dependable bows and hatchets. Cold, hungry, outgunned, his troops were easily routed in what historian James McPherson called "the most one-sided victory won by an outnumbered Union army during the war."[121]

In October 1862 Van Dorn attempted to redeem his Pea Ridge failure with an assault upon the rail junction at Corinth, Mississippi. Combining his ten thousand men with Sterling Price's eleven thousand, the Confederates brought equal numbers against the Union side. The Federals, however, were dug in well, supported by backup trench works and considerable reserves. For two days Van Dorn smashed away at the Union center. A few of his troops broke through only to be wiped out by the hundreds of bluecoats waiting in the inner network of embankments.[122]

Broken militarily and by some accounts mentally, Van Dorn disengaged, only to double back with the intent of attacking Corinth again. Demoralized and depleted (one brigade lost 1,295 of 1,895 soldiers), his junior officers talked him out of it. The Confederate army never again mounted a major offensive in Mississippi.[123]

He later served with greater ability as a cavalry commander, but his legacy cost the Confederacy dearly. Other generals lost cities, supply depots, hilltops. Van Dorn lost most of Missouri and Mississippi in the first two years of the war.

Earl Van Dorn met an untimely end when an outraged husband, Dr. George Peters, entered the general's headquarters at Spring Hill, Tennessee, and murdered him. Allegedly, Van Dorn had assailed one breastworks too many.

---

6. JOHN C. FRÉMONT (U.S., GEORGIA, 1813–90)

 Famed as the Pathfinder for his explorations through the Rockies, former governor and senator of California and first presidential candidate for the Republican Party, youthful, self-assured, charismatic John Charles Frémont was one of the most famous American public figures in 1861.

His credentials landed him command of the enormous Union Department of the West, which was basically Illinois and everything west of the Mississippi. Unfortunately for the Union, Frémont proved to be one of the most cocky, undisciplined, witless generals in blue, incapable of controlling himself or his territory. From his headquarters in St. Louis, Frémont surrounded himself with a staff of swinish lackeys, handed out lucrative government weapon and ordnance contracts like shark bait, and neglected to define how or if he was going to create stability among a bitterly divided populace. A devastating Union loss at WILSON'S CREEK in southwest Missouri, followed by escalating guerrilla activity in the state's western counties, inspired Frémont to panic.

On August 30, 1861, Frémont declared martial law in Missouri, threatened to execute captured guerrillas, and vowed to emancipate the slaves of those sympathetic to the enemy. In one motion he managed to outrage loyal Missourians, the Confederate military, and the four slave states not yet lost to secession, all without a single military success to make such a proclamation credible.

Lincoln, ever the calculating moderate, deftly suggested Frémont revise his statement. In response, Frémont sent his wife, Jessie, to Washington to inform the president how inappropriate it was for Lincoln to muzzle her intellectually superior husband. Lincoln in turn exercised superior authority and transferred Frémont to the Shenandoah Valley.

Lincoln's reassignment of the brash Frémont helped placate the Union faithful within the Border States and ended talk of retaliatory executions of Federal soldiers, but it also gave Frémont another chance to embarrass the president. The Pathfinder could not find his courage in the Valley, proving lethargic, timid, unorganized, and an easy target for THOMAS J. "STONEWALL" JACKSON at the battle of Cross Keys.[124]

After his defeat in the Shenandoah, Frémont was reassigned as a corps commander under the lower-ranked John Pope. Rather than acquiesce, Frémont resigned and spent the remainder of his fruitless war awaiting reassignment.[125]

While stationed in St. Louis, John C. Frémont maintained a force of 150 bodyguards.

---

7. NATHANIEL P. BANKS (U.S., MASSACHUSETTS, 1816–94)

Born among the spinning mills of Massachusetts and working in them as a child, Nathaniel Prentiss Banks became the quintessential self-made success. He taught himself Latin, Spanish, and classic literature, served in the U.S. Congress, and became president of a railroad. Honest, industrious, a prominent antislavery voice while governor of Massachusetts, he received an appointment as a major general of U.S. Volunteers despite having no military experience whatsoever.

Fond of the frills and splendor of his rank, Banks had the misfortune of contesting generals of better substance. In May 1862 THOMAS J. "STONEWALL" JACKSON took three days to push Banks completely out of the Shenandoah Valley. Having swiped supplies from him almost routinely in the affair, Jackson's men called Banks "Old Jack's commissary general." Jackson bettered Banks again later that summer, routing the former governor days before SECOND MANASSAS.[126]

Transferred in early 1863 to replace volatile BENJAMIN F. BUTLER in the Department of New Orleans, Banks attempted to absolve his past shortcomings by striking at Port Hudson, Louisiana, and its fortifications along the Mississippi. Three frontal assaults yielded nothing but thousands of casualties. Only when upriver VICKSBURG fell to ULYSSES S. GRANT did Port Hudson surrender.

Finally, there was the spring 1864 Red River campaign, a dismal, fractured foray into northern Louisiana. Lincoln believed it could snare tons of cotton, inspire clandestine Unionists, and demonstrate Federal might in the far West. As with most disasters, things began well. Working in tandem with a fleet of gunboats and ironclads under Adm. David D.

Porter, Banks and fifteen thousand men proceeded north along the river with minimal trouble. Then Banks marched away from the river and his naval support, and Confederates routed his isolated forces in a string of engagements. Banks in fact won several of these battles only to retreat each time. For his efforts, Banks lost eight thousand men, sixty pieces of artillery, and nearly a dozen ships. A subsequent congressional investigation was nearly as unkind to Banks as the Confederates had been. Banks's superior officer Grant casually referred to the incident as "Banks' disaster."[127]

Before the war, Nathaniel Banks, Ambrose E. Burnside, and George B. McClellan worked for the Central Illinois Railroad, a company that also called upon the legal services of an attorney named Abraham Lincoln.

---

8. JOHN BELL HOOD (C.S., KENTUCKY, 1831–79)

As a commander of a brigade or division, the gallant Texas émigré with the hound-dog eyes could count himself among the more able of the Confederacy. As head of an army, his tenure was arguably the worst of the entire war.

Initially, courage alone served Hood well. He led his Texas Brigade to glory in the battles of the SEVEN DAYS, where his men hit and drove the Federals at Gaines's Mill. In vicious combat near the Dunker church at ANTIETAM, his men were the bedrock of the Confederate defenses. At GETTYSBURG he was knocked out early with a severely wounded arm. He then lost a leg at CHICKAMAUGA, again leading his men into the fray.[128]

While his exploits contained elements of astute bravery, they were also seeded with portents of his limitations. Hood was continually inattentive to matters of logistics, supply, and communication. He was also ignorant to the benefits of swift couriers and competent staff, prone to blame others while praising himself, and as it turned out, not a brilliant fighter after all.[129]

Impatient with JOSEPH E. JOHNSTON's strategy of gradual withdrawal in Georgia, Jefferson Davis replaced Johnston with Hood. At the head of the Army of Tennessee, Hood moved to the offensive and lost battles in quick order: Peachtree Creek, Atlanta, Ezra Church, and JONESBORO.

Coming to the conclusion he could not stop the rolling Union army directly, Hood planned to lure them away from Georgia by marching north toward Union states. It did not work. Elated with the progress he was making in Hood's absence, WILLIAM TECUMSEH SHERMAN responded, "If he will go to the Ohio River I'll give him rations."[130]

While Sherman and sixty thousand Federals marched largely uncontested across Georgia, Hood plodded north to horrendous slaughter at FRANKLIN and Nashville. In a month's time Hood managed to turn the second largest army of the Confederacy, more than forty thousand strong, into a decimated and demoralized mob of twelve thousand.[131]

After the bloodbath at Franklin, Hood did the same thing Burnside did after Fredericksburg and Grant did after the Wilderness: He wept uncontrollably.

---

9. BENJAMIN F. BUTLER (U.S., NEW HAMPSHIRE, 1818–93)

Rotund, balding, cross-eyed, gravel-voiced Benjamin F. Butler was a walking contradiction. He favored states' rights, yet in the early days of the war he threatened to arrest the Maryland legislature if it tried to secede. An ardent Democrat, he won the hearts of Radical Republicans for his protection of runaway slaves as "contraband." In the 1850s he was a political champion for women's rights, yet his infamous 1862 Woman's Order directed the women of New Orleans who showed any disrespect to a Union soldier to be treated as prostitutes. He was among the first to employ weapons of the future, such as observation balloons and the Gatling gun, yet he was one of the most backward as a tactician.

Proof of his incompetence emerged at Big Bethel, Virginia, the first land battle of the war. Butler's seven regiments outnumbered the opposition four to one. The odds were leveled when Butler's poorly directed columns fired on each other before the battle, accounting for one-third of the Federal casualties in the defeat.[132]

Recovering his reputation somewhat with successful land and naval operations in North Carolina, Butler was assigned to the captured city of New Orleans. He subdued the hostile population with ruthless measures, including seizure of property, his Woman's Order, and hanging a civilian for removing a Union flag from a Federal building. Butler's harshness and alleged profiteering persuaded Lincoln to relocate him.[133]

After security work in riot-prone New York, the still influential Butler secured a chance to take the Confederate capital in May 1864. Grant ordered Butler to advance on Richmond from the southeast while he occupied Lee's Army of Northern Virginia to the northeast. Landing thirty-three thousand men on a Virginia peninsula called the Bermuda Hundred, Butler planned to take Richmond and its few thousand defenders just fifteen miles distant. But first he set up a base camp and lost ten precious days. A numerical superiority of roughly twelve to one dwindled to even numbers as the Confederates rushed in reinforcements, eventually attacking Butler and pushing him back to his landing site.

There was one last opportunity to redeem himself. Guarding the cape below Wilmington, North Carolina, was Fort Fisher, an L-shaped earth-and-lumber menace hundreds of yards long and host to forty-seven cannon. It was the last stronghold protecting the final open port of the Confederacy. Grant instructed Butler to reduce the fort. Butler figured a boat filled with 215 tons of explosives would do, followed by an amphibious assault. Detonated too far away, the floating bomb left the fort's soft outerworks unharmed. After a weak naval bombardment, Butler sent in landing parties only to withdraw them soon after with light casualties. Later in the war, while defending his actions to a congressional committee, Butler proclaimed that nothing but a prolonged siege could possibly subdue the mighty bastion. During his deposition, news came to the meeting that Fort Fisher had just surrendered to Butler's replacement.[134]

For Butler's iron-fisted occupation of New Orleans in 1862, Jefferson Davis offered a reward for his capture, dead or alive—the same Butler who had nominated Davis for U.S. president fifty-seven times during the 1860 Democratic National Convention.

---

10. JOSEPH E. JOHNSTON (C.S., VIRGINIA, 1807–91)

The man looked like a general: dignified, proud, intelligent, with a presence as clean and smart as his reputation. Joseph E. Johnston also knew how to act like a general, offering nothing but punishment to the cowardly, giving commendations and furloughs to the brave, performing acts

 of indisputable wizardry with organization, morale, maneuvers, and supply. His adversaries, Sherman and Grant in particular, considered him one of the most able generals the South offered. Yet Johnston had one enduring fault: He continually surrendered ground.[135]

In command of Virginia's defenses at the beginning of the Peninsula campaign, the outnumbered Johnston forced the Army of the Potomac to a crawl, preventing any major assaults or flanking maneuvers. GEORGE B. MCCLELLAN and company progressed just fifty miles in two months, but those fifty miles included nearly everything between the York and James Rivers, from the Atlantic Ocean to the gates of Richmond. Only after being wounded in the battle of Seven Pines (a.k.a. Fair Oaks) was Johnston relieved of command and replaced permanently with ROBERT E. LEE.[136]

East of Vicksburg in the late spring of 1863, Johnston regressed again, where his aversion to chance spared his army but allowed the Federals to surround and eventually conquer the citadel on the Mississippi. Sent east to Georgia in 1864 to replace BRAXTON BRAGG after the debacle at Chattanooga, Johnston restored order, rations, morale, and his policy of steady withdrawal. In ten weeks he gave up one hundred miles, backing ever southward, until his opponent came within sight of Atlanta. His exasperated president replaced him with the aggressive JOHN BELL HOOD.

An admiring infantryman in the First Tennessee Volunteers, Sam Watkins boasted, "History does not record a single instance of where one of his lines was ever broken—not a single rout." To accomplish this, Johnston relinquished towns, cities, rail lines, and thousands of square miles, and with them he forever lost the physical and political support they once provided. His reliance on strategic withdrawal might have worked had he a Russian winter or a row of Urals to hide behind or foreign allies to reward his pesky endurance with armed intervention. His promises of mighty counterattacks, however, went unfulfilled, and his stubborn but steady retreats offered little beyond a slow death for a South that could not spare the ground or the time.[137]

In 1891, out of respect for his fallen former enemy, Joseph E. Johnston refused to wear a hat in the bitter cold of William Tecumseh Sherman's funeral procession. In ten days Johnston was dead of pneumonia.

TOP TEN BLOODIEST BATTLES

Compared to other battles in U.S. history, Civil War engagements were exceedingly lethal. The amphibious landing of 110,000 at Iwo Jima cost 5,931 American lives and wounded 17,372 more. Roughly the same numbers and losses were involved at CHICKAMAUGA, but Iwo Jima spanned thirty-six days. Chickamauga lasted thirty-six hours. In Vietnam the ten-day battle for Ap Bia (a.k.a. Hamburger Hill) killed 46 Americans. The Fifth New York Regiment lost almost three times as many men in one hour at Second Manassas.

Most of the worst battles in the Civil War had two factors: large armies and ROBERT E. LEE. Nine of the top ten bloodiest battles involved one hundred thousand soldiers or more, and seven involved Lee.

When considering Civil War combat, it is important to keep in mind that these battles were not precise on-off events. They better resembled a series of bell curves, where foes measured, probed, and parried their way into larger transactions, scaling back when weather, darkness, or the fortunes of war dictated. Although measured in days, much of the carnage happened in short bursts over a few hours and usually in concentrated areas rather than along an entire line.

The following battles have the ten highest counts of combined killed and wounded. Add the casualties of the missing and captured, and the total losses are thousands greater.[138]

1. GETTYSBURG, PENNSYLVANIA
(JULY 1–3, 1863; 33,000 KILLED OR WOUNDED)

The bloodiest battle ever in North America was also among the largest, with a combined number of combatants exceeding 160,000. It was also one of the harshest in terms of percentage. The North endured 21 percent casualties; the South lost 30 percent killed, wounded, missing, or captured—the worst Confederate dispossession of the entire war.

The first day began with a chance encounter of Union cavalry and a Confederate brigade northwest of Gettysburg. As couriers fled back to warn the main forces, advanced units fought for control of the town. By nightfall the Confederates held Gettysburg while the Union held higher ground to the south. Already, hundreds were dead or dying.

Gettysburg was the largest battle of the war, and consequently the three days of fighting are perceived as the most heroic by both sides.

The worst of the second day came when Union Gen. Daniel E. Sickles moved his corps forward (west) in hopes of gaining a better vantage point but creating a conspicuous bulge on the left side of the Union line. Late in the afternoon, Confederate forces launched into him. Once nameless country fields became immortalized as hallowed sites in American history: the Peach Orchard, the Wheatfield, Devil's Den. Portions of ground exchanged hands six times.

The third day brought the catastrophic PICKETT'S CHARGE. Half of the thirteen thousand infantry sent forward against Union forces on Cemetery Ridge did not return.

More than three thousand horses were killed at Gettysburg.

---

2. CHICKAMAUGA, GEORGIA
(SEPTEMBER 19–20, 1863; 28,400 KILLED OR WOUNDED)

East of a meandering creek, a Confederate line ran north and south for four miles. The Southerners were led by stubborn, luckless, and vain

BRAXTON BRAGG, who was fixed on dislodging William S. Rosecrans's Army of the Cumberland from northern Georgia. Tangled in dense woods and heavy thicket, with troops deployed in darkness, each side lost track of regiments and reserves. Dense smoke from batteries and rifle volleys only added to the confusion. Rosecrans attempted to close an imaginary gap in his lines but created a real one nearly a quarter mile wide. Confederate Gen. JAMES LONGSTREET, having recently arrived with reinforcements from the Virginia theater, rammed eleven thousand men through the opening. Union brigades fought fiercely to repulse the infiltration, which simply encouraged the Confederates to commit more men to the effort.[139]

In the end, the Confederates took the field but at the price of 26 percent casualties. Of 66,300 Confederate effectives, more than 2,300 were killed and 14,700 wounded. The Union lost 1,700 killed and almost 10,000 wounded out of 58,200 engaged. Rosecrans suffered almost 20 percent casualties and retreated in haste to Chattanooga, where he was summarily relieved of his duties.[140]

At Chickamauga the tide of battle turned with the timely arrival of Longstreet's corps—temporarily attached to Bragg's army in the fall of 1863.

JOSEPH M. BROWN, *THE MOUNTAIN CAMPAIGNS IN GEORGIA* (1895)

Chickamauga is said to be a Cherokee word meaning "River of Blood."

3. ANTIETAM, MARYLAND
(SEPTEMBER 17, 1862; 23,400 KILLED OR WOUNDED)

Close on the heels of his stunning victory at Second Manassas, Lee marched into Maryland with fifty-one thousand men. In opposition, GEORGE B. McCLELLAN had seventy-five thousand. Unlike their ever-hesitant commander, the boys in blue were aching to end a string of defeats and stalemates, willing to push harder on the enemy than ever before. McClellan's men caught up to Lee's outnumbered force outside Sharpsburg, Maryland, along winding Antietam Creek. The ensuing battle was more like three battles.

North of town, a Union cannon barrage broke through a morning mist, cutting into a forty-acre corn field that hid the Confederate left flank. With waves numbering in the thousands, attacks and counterattacks

Despite Union blundering, victory was at hand—until the arrival of A. P. Hill's division broke the Federal attack.

flooded across the tree-lined fields. When the Confederates fell back, five thousand Federals rushed after them, entering a forested area known as the West Woods. Rebel reinforcements were waiting for them. Nearly half of the Union soldiers who entered the woods were killed or wounded in twenty minutes.

Fighting then shifted to the center of the line, where a Union division stumbled upon twenty-five hundred Confederates sheltered in a sunken farm road. A fight for the position escalated, and reserves from both sides ran into the fray. After three hours, the bluecoats gained a position where they could fire down the length of the road, breaking the Confederate hold. Approximately five thousand men were wounded or killed in a place known afterward as Bloody Lane.[141]

Later that day, on the south end of the line, Union Gen. AMBROSE E. BURNSIDE forced his corps across Antietam Creek at a single, narrow stone trestle later called BURNSIDE'S BRIDGE. Confederate Gen. Robert A. Toombs positioned his understaffed brigade with brilliant dispatch, inflicting horrible, constant, and easy damage upon Burnside's charging regiments. Despite their successes, the Confederates' right flank started to give way under the weight of Union numbers, until A. P. Hill's division arrived at 4 P.M. from recently conquered Harpers Ferry and slammed into the Union left, adding to the horrible totals.[142]

More than five thousand soldiers died at Antietam, making September 17, 1862, the single bloodiest day in U.S. military history.

After the battle, surviving members of the Tenth Georgia counted forty-six new bullet holes in their regimental flag.

---

4. THE WILDERNESS, VIRGINIA
(MAY 5–6, 1864; 22,000 KILLED OR WOUNDED)

ULYSSES S. GRANT, recently named to head the affairs of the eastern theater, chose to begin the 1864 campaign in the early days of May. Starting from their winter encampment near Washington, Grant and the Army of the Potomac headed southwest toward ROBERT E. LEE and his armies near Orange Court House.

Outnumbered, with the opposition approaching, Lee engaged his new nemesis in the thicket called the Wilderness, using the dense brush

The first engagement between Grant and Lee took the Federal commander by surprise. For Lee the surprise was that Grant did not retreat afterward.

and narrow roads to negate Union supremacy in numbers and artillery. The plan worked but not without consequences. Officers and men from both sides quickly became lost. Fellow regiments fired on each other. By necessity, fighting occurred in extremely close proximity. Smoke, forest fires, and broken communication lines added to the terror.[143]

Lee's gamble resulted in one of the most lopsided counts in the war. While the Confederates lost at least 7,750 men, Union casualties amounted to more than 12,100 wounded and 2,246 dead. Grant later wrote, "More desperate fighting has not been witnessed on the continent than that of the 5th and 6th of May."[144]

An estimated eight hundred wounded men burned to death in the battle of the Wilderness, unable to crawl away from advancing brush fires.

5. CHANCELLORSVILLE, VIRGINIA
(MAY 1–4, 1863; 21,700 KILLED OR WOUNDED)

ROBERT E. LEE's counterstrike at Chancellorsville came as a lethal surprise to Joseph Hooker's Army of the Potomac. Outnumbered nearly two to one, Lee defied all logic and split his army of sixty thousand effectives three ways, allowing the battle to engage large portions of both armies simultaneously. Such aggressive tactics can (and in this case did) succeed if the initiative is maintained, which requires exceptionally lethal intensity of engagement. Lee and his army maintained the initiative for four days, defeating "Fighting Joe" Hooker and his Army of the Potomac.[145]

By the time the Union finally withdrew from the field, Hooker had lost 12 percent of his voluminous 110,000-man army. For his greatest tactical achievement, Lee sacrificed 19 percent of his men. The South also lost the irreplaceable corps commander THOMAS J. "STONEWALL" JACKSON, who rode into the darkness of May 2 looking for opportunities to mount a rare night assault. His own pickets mistook him for the enemy, wounding Jackson and killing two of his staff.[146]

The raincoat Stonewall Jackson wore at Chancellorsville is currently on display at the Virginia Military Institute Museum in Lexington. Bullet holes are visible on the left sleeve.

At Chancellorsville, Lee defeated an overwhelming force through sheer audacity: dividing his army not once but twice in the face of superior numbers. His victory was not cheap, and some say the South never recovered from the loss of Stonewall Jackson, who was wounded by his own men.

BATTLES AND LEADERS

6. SHILOH, TENNESSEE
(APRIL 6–7, 1862; 19,900 KILLED OR WOUNDED)

Inexperience can take credit for many of the losses at Shiloh. Eight out of ten men on the field had never experienced combat. There were few breastworks or trenches, allowing the two massive armies to come into very close contact before a full battle was evident. Once the fighting began, both sides took wrong turns, shot at their own troops, fumbled with communications, and fought without coordination. The chaos was too much for many green recruits, and thousands from both sides fled in panic.

In hopes of cracking the Union center at the outset, Confederates concentrated eighteen thousand men on a sunken road held by forty-five hundred Union men under Brig. Gen. Benjamin M. Prentiss. Rather than simply contain them, the Rebels launched eleven assaults and a sixty-two-gun barrage into the Union stronghold. All of Prentiss's men were killed, wounded, or captured in what became known as the Hornets' Nest.

A massive counterattack on the second day allowed the Union to take the field. Perhaps most tragic, there were inadequate plans in place on

News of the high casualties at Shiloh stunned the nation. Worse was to come.

LIBRARY OF CONGRESS

either side to care for the wounded. Hundreds died who might have otherwise been saved.

Before Shiloh, the bloodiest battle in the war had been FORT DONELSON (February 12–16, 1862) with forty-six hundred dead and wounded over five days. Shiloh surpassed those numbers in a matter of hours.[147]

Just before the Confederates stormed the Federal encampments, Union Gen. William Tecumseh Sherman sent a note off to U. S. Grant that read: "I do not apprehend anything like an attack on our position."

---

7. STONES RIVER, TENNESSEE
(DECEMBER 31, 1862–JANUARY 2, 1863; 18,450 KILLED OR WOUNDED)

The ground was no place for a battle. Flocks of dense timber divided the fields. Broods of limestone rose from the soil. A passing river ran wide. Hence, options for maneuver were few. Opportunities for getting lost, separated, or trapped were plentiful. William S. Rosecrans's army of forty-one thousand was ready to push BRAXTON BRAGG's Confederate army of thirty-five thousand out of Tennessee. Bragg was ready to return the favor. By December 31, 1862, the melee was on.

Facing off along the banks of a wide and quiet creek, each side planned to ring in the new year with gunfire and victory. The Confederate Army of Tennessee struck first, hitting the right side (west) of the Federal Army of the Cumberland, launching a series of full-scale attacks. Rosecrans rallied his troops, his uniform stained with the blood and brains of a staff officer decapitated by artillery.

It was soon apparent that the right side of the Federal line was starting to bend backward, wheeling as if its left flank were hinged to the river. Bragg immediately resolved to break the hinge, an oak-ringed hill dubbed the Round Forest. Four separate Confederate waves rushed forward. Each one fell in bloody heaps, butchered by fifty Union cannon and thousands of rifles barbing the hilltop.

New Year's Day passed, and neither army moved. On January 2, against the wishes of his junior officers, Bragg sent forty-five hundred troops to take areas east of the river. Within an hour, fifty-eight Federal cannon and a fierce infantry counterattack reduced this number to twenty-eight hundred. Bragg quietly slipped away and left Tennessee to the Federals. The two armies did not fight again for six months.

In terms of numbers, the battle was modest. Chancellorsville involved more than twice the number of effectives, and Fredericksburg nearly three times. In terms of percentage, Stones River is the worst major engagement loss of Federal soldiers for the whole of the war, with more than 22 percent killed or wounded. The Confederates fared even worse, losing an astounding 27 percent. Most of the destruction transpired during the first ten hours.

The affair had cost so much so fast because it possessed a unique nature. For other battles, fighting was often sporadic. On the first day of Stones River, the sides clashed not in a few locations and not for short periods, but along the entire line through every minute of daylight.

On the night before the battle, bands from both sides played various tunes. When they began to play "Home Sweet Home," thousands of voices from both sides joined in.

---

8. FREDERICKSBURG, VIRGINIA
(DECEMBER 13, 1862; 17,900 KILLED OR WOUNDED)

Along the west bank of the Rappahannock, halfway between Washington and Richmond, 200,000 soldiers faced each other on a front that stretched across six miles. Their backs to the river, the Federals held the numerical advantage with 122,000 on hand, but the Confederates held higher ground. The day began with a Federal assault of 50,000 upon the hills and woods to the south. Hours of bitter fighting and artillery duels dissolved the attack, and the battle swung to the north end of the line.

At 1 P.M., Union Gen. AMBROSE E. BURNSIDE committed one of the worst atrocities of the war by ordering tens of thousands of men against an impregnable position at MARYE'S HEIGHTS. Only the early winter nightfall ended the suicidal attacks. December 13, 1862, became the second bloodiest day in U.S. military history, outdone only by a previous battle involving another hideous blunder by Burnside.[148]

The night after the battle, Federals on the front line made protective breastworks by stacking corpses.

LIBRARY OF CONGRESS

Fredericksburg began with a costly river crossing. The situation only worsened.

9. SECOND MANASSAS, VIRGINIA
(AUGUST 29–30, 1862; 17,200 KILLED OR WOUNDED)

Near Manassas Junction in late summer of 1862, John Pope, commander of the Federal Army of Virginia, let his massive ego get the better of him. On August 28 and 29, he falsely interpreted nearby maneuvers of the Army of Northern Virginia as a general retreat. Attacking piecemeal, he sent division after division of his thirty-two-thousand-man force into well-defended Confederate lines numbering more than twenty thousand.[149]

Stinging from defeat and bolstered by the arrival of thirty thousand reinforcements from the Army of the Potomac, Pope continued the attack the following day. What happened next was the largest collective attack of the Civil War.

JAMES LONGSTREET, having arrived the previous day with twenty-eight thousand men, countercharged with nearly his entire force (more than twice the number in PICKETT'S CHARGE at GETTYSBURG), destroying large portions of Pope's command. Only a series of fierce and costly defensive stands prevented a complete rout of Union forces.[150]

The Manassas countryside was twice the scene of routed Federal armies.

In the Civil War, no Union brigade lost a higher proportion than the Indiana-Wisconsin Iron Brigade. Virginia's Stonewall Brigade lost more men than any on either side. At Second Manassas, the two brigades had the misfortune of fighting each other.

10. SPOTSYLVANIA, VIRGINIA
(MAY 7–12, 1864; 16,000 KILLED OR WOUNDED)

Second in the unholy trinity of the May 1864 Eastern campaign (WILDER-NESS, Spotsylvania, COLD HARBOR), Spotsylvania involved the most continuous hand-to-hand fighting of the war.

Anticipating ULYSSES S. GRANT's attempt to wedge into Richmond by way of the crossroads town, ROBERT E. LEE beat him to it with enough time to create extensive trench works along strategic ridges. These included an odd muleshoe-shaped salient at the center of his lines. Union attacks on the Confederate flanks garnered nothing, but when a May 10 assault on this salient netted nearly one thousand prisoners, Grant decided to press the initiative.

On May 12, before dawn, a corps of sixteen thousand men in blue drove the defense works, taking the trenches and even more prisoners. Knowing his army had been split in two, Lee vowed to retake the position. The result was almost twenty hours of continuous combat amid heavy rain showers in an area covering a few acres. The killing churned the mud a deep crimson red. Men struggled to fight on top of piles of dead and wounded. Oak trees in the vicinity toppled over, their trunks gnawed away by bullets. By itself this contest for the Bloody Angle produced five thousand Confederate and seven thousand Union casualties.

After the battle, Union soldiers on burial detail came upon bodies piled four deep. Some had drowned in a mixture of corpses and mud. Several of the dead were so riddled with bullets as to appear "more like piles of jelly than the distinguishable forms of human life."[151]

More Americans died at the Bloody Angle than at Omaha Beach on D-Day in 1944.

Just days after their first encounter at the Wilderness, Lee and Grant clashed again, this time near the tiny crossroads village of Spotsylvania. The worst fighting occurred near a salient that came to be known as the Bloody Angle.

LIBRARY OF CONGRESS

TOP TEN DEADLIEST MILITARY PRISONS

During and after the war, former prisoners and the press circulated stories of torture, deliberate starvation, and wanton acts of murder in enemy prison camps. Over the years there has been much debunking of such emotionally charged testimonials as acts of propaganda or malevolence.

In spite of ongoing blame and excuses, some disturbing arithmetic prevails. A Civil War soldier marching into battle stood a one-in-thirty chance of dying. If he stepped into one of the 150 stockades, warehouses, or forts serving as prison camps during the war, his odds fell to one in seven. More than fifty-seven thousand soldiers died in prison during the war, just shy of all American soldiers lost from all causes in Vietnam.

Carelessness, rather than conspiracy, appears to be the seed of such ruination. Neither side was prepared nor apparently very motivated to care for the hordes of captured foes, the totals of which are phenomenal. More than 211,000 Union and 265,000 Confederate servicemen were captured, or about one out of every eight men who served. Many were spared prison time, that is, until the BREAKDOWN OF THE PRISONER EXCHANGE in 1863. Afterward, prisoner fatalities skyrocketed for want of services.

Many starved to death. Most died from disease, primarily typhoid, smallpox, dysentery, and diarrhea. Acts of torture occurred as did remarkable moments of kindness. Some camps allowed enemy officers short furloughs, while others forbade shoeless men to possess as much as a blanket in the dead of winter.[152]

Listed here are the ten deadliest military prisons, based on very conservative numbers of prisoner fatalities at each institution.[153]

1. ANDERSONVILLE (C.S.)

LOCATION:	ANDERSONVILLE, GEORGIA
CAPACITY:	10,000
PEAK:	33,000
DEATHS:	12,919

To this day, historians struggle to explain the horror of Andersonville. The name itself stands above all others as the most infamous of Civil War military prisons. Opened in February 1864, it was built to relieve the Richmond area of the drain of resources involved in housing thousands of

LIBRARY OF CONGRESS

Andersonville's indescribable squalor epitomized the worst of the prison camps.

Union captives. Regrettably, the remote location in central Georgia was poorly suited to hold so many men. Despite a severe shortage of resources, Andersonville became the fifth-largest population center in the Confederacy, occupying an area of less than twenty-seven acres.[154]

An open stockade surrounded by high timber walls, the place was officially known as Camp Sumter. No shelter was provided for the captives. Some prisoners managed to build crude huts out of scrap wood. Most used old tents, fashioned lean-tos, or clawed holes into the ground for protection from the sweltering sun and driving rains. A slow-running stream called Sweet Water Creek ran through the middle of camp and served as sewer, latrine, and water source.[155]

The inmates, all enlisted men, received meager rations. By August 1864 it was common for a day to pass without food. Guards often suffered the same fate, as did several Confederate armies elsewhere. Prisoner rations declined to mere tablespoons of grain or meat, often contaminated enough to permanently damage digestive systems. Grown men shrank to less than eighty pounds. Those who did not succumb to diarrhea, dysentery, gangrene, pneumonia, scurvy, suicide, or sunstroke were harassed by a large gang of camp "raiders" who worked together to harass, rob, and murder fellow inmates.[156]

After the war, many Northerners argued that for Andersonville alone, the South should suffer a vengeful reconstruction.

There is one lone U.S. National Park serving as a memorial to all American POWs in history: Andersonville.

2. CAMP DOUGLAS (U.S.)

LOCATION:	SOUTH CHICAGO, ILLINOIS
CAPACITY:	6,000
PEAK:	12,000
DEATHS:	4,454

Federal victories at FORTS HENRY AND DONELSON in 1862 brought with them a burden of thousands of prisoners. In haste, officials at the Camp Douglas military training facility walled off an area to contain the influx.[157]

Initially, the prison of enclosed barracks functioned under capacity, and captives received adequate amounts of food and clothing. After Union forces captured thousands more Confederates at SHILOH and Island No. 10 in the spring of 1862, the facilities at Camp Douglas turned abysmal. Built in a low-lying area, the camp flooded easily, even after light rainfalls. Open latrines had no place to drain, creating a vast compound of deep filth and nauseating stench. During an inspection of the quarters in 1862, members of the U.S. Sanitary Commission were so repulsed by the conditions, they demanded the prison section of Camp Douglas be abandoned altogether. Camp officials dismissed the report.[158]

The winter of 1862–63 brought several weeks of subzero temperatures. Many of the barracks, some filled to twice their capacity, had no heat source. Roofs and walls were wrought with gaping holes. Some prisoners had no blankets or coats. With a prevalence of exposure, pneumonia, and typhoid, the death rate surpassed 10 percent a month, the highest of any camp in the war—including Andersonville.

Despite the death toll, the prison continued to operate with some engineering improvements into the summer of 1865.[159]

The Confederate dead of Camp Douglas are buried in at least five different places in Chicago. Not all burial sites are known, and it is believed some graves have undergone real estate development.

3. POINT LOOKOUT (U.S.)

LOCATION:	POINT LOOKOUT, MARYLAND
CAPACITY:	10,000
PEAK:	22,000
DEATHS:	3,584

Point Lookout is a sandy flat peninsula jutting between the Potomac River and Chesapeake Bay. During the Civil War it was home to Camp Hoffman, a Federal military installation. Within its south walls sat a vast field of ragged tents, each filled far beyond its capacity with captive Confederates.

In response to the horrid conditions of Confederate prisons, Secretary of War Edwin M. Stanton forbade the construction of barracks at Point Lookout and elsewhere. He also permitted the reduction of prisoner rations. What made Point Lookout particularly inhuman was its succession of cruel commandants who enforced Stanton's mandates with impunity and further reduced distribution of firewood and blankets.[160]

Prisoners did have occasional access to the sea front, allowing them to scrounge for clams, dead birds, fish, oysters, and wharf rats and to bathe. As much as the surrounding waters provided life, they also brought misery. Winter storms flooded the camp. Exposure and waterborne diseases killed hundreds a month. Wells within the stockade were thick with iron and salt, and everyone who drank from them became ill. The bay and the river acted as one vast moat, making escape nearly impossible.[161]

Opened in 1863, Point Lookout was supposed to be a temporary holding station, a stopover for prisoners bound for other camps. Instead, it became the largest Union prison in the war, holding at one time more than twenty-two thousand inmates.[162]

The first POWs to arrive at Point Lookout were captives from Gettysburg.

---

4. SALISBURY (C.S.)

LOCATION:	SALISBURY, NORTH CAROLINA
CAPACITY:	2,000
PEAK:	10,000
DEATHS:	3,479

A textile plant before the war, the sixteen-acre heavily wooded Salisbury Camp opened in 1861 and was initially hospitable. Its first six hundred inmates were housed in a large four-story factory building and in smaller tenements. There were adequate provisions, lenient commandants, and occasional games of the new sport of baseball.[163]

By October 1864 five thousand new prisoners arrived, followed soon by thousands more, crammed into a camp designed for two thousand. Among the more than ten thousand prisoners were Confederate convicts. In this volatile mix, gang fights and murders were common.[164]

Food, space, clothing, and water shortages quickly became chronic. By winter 1864 wells became contaminated, and a typhoid epidemic erupted. At one point nearly eighty men died every twenty-four hours. Piles of bodies were thrown into open burial pits. Clothes of the dead were given to the living. Men burrowed into the ground for shelter. Shoeless guards as young as twelve years old were nearly incapable of maintaining order, consequently giving rise to the number and frequency of prisoners murdering prisoners.[165]

Salisbury Prison had only one inmate die in its first two years of operation.

---

5. ELMIRA (U.S.)

LOCATION:	ELMIRA, NEW YORK
CAPACITY:	5,000
PEAK:	9,400
DEATHS:	2,993

Elmira Prison was, like Camp Douglas and Camp Hoffman, a military training camp converted into a stockade. Situated close to the Pennsylvania border and opened in July 1864, "Hellmira" was eight acres enclosed by twelve-foot-high fences. On the south side of the enclosure was a one-acre lagoon used as a latrine and sewer. Thirty-five single-story barracks were designed to hold ninety men each, but camp and government officials determined the barracks could accommodate twice as many.[166]

Most of the prisoners came from overcrowded Point Lookout. Thousands arrived sick and emaciated, with ragged clothes and no blankets. Barracks, including a few new ones constructed with prisoner labor, offered minimal protection from the elements. Tents were issued to address overcrowding, but even those were too few. Hundreds of prisoners lived continually in the open. In response to Southern prison conditions, Washington occasionally reduced rations to bread and water, creating a drastic rise in scurvy cases. The men began using dead rats as currency. Unsanitary conditions and poor medical treatment caused outbreaks of dysentery followed soon by eruptions of pneumonia and smallpox. With poor water, reduced rations, overcrowding, and rampant illness, Confederate prisoners began to die at a rate of ten a day.[167]

In 1865 the nearby Chemung River ran its banks. The St. Patrick's Day Flood left as much as four feet of icy water in the barracks. Mud, refuse, and feces infiltrated everything, illnesses spread like wildfire, and March became the deadliest month in the camp's year of service. In thirty-one days, 491 inmates died.[168]

> Elmira had two observation towers constructed for onlookers. Citizens paid fifteen cents to gander at the inmates. Concession stands by the towers sold peanuts, cakes, and lemonade, while the men inside starved.

6. FLORENCE (C.S.)

LOCATION:	FLORENCE, SOUTH CAROLINA
CAPACITY:	UNKNOWN
PEAK:	15,000
DEATHS:	2,973

In the autumn of 1864 thousands of inmates at Andersonville and elsewhere were informed they were paroled. All that was left was a long trip northward under heavy guard for an official exchange. In reality, Confederate officials were simply transferring these prisoners to a new stockade near Florence, South Carolina.

The disappointment was so extreme, and the conditions at Florence so decrepit, a great many POWs suffered mental breakdowns. Men experienced complete memory loss. Some spoke in babble or became mute. A few men dug holes, crawled in, and attempted to bury themselves.[169]

Veterans of Andersonville considered Florence worse. Both camps were open-air stockades, surrounded by walls of raw timber, with a small creek running through, and no permanent shelter. Food, clothing, and space, however, were even scarcer at Florence. Up to twelve thousand men occupied less than twenty-four acres, six acres of it unusable marshland. Often the only food was coarse flour, which men mixed with the creek water to eat as a mush. During some periods, men died at a rate of two per hour, and the dead were often left inside for days until new burial trenches could be dug. Dysentery and scurvy were most common. To promote "order," guards occasionally shot prisoners.[170]

The sixth deadliest Civil War prison, Florence was in operation for just eighteen weeks.

7. FORT DELAWARE (U.S.)

LOCATION:	PEA PATCH ISLAND, DELAWARE
CAPACITY:	10,000
PEAK:	12,600
DEATHS:	2,460

Several Union prisons were labeled "Andersonville of the North." Fort Delaware arguably deserves the comparison. Situated on an island of seventy acres, capped by a granite pentagonal fort with thirty-foot-thick thirty-five-feet-high walls, and surrounded by dilapidated barracks, the coastal-bastion-turned-penal-colony received its first hundred prisoners in July 1861. Two years later, the inrush of captures at GETTYSBURG swelled the inmate count beyond twelve thousand. Hundreds of men who survived Devil's Den and Pickett's Charge died here.

Shelters were little more than shacks of rough pine board. Flies, mosquitoes, rats, and lice thrived in summer. Storms beat the island in winter. Prisoners were allowed to possess a coat or a blanket but not both. Many frigid mornings found men dead of exposure inside their barracks.[171]

Along with dismal rations, wet sandy ground, and wretched overcrowding, Fort Delaware's cruelties began to include torture, fostered by Albin Francisco Schoepf, the camp commandant from the summer of 1863 to the war's end. With his permission, prison guards employed gagging, hanging by thumbs, clubbing, random shootings, and other transgressions bordering on torture.[172] As many as thirty thousand Confederates were confined here throughout the war.

Among the inmates were nearly three thousand political prisoners, including Jefferson Davis's private secretary Burton Harrison.

8. CAMP CHASE (U.S.)

LOCATION:	COLUMBUS, OHIO
CAPACITY:	4,000
PEAK:	9,400
DEATHS:	2,260

Camp Chase was actually three sections, the first covering an acre, the second and third covering five acres each, with the entire complex surrounded by sixteen-foot double walls. When the camp first opened in 1862, prisoners enjoyed a degree of freedom.[173]

Officers and political prisoners could travel into Columbus, provided they signed an oath to not escape. In turn, townspeople toured the camp for a small fee. As the war worsened and tolerance for the Rebel presence waned, officers and political prisoners were transferred to another camp, and harsh discipline became the norm for those who remained. Guards strictly enforced order and often shot prisoners for minor infractions.[174]

As with so many of the worst prisons, Chase eventually suffered from overcrowding and poor drainage as well as food shortages and standing pools of feces. Prison barracks were small and shabby. Snow and rain seeped through roofs and floorboards. The autumn months of 1864 were the deadliest for inmates and guards; hundreds died from smallpox.[175]

The camp was named in honor of Lincoln's secretary of the treasury, Salmon P. Chase.

---

9. ROCK ISLAND (U.S.)

LOCATION:	ROCK ISLAND, ILLINOIS
CAPACITY:	10,000
PEAK:	8,600
DEATHS:	1,960

In the Mississippi River, barely three miles by one-half mile, rests aptly named Rock Island. In 1862 the U.S. government established an arsenal there and soon after created a small enclosure of prison barracks on the island's north side.

In early December 1863 the first Confederate prisoners arrived, mostly captives from Lookout Mountain and Missionary Ridge from the battle of CHATTANOOGA. Weakened by hunger, illness, the cold, dehydration, and the brutal trek from the Georgia border by rail, men began to die right away. The first fatalities were from pneumonia, followed by diarrhea, exposure, and smallpox. Within weeks, the camp population climbed to six thousand, and the temperature fell below zero. Snow, wind, and ice sifted into the temporary barracks. Frostbite became prevalent. Eighty-six men were dead by Christmas. A week later a blizzard hit. There was yet no hospital.[176]

Disease and exposure claimed hundreds of lives each month. Once the weather warmed, the camp's inadequate drainage became nauseatingly apparent. A marsh of excrement began to pool at the stockade's southwest corner. Improvements were made in waste removal—nearly a year after the problem began. In total, around 16 percent of the prisoners perished.[177]

In the epic fiction *Gone with the Wind,* noble hero Ashley Wilkes was a POW at Rock Island.

10. CAMP MORTON (U.S.)

LOCATION:	INDIANAPOLIS, INDIANA
CAPACITY:	2,000
PEAK:	5,000
DEATHS:	1,763

Constructed on the Indiana State Fairgrounds, the five-acre enclosure included five wells, undulating ground, and maple trees. A few large buildings served as quarters but were little more than barns and exhibition halls, with prisoners sleeping in animal stables or on the bare ground.[178]

Despite the efforts of a compassionate first commandant, Col. Richard D. Owen, the prisoners began to suffer from unimaginable overcrowding and open latrines. Rations lacking in vegetables caused a massive outbreak of scurvy. Over time the entire enclosure and all wells became contaminated with human waste. Resulting disease, combined with frigid winters, killed nearly 20 percent of those incarcerated. Hundreds attempted escape with limited success.[179]

After the war former prisoners returned to the site to build a monument dedicated to Colonel Owen.

TOP TEN MILITARY BLUNDERS

Hindsight is twenty-twenty, and in the case of the Civil War, it's armed with a microscope. Enthusiasts, reenactors, and scholars repetitiously dissect the remains of the war, and many cannot help but experiment with the variables. In roundtables, conferences, and print, hypotheses emerge as to what might have been had different decisions prevailed.

Second-guessing is hardest to curb when contemplating the major blunders of the war, when turning points failed to turn, when leaders failed to lead, when the biggest gambles went bust. Criticism, however, must be placed in context. Unlike students of the war, military leaders at the time rarely had accurate information, adequate time, second tries, or liberty from risk.

Excused from this topic are "failures to pursue the enemy," when successful battles were not immediately followed by an aggressive chase (examples include Confederate victories at FIRST MANASSAS and CHICKA-MAUGA, and Union wins at ANTIETAM and GETTYSBURG). Then and now, criticism against reluctant victors may be valid to a certain degree, but more often than not, the victor was as exhausted as the vanquished after heavy combat. Pursuit meant facing furious rear-guard actions and defensive stands. Darkness, terrain, spent resources, and weather often negated the option to track down the defeated. Fresh reserve units, if there were any, were usually too small to take on the enemy's main body, especially across ground strewn with the broken and bloody refuse of a major engagement. Thus any successes of such actions should remain purely in the mist of conjecture.

Still, there were plenty of occasions where plans were beyond poor and execution bordered on the ridiculous. Presented in this list are the ten best examples of the worst military mistakes of the war, ranked by their cost in land, time, and lives lost.

1. BREAKDOWN OF THE PRISONER EXCHANGE (OCTOBER 1863–JANUARY 1865)

A hidden benefit of the war's slow start was the absence of a prisoner glut. By the summer of 1862, however, the gradual escalation of hostilities turned the trickle of military captives into a ground swell. To address the problem, the Federal and Confederate governments negotiated an agreement based on a War of 1812 cartel between Great Britain and the United States. Rather than confine captives, North and South chose to exchange prisoners of war, or failing that, to "parole" them, whereby soldiers were not to return to their units until notified they had been officially exchanged.

The system began to deteriorate during the September 1863 battle of CHICKAMAUGA. Federals discovered Confederate parolees in the battle who had not been exchanged. Prisoner trades halted altogether in late 1863 when the South retaliated against the Union's formation of black regiments. The Confederate Congress and military refused equal treatment of white and black prisoners, going so far as to send former bondsmen back into slavery, subjecting others to hard labor, or executing black captives (done with chilling passion at the 1864 battles of Fort Pillow and THE CRATER).[180]

Neither side made a serious effort to resolve the impasse, viewing the aging war as one of attrition, where resupplying the opposition with exchanged troops was considered counterproductive if not suicidal. What proved to be suicidal was the halting of the exchange. Prisons quickly filled to three times their capacity. Both sides were either unwilling or incapable of providing the medicines, transport, support staff, and rations necessary to service the hundreds of thousands incarcerated. With no outflow, a workable system reached critical mass, and prisoners began to die by the thousands. Not until January 1865 did the Confederacy consent to equal treatment of black and white prisoners, and the parole-exchange system resumed.[181]

During the war, and mostly during the fifteen-month period of the failed exchange, more than fifty-one thousand men died in military prisons. The death toll exceeded the number killed in action at GETTYSBURG, CHICKAMAUGA, ANTIETAM, THE WILDERNESS, CHANCELLORSVILLE, SHILOH, FIRST and SECOND MANASSAS, STONES RIVER, COLD HARBOR, SPOTSYLVANIA, FREDERICKSBURG, PEA RIDGE, and WILSON'S CREEK combined. Moral issues aside, the physical cost of the exchange breakdown weakened both sides for the remainder of the war and for years to follow.

Approximately 470,000 soldiers were captured during the Civil War, which was more than the population of Arkansas at the time.

2. HOOD'S ASSAULT ON SCHOFIELD
(BATTLE OF FRANKLIN, NOVEMBER 30, 1864)

The whole of the battle of Franklin proper lasted just five hours, long enough for Confederate Gen. JOHN BELL HOOD to send the second largest Confederate army to its doom. Compared to PICKETT'S CHARGE, Hood attacked with nearly twice as many men (21,000), using almost no artillery support, covering twice as much open ground (two miles), against better defenses. For this attempt, Hood lost more than thirty battle flags, thirteen generals killed or wounded, and 7,250 men dead, wounded, or missing. By comparison, the Union lost 2,300 dead, wounded, or missing.[182]

It began south of Atlanta as a scheme to halt WILLIAM TECUMSEH SHERMAN's March to the Sea. While Sherman and sixty thousand Federals moved toward Savannah, Hood and thirty-five thousand Confederates headed in the opposite direction, hoping to cut Sherman's supply line and force him to withdraw from Georgia. It worked—partially. Sherman sent thirty thousand men under John M. Schofield to aid GEORGE H. THOMAS's force of equal size stationed at Nashville. When poor timing, execution, and planning allowed Schofield's men to slip past his army at Spring Hill, Tennessee, Hood blamed his men for maintaining the costly caution of their former commander, JOSEPH E. JOHNSTON. Hood concluded an act of discipline was in order.[183]

Hood caught up with Schofield at Franklin, fifteen miles south of Nashville. The Federals had dug in and repaired earlier fortifications along the southern edge of town. Hood's artillery had not yet caught up with the infantry, but this did not deter the Confederate commander. Any assault rested squarely and entirely on his infantry and over open ground. Hood ordered the attack.

Hood's mistake at Franklin cost the Confederacy 25 percent of the Army of Tennessee, but his failure was not over. Two weeks after Franklin, at the battle of Nashville, Thomas and Schofield combined their armies—seventy thousand men—then swept down and decimated the nineteen thousand that remained of Hood's army.[184]

Five Confederate generals died in three days at Gettysburg. Six Confederate generals died in less than four hours at Franklin.

---

3. PILLOW'S CANCELED BREAKTHROUGH
(BATTLE OF FORT DONELSON, FEBRUARY 14–16, 1862)

In early 1862, during a single engagement, the South lost more men to capture than it had in all previous engagements of the war combined, more than all the casualties ROBERT E. LEE would suffer at CHANCELLORS-VILLE, more than three times all the Confederate dead at GETTYSBURG. During the battle, an opportunity to escape capture presented itself, until a Confederate general closed it himself.[185]

In northwest Tennessee, carved into a ridge of hills just north of Dover, stood Fort Donelson, the Confederacy's Gibraltar of the Cumberland River. A dozen miles west, her sister bastion of Fort Henry on the Tennessee River had recently succumbed to a combination of rising waters, gunboats, and ULYSSES S. GRANT. Donelson was next.

To defend the fort, thousands of Confederate soldiers from nearby areas poured in, until 17,500 held Donelson, the town, and three miles of trenches and rifle pits atop the surrounding hills. Last to arrive was a brigade under Gen. John B. Floyd, a man of no military experience beyond a few embarrassing defeats in northwest Virginia. Fortunately for the Union, Floyd was senior officer at the fort. Beneath Floyd was temperamental braggart extraordinaire Gideon J. Pillow, an accomplice in LEONIDAS POLK's invasion of neutral Kentucky. Third in line was Simon Buckner, a marginally capable soldier who in 1854 loaned money to a penniless army buddy named Grant.[186]

As Union artillery, gunboats, and 27,500 troops began to slip around Donelson, Floyd opted to abandon the fort rather than be caught in a siege. He ordered Pillow to lead an escape south along the river the next morning.

Initially, the plan went well. The Confederates crashed through, peeled Grant's right flank away from the Cumberland, and opened an escape route for the entire garrison. Then Pillow did the inexplicable. He stopped his men and ordered them back into the defenses.

History has not conclusively determined why Pillow reversed the breakthrough. Whatever the cause, his subordinates were livid. While Pillow vacillated on the south side, Grant broke through from the north. The Union army was poised to crush the entire area the following morning. Realizing their predicament, Floyd took four of his regiments and escaped by steamship in the night while Pillow and a fellow officer paddled away on a small boat. It was left to Buckner to beg his old friend Grant for mercy. Grant threw friendship aside in his infamous response: "No terms except an unconditional and immediate surrender can be accepted. I propose to move immediately upon your works." Buckner surrendered.[187]

Grant estimated his men captured in excess of 14,600 prisoners. Hundreds of these would-be escapees would later rot and die in the Chicago prison of CAMP DOUGLAS.[188]

The senior officer at Fort Donelson, John B. Floyd, was from 1857 until December 1860 the secretary of war of the United States.

---

4. PICKETT'S CHARGE (BATTLE OF GETTYSBURG, JULY 3, 1863)

Imagine a long femur bone, thick and solid at the ends, thin and breakable at the center. This is how ROBERT E. LEE envisioned the Union line by the third day at GETTYSBURG. The hip joint of Culp's Hill and the knee joint of the Round Tops proved heavily defended on Day 2. On Day 3 Lee believed he could crack the bone at its shank of Cemetery Ridge, first blasting it with some 170 cannon, followed by a strike of massed infantry.

Lee was an aggressive commander, but most of his offensives were calculated, using surprise, cover, speed, and multiple points of attack to maximize his chances. On Day 3 at Gettysburg, Lee had no element of surprise: His artillery barrage signaled where he intended to attack. A planned diversionary assault on the Union right occurred prematurely and failed. Preliminaries aside, Lee sent foot soldiers on a frontal assault across a mile of open ground, most of it within range of enemy artillery and infantry shielded by walls and breastworks.[189]

At 3 P.M. three divisions stepped out of the woods of Seminary Ridge and marched toward eighty cannon and ten thousand Union soldiers. Of thirteen thousand Confederates to go forward, only half returned an hour later. A few hundred reached the Federal lines and were killed or captured soon after. Lee instructed George E. Pickett to brace his division for a possible counterattack. Pickett responded, "General Lee, I have no division now." So obvious and immediate was the failure that Lee begged forgiveness from at least one officer, although perhaps not from the enlisted men as legend has suggested.[190]

Two months after Gettysburg, Lee offered his resignation to Jefferson Davis, which the Confederate president abruptly rejected. Lee went on to lead his weakened Army of Northern Virginia for the remainder of the conflict, but desertion from his ranks increased considerably after Gettysburg, and never again would a major invasion of the North take place.[191]

The name Pickett's Charge is erroneous as James Longstreet was the commanding officer, and the largest of the three divisions in the charge belonged to James J. Pettigrew, not Pickett.

---

5. POLK ENTERS KENTUCKY (SEPTEMBER 3, 1861)

In a contest over the Mississippi River, an inept Union general almost committed one of the costliest mistakes of the war, then an equally incompetent Confederate general beat him to it.

From the outset of the war, the sprawling state of Kentucky had declared its neutrality. Presidents Lincoln and Davis both vowed to respect the wishes of their mutual birthplace. Although beneficial to both men, neutral bluegrass was as good as gold for Davis. Resting on five hundred miles of the Confederacy's border, from western Virginia across the length of Tennessee's vulnerable north boundary, Kentucky stood directly between the Southern heartland and five Union states. The only land avenues left into Dixie were tumultuous Missouri and the stone wall of Virginia.[192]

All this mattered little to self-aggrandizing Union Gen. JOHN C. FRÉMONT and equally shortsighted Confederate Gen. LEONIDAS POLK. Both eyed Kentucky's jagged westerly tail as prime, unclaimed real estate for controlling the mighty Mississippi. As it turned out, both generals targeted Columbus, Kentucky, a small, undefended town tucked neatly in a strategically exquisite bend in the river. Consulting neither their presidents nor their War Departments, each man positioned himself for the first strike, Polk in Union City, Tennessee, and Frémont across the waters in Belmont, Missouri.[193]

Polk was the first to move. He crossed the Tennessee-Kentucky border on September 3, 1861, and snuggled into Columbus the following day. Hearing of Polk's unilateral act of political idiocy, Tennessee Gov. Isham Harris, Confederate Secretary of War Leroy Walker, and Jefferson

Davis demanded Polk withdraw back to Tennessee. An indignant Polk took the orders under advisement and declined.[194]

Repercussions were swift. Armed with the moral high ground, Union forces took two days to occupy Paducah in the west and Frankfort in the north. In two weeks, the government of Kentucky declared allegiance to the Union. A vast roadblock to the Confederacy had become an open passage.[195]

Frémont's man in charge of the Union assault force designated to attack Columbus—a promising brigadier named Grant.

6. ASSAULT ON MARYE'S HEIGHTS
(BATTLE OF FREDERICKSBURG, DECEMBER 13, 1862)

By November 1862 the public and government of the North were impatient for any sign of military progress. To speed things along, Lincoln relieved the overly cautious GEORGE B. MCCLELLAN and placed the more agreeable AMBROSE E. BURNSIDE at the head of the Army of the Potomac.

The Sunken Road at the base of Marye's Heights proved to be impregnable in December 1862.

BATTLES AND LEADERS

In short order, Burnside pressed toward Richmond via Fredericksburg with most of his army of 120,000 on hand.

Burnside lost precious days in early December while waiting for the arrival and assembly of pontoon bridges so he could cross the frigid Rappahannock. The delay gave ROBERT E. LEE plenty of time to collect and entrench most of his 75,000 men on the west side of evacuated Fredericksburg. To reinstate a factor of surprise, Burnside attempted the unfathomable: He crossed the Rappahannock anyway, heading straight toward Lee's defenses. To add to the effect, Burnside launched multiple assaults upon the most impenetrable part of the Confederate line, a half-mile-long stone wall shielding thousands of Confederate infantry and covered by dozens of cannon on the slopes of Marye's Heights directly behind.

Despite the courage of the Union infantry who would not relent, the well-protected opposition slaughtered each wave with ease. Of the 12,700 Federal soldiers killed or wounded at the one-day battle of Fredericksburg, most fell within sight of the wall. Upon learning the horrible news, Lincoln uttered his now famous lament, "If there is a worse place than Hell, I am in it."[196]

As night fell on the battlefield, the aurora borealis could be seen overhead, a very rare occurrence that far south.

---

7. THE CRATER (PETERSBURG, JULY 30, 1864)

June 1864 the Army of the Potomac laid siege to the defenses of Petersburg, aiming to penetrate the southern flank of a thirty-mile front protecting Richmond and its rail arteries. Impatient to get through the Rebel trenches just 150 yards away, members of the Forty-eighth Pennsylvania, many of whom were coal miners, made a suggestion. A tunnel charged with a good deal of explosives could break open the fortified line. With tacit approval from Gens. AMBROSE E. BURNSIDE, George Gordon Meade, and ULYSSES S. GRANT, the miners began their work in earnest. What resulted was an engineering marvel. The finished mine had a length of five hundred feet, complete with ventilation system. An end chamber eighty feet wide and twenty feet below the Confederate line contained eight thousand pounds of black powder.

The battle of the Crater failed because the shock of the explosion awed the Union troops poised to attack as much as it stunned the Confederate defenders.

Burnside selected and trained his largest and most rested unit, an inexperienced but motivated division of African American soldiers, to lead an assault immediately following the blast. Just hours before the planned detonation, Burnside's immediate superior, Meade, overturned the attack order. Grant concurred, fearing abolitionist outrage should the troops suffer heavy casualties. A white division would lead the way, one chosen by lots. The shortest straw went to Brig. Gen. James Ledlie, a man of questionable competence and an alcoholic.

At 4:45 A.M., July 30, the charge went off. A deafening ball of fire and earth mushroomed into the dim morning sky. Smoke rolled, debris rained, and an entire Confederate regiment and battery disappeared. Ledlie's division, however, did nothing for almost an hour, awed by the chasm 170 feet long, 60 feet wide, and 30 feet deep. Meanwhile, Ledlie cowered in a shelter hundreds of yards away with a bottle.

Untrained on what to do next, Ledlie's men eventually charged *into* the crater rather than *around* it and became trapped in the powdered soil, unable to climb out in any direction. Re-forming soon after the blast,

Confederates lofted volley after volley of artillery and rifle fire into the hole. In support, Burnside's entire Ninth Corps, including his select black division, ran into the fold, creating a tangle of living and dead with nowhere to go. The shooting lasted for hours.

In total, the North lost more than four thousand killed, wounded, and missing. The South lost thirteen hundred, and their lines outside Petersburg would hold for another eight months. Grant would later call the battle of the Crater "the saddest affair I have witnessed in the war," a comment coming *after* the bloodbaths of WILDERNESS, SPOTSYLVANIA, and COLD HARBOR.[197]

Two years after the battle, human remains were still visible in the crater.

8. GRANT'S ASSAULTS AT COLD HARBOR (COLD HARBOR, JUNE 3, 1864)

To enfilade is to fire upon an enemy line from the side. Such an operation, on the rare occasion it is feasible, can be brutally effective. Shots long or short on range are still likely to fall upon the target. Only the opponent's flank has an open line of fire for a response. To attempt an assault past

At Cold Harbor more than seven thousand Federals fell in the first few minutes.

LIBRARY OF CONGRESS

enfilade is consequently treacherous. Advancing past enfilade and upon a heavily defended position borders on the ludicrous, but that is exactly what ULYSSES S. GRANT ordered his men to do at Cold Harbor.

At 4:30 A.M. on June 3 Grant sent fifty thousand men toward entrenched and enfiladed Confederate defenses. More than seven thousand men in blue were killed or wounded in fifteen minutes. Following waves diminished in intensity as officers and men quickly realized the futility of the situation. Eight hours passed before George Gordon Meade and Grant ceased sending men. Four days passed before Grant consented to a truce for the retrieval of the wounded between the lines, but by that time most of the wounded had perished. Only later did Grant write, "I regret this assault more than any one I have ever ordered."[198]

After Cold Harbor, the Army of the Potomac and Grant were never truly aggressive again. When Union forces advanced on critical Petersburg later that June, lead units outnumbered the paltry twenty-five hundred Confederates seven to one and overran the outer defenses quickly. The Federals, however, made little effort to press their advantage, and support units hesitated to aid them. The following month's catastrophe at THE CRATER illustrated the indecision and apprehension of a once confident command. By the autumn of 1864, Grant still held a three-to-one advantage over the Confederates, which grew to five to one by the spring of 1865. Before Cold Harbor, Grant and company moved eighty miles in one month. Afterward, the grand Army of the Potomac moved ten miles in eight months. Not until ROBERT E. LEE's units failed miserably in two desperate breakout engagements (Fort Stedman and Five Forks) did Grant order a general offensive, sweeping through Richmond and Petersburg and thus ending the longest siege in U.S military history.

Nearly three thousand people died in the terrorist attacks of September 11, 2001; approximately the same number died in the first fifteen minutes at Cold Harbor.

---

9. HOOKER'S SWITCH TO THE DEFENSIVE (CHANCELLORSVILLE, MAY 1–4, 1863)

It looked as if ROBERT E. LEE and the Army of Northern Virginia were finally trapped. Facing them were forty thousand Federal troops near the old battleground of FREDERICKSBURG. Sweeping around the Confederate left were fifty-five thousand more men led by AMBROSE E. BURNSIDE's new replacement, the brash and confident Joseph Hooker.[199]

Union morale was ablaze. Lee was not moving, seemingly unable to advance or withdraw, on the verge of being surrounded. Yet as Hooker's men began to close in behind Lee's forces and encountered predictable resistance, Hooker suddenly lost his nerve. He ordered his advancing columns to withdraw back to the crossroads of tiny CHANCELLORSVILLE. Union officers and men were baffled. Not only did their commander surrender a very rare opportunity to crush Lee, he also backed himself into a veritable trap. Massive thickets and dark forests surrounding Chancellorsville rendered Hooker's artillery practically impotent. Worse, the heavy woods made enemy positions, numbers, and movements almost invisible. Rather than act on reports that Lee had divided his army into several disjointed parts, Hooker remained stationary, convinced that the opposition was actually retreating.[200]

As Lee began his sudden and simultaneous attacks on May 2, Hooker panicked, gave up high ground, and withdrew even farther. When the battle resumed the next day, a Confederate shell crashed within feet of Hooker. Despite showing signs of a concussion, he refused to relinquish command. Later on, when Union forces at Fredericksburg broke through infamous MARYE'S HEIGHTS to rescue his wing, Hooker made no effort to join them. By May 6 the whipped Hooker backed over the Rappahannock, bloodied and disgraced.

Chancellorsville proved to be Lee's greatest fight and the apex of the Confederate movement, yet the moment would not have been possible without the consent and cooperation of a general who before this engagement had been known as "Fighting Joe."[201]

Hooker got his nickname when a newspaper covering his progress in the Peninsula campaign used the headline "Fighting—Joe Hooker."

---

10. BURNSIDE'S BRIDGE (ANTIETAM, SEPTEMBER 17, 1862)

Ideally, an avenue of attack includes natural and/or weaponry cover, wide approaches to accommodate the numbers involved, and secure rear areas for prompt reinforcement or withdrawal. Outside Sharpsburg, Maryland,

For more than three hours Burnside's corps was stalled at the bridge that now bears his name. Here fewer than six hundred Georgians held off twelve thousand Federals, wreaking five hundred casualties.

on September 17, 1862, AMBROSE E. BURNSIDE used the worst avenue of attack of the entire war.

Over open ground, under heavy enemy fire, and with minimal artillery support, Burnside attempted to send his Ninth Corps, twelve thousand men, over Antietam Creek by way of a single arching stone bridge less than thirteen feet wide. He tried, not once or twice, but four times.

By using the bridge, Burnside presented a small and compact target that could not fan out to return effective fire, move wounded to the rear, or provide any cover to the thousands behind them in cue. Cutting them down with deadly effect was former Confederate Secretary of State Robert A. Toombs and his fellow Georgians, fewer than five hundred men, outnumbered twenty to one.

Union forces did manage to cross the creek three hours later when they discovered they could wade across the Antietam a few hundred yards upstream. Their success was short lived, however. Coming up from Harpers Ferry, A. P. Hill and three thousand Confederates (several of them wearing captured blue uniforms) smashed into Burnside's left flank, killing hundreds before nightfall.[202]

More than two thousand men in blue were casualties, and vital time was lost. An inept execution of an inept order negated the chance for a quick and massive advance. What could have been a rout turned out to be a costly and marginal win.[203]

Burnside later became the first president of the National Rifle Association.

TOP TEN HEROINES

Popular history may characterize the Civil War as a flourish of opportunity for women. The case is marginally true. In 1861 75 percent of the nation's primary and secondary teachers were men, a ratio reduced to nearly 50 percent by 1865. Women held 25 percent of the manufacturing jobs at the start of the war, then almost 33 percent by the end. Hundreds of new civil appointments went to women, particularly in the Treasury Departments of both governments. An understaffed medical profession reluctantly gave ground to female participation.[204]

In most instances, these modest increases came not by some war-induced enlightenment of women's abilities but by a shortage of labor. In fact, exemplary performances in office, school, and hospital environments were often downplayed as "instinctual" to the feminine psyche. Women were also compelled to accept lower pay, often half that of men.[205]

Discrimination and poor wages were only part of the task. Harassment was common, sexual and otherwise. There were a few among the gender who perpetuated myths of "feminine fragility," being flirtatious, lazy, and incompetent in their jobs.[206]

Then there was the chance of death. Female nurses were just as susceptible to illness as the soldiers they tended. Working with typhoid cases was especially dangerous, killing scores. Hundreds worked in munitions, where the dangers of the workplace went beyond inequality. A Richmond laboratory explosion killed forty women. A Washington arsenal fire consumed nineteen.[207]

For the most part, women worked in the home, which in the mid-nineteenth century was not a domicile of leisure but a hospital, school, office, and for many families, a factory. Although some women found a new sense of freedom and independence during the war, many experienced an increase in burden, already heavy before the onset of a national insurgency.[208]

Most heroines of the war remain unsung. Of the two million slave and fifteen million free women involved, fame usually fell upon the unmerited, such as the self-promoting spy Belle Boyd or the privileged and untested diarist Mary Chesnut. Below are standouts among the largely overlooked. To an extreme, the following risked their financial, professional, or physical safety in the service of their country and cause. Directly or indirectly, most advanced women's status in male-dominated environments. All inspired a generation with their courage and commitment.[209]

1. CLARA BARTON (MASSACHUSETTS, 1821–1912)

Throughout the war and on both sides, eight out every ten nurses were men, and very few traveled to the front lines. Clara Barton made herself the exception. Five feet tall, of light build, with a soft voice and a relentless work ethic, she was an odd semblance of unbound tenderness and absolute tenacity.

Thirty-nine years old when the war broke out, she witnessed soldiers of FIRST MANASSAS (First Bull Run) returning from the battlefield. Some of the wounded had walked the twenty-three miles back to Washington for lack of ambulances. Caring for the men with supplies from her own home, she vowed to become a nurse.[210]

Affiliated with no organization or charity, she served in several battles, including SECOND MANASSAS, FREDERICKSBURG, Battery Wagner, and the WILDERNESS. Chartering wagons, collecting food and medicine, helping with surgeries, and dressing wounds, she personified calm resilience. Remarkably focused under fire, she often found her clothes drenched with blood and pierced by lead. At ANTIETAM, Barton was caring for a wounded soldier when a bullet passed through her sleeve and into his chest, killing him instantly.[211]

A divinity to the enlisted, perhaps her greatest service was to the families of those missing in action. Late in the war, Lincoln enlisted her to identify the unknown buried at ANDERSONVILLE. With a team of forty casket makers and other assistants, she exhumed more than 12,000 bodies and managed to identify all but 451 of them.[212]

Continuing her assignment at other sites, she encountered constant obstruction. Leading her detractors was the U.S. War Department, unappreciative of her divulging its lethargy in assisting families of missing veterans. Despite the challenges, including tremendous personal debt, she and her crew wrote and received tens of thousands of letters, exhumed nearly as many graves, and identified ten thousand more bodies. Such a service was particularly important to widows and dependents. Aside from learning the fate of their loved ones, they could collect pensions, as the government required proof of death before payment. Yet by Barton's own calculations, at least forty thousand Union dead had no known burial place and would remain missing forever.[213]

After the war, she traveled as a public speaker, sharing her experiences and supporting veterans programs. To one audience, she revealed the extent of her tolerance for battle: "Men have worshipped war, till it has cost a million times more than the whole world in worth, poured out the best blood and crushed the fairest forms the good God has ever created. . . . All through and through, thought, and act, body and soul—I hate it."[214]

Barton went on to become the founder and first president of the American Association of the Red Cross. She continued her work as a nurse during the Spanish-American War at the age of seventy-seven.[215]

Although the War Department routinely undermined her services during and after the Civil War, the American public was far more appreciative. For generations, hundreds of newborn girls were named Clara Barton.

---

2. MARY ANN BICKERDYKE (OHIO, 1817–1901)

For both armies, nursing was an afterthought. Soldiers physically or mentally incapable of combat service were often charged with hospital duty. Training was minimal or nonexistent, and the orderlies served on a rotational basis. Neglect, theft, and abuse of patients were prevalent.[216]

Into this scene came widowed Quaker Mary Ann Bickerdyke, a stocky, unpolished, and fierce opponent of the Union Medical Bureau. Examining a row of overcrowded hospital tents at a Union camp in Illinois, she labored to contain her anger: "The mud floor was foul with human excrement . . . patients lay in shirts and underdrawers, filthy with vomit, rank with perspiration."[217]

Bickerdyke immediately rectified the situation. She obtained better food and living conditions for the men, organized kitchens, established wash teams, replaced beddings, dressings, and clothes, assisted with surgeries, and fired anyone who resisted, despite having no authority to do so. Traveling with ULYSSES S. GRANT's forces to FORT DONELSON and VICKS-BURG, she quickly earned the admiration of the enlisted and emphasized to doctors and soldiers alike the relationship between cleanliness and health. When officers or surgeons complained of her iron-fisted tactics, both Grant and WILLIAM TECUMSEH SHERMAN advised them to step aside. Grant commented to one objector, "Mother Bickerdyke outranks everybody, even Lincoln."[218]

On his Atlanta campaign, Sherman specifically requested her help for the Fifteenth Corps, permitting her to trade, demand, and confiscate anything needed for "her boys." At the conclusion of the war, for the Grand Review of the Armies, Sherman instructed Bickerdyke to ride in the parade at the head of the grateful Fifteenth.[219]

Bickerdyke served all four years and in nineteen battle zones. Remaining with her corps until the last soldier was discharged in 1866, she labored the rest of her life, assisting veterans from coast to coast. Alternately called a cyclone, a tornado, a damned nuisance, she preferred the name the men awarded her—Mother.[220]

For her fast and furious commitment to the service, the U.S. government granted Mother Bickerdyke a pension of three hundred dollars a year, which she did not receive until 1886.

---

3. ORDERS OF CATHOLIC NUNS

During the height of a battle, Confederate soldiers sighted unarmed women entering the field. One exclaimed, "My God! . . . What are they doing down there? They'll be killed." A compatriot informed him, "Those are the Sisters. They are looking for the wounded. They are not afraid of anything."[221]

Before the war the largest military hospital was in Kansas, boasting a total of forty beds. At the same time the Catholic Church operated nearly thirty hospitals across the country. While nursing schools would not appear in the United States until the 1870s, the sisterhood had a tradition of nursing dating back to the Middle Ages. To a society frightened by the prospect of untrained, unmarried, unchaperoned ladies caring for armies of grown men, the nuns appeared as heaven sent.[222]

Among them were the Sisters of Mercy from Shelby Springs, Alabama, the Sisters of St. Dominic out of Memphis, and the Sisters of Charity from Cincinnati. An order from Emmitsburg, Maryland, traveled to GETTYSBURG, gathered the wounded, blessed the dead, and assisted surgeries done in Gettysburg's St. Francis Xavier Church.[223]

Throughout the war, more than six hundred sisters from a dozen orders served, and yet they were ridiculed. Dressed in their habits, most were foreign-born, lending an air of suspicion to their presence. Additionally, the sisters served on both sides, making no distinction between Union and Confederate wounded. A common accusation against them was that of espionage. Yet the majority of surgeons, civilians, and soldiers were grateful. Jefferson Davis thanked the orders for their work in the Confederacy's "darkest days." Lincoln added, "They were veritable angels of mercy."[224]

Catholic nuns tended to the wounded and sick of the American Revolution and the War of 1812. During the Crimean War, the majority of Florence Nightingale's crew of thirty-eight nurses were members of Anglican and Catholic sisterhoods.

---

4. HARRIET TUBMAN (MARYLAND, 1821(?)–1913)

Born into slavery as Araminta Ross, she escaped from slave state Maryland and arrived in Pennsylvania in 1849 alone and penniless. Two years later she began the first of nineteen forays southward, risking reenslavement and death, leading by some estimates 270 people to freedom. In ten years on the Underground Railroad, she was never caught and "never lost a passenger." In 1861 Washington actively sought her talents.[225]

Her admirers included cabinet members William H. Seward and Edwin M. Stanton. Consequently, Tubman moved through the lines and among the camps with considerable freedom. Assisting the military as a spy, scout, and nurse, she worked primarily in South Carolina. Coordinating the assistance of local freedmen and slaves, she labored to improve the care of refugee slaves, collected intelligence for the military, and sought out any opportunity to find and free more people. On one occasion she quadrupled her antebellum tally, liberating 756 slaves during an expeditionary raid.[226]

After the war she returned to her adopted home in Auburn, New York. In spite of continual poverty, she raised money for freedmen remaining in the South, endorsed women's rights, and in 1908 opened a home for the aged and poor.

Her distinguished life forged associations with Ralph Waldo Emerson, FREDERICK DOUGLASS, THOMAS GARRETT, WILLIAM LLOYD GARRISON, and WENDELL PHILLIPS. Her friend JOHN BROWN referred to her as "General" and considered her "one of the best and bravest persons on this continent."[227]

> Tubman managed to be a spy, nurse, scout, suffragette, and rescuer despite being illiterate.

5. MARY LIVERMORE (MASSACHUSETTS, 1820–1905)

 Of the many private organizations North and South, the U.S. Sanitary Commission was by far the largest. Lincoln sanctioned the commission in the first summer of the war, permitting what he called the "fifth wheel to the coach" to review camps and hospitals, report their findings, and nothing more. Yet it became clear early on that the U.S. military, designed to handle a peacetime strength of sixteen thousand, was wholly unprepared to care for a volunteer force of more than a half million.[228]

After inspecting decrepit camps, inadequate supply networks, and squalid hospitals, the Sanitary Commission became a volunteer force of its own, growing to five hundred officers (mostly men) and more than ten thousand volunteers (mostly women, including MARY BICKERDYKE). Among its executives was editor, teacher, activist, and preacher's wife Mary Livermore of Chicago, who embodied the commission's objective of bringing rations, medicines, and better living conditions for every Union soldier.

After cofounding a chapter in her hometown, she became a national director. Traveling across the North, she recruited doctors, nurses, businessmen, and veteran's families, organized charity drives, collected and shipped provisions for the enlisted, and chartered thousands of branch offices. Leading the fight against an inflexible and outdated military Medical Bureau, she helped make the Sanitary Commission a bountiful provider for the legions of servicemen who depended upon it for survival.[229]

There was one female reporter at the 1860 Republican National
Convention: the multitalented Mary Ashton Livermore.

---

6. SALLY LOUISA TOMPKINS (VIRGINIA, 1833–1916)

The Southern celebration of the feminine ideal had a decidedly negative
effect. When it came time to mobilize a nursing corps, the turnout was
alarmingly low, and most Confederate hospital orderlies throughout the
war were slaves.[230]

Among the exceptions was Sally Louisa Tompkins. A Richmond
philanthropist, she converted a judge's home in the Confederate capital into a hospital where she and six assistants took in the wounded of
FIRST MANASSAS.

As Virginia became a vast war zone, so Richmond became an extensive network of makeshift hospitals. Few, however, rivaled the efficiency
and reputation of Tompkins's ward. To lend power to her practice, Jefferson Davis gave her the rank of captain. She refused the pay but used the
rank to procure rations and supplies.[231]

From August 1861 to April 1865 she and her staff received more than
thirteen hundred cases, many of them severe. The hospital kept all but
seventy-three men alive, an astounding achievement, considering the
overall Confederate average of deaths from wounds was four times
higher. Continuing her work well after Appomattox, she gradually
resumed her prewar commitment to social charity.[232]

Sally Louisa Tompkins was the first and only woman given an officer's
commission in the Confederate military.

---

7. DOROTHEA DIX (MAINE, 1802–87)

At sixty years of age and a famous advocate for medical reform, especially
for the care of the mentally ill, authoritative and inexhaustible Dorothea
Dix was a reasonable choice for superintendent of the U.S. Women
Nurses Corps.

In her recruiting efforts, Dix established strict guidelines for prospective attendants: "No woman under thirty years need apply to serve in

government hospitals. All nurses are required to be very plain looking women." She also imposed restrictions on dress, travel, and socializing.[233]

In her own words, she revealed the dichotomy of Dix. Opinionated, terse, arbitrarily selective in times of desperate nursing shortages, she eventually alienated a large portion of her male and female colleagues. At the same time, she forced efficiency upon a slipshod medical department, selected the best available caretakers within her narrow criteria, and secured pay for them while never accepting her own wages. Overall she managed a staff of more than two thousand—roughly equivalent to a brigade—all the while attempting to remove prejudice against women and bring a superior level of care to the men.[234]

Dispossessed of most of her authority by the end of the war, she resigned her position in September 1865. Dix returned to her pioneering work in the betterment of care for the mentally ill, finally retiring when she reached her eightieth year.[235]

U.S. Medical Bureau officials selected Dorothea Dix as superintendent of nurses over a more qualified nominee—Elizabeth Blackwell, the first trained female physician in American history (Geneva Medical College, 1849).

---

8. ELIZABETH CADY STANTON (NEW YORK, 1815–1902) AND SUSAN B. ANTHONY (MASSACHUSETTS, 1820–1906)

Elizabeth Cady grew up around her father's New York law office, where she saw numerous married women ask for help against abusive husbands only to be told they had no legal recourse. Susan Brownwell developed a deep sense of independence while working her family farm outside Rochester, New York. Both were involved in social reform for years before meeting in 1851.

Thereafter, they teamed together and became the most prominent voices for women's rights in the nineteenth century.[236]

Stanton, the more extroverted and articulate of the two, handled the lion's share of writing and public speaking while Anthony performed most of the managerial duties. Ardent abolitionists, they paralleled the plight of marriage with slavery. Specifics varying by state, betrothed women had limited or no control over their own money and property. In several states, physical abuse was insufficient grounds for divorce. In matters of dress, speech, and child-bearing, obedience was expected. The overriding concern, Anthony informed a fellow activist, "was *Human Rights*—not *Woman's* Rights."[237]

During the war Anthony and Stanton minimized their message of gender issues and focused on abolition. Annoyed by the minimal scope of Lincoln's emancipation edict, they formed the Women's National Loyal League, supporting the Union but calling for total emancipation. The two petitioned for the eradication of slavery from the Constitution and collected four hundred thousand signatures for what would become the THIRTEENTH AMENDMENT.[238]

Yet the end of the war did not bring the social transformations they had hoped for. In response, Stanton and Anthony founded the National Women's Suffrage Association and continued their lifelong mission for equal rights and opportunity. Together they ushered a gradual public recognition of women's issues and encouraged individuals to grant themselves the right of self-determination. Despite their work, neither lived to see the 1920 passage of the Nineteenth Amendment, which granted women the right to vote.

Created by Susan B. Anthony and Elizabeth Cady Stanton, the National Women's Suffrage Association changed its name in 1920 to the League of Women Voters.

---

9. ANNIE ETHERIDGE (WISCONSIN, 1840–1913)

Born Lorinda Anna Blair, she came to be known as "Gentle Anna," a selfless caretaker of Michigan's soldiers.

When her husband, James Etheridge, joined the Second Michigan, she volunteered as a nurse. Through FIRST MANASSAS, SECOND MANASSAS, ANTIETAM, FREDERICKSBURG, CHANCELLORSVILLE, GETTYSBURG, and SPOTSYLVANIA, she served the Second, Third, and Fifth Michigan, among others. On hospital ships, in camp, on the move, the sunny, reticent, yet restless Anna shared the same food, slept on the same ground, and marched the same miles as the enlisted. Several holes in her clothes attested to her indifference to gunfire. Similar to Clara Barton's Antietam experience, Etheridge was caring for a soldier on the front lines of Fredericksburg when shrapnel struck and killed him.[239]

In 1864 ULYSSES S. GRANT streamlined his operations and ordered women away from the Army of the Potomac. Officers of all ranks signed a petition asking Grant to make an exception for Etheridge. Grant did not, and Etheridge worked at the City Point Hospital during the long siege of Petersburg.[240]

After the war Etheridge continued to serve her regiments. Working in the U.S. Pension Office, she secured annuities for Michigan veterans, war widows, and their dependents.

Annie Etheridge died in 1913. In recognition of her service and sacrifice to the Union army, the U.S. government buried her with full honors in Arlington National Cemetery.

---

10. KATE CUMMING (SCOTLAND, 1828–1909)

As the war entered its second year, twenty-seven-year-old Kate Cumming struggled with an inconsistency. England's Florence Nightingale had many admirers, and yet many deemed it socially unacceptable to emulate her work.[241]

When Cumming learned of a deadly battle at SHILOH, she traveled from her home in Mobile, Alabama, to the Confederate base at Corinth, Mississippi. Against her family's wishes, she went to care for the wounded. For ten straight days she changed bandages, gathered food and water, searched in vain for medicines, and never had the opportunity to change out of her blood-soaked dress.

After returning briefly to Mobile, she assisted the Army of the Tennessee for the rest of the war, first as a nurse and then as one of the few field-hospital matrons of the South. Although not alone in her sacrifices, she was unique in one respect. She publicly questioned the commitment of Confederate women: "Are the women of the South going into the hospitals? I am afraid candor will compel me to say they are not!" Of those restricted by age or health, she wondered why so many did not bother to sew shirts, send food, darn socks, or wrap bandages. "I have no patience with women whom I hear telling what wonder they would do if they were only men, when I see much of their legitimate work left undone." Many accepted her challenge and committed themselves to uncharted territory.[242]

Following the war, she wrote *A Journal of Hospital Life,* one of the most precise and insightful renditions of medical care in the Confederacy and an astute dismantling of Southern womanhood's china-doll image. After its publication, she became a schoolteacher, participated in veterans affairs, and urged women to care for the disfigured and disabled veterans of the South.[243]

The consummate Southern nationalist, Kate Cumming was born in Scotland, immigrated with her family to New York, then moved to Montreal before settling in Alabama.

Pursuing the War

TOP TEN GENERAL HISTORIES

No event in American history has had as much written about it as the War Between the States. By conservative estimates, there are some fifty thousand texts on the subject plus countless articles, essays, and dissertations.

Among them, several hundred books attempt to address the war as a whole, a monumental endeavor mastered by a few. The quality of general histories ranges from excellent to inane, with the latter represented by the nauseating misinterpretations of *The Civil War in the United States* by Karl Marx and Frederick Engels and the exceedingly self-serving *McClellan's Own Story* by the former commander of the Army of Potomac. To the other extreme are fine works of lasting merit. Presented here are the ten best examples for general audiences based on each work's historical accuracy, balance of coverage, cited evidence, objectivity, and readability.

1. *BATTLE CRY OF FREEDOM: THE CIVIL WAR ERA*
   JAMES M. McPHERSON (1988)

No other general history on the Civil War is as simultaneously detailed and succinct as McPherson's Pulitzer Prize winner, a product all the more impressive as it is a single-volume work.

Beginning with a snapshot of the nation as a whole in the mid-nineteenth-century and moving into a compelling reexamination of the war with Mexico and its effects on a country in transition, McPherson commits considerable space to the foundations of sectional discord. Only the most impatient reader will miss his intent. The Princeton professor interprets the war as inseparable from a synthesis of national transformations, primarily industrialization and its effect on human labor, and westward expansion's disruption of regional balances.

McPherson's greatest strength is his ability to blend a multitude of facts into flowing prose, crafting more illuminating evidence within a page than some historians accomplish in a chapter. Few corners of the struggle are left untouched, from the plight of the slave to the paper trails of the desk clerk, from the struggles on the home front to the logistics of warfare. Each subject is presented with considerable documentation and sobriety, establishing a level of credibility for this work rarely matched by other histories of popular appeal.

Although pleased with the final product, neither McPherson nor his publisher expected *Battle Cry of Freedom* to sell well. Since its release in 1988 it has sold more than six hundred thousand copies.

---

2. *THE CRISIS OF THE UNION* AND *THE WAR FOR THE UNION* ALLAN NEVINS (1947–71)

A bulwark of facts, a tight weave of drama, the work of Allan Nevins is no light affair, because, as he shows, the war was no picnic.

Nevins divides his presentation into a four-volume examination of events before the war (*The Crisis of the Union*) and a four-volume account of the war itself (*The War for the Union*), examining the social, political, and military synthesis in depth. Several newer works are superior in resource materials, a few histories possess better prose, but none save McPherson surpass Nevins in creating a balance between story and evidence. Such an accomplishment is no mean feat, considering Nevins wrote the series while Civil War sentimentalism was still in vogue.

There are times when Nevins drops a litany of surnames, which may read like delectable gossip to committed Civil War buffs but may feel more like a Wilderness thicket to new readers. He is also heavy-handed in his criticism of certain officers and congressmen, the hapless Jefferson Davis and the vengeful Radical Republicans in particular. Still, his shortcomings pale in comparison to his skills. Nevins is as entertaining as he is wise, capable of explaining a complex issue with a single sentence of ingeniously blended words, much in the same grass-roots flavor of Samuel Clemens. Frequently cited by writers past and new, Nevins is often overlooked by a public more attentive to shorter and more recent publications.

Shortly after finishing his final volume on the war, Nevins died.

---

3. *A CENTENNIAL HISTORY OF THE CIVIL WAR*
BRUCE CATTON (1961–65)

The elder statesman of popular American history, Bruce Catton is the quintessential enunciator of Civil War bravado, earning him praise among the public and a cooler reception among academic purists. He began his three-volume work (consisting of *The Coming Fury, Terrible Swift Sword,* and *Never Call Retreat*) in 1955 and completed it a decade later. Resting heavily on the financial backing and creative direction from publication giants Doubleday and the *New York Times,* the end result was, predictably, suited for a general audience (primarily a Northern one) and centered on military events and famous names.

Catton emphasizes the war in the East, yet he does so to reflect the political and popular preoccupations existing in the era. The warring sides committed more men, materiel, and money to the fight between the capitals than in any other arena, civilian or military. To the American majority, survival in the East meant survival, period.

Less convincing, although tempting in its charm, is his overall presentation of the war as a battle of personal wills between a handful of players. Catton illuminates wonderfully these personalities and the struggles they faced, although in doing so he undermines the effect of the war on the remainder of the nation.

Resource materials are of astounding quantity. Woven as they are into sometimes long-winded, melodramatic renditions, they are nonetheless good history, factual and flowing, exemplified by his description of the Confederate enlisted as they were about to embark on PICKETT'S CHARGE: "They were old soldiers and had been in many battles, but what they saw took their breath away, and whether they had ten minutes or seventy-five years yet to live, they remembered it until they died."

Leaving Oberlin College to serve in the First World War, Bruce Catton never took a college history course.

4. *THE CIVIL WAR: A NARRATIVE*
SHELBY FOOTE (1958–74)

Ken Burns's documentary *The Civil War* made Shelby Foote a household name, and to a large degree it was fame well deserved. In the 1950s this Mississippi-born novelist set out to write what had not yet been accomplished: a military history both sympathetic to the South yet respected by the North. Foote accomplished this and more with a three-volume, three-thousand-page narrative that is both detailed and sinuous (consisting of *Fort Sumter to Perryville, Fredericksburg to Meridian,* and *Red River to Appomattox*).

In a style he calls, "Accepting the historian's standards without his paraphernalia," Foote writes without footnotes, substantial annotations, or other evidential tools. For this and his excessive admiration for cavalry commander NATHAN BEDFORD FORREST, Foote has been criticized. He also offers little in the way of new evidence.

In spite of this, Foote humanizes the great characters, turning once unreachable icons into believable, knowable flesh and blood. He recognizes the fight between the capitals as a stalemate and instead focuses on the underrated battles in Tennessee, Georgia, and Mississippi. He also brings his talents as a novelist. It is one thing to know that John Wilkes Booth shot Lincoln in Ford's Theatre. It is quite another to read of "a half-muffled explosion . . . a boil and bulge of bluish smoke in the presidential box, an exhalation as of brimstone from the curtained mouth, and a man coming out through the bank and swirl of it."

Some paint the war in glory; others present it as a series of outcomes as predictable as a controlled experiment. Foote offers a third view. The Civil War, and history itself, was ultimately how people related to one another, no matter their rank or station.

Shelby Foote completed this three-volume history in a little under two decades.

5. *ENCYCLOPEDIA OF THE AMERICAN CIVIL WAR:*
A POLITICAL, SOCIAL, AND MILITARY HISTORY
EDITED BY DAVID S. HEIDLER AND JEANNE T. HEIDLER (2000)

There are reference works, and then there is David Heidler and Jeanne Heidler's encyclopedia. Piled into this five-volume compilation are more that sixteen hundred alphabetized subject entries, seventy-five sharp and useful maps, and illustrations numbering in the hundreds. The last volume contains a chronology of events from the antebellum period to Reconstruction, an ample glossary, lists of general officers, extensive bibliographical information, and samples of key government documents from both sides.

Most reassuring is the brigade of contributing authors. There are no fewer than three hundred, all of them venerable experts in their respective discipline. In the nature of encyclopedias, some of the entries are dry and diminutive, but each includes reputable suggestions for further reading. Whether as a guide to serious research or as a playground for impulsive sampling, this is an investment worth making.

Also available in a condensed one-volume work, the five-volume encyclopedia is a bit steep—$425—about twice the monthly pay of a major general in the Union army.

---

6. *THE CIVIL WAR ARCHIVE: THE HISTORY OF THE CIVIL WAR IN DOCUMENTS*
EDITED BY HENRY STEELE COMMAGER (2000)

Originally titled *The Blue and the Gray,* Commager's long-respected collection of primary resources functions better under its newer title, as it is truly an archive in miniature. Showcased are eyewitness accounts of elections, battles, prisons, and hospitals. Also presented are reflective memoirs from ULYSSES S. GRANT, Mary Chesnut, Jefferson Davis, and others. Momentous laws are included, such as the Confederate Constitution, the HOMESTEAD ACT, and the THIRTEENTH AMENDMENT. Added are marching songs like "Dixie," "Bonnie Blue Flag," and "John Brown's Body." All serve as enlightening evidence of how people treated the war and vice versa.

In the vein of traditionalist history, Commager offers a disproportionate amount of material on the eastern theater, although he concedes the war was won and lost in the dynamic West. Nonetheless, the work is a tempting dip into the oceans of artifacts, from the anxious fury of secession to the bitter fight of Reconstruction.

In the 1950s Henry Steele Commager was a leading national critic of Sen. Joe McCarthy.

7. *THIS TERRIBLE WAR: THE CIVIL WAR AND ITS AFTERMATH* EDITED BY MICHAEL FELLMAN, LESLEY J. GORDON, AND DANIEL E. SUTHERLAND (2003)

With the exception of James McPherson's insightful but temperate *Ordeal by Fire* (1982), there was no classroom textbook on the Civil War worth much bother. That is, until three accomplished historians offered *This Terrible War.*

With lively writing, Fellman, Gordon, and Sutherland use only 450 pages yet leave few stones unturned. Along with the traditional issues of slavery and military operations, the work also covers lesser known but just as illuminating subjects, such as labor strikes, race relations, postwar trials, and the systematic demise of Reconstruction. Most inventive is the table of contents, essentially an index of hundreds of subject headings. Far from distracting, the format works like a storyboard, presenting the big picture while directing a reader to any desired scene.

Included are topographical maps, intuitive quotes, and twenty-nine primary documents, including JOHN BROWN's last speech and a segregationist state code written into law after the war. Absent are footnotes or endnotes, but there is an extensive bibliography of selected works.

The final chapter is a unique and welcomed creation, chronicling the war's treatment in popular culture from motives behind the monuments to enduring myths, legends, and sense of loss.

Union Gen. Winfield Scott and author Lesley J. Gordon both attended the College of William and Mary.

8. *THE CIVIL WAR DAY BY DAY: AN ALMANAC, 1861–1865* BY E. B.LONG AND BARBARA LONG (1985)

Bruce Catton's chief researchers for the *Centennial History* project (see Number 3 above) were E. B. Long and Barbara Long. After years of diligent research for Catton's three-volume history, the Longs found they had a surplus of serviceable data. Contemplating an encyclopedic volume or a fact book to accompany Catton's releases, the authors decided instead on an almanac. Civil War readers are fortunate they did.

No other time-line book contains the balance, clarity, and informative quantity found in this contribution. Sifting through manuscripts, books, reports, newspapers, and various periodicals, the Longs managed to cover nearly every day of the four-year war. Seen in its calendar march, the conflict comes into focus. Political, economic, and military events appear as they did to the people living them, as a stream of hope and dread, glory and ruin, healing and revenge.

For Bruce Catton's trilogy and his own almanac, E. B. Long reportedly collected more than nine million words of research notes, visited 125 archives and libraries, and traveled more than sixty thousand miles.

---

9. *THE WAR OF THE REBELLION: A COMPILATION OF THE OFFICIAL RECORDS OF THE UNION AND CONFEDERATE ARMIES* (128 VOLS., 1880–1901) AND *OFFICIAL RECORDS OF THE UNION AND CONFEDERATE NAVIES IN THE WAR OF THE REBELLION* (30 VOLS., 1894–1922)

A must browse. Known simply to researchers as the OR, the Official Records serve as the backbone for any respectable military account of the war. Available in most academic libraries or to anyone with a load of cash, the collection is a gold mine of reports, dispatches, memoranda, and letters from the armed forces of the gray and blue.

In 1864 the U.S. Congress planned for an assembly of the conflict's most important records so future generations could read of what transpired. To accomplish this, they allocated fifteen thousand dollars. Fourteen presidents and three million dollars later, the final volume in the series was finished.

Clerks, researchers, historians, and former officers from the Union and Confederacy searched tons of official materials (Confederate records alone filled a three-story warehouse). Omitted were any items not from the two armed forces, postwar reports, duplicates, contracts, discharges, invention proposals, and anything deemed historically insignificant. What remained was a literary monument of two hundred thousand pages. It is the voices of the ghosts themselves.

A surprising casualty within its leaves is accuracy. Numerous accounts were written during or immediately after events, when officers and men had few verified facts at their disposal. In many instances, commanders also wrote for effect, bending the truth to hype or critique themselves or their subordinates in recent performances. These factual foibles are one of the greatest elements of the compendium, for they illustrate with lucid panache how human beings function under duress. To the soldier or sailor, a battle does not appear as convenient maps with colorful legends. It is a perpetual struggle for time, space, and resources. In fact, when learning of the impending publication of the records, several former officers begged to edit their old reports to spare themselves embarrassment, a request the War Department fortunately rejected.

The OR ranks ninth on the list because of its indigestible size, boggling disorder, and nearly exclusive concentration on military affairs. Fortunately, a few works are available to assist with this behemoth, including *A User's Guide to the Official Records of the American Civil War* by Alan C. Aimone and Barbara A. Aimone (1993) and *Military Operations of the Civil War: A Guide-Index to the Official Records of the Union and Confederate Armies, 1861–1865* by Dallas Irvine (1968–80).

When the project to compile the Official Records began, Calvin Coolidge was not yet born. By the time the final volume was complete, Silent Cal was serving his second term as president of the United States.

---

10. *THE CIVIL WAR: AN ILLUSTRATED HISTORY* BY GEOFFREY C. WARD (1990)

Fashioned from the filmscript of the Ken Burns documentary, with additional material from prominent historians, this would have been a mildly celebrated work of mass appeal if it did not reside in the shadow of its exceedingly popular parent video.

Often "illustrated" means a work is padded with pictures and thin on substance. Such is not the case in this rendering. The readable text benefits from its established authors, who present their particular spin and expertise, making *The Civil War* as wide in spectrum as most other collective works. Images (photographs in particular) are unique, and all are reproduced with impressive clarity. Adding to the prints and prose are numerous quotes from the era, which again are an assembly of fine balance, with the famous, infamous, and previously unknown lending their color to this tapestry.

Downgrading this edition is its relative brevity and emaciated bibliography. The shortest book in this list (420 pages), however, is also the shortest path to understanding the fundamental issues and emotions of a very long war.

The publisher paid the authors a rather handsome advance on the book—$375,000.

TOP TEN CIVIL WAR FILMS

Among the approximately 350 feature-length Civil War films made, it is difficult to find ten of any great quality, a wonder considering the rebellion's inherent emotion. Producers and screenwriters often use the war as a blurred backdrop or a vehicle for careless dramatic license. Despite the underwhelming crop of prospects, the genre provides an intriguing depiction of how Americans perceived the war over time.

During the silent era, the War Between the States was a popular topic, with forty major titles produced. Commonly pitting family against family in a metaphoric blood feud, most of these plots included firefights and acts of espionage. In a purgative display of prevailing American desire, stories typically concluded with acts of forgiveness and reconciliation.[1]

As the medium matured into talkies in the 1920s, nearly all releases failed miserably. Battle scenes proved unpopular, especially to a country fresh from entanglement in World War I. In the decades that followed, the Civil War faded under the hefty pressure of public indifference, working only as an afterthought in epic love stories and scaled-down westerns.

During the civil rights movement and Vietnam, producers paired the depth of existing social unrest with the breadth of the Civil War. Most storylines dealt with racial injustice, youthful disillusionment, and the horrors of war. At the turn of the millennium, Civil War films have come full circle, returning to the silent era's use of martial military showdowns and the convenient bliss of eventual reconciliation.

The following are the best achievements in Civil War full-length film production based on quality of writing, directing, acting, and cinematography. Some are compelling portrayals of the war itself. Others are pivotal achievements in film history. Each possesses varying degrees of accuracy, although none are precise. All are required viewing for anyone wishing to comprehend the dynamic union of the war and its place in popular culture.[2]

1. *GLORY* (1989)

TRISTAR

PRODUCER:	FREDDIE FIELDS
DIRECTOR:	EDWARD ZWICK
STARRING:	MATTHEW BRODERICK, DENZEL WASHINGTON, MORGAN FREEMAN

Glory depicts the mustering, training, and early deployments of the fabled Fifty-fourth Massachusetts. The film climaxes with the ill-fated July 1863 assault upon Battery Wagner in Charleston Harbor, where Col. Robert Gould Shaw (Matthew Broderick) and many of his men lost their lives.

Well directed and executed, the story of the Fifty-fourth stands far above all other Civil War films as the finest yet made. Outstanding within this strong although sometimes melodramatic work are the sights and sounds of battle, which mimic hauntingly the very sensations many veterans described in their memoirs—gleaming bayonets, hissing bullets, and the unworldly spin of artillery shells. For their effort, the film's creators rightfully landed Oscars in the categories of sound and cinematography.

Glory is by no means a documentary. Aside from Shaw, all other characters portrayed in the unit are fictional. Although the film implies otherwise, most of the Fifty-fourth were freemen, having lived their whole lives in the North. Nor were they the first black regiment raised or the first to engage in battle. A scene where the soldiers refused pay rather than submit to reduced wages is based on fact, but it first occurred with another regiment. The major events in the picture, however, occurred largely as portrayed—the sacking of Darien, Georgia, the assault on Battery Wagner, Confederates burying Shaw's body with those of his troops.[3]

The subtle gems in *Glory* are readings from Shaw's letters to his New England abolitionist family. His sincere missives reveal a man both insightful and insecure, trying his best to lead others who had a greater stake in the war than he did. Sadly, these short narratives are underutilized, and the film treats them more like a time-killing montage rather than a profound looking glass.[4]

Within the ranks of the Fifty-fourth Massachusetts were two sons of FREDERICK DOUGLASS.

---

2. *GETTYSBURG* (1993)

TURNER PICTURES AND NEW LINE CINEMA
PRODUCER: MACE NEUFELD AND BOB REHME
DIRECTOR: RON MAXWELL
STARRING: TOM BERENGER, JEFF DANIELS, MARTIN SHEEN

Somewhat less accurate but even larger than *Glory* is *Gettysburg,* adapted almost verbatim from Michael Shaara's novel *The Killer Angels.* Included in this detailed movie are the scramblings for position during the battle's first day, the pivotal fight for Little Round Top, and PICKETT'S CHARGE.

Much of the movie examines personal relationships within the carnage, namely between Col. Joshua Chamberlain (Jeff Daniels) and his subordinates in the Twentieth Maine and between the conflicting natures of opportunist Robert E. Lee (Martin Sheen) and pragmatist James Longstreet (Tom Berenger). At times these dialogues paint vividly the ad hoc nature of engagement and the human reactions to duty and the unknown. Many of the orations, however, appear contrived and convenient, allowing mortal men to eloquently confess "what it all means" while simultaneously dodging shells and bullets.

There are extremes in the quality of special effects. Firefights, especially the grandiose Confederate artillery assault upon Cemetery Ridge, are impressive. Yet men, ground, and trees stay relatively intact when the actual physical destruction was otherworldly. Such limited damage is excusable, as the producers worked to maintain broad audience appeal.

The weakest facet of the film is the frail performance of Sheen as Lee. The Marble Man appears as a short and simple stumbler, with accent and makeup of community theater quality. Still, *Gettysburg* is an insightful, moving, and measurably viable rendition of three days that changed and characterized American history.[5]

Among the thousands of extras in Gettysburg were media kingpin Ted Turner and documentarist Ken Burns.

---

3. *RED BADGE OF COURAGE* (1951)

MGM
PRODUCER: GOTTFRIED REINHARDT
DIRECTOR: JOHN HUSTON
STARRING: AUDIE MURPHY

Rendering Stephen Crane's novel to screen, *Red Badge of Courage* may be unsurpassed in its portrayal of cowardice, heroism, confusion, remorse, and death within combat. Both the novel's author and the film's director consulted Civil War photographs for a better concept of actual imagery, and few war films since, even those aided by special effects, have been as moving.

The central figure is a young private (Audie Murphy) who abandons his unit during the height of a battle. He then plummets into a night of inexorable shame, incapable of determining right from wrong. He eventually resolves his anguish by charging the enemy the following day. To his astonishment, he is praised and rewarded for his brief act of madness.

The studio cut nine minutes from the already brief original, editing scenes of violence and language that would be viewed as timid by today's standards. Studio head L. B. Mayer had no faith in the film altogether, saying *Courage* "has got no laughs, no songs, no entertainment value." Had these nine minutes remained, believed an incensed Huston, *Courage* would have been the finest film of his illustrious career.[6]

The film did not fare well commercially or critically. Only after Vietnam was *Red Badge of Courage* elevated to its current status as an insightful examination of human behavior.[7]

Actor Audie Murphy was the most decorated American soldier of the Second World War.

---

4. *THE BIRTH OF A NATION* (1915)

EPOCH PRODUCING CORPORATION
PRODUCER: D. W. GRIFFITH
DIRECTOR: D. W. GRIFFITH
STARRING: LILLIAN GISH, HENRY B. WALTHALL

Few films have received as much praise and condemnation as the 1915 silent epic *The Birth of a Nation*. President Woodrow Wilson proclaimed it was "like writing history with lightning." Some theaters ran the movie for seven months. Many film historians rank it as one of the revolutionary achievements of the medium. Yet D. W. Griffith's opus may never be shown in public again.[8]

When most films were one or two reels, *Birth of a Nation* ran twelve. When most sets and casts were modest in size, Griffith used huge and elaborate scenes with battle segments involving thousands of extras.

Based on Thomas Dixon Jr.'s fictional novel *The Clansman*, the film shadows the intertwined fates of the Stoneman family of the North and the Camerons of the South. Much of the plot revolves around the Camerons, who suffer the humiliation of losing the war, the injustices of Reconstruction, and the ensuing fears of slave liberation. The story concludes with the newly created and ennobled Ku Klux Klan riding forward, ready to preserve the integrity of the fragile South against the intruding black race.

Throughout the film, Griffith depicts slaves as almost simian in behavior, playful and childish, with definite animalistic intentions. So venomously racist, so excruciatingly degrading, Griffith's "masterpiece" sparked riots and protests after its debut. President Wilson and others learned to regret their praises. Theater owners, even those sympathetic or objective, began to refuse its display.[9]

A landmark in film history, *Birth of a Nation* was the first epic ever released. It also served as proof that the war continued long after Appomattox.[10]

One of the film's many admirers was a young Russian by the name of V. I. Lenin.

---

5. *GONE WITH THE WIND* (1939)

MGM

PRODUCER: DAVID O. SELZNICK

DIRECTORS: VICTOR FLEMING, GEORGE CUKOR, SAM WOOD,
              WILLIAM MENZIES, SIDNEY FRANKLIN

STARRING: CLARK GABLE, VIVIEN LEIGH, HATTIE MCDANIEL

The most popular Civil War film of all time does not include a single battle scene. Instead, it spends its energies on a tumultuous although compelling love story. Still, the movie remains one of the most significant studies because of its influence on the American public.[11]

Gone with the Wind forged the enduring mythical image of the cotton South, with ornate mansions and dashing men, healthy and adorned slaves, and sweeping plantations. In fact, there may have been as few as twenty such estates the size of Tara. Many of these suffered much worse shortages, damage, and anarchy during the war than the comparatively tame hardships endured by Scarlett and friends.

Based on Margaret Mitchell's novel of the same name, the film is rightly criticized for its farcical portrayal of house slaves as panicky comic relief. Nonetheless, the work is remarkable considering its release date of 1939. A piece of such vivid grandeur and moving score had not yet been done, and audiences to this day are enamored by its magnificence.[12]

Hattie McDaniel's Academy Award for best supporting actress was the first Oscar ever given to an African American.

---

6. *ANDERSONVILLE* (1996)

TURNER PICTURES

PRODUCER: DAVID W. RINTELS
DIRECTOR: JOHN FRANKENHEIMER
STARRING: JARROD EMICK, FREDERIC FORREST, TED MARCOUX,
              WILLIAM H. MACY

For pure dramatic effect, few movies can match the offering of *Andersonville,* a made-for-cable story of life and death in the infamous stockade. The 1996 production could not have come closer to the camp's actual filth and depravation without effectively harming the actors and repelling most viewers.

Centering on a Massachusetts unit's capture, imprisonment, and fight to survive, *Andersonville* benefits from believable characters in an unbelievable setting. Most impressive are Cpl. Josiah Day (Jarrod Emick) and Martin Blackburn (Ted Marcoux), honor-bound men finding themselves slipping from disbelief into resignation as their bodies and chances fade away.

Certainly, director John Frankenheimer emphasized entertainment over accuracy. The camp was far more crowded than is depicted. At the real ANDERSONVILLE, guards were almost as emaciated and poorly clothed as the prisoners. One scene shows Federal prisoners rejecting Confederate recruiters en masse. Recruiters were actually successful in convincing some Andersonville prisoners to fight for the gray, just as there were Southern prisoners who ended their imprisonment in places such as CAMP DOUGLAS and ROCK ISLAND by volunteering for service in the Union army.

The film's running time of nearly three hours could be whittled to two, and minor detractions include the rare clumsy line, choppy editing, and unfortunate gaps required for commercial slots. Yet even a jittery, over-the-top rendition of Commandant Wirz (Jan Triska) cannot dilute the impact of the compelling subject. Most impressive is the set design of the stockade. The high drama of the film replaces the reality of the long, slow death that was Andersonville, but the terrain and walls on screen are very much the same as those seen by the actual inmates.[13]

Several reels mysteriously disappeared during production of *Andersonville*. At great expense, the lost scenes filmed in Georgia had to be reshot at a later date in North Carolina.

---

7. *THE GENERAL* (1927)

UNITED ARTISTS
PRODUCER: JOSEPH SCHENK
DIRECTOR: BUSTER KEATON
STARRING: BUSTER KEATON

Keaton plays Johnny Gray, a plucky train engineer who attempts to join the Confederate army but is rejected because his skill is too vital to the war effort. When his love interest is taken captive by a mob of engine-stealing blue bellies, Gray steams to the rescue with an army of Confederates in support.

The work, thick with intricate stunts and impressive cinematography, ends with Johnny saving his girl and the Confederates winning a decisive victory.

The legendary Keaton never made a better film, and *The General* often is considered one of the top one hundred films of all time, with supreme timing, pace, purpose, and shot variation. Yet this movie is most significant for what it is: the one and only critically acclaimed Civil War comedy ever made.[14]

Adored today, *The General* was a commercial and critical flop in its time. Star and director Keaton was devastated by its failure.

---

8. *SHENANDOAH* (1965)

UNIVERSAL STUDIOS
PRODUCER: ROBERT ARTHUR
DIRECTOR: ANDREW MCLAGLEN
STARRING: JAMES STEWART, GEORGE KENNEDY, GLENN CORBETT,
              KATHARINE ROSS

Charlie Anderson (Jimmy Stewart) is widower patriarch to an extended subsistence farm family. The character hopes to stay neutral in a war that eventually destroys much of his life.

An inappropriately flighty soundtrack and a syrupy feel-good ending degrade this brave presentation of unspoken truths: Few people had a role in the war's initiation, many wanted no part in its continuation, and countless suffered despite their wishes. A fictional character in a fictional town, Anderson is nonetheless an excellent sampling of many Border State farmers caught in the middle, subjected to the devastating whims of roaming armies and subhuman looters.

Unkind to war as a whole, *Shenandoah* precedes by years a flood of antiwar films spawned by the American struggle with Vietnam.[15]

A story set in the Virginia valley, *Shenandoah* was actually filmed in Oregon.

---

9. *GODS AND GENERALS* (2003)

TURNER PICTURES
PRODUCER: RON MAXWELL
DIRECTOR: RON MAXWELL
STARRING: ROBERT DUVALL, JEFF DANIELS, STEPHEN LANG

Incredible how a film can consume more than fifty million dollars, last nearly four hours, and achieve so little. Based on Jeff Shaara's novel of the same name, the prequel to *Gettysburg* is poorly directed, haphazardly shot, and stifled by weak performances.

The work, however, does offer a fresh and mostly factual treatment of THOMAS J. "STONEWALL" JACKSON. Although not nearly as personable, talkative, nor bipolar as Stephen Lang plays him, the high-voiced, shy, and judgmental Jackson was indeed very gentle with children and his wife. Owning slaves, he did have a personal servant who was a freedman. He readily executed disobedient soldiers, became a new father just before FREDERICKSBURG, and was tone deaf. Jackson's wounding and death happened almost exactly as portrayed, right down to the clothes he was wearing. And yet his true-to-life First Brigade speech appears completely out of context, as are his personal feuds with other Confederate generals. Worse, the film makes him all but invisible at Fredericksburg, where in fact Jackson's and Jeb Stuart's men saved the critical south flank after hours of relentless combat.[16]

Altogether, the script supplants dialogue with diatribe, scenes lack any trace of sequence, special effects are anemic, field hospitals appear comically placid, and ROBERT E. LEE (Robert Duvall) always seems to be on the verge of a nap. Yet the names and dates are accurate if not the personalities. In short, *Gods and Generals* is made of, by, and for reenactors. Film buffs may have a harder time with it.

Playing the part of Jackson, actor Stephen Lang also appeared in *Gettysburg* as George E. Pickett.

---

10. *RIDE WITH THE DEVIL* (1999)

UNIVERSAL STUDIOS
PRODUCER: TED HOPE
DIRECTOR: ANG LEE
STARRING: JEWEL KILCHER, TOBEY MAGUIRE, SKEET ULRICH, JEFFREY WRIGHT

Well received both critically and commercially, *Ride with the Devil* is among the worst Civil War films ever. Otherwise impressive director Ang Lee offers a fictional piece with no sense of direction, pointless scenes, disappearing characters, and more loose ends than a battalion with dysentery. Yet *Ride* is appealing to the American eye for one sublime, intense reason: It is the Civil War that much of America wishes to see.

The plot: A band of pro-Confederacy men fight to defend their Missouri homes against invading Yankees. Along the way, they take part in

William Quantrill's sacking of Lawrence, Kansas. Later, the afraid-of-commitment youngster of the gang (Tobey Maguire) reluctantly weds his dead buddy's pregnant mistress (Jewel Kilcher), and they gallop off to California and a new tomorrow while resolving nothing.

To be sure, Lee did not make much of a Civil War movie. He did, however, fashion the perfect Civil War. Chase scenes, gory special effects, requited love, and a single obedient slave who finds respect and freedom, *Ride* is required viewing for the Civil War student, because it reflects the enduring and yet unfulfilled popular desire for reconciliation and closure between North and South, between black and white.

In depicting an 1861 shootout, several actors used Remington Model 1858 revolvers. Although patented in 1858, that model was not manufactured until 1863.

TOP TEN WAYS TO BE
AN ACCURATE REENACTOR

Reenacting has become an art as well as a science for Civil War aficionados. From the thousands of hobbyists to the legions of expert organizers, these artisans in field theater loyally involve themselves and the general public in the history of sights and sounds otherwise lost.

Not a few of them are full-fledged encyclopedias in the art of Civil War soldiery, skilled in small arms and artillery, fluent in epaulets and chevrons, with exhaustive knowledge of the conflict's officers and enlisted. Yet most will admit they are not a perfect representation of their subject.

If one is inclined to join up with the local weekend warriors but afraid of sporting inaccurate shoe stitching or implausible canteen covers, here are a few ways to match the most die-hard. Some tricks are more subtle than others, and each is ranked by its respective level of feasibility. If the desire is there to look as much like Billy Yank or Johnny Reb as possible, consider some of the following.

1. WEAR ILL-FITTING EVERYTHING

Government-issue articles, produced by the thousands, gave little consideration for the variety of body types. Men of all sizes had to deal with clothes of clownish proportions. Shoes were made to fit either foot. There were one-size-fits-all hats. Pants were especially vague in their construction. All combined to rid a soldier of any sense of grandeur.

Tailoring and trade rectified some of the more ridiculous problems. Soldiers with extra cash procured better fits from locals or sutlers (civilian peddlers), and many committed much of their pay for such purposes. Union boys had it better in this case, as their War Department allotted forty-two dollars per year for a clothing allowance.[17]

If by chance you already have a well-fitted kit but want to look more like a battle-tested artillerist rather than a paper-pushing adjutant, proceed to step 2, going for the worn look.

> The term *shoddy* comes from the Civil War. A fabric consisting of recycled wool and cotton cloth, it was used by unscrupulous manufactures to make uniforms and blankets.

2. GO FOR THE WORN LOOK

Most reenactors spend a pretty shinplaster on their replicated duds, subsequently treating their uniforms better than a Sunday suit. Even those attempting to represent the mismatched nature of Civil War outerwear, sporting a homespun shirt or a hand-me-down hat for example, still appear pristine compared to the real campaigners. To an actual soldier, there were four kinds of clothes: lost, tossed, dress, and damaged.

Marching and fighting was as hard on the weave as they were on the warrior. Brush, brambles, and the jagged ensemble of soldier equipment tore away at cloth. Rain and mud had a particular appetite for cotton and wool. Although regulations sternly recommended he maintain appearances, a soldier became unavoidably haggard while on the move. Yet he managed. Before he learned how to cook, fight, or march, he usually mastered a needle and thread, or developed a talent for finding someone handy with a housewife (slang for a sewing kit).[18]

Take note: There are comparatively few reenactments of post-1863 battles, when the war transformed to one of attrition. Understandably, not many Confederate reenactors wish to dress the part. For the South, supply-hoarding governors and the oppressive blockade turned whole armies into the walking ragged. Legions of gray and butternut began to resemble a sentry of threadbare scarecrows. In short, battles of 1864–65 hold very little martial beauty or what-if mystique for the reenactor or audience.

> When officers and enlisted men donned formal dress uniforms, they called it "ragging out."

3. COMPLAIN OF DYSENTERY OR DIARRHEA

Sure, it's not going to win many hearts at the postbattle square dance, but it will sound authentic. A soldier's chance of getting the "fluxes" during his stint was approximately 99 percent. Most men had it three or four times before being discharged or killed. When commanders calculated how many effectives they had for duty, they first took the sum total of their forces and subtracted the reported cases of the "quickstep." At sick call, the entry question a doctor asked was, "How are your bowels?" At any one time, 5 to 40 percent of an entire field army could be under its lurid spell. In the war between the blue and the gray, diarrhea won.

The men normally avoided getting chatty on the subject for various reasons. Primarily, news of illness was hardly news, and spreading the word was almost as damaging to morale as spreading the disease.[19]

> A doctor's cure for the fluxes: opium, quinine, caster oil, lead tincture, and/or whiskey. A soldier's cure for the fluxes: fasting, hot tea made from tree bark, flannel cloth around the waist, and/or whiskey.

4. LOSE THE EXTRAS

Although the impetus might be to collect all the right equipment and leave nothing out, the most authentic move is to unload.

When heading off to war, eager volunteers weighed themselves down with perceived necessities: pistols, Bowie knives, overcoats, gloves, compasses, mess kits, spare shirts, spare pants, and for the extracautious, armored chest plates. On the first mile of their first march, many soldiers must have felt ready for anything. By about the second mile, they were usually ready to convert to the theology of thrift.[20]

Most men learned to replace equipment with ingenuity. No need for heavy pots when a tin cup worked just as well. Half of a canteen made an excellent frying pan-dinner plate-shovel. The best way to keep food from rotting was to eat it. A few good men discovered that a corked rifle barrel held quite a bit of whiskey.

Soldiers heading for a big scrape also knew to jettison playing cards, pipes, dice, gambling IOUs, anything even remotely associated with sin. If killed in battle and the body identified, a soldier's effects were sent home. The last thing a private wished to impose upon his mother was evidence that her dear lost boy had succumbed to some seductress vice.

> Bare minimum, an infantryman carried a rifle, bayonet, scabbard, haversack with three days' rations, cartridge box with forty rounds of ammunition, a blanket roll, and a canteen. Total weight—about thirty pounds.

5. LOSE SLEEP

More often than not, the possibility of an impending engagement was not a mystery to the men in the ranks, and the time required for preparation left little opportunity for rest.

Prep time superseded sleep: cleaning weapons, limbering horses, filling haversacks, collecting ammunition, picket duty, skirmish duty, and standing by. Officers used the cloak of darkness to mobilize or dig in. Getting ready usually lasted all night.

Federal units were up at 2 A.M. preceding the battle of FIRST MANASSAS. THOMAS J. "STONEWALL" JACKSON and his soldiers traveled day and night from the Shenandoah to take part in the SEVEN DAYS. Union soldiers were awake twenty hours and more, preparing for a hopeless dawn attack on COLD HARBOR. In frigid winters, men stayed up all night to keep from freezing to death. In summer, officers marched men through the darkness to avoid the blistering sun.

> Over the three-day battle of STONES RIVER, William S. Rosecrans stayed awake almost the entire time. At the one-day battle of Antietam, GEORGE B. MCCLELLAN slept in and missed a third of it.

6. LOSE THE GLASSES

Pince-nez, glasses, or other eyewear might have conveyed a look of scholastic prowess among the learned elite, but such optical aids were considered a sign of infirmity to the manly sort in the middle 1800s, equivalent to a cane or an ear horn. Accordingly, nineteenth-century spectacles were not designed for excursion. With straight temples and no nosepieces, anything more than a stroll caused the specs to slide down the face. Exceptionally fragile, glass lenses and flimsy frames had shorter life spans in battle than flag-bearers. Soldiers dependent on corrective lenses either opted out, were weeded out, or went without.

For the reenactor who needs vision correction but cannot wear contacts (perhaps an Arkansan with astigmatism or a bifocaled bluecoat), there are many sources of period frames. Antique stores are the least expensive, and most optometry suppliers can custom fit new lenses. Web-based providers of period eyeglasses are plentiful. Some reenacting suppliers can be of service. Choose oval glasses or octagonal. Circular frames were available during the war but were out of style.

> Examine closely any military portrait or group photo during the war. An extremely rare find is the sight of a Civil War soldier sporting eyewear, literally one in a million.

7. LOSE THE WEIGHT

The average soldier was a scant 145 pounds. Questionable rations, hard labor, marches in excess of twenty miles, bouts of illness, and tough outdoor living kept the fighting man lean, even gaunt. As early as ANTIETAM in 1862, Northern soldiers and citizens remarked how thin the Confederates looked, a condition soon shared by field soldiers on either side.

Wartime desk clerks might have allowed themselves the pleasure of a little pudge, some officers might have taken the better portions of issued fare, but the infantry rank and file lived underweight despite a diet laden with fat and grease. However frail he might have appeared, the soldier with the diminutive carriage tended to last longest. Diaries are ripe with stories of giants in camp, but the same accounts praised the thin, more efficient soldier in the endurance events of marching and fighting.

> Two soldiers not on the diet plan were Gens. Winfield Scott and George H. Thomas. Scott topped three hundred pounds at the beginning of the war, and Thomas reached the three-hundred mark soon after the war ended.

8. NEGLECT YOUR SKIN

Constant exposure to the elements ravaged the skin of any private or sailor. Burning sun, driving winds, cold rain, and frigid winters aged a soldier's complexion well beyond his years. Working in, marching through, and sleeping on brush and dirt accelerated the process further.

Adding to the misery was a soldier's uniform. Collars, cuffs, and waistbands, much of them wool, became greasy with sweat, mud, rain, and dirt. Inevitable chafing rubbed certain areas raw and made them susceptible to infection. A regular concern for orderlies and doctors was the problem of boils around the areas where clothes sanded away at the flesh.

On top of all this, and usually worse, were the eternal companions of vermin. Mosquitoes, ticks, mites, fleas, chiggers, lice (a.k.a. graybacks, rebels, or tigers), and the occasional rat would tear at a soldier's hide, especially at night. Even in the coldest winters, a man's coat was a tenement of gnawing little beasts, driving the most pious to fits of colorful blasphemy. Most soldiers preferred to fight soldiers rather than insects, as there was a measurable chance of victory with the former. In the war against the wigglers, the contest was an inglorious, infectious degradation, ceasing only after death or a hot bath and a new suit of clothes.[21]

Although few soldiers in the war routinely bathed, even fewer were inclined to brush their teeth.

---

9. DISPLAY A SENSE OF DEPRESSION AFTER THE BATTLE

Veterans of many wars describe battle with disturbing similarity. An initial fear often fuels a heightened sense of readiness. Entering the firestorm triggers an intense, almost maniacal force of concentration. Many speak of hearing nervous laughter emanate from themselves or others. A strange numbness prevails. Gone is any perception of time.

After participating in mock combat, many reenactors speak of sensations mildly resembling the above, an honest adrenaline rush that leaves several feeling as if they had indeed "traveled through time."

Of course, the two experiences are oceans apart and completely unbridgeable. Reenactors shake hands, set off for a nice meal, visit the sutler's store, or get ready for a formal dance or a box social. For Civil War soldiers and many like them who survived moments of elongated terror, there was commonly a postcombat letdown, apparently similar to running into a wall. A deep, quiet sadness prevailed, with threads of guilt and despair dominating the psyche. Men spoke of a tiredness somehow deeper than exhaustion.[22]

According to the *Medical and Surgical History of the Rebellion,* soldiers most prone to depression were those with "highly developed imaginative facilities" and "young men of feeble will."

---

10. BE ABSENT

When picturing a typical infantry regiment in the Civil War, keep in mind that most of it was not there. Ideally numbering one thousand to eleven hundred men (Confederate regiments were intended to be larger), such units typically hovered around half to quarter strength. Thus any reenactor can add a sense of realism by subtracting himself from the equation.

Furloughs were common, where a few men or a few hundred from a regiment were on leave for two hours to two months. Naturally, sickness thinned the ranks. One in ten who served was captured sooner or later. By 1865 the dead and the wounded constituted one million men.

For a sincere display of realism, show up for the weekend activities but don't take part in the battle. Every battle produced stragglers, men who failed to keep up with the marching columns, whether by injury, illness, fatigue, or choice. Within this last group were "skulkers," men who conveniently slinked off and hid once the front came into view. Of like nature were "skedaddlers" who made it as far as the shooting then flew rearward in a panic.[23]

Altogether, an estimated 200,000 deserted from the Union army and navy. Some 120,000 did the same from Confederate forces.

TOP TEN NATIONAL BATTLEFIELD SITES

Bloody Hill at WILSON'S CREEK, the Bloody Pond of SHILOH, the Bloody Angle of SPOTSYLVANIA—these places still exist although their preservation was slow and uncertain and many like them are gone. For years, Americans wanted to forget the war, sharing in Robert E. Lee's postwar wish "to obliterate the marks of civil strife and to commit to oblivion the feelings it engendered." Some traveled to hallowed grounds but did so to find bodies of loved ones and return them home or to reap the soil of its valuable scrap iron and lead.[24]

No national process existed to save land for posterity, except for burial sites. In July 1862 the U.S. Congress granted executive authority to buy and receive land for the creation of military cemeteries. Using rather morose wording, the legislation read, "For the soldiers who *shall* die in the service of their country" (italics added). In doing so, Northern legislators unwittingly created the nucleus for future national military parks.[25]

Cemeteries became rendezvous points for aging veterans. By the 1880s full-fledged reunions emerged, and with them a desire for reconciliation. Concurrently, many former soldiers were successful businessmen and politicians. Armed with the levers of law and money, veterans worked to preserve land sewn with the bones of their comrades. In 1890 Chickamauga and Chattanooga became the first federally protected battlefields in the United States.[26]

Of the hundreds of local, state, federal, and private holdings, the following are the ten best in terms of preservation of landscape, size, quantity of markers and information, accessibility (parking, trails, ramps, etc.), and viewshed (sight line of surrounding area). All are protected by the National Park Service.[27]

1. GETTYSBURG NATIONAL MILITARY PARK AND CEMETERY (GETTYSBURG, PENNSYLVANIA)

What began in 1895 as an eight-hundred-acre park is currently almost six thousand. More than a day is needed for the grounds alone. There is the geological oddity of Devil's Den, the stone-crowned Round Tops, Meade's headquarters, the Wheatfield that changed hands six times, and the awful mile of open ground between Seminary and Cemetery Ridges. Also within the grounds is the national cemetery where Lincoln delivered his immortal address. To the east of town is the East Cavalry Battlefield Site, where Union horsemen intercepted Jeb Stuart's cavalry attack on the final day.

The surrounding viewshed is reasonable, thanks to strict zoning laws in the borough of Gettysburg. Outlying areas are less restricted, which has

prompted bitter fights between preservationists and real estate developers.[28]

Crowds are a potential distraction. More tourists come to this small Pennsylvania town each year than there are residents of Nebraska—nearly two million. This influx and attention, however, translates into the largest budget of any Civil War site. As of 2003, plans are under way to build a $95 million museum and visitors center.[29]

The park contains more than twenty-six miles of roadways, with more than fourteen hundred markers, monuments, and memorials. There are picnic areas, walking paths, observation towers, an amphitheater, licensed personal tour guides for hire, and a museum. A featured attraction is a 360-degree painting of PICKETT'S CHARGE, one of the last surviving cylcoramas in the country. More than a century old, the oil-on-canvas work occupies nearly ten thousand square feet and is accompanied by a twenty-minute light-and-sound display.

> Gettysburg hosted the largest Civil War reunion ever. On the fiftieth anniversary of the battle, more than fifty thousand veterans of blue and gray traveled to take part in a weeklong commemoration. Due to an oppressive heat wave, nine veterans died.

2. ANTIETAM NATIONAL BATTLEFIELD SITE AND CEMETERY (SHARPSBURG, MARYLAND)

The battle of Antietam lasted eleven hours. The fight for the Antietam battlefield has been ongoing ever since. Fortunately, private and government efforts to save the area have thus far succeeded.

As with other national sites, Antietam began as a cemetery. The state of Maryland set aside eleven acres in 1865 to inter the Union dead of Antietam and other battles. In 1890 Congress declared the site a federally preserved battlefield. The park has grown over the years, from eighteen hundred acres in 1960 to thirty-three hundred acres in 2000.

The area's greatest attribute is its enduring faithfulness to appearance. The town of Sharpsburg retains a provincial character, even though the park attracts 330,000 visitors yearly. The horizons are largely free of modern construction. Miles of snake-rail fences continue to wind around fields. Melancholy and narrow, BURNSIDE'S BRIDGE remains astride Antietam Creek.

The park contains an eight-mile driving tour, battle markers, monuments, and an observation tower. The visitors center has a small museum, an orientation film, and an hourlong documentary at noon. Summer activities include guided tours and living-history presentations. Unique to the park is the historic Piper family home, now a bed and breakfast, but in 1862 the house served as Confederate Gen. JAMES LONGSTREET's headquarters.[30]

> At the center of Antietam Cemetery stands *The Private Soldier.* The granite statue stands more than twenty-one feet high and weighs over thirty tons. In tribute to the 4,776 Union soldiers buried there, the statue faces north.

3. SHILOH NATIONAL MILITARY PARK AND CEMETERY (SHILOH, TENNESSEE)

Established in 1894, Shiloh remains the most serene and least encumbered of the inaugural battlefield parks. Its four thousand acres of groves and fields stand nearly as they did in 1862, when Confederate Gen. Albert Sidney Johnston struck here to protect the rail city of Corinth to the south.

Shiloh's distinctive landmarks and well-planned tour route make the battle easy to visualize. One can traverse the road known as the Hornets' Nest and look out upon the row of artillery that finally broke this Union line. To the south grows the Peach Orchard, where Confederates hit the Union left flank in force, sending a hail of bullets through the blossoming trees. Nearby is Bloody Pond, an eerily placid pool once turned red from the corpses of horses and men. Last stop is Pittsburg Landing, where

Union soldiers cowered from the Confederate onslaught and Don Carlos Buell landed twenty thousand reinforcements to turn the tide of the fight.

Shiloh's visitors center has an orientation film and museum. The bookstore is in an adjacent building. There are picnic tables and a pavilion. Seasonal activities include rifle-firing demonstrations and other interpretive programs. Summer weekends have ranger-led activities and periodic living-history events. The auto tour is more than ten miles long, and numerous footpaths accompany the fourteen stops. The grounds contain 150 monuments, 217 cannon, and 450 informational tablets. More than 320,000 visitors come to the park each year.

Shiloh National Park is also home to several Native American burial mounds.

---

4. PEA RIDGE NATIONAL MILITARY PARK (PEA RIDGE, ARKANSAS)

Site of the March 1862 battle that secured Missouri for the Union, Pea Ridge is considered by many to be the best preserved battlefield in the United States. Shelved away in northwest Arkansas, the site of forty-three hundred acres is a healthy distance from excessive civilization (the nearest hotel is nine miles south). It is also free of stifling crowds. Yearly attendance of the park does not exceed ninety thousand.

A late addition to the family of military sites (1956), the park contains a seven-mile auto tour with ten stops. The most stunning is certainly Stop 6, the East Overlook. It is the finest panoramic vista of any Civil War park, providing almost a full view of the battlefield as well as the heights and valleys of a remarkably pristine horizon. It was from this point and nearby

Elkhorn Tavern where nine thousand Federals pushed nearly fourteen thousand off Pea Ridge and deep into the Arkansas interior.

A short orientation film, *Thunder in the Ozarks,* is shown in the visitors center, which offers permanent and traveling museum exhibits.

The park also has picnic areas and ten miles of hiking and horse trails. There are living-history presentations in the summer. The Elkhorn Tavern has been reconstructed and is open for tours from June to October. Although most of the facilities are fully accessible, the tavern has stairs, and a few tour stops have inclines not recommended for wheelchairs.

Protected within the park boundaries are two and a half miles of the 1838 Trail of Tears, the route of the Cherokees forcibly relocated to Oklahoma.

---

5. CHICKAMAUGA AND CHATTANOOGA NATIONAL MILITARY PARK (CHATTANOOGA, TENNESSEE)

NATIONAL PARK SERVICE

In 1889 area residents and veterans from North and South petitioned Congress to spare the unique landscapes and battle sites along the Chickamauga River. By recommendation from the House Committee on Military Affairs in 1890, Chickamauga and Chattanooga became the first Civil War national battlefield parks in the United States. Totaling more than eighty-two hundred acres, they remain the largest.[31]

Of the two places, Chickamauga benefited from its rural location and remains far more contiguous. Chattanooga had 2,500 residents in 1860. By 2000 the city surpassed 160,000. With the exception of Lookout Mountain's peak, preserved sections along Missionary Ridge and in town are modest in size.

Yet Chattanooga must be seen to be comprehended. Missionary Ridge runs for twenty miles and slopes four hundred feet upward. Lookout Mountain towers twenty-one hundred feet above sea level. From these vantage points, it is easy to see how thirty thousand bluecoats could get trapped in the valley. Once more, the successful Federal breakthrough on November 25, 1863, appears all the more remarkable.

A short drive south, Chickamauga provides a different scene altogether. The dense underbrush, dark woods, and irregular clearings of the park illustrate how this September 1863 battle devolved into a frightful hive of disjointed, confused, hand-to-hand fighting. Together, Chattanooga and Chickamauga provide unrivaled opportunity to compare extremes in terrain and, for that matter, results.[32]

The parks contain 250 cannon, 700 monuments, and 650 markers. Both have self-guided driving tours and miles of footpaths. Situated atop Lookout Mountain, the Chattanooga visitors center displays the historic James Walker painting, *The Battle Above the Clouds.* The nearby Ochs Museum and Overlook, however, are not wheelchair accessible. The Chickamauga visitors center on Lafayette Road features a multimedia presentation and an exhibit of more than 350 shoulder arms. Summer activities at both sites include living-history presentations and military reenactments. On average, 790,000 people visit the parks each year.

August 19, 1890, President Benjamin Harrison signed the bill that formed the national battlefields of Chickamauga and Chattanooga. A great grandson of a signer of the Declaration of Independence, Harrison was also a Union officer during the Civil War.

---

6. VICKSBURG NATIONAL MILITARY PARK AND CEMETERY (VICKSBURG, MISSISSIPPI)

At first there were to be only four major national military parks—one battlefield for each region. The Southwest's lone representative was SHILOH until relentless pressure from civilians and veterans enlightened Congress to protect the siege lines and forts of Vicksburg in 1899.[33]

Today the park stands as one of the most impressive military memorials in the country, hosting more than 1,300 monu- ments and markers. Among them is Illinois's moving tribute to its soldiers. On the interior walls of its tow- ering Grecian dome are sixty bronze tablets bearing the 36,325 names of men from Illinois who served in

the Vicksburg campaign. Missouri's compelling monument honors its forty-two units that fought in the siege—fifteen for the Confederacy and twenty-seven for the Union. Anchoring the park to the old banks of the Mississippi is Vicksburg National Cemetery. Completed in 1866, it is the largest burial site of Union soldiers in the country, with more than 17,000 interments, most of whom are unknown.

Also in the park are twenty miles of original and reconstructed trench works, 144 cannon, hiking and equestrian trails, seventeen miles of paved road, picnic areas, and a visitors center with several exhibits. Summer activities include guided tours and presentations on the weekends, including demonstration firings of cannon and rifles. The thirteen-gun ironclad *Cairo,* resurrected from the murky Yazoo River in the 1970s, is on display next to an accompanying museum. Over a million tourists come to the park each year.

> The first resident commissioner of the military park was William Rigby, who held the position from 1899 until his death in 1929. Rigby had worked for the government before, as a soldier of the Twenty-fourth Iowa at the siege of Vicksburg.

7. PETERSBURG NATIONAL BATTLEFIELD
(PETERSBURG, CITY POINT, AND FIVE FORKS, VIRGINIA)

Few remnants of the Civil War are as haunting as trenches and forts. Miles of these mounds and walls, scraped from the soil of the Confederacy, remain visible, but time and urbanization are steadily pressing them back into the earth. For the best collection of these fading structures, look to the Petersburg National Battlefield.

The siege of Petersburg lasted five times longer than Chattanooga, six times longer than Vicksburg, and nine times longer than Yorktown. There were eleven major offensives, countless skirmishes, constant sniper and artillery activity, cavalry raids, and the tunneling of mines and counter-mines. At stake was Richmond's last rail lines south, protected by more than seventy miles of trenchworks and forty thousand soldiers.

Petersburg National Battlefield is by necessity a collection of several protected areas. Ten miles northeast is City Point. A wharf on the James and Appomattox Rivers, City Point was the supply depot for 120,000

Union troops. Present are ULYSSES S. GRANT's headquarters and a pre-served plantation homestead.

The main park is just northeast of Petersburg. At the visitors center maps, exhibits, and displays provide background to the siege. There is a four-mile auto tour, with stops at two preserved batteries, eight forts, and THE CRATER. Southernmost on the loop is Poplar Grove Cemetery, where more than six thousand Union soldiers are buried. Two of every three bodies there were never identified.

During the summer months, park rangers provide short tours of major points of interest. There are also living-history programs plus rifle, mortar, and cannon demonstrations. The main park is one of the few that cater to cyclists, with miles of park roads having bike lanes. In addition, there are many hiking and equestrian trails.

In terms of viewshed, the park network fairs well considering its prox-imity to populous Richmond. Petersburg itself is not overly intrusive. In 1860 the city numbered eighteen thousand. The population has not quite doubled in 140 years. Yet the diffuse locations of forts and trenches make Petersburg expensive to maintain. The park has half the annual budget of Gettysburg but one-twelfth the number of visitors. Despite the cost, preservationists continue to seek ways to improve the park and protect trenches and forts still on private land.[34]

President Lincoln spent two of the final three weeks of his life at City Point near Petersburg, overseeing the final push against the Army of Northern Virginia.

---

8. WILSON'S CREEK NATIONAL BATTLEFIELD (WILSON'S CREEK, MISSOURI)

Little beyond tree lines have changed around the meandering stream and rolling hills of southwest Missouri, where on August 10, 1861, Union Brig. Gen. Nathaniel Lyon and six thousand Federals attacked twelve thousand Confederates under Sterling Price. In terms of pristine beauty, the site rivals Pea Ridge.

A five-mile driving tour around the seventeen-hundred-acre park documents the fateful day. Tour Stop 4 (Franz Sigel's Last Position) marks the critical Union flank attack, doomed to failure when the German general mistook an enemy column for his own troops. Centerpiece of the park and the battle is appropriately named Bloody Hill at Tour Stop 7. Lyon's main force of forty-two hundred tried to hold this ground. Hopelessly outnumbered, Lyon lost the hill, nearly 18 percent of his force, and his own life.

At the visitors center, brief video and fiber-optics presentations describe the contest. Over the summer months, the Ray house (used as a Confederate hospital after the battle) is open weekends. Sundays have living-history cavalry drills plus rifle and artillery demonstrations. There are picnic areas and seven miles of trails for hiking and horseback riding. More than two hundred thousand people come to the park every year.[35]

The Union lost a higher percentage of soldiers at Wilson's Creek than at Antietam.

---

9. MANASSAS NATIONAL BATTLEFIELD PARK (MANASSAS, VIRGINIA)

Established in 1940, Manassas is a place where destinies change at the eleventh hour. In both battles, Union generals telegraphed Washington to declare victory only to be corrected soon after by grand Confederate counterattacks. In the late twentieth century, last-minute public intervention ceased construction of a mall and a theme park nearby. Despite tremendous odds, Manassas has grown to five thousand acres. Only Chickamauga-Chattanooga and Gettysburg surpass its size.[36]

The visitors center has a small museum and shows a short audiovisual presentation throughout the day. A forty-five minute documentary, *The End of Innocence,* can be seen for a nominal fee. Along the rolling hills and fields near the center, a footpath leads to the most prominent points of FIRST MANASSAS. On the thirty-minute walk is the grave of Judith Henry, the only civilian to die in the battle. Behind the Henry house is the high ground where THOMAS J. JACKSON earned the nickname Stonewall. Visible to the east is Chinn Ridge, where the Union right flank began to collapse.

A driving tour of twelve miles covers the ground of SECOND MANASSAS. Among the twelve stops is the unfinished railroad bed to the northwest, where desperate hand-to-hand fighting produced thousands of casualties. To the south and west are the New York monuments. On this low hill, 123 men of the Fifth New York regiment died in five minutes, the worst loss of any regiment in any fight of the entire war. To the east the Henry Hill marks a successful last stand of Union forces.[37]

The driving tour reveals a third battle, a continuous struggle with development. Virginia Highway 234 and Highway 29 intersect the otherwise grand park. The Stone House, a two-story building used as a hospital during both battles, shakes from the intersection just paces away. The Stone Bridge over Bull Run, a key attack and escape route in both contests, today cowers under the shadow of a highway viaduct. Despite the most noble and diligent work by preservationists, the westward expansion of population and development continues to envelope the area, much the same way COLD HARBOR and FREDERICKSBURG have been overrun.[38]

> From 1921 to 1935, a private organization—the Sons of Confederate Veterans—bought and preserved the buildings and land on Henry Hill.

10. STONES RIVER NATIONAL BATTLEFIELD AND CEMETERY (MURFREESBORO, TENNESSEE)

Saved as a military park in 1927, Stones River appears much as it did at the time of the battle, down to the fields of unpicked cotton among the cedars. Although small (714 acres), the park benefits from as yet underdeveloped surroundings.

A primary site on the driving tour is Sheridan's Stand, where a Union division withstood close-range artillery fire and three infantry assaults before it fell back. Also on the route, the national cemetery holds more than six thousand graves. During the battle, Federal artillery fired from this high ground, covering the last line of Union defenses. Key to the park is Stop 8, the infamous Round Forest. This tree-capped knoll anchored the Union left flank. On the first day of battle, four Confederate attacks tried to take the hill and were slaughtered.

Several stops contain short walks on flat ground. A few paths may be difficult, since they pass over the same limestone outcroppings that trapped caissons and ricocheted shells lifetimes ago. Marginally distracting is U.S. Highway 41, passing near the main section of the park. Crossing the north side of the grounds are the Nashville Pike and a rail line, the same road and rail beds that existed at the time of the battle.

Inside the visitors center, a small museum and a slide presentation give a battle synopsis. During summer and autumn, ranger-led walks happen daily, and living-history programs can be seen on most weekends. Stones River sees 180,000 visitors each year.

Inside Stones River National Cemetery is a monument to the Union's Hazen Brigade. Erected in 1863, it is considered to be the oldest Civil War monument in existence.

TOP TEN WAYS TO GET INVOLVED

In effect, Americans are already involved with the Civil War. Millions vote for representatives and pay taxes determining the future of historic sites. Millions more are descendants of Union and Confederate veterans. Every citizen is an heir to the social, economic, and constitutional changes created by the sectional struggle.

Of course, one of the best ways to better comprehend the war's place in the past and present is exactly this—reading—but sometimes there comes an urge to step beyond the bookstore, to encounter the tangibles of the past. Thankfully, nothing has brought the past closer than modernity.

The Civil War is more accessible now than it has been for generations. Several of the activities listed here were not available a century ago. There has been a steady increase in the number of publications and educational television programs over the years, and the Internet has become the principle means of communication between buffs, historians, and organizations.

Following are ten among many pursuits for beginners, hobbyists, schoolteachers, and students wishing to expand their Civil War horizons. Ranking is according to the minimum investment in time and funds required for participation, from least to most.

1. JOIN A CIVIL WAR ROUNDTABLE

In 1940 a handful of people gathered in a Chicago bookshop to share their interest and curiosity in the Civil War. From those humble beginnings grew a vast network of roundtables, currently topping three hundred in number, dotting the United States and several foreign countries.[39]

Far from being exclusive, such discussion groups welcome all levels of appreciation. Activities vary, but most roundtables schedule guest speakers, review the latest films and books, share news and experiences, and are involved in historic preservation. Some organize field trips and restoration projects.

For a modest membership fee, a roundtable is the least expensive and best gateway to a wide range of opportunities, perspectives, and information. Check the Web or local newspapers to find the closest group. If there are none in your area, consider creating one. A central clearinghouse of associates has instructions on how to get started: Civil War Round Table Associates, P.O. Box 7388, Little Rock, AR 72217. See also: the United States Civil War Center (www.cwc.lsu.edu).

Award for the roundtable farthest from Chicago goes to the American Civil War Round Table of Australia, which holds meetings in Sydney and Melbourne.

---

2. DONATE MONEY

When time or location limit chances for greater participation, contemplate a donation. Reputable organizations turn dollars into preservation programs, land acquisitions, site restoration, research grants, and other means of protecting national heritage. Look for an IRS rating of 501(c)(3). Donations to these not-for-profit organizations are tax deductible.

Twenty dollars or more can buy membership into a wide selection of trusts, such as the Friends of Resaca Battlefield, the Salisbury Confederate Prison Association, and the Friends of the Wilderness Battlefield. Along with gaining the satisfaction of preserving a part of the Civil War, there are perks for various levels of contribution. Almost all programs distribute newsletters and progress reports to members.

Not a joiner? A small collection can help public libraries replace worn or outdated Civil War materials. University and college history departments are in constant need of financial support. There are "adoption" programs for monuments, positions, cannon, etc. Contact local and state historical societies for opportunities or see the Conservation Fund: Civil War Battlefield Campaign (www.conservationfund.org) or the Civil War Preservation Trust (www.civilwar.org).

> The Civil War Preservation Trust has more than four hundred thousand members—roughly the same size as the entire Confederate army in 1863.

3. COLLECT MEMORABILIA

There is nothing quite like owning a piece of history, and history often neglected is that of commemoration. After the horrors of the war dissipated, nostalgia took over, generating an extraordinary mixture of images, keepsakes, mementos, and in the case of Lincoln and Lee, a slew of iconography.

The years between 1880 and 1930 offer some of the best material, the decades when veterans were still alive and wanted to remember. Reunions produced patriotic ribbons and buttons, regimental reports and rosters, and moving photos of aged comrades.

Images are enlightening and readily available. Early twentieth-century postcards and stereoviews show famous towns, battlefields, and monuments untouched by tourism and real estate development. Late nineteenth-century lithographs of pivotal engagements are peculiar, depicting neat and tidy trenches, geometric attack formations, and not a spot of blood. As for paintings, some twenty different renditions exist of Lee and Grant's historic meeting at the McLean home at Appomattox. Each image is different, as there were no artists present, and souvenir hounds gutted the room soon after.

Sheet music, veterans badges, lead soldiers, and tintypes, history itself is often not how it was but how following generations perceived it to be.

Helpful guides to this examination include Richard Friz, *Official Price Guide to Civil War Collectibles* (1999) and Stuart L. Schneider, *Collecting Lincoln* (1997).

There are some one hundred billion likenesses of Abraham Lincoln in existence. Most of them are in the form of U.S. currency.

---

4. COLLECT ARTIFACTS

In the process of forging two nations into one, the Civil War produced a king's ransom in relics. In bayonets and buttons, muster sheets and musket balls, legal tender and letters home, there are finds to acquire and deals to be made.

Swap meets, antique shows, and weekend reenactments are common sources. For the fortunate few, discoveries still happen at estate sales and in family attics. Beware of Internet auctions as they are high-risk ventures. The best defense against mistaking replicas for the real thing, or overpaying for authentic pieces, is prudence. Work with reputable dealers, never let excitement cloud judgment, and consult the following: James P. Mesker, *A Practical Guide to Collecting Civil War* (2001) and John F. Graf, *Warman's Civil War Collectibles* (2003).

Lincoln's personal copy of the Emancipation Proclamation would be worth millions if it were available. Donated to the Chicago Historical Society in 1864, it was destroyed in the Great Fire of 1871.

---

5. VISIT A HISTORIC SITE

When asked how to study a great event of the past, historian Barbara Tuchman offered one simple piece of advice: "Go to the place." Text, photographs, and maps cannot replace a firsthand education of the five senses. Opportunities are plentiful. Hundreds of forts, prisons, cemeteries, birthplaces, homes, and battlefield sites live on in public and private hands. Incredibly, each of the forty-eight contiguous states possesses at least a few historic sites related to the war.

Any chance to personally experience these places is worth the effort, whether it requires a drive across town or a long weekend. To walk the hallowed fields, to look upon the historic artifacts, to feel the cold head-stones, such experiences provide an education unobtainable by other means. Consult the following to get started: Alice Cromie, *A Tour Guide to the Civil War* (2002); Julie Shively, *The Ideals Guide to American Civil War Places* (1999); and Frances H. Kennedy, ed., *The Civil War Battle-field Guide* (1998).

In the United States there are more than twenty federal historic sites, forty museums, and seventy national cemeteries dedicated to the Civil War.

---

6. DONATE TIME

Many of the people assisting archivists, painting cannon carriages, manning desks, and maintaining trails at parks and facilities are volunteers. From cleaning monuments to repairing fortifications, on projects lasting a few hours to several months, charitable work has been and remains a pillar to preservation.

For the activist, there are editorials to write, legislation to watchdog, and representatives to influence. Too often public officials and the public at large dismiss the value of history in schools and historic preservation in communities. Historical advocacy can turn general indifference into communal interest.

Consult the nearest Civil War roundtable or local and state historical societies for information on how to help. For opportunities in national battlefield parks, please consult the National Park Service Web site (www.nps.gov).

Of the three million soldiers in the Civil War, approximately 1 percent were regular army, 9 percent were draftees or substitutes, and the rest were volunteers.

---

7. TRACE GENEALOGY

By marriage or direct lineage, millions of Americans have forefathers who were veterans of the Blue and the Gray. Germans, Mexicans, African Americans, Irish, Welsh, English, Dutch, Native American, Russian, Spanish, and dozens of other heritages served in the Brothers' War.

Descendants of Union soldiers are at an advantage, as Federal record-keeping surpassed the detail and preservation of the Confederate infrastructure. Likewise, the paper trail on officers, their assignments and promotions, is an easier road than searching for an enlisted man.

Even if there is no long-lost uncle to be found in uniform, the search will still produce results. Revealed through family trees, letters, newspapers, marriage records, and fading portraits, history takes on a dimension much deeper than that of lists of famous names and dates.

To organize the search, consider purchasing genealogy software. Try the following for guidance: Betram H. Groene, *Tracing Your Civil War Ancestor* (1989); American Genealogical Research Institute Staff, *How to Trace Your Family Tree* (1998); the National Park Service Civil War soldiers and sailors database (www.itd.nps.gov/cwss); and the National Archives and Records Administration, Washington, D.C. (www.nara.gov).

There is no living descendant of Abraham Lincoln. The last surviving member of the line was great-grandson Robert Todd Lincoln Beckwith, who died in 1985.

---

8. JOIN A DESCENDANT ORGANIZATION

When veterans of the war passed away, their children formed heritage associations. These leagues of lineage endure today, maintaining the memories and promoting the ideals of their predecessors.

Seeking membership indicates one is far beyond a novice level of Civil War involvement. To be admitted, applicants must prove they are direct descendants of a Civil War veteran or a veteran's sibling. Some groups allow nondescendants to join as associates rather than as full members.

Heavily patriotic if not dogmatic, these organizations conduct regional meetings and annual conventions, participate in living-history programs, and conduct community service. A few provide academic scholarships to descendants, and nearly all assist with further genealogical research. To find out more, consult the following: Daughters of Union Veterans of the Civil War (www.duvcw.org); Sons and Daughters of U.S. Colored Troops (www.sdusct.org); Sons of Confederate Veterans (www.scv.org); Sons of Union Veterans of the Civil War (www.suvcw.org); and United Daughters of the Confederacy (www.hqudc.org).

In September 1994 the United Daughters of the Confederacy celebrated its one hundredth anniversary. The organization received several letters of congratulations, including one from Southerner President William Jefferson Clinton.

9. REENACT

For generations no one thought to try and duplicate the tough look and hard life of Civil War soldiers. But when a few skirmish societies formed to commemorate the war's centennial, a handful of rifle demonstrations planted the seed of what is now a multimillion-dollar industry of replica equipment and period uniforms.

It is a deceptively expensive hobby but a remarkably flexible one. Contrary to popular belief, opportunities for reenacting go far beyond battle simulations and can involve the whole family. Along with the stereotypical infantryman, reenactors portray marines, shipmen, politicians, clergy, telegraphers, doctors, nurses, and blacksmiths. Events are held at plantations, forts, private homes, and public parks during historic festivals or on anniversaries. They can involve groups of a handful to several hundred.[40]

The best way to start is to attend an event and speak with the participants. Take note of the demands on time, money, and especially the body. Spending hours and sometimes days in all types of weather, weighed down by heavy wool and accouterments, eating period grub, and walking for miles is all part of the experience. Many companies and groups are eager for new recruits so long as the rookies are ready and willing to spend hours and hours in preparation and practice. The payoffs include the gleam of bayonets, the sounds of the charge, the twirl of hoop skirts at the formal dance, and a few other perks not found at the usual business office.[41] See William C. Davis, *The Civil War Reenactor's Encyclopedia* (2002); Robert L. Hadden, *Reliving the Civil War: A Reenactor's Handbook* (1999); and the Civil War Reenactors home page (www.cwreenactors.com).

There are more than forty thousand Civil War reenactors in the United States, equivalent to the population of Washington, D.C., in 1860.

10. FIND AND SAVE AN UNPROTECTED SITE

In 1991 Congress authorized an assessment of Civil War battlefields. A commission of authorities, including filmmaker Ken Burns, prolific author Ed Bearss, and Pulitzer Prize–winner James M. McPherson, collected and presented the findings. Out of 384 principal battlefields, one-third were completely lost due to real estate development, an additional third were under immediate threat, and just one-sixth were under some degree of public protection.

These were just the battlefields. The commission also expressed concern over other places of Civil War relevance, such as historic homes, trench works, forts, birthplaces, campsites, monuments, memorials, and prisons.

As it is not economically viable for federal, state, and local budgets to save and protect everything pertinent to history, compromises are made and much is left to individual citizens. Unfortunately, many Americans have little concept of their own history, partially because so much of it has disappeared.

Some places are irretrievable, such as Big Bethel, Virginia, site of the first land battle of the war, now covered by a man-made reservoir. But there are still innumerable candidates for search and rescue. The Friends of the Florence Stockade saved a large portion of the land where the sixth deadliest Civil War prison once stood. An artist and his wife purchased forty acres of the battleground of Cross Keys—by accident. Scores of Civil War field hospitals and headquarters are still around because they remain as they always were—private homes.[42]

For inspiration and instruction on how to recover treasures of history, please see: Frances H. Kennedy and Douglas R. Porter, *Dollar$ and Sense of Battlefield Preservation* (1994); National Trust for Historic Preservation (www.nthp.org); and American Battlefield Protection Program of the National Park Service (www.nps.gov/abpp).

Sometimes Mother Nature plays a hand in destroying historic sites. Don't bother looking for the battle sites of Belmont, Missouri, or Island No. 10 in Kentucky. Both have been swept away by the Mississippi River.

EPILOGUE
TIME LINE
NOTES
BIBLIOGRAPHY
INDEX

EPILOGUE

IN 1861 ELEVEN STATES attempted to divorce themselves from a political union, citing irreconcilable differences and seeking custody of land and people. By 1865 the demand for separation had been irrefutably denied.

For all the destruction wreaked over four years, much had not changed. The U.S. military, although dramatically reduced in number after the war, continued its peculiar role as an instrument of domestic rather than international policy. Federal occupation of the Southern states persisted for twelve years after Appomattox. The prewar conquest of Native Americans resumed, halted only momentarily along the banks of the Little Bighorn in 1876. After a brief euphoria over African American freedom, a swath of segregationist Black Codes replaced slavery as the next roadblock to civil equality. As wars go, the Civil War was only the twelfth in which the country had been involved since its revolution (and just one of thirty to date). The victor had manifested the ideals of Union and abolition only to struggle ever after with the magnitude of their realism.

Yet incredible change was wrought by the conflict. A once mighty rebellion had imploded, reduced to a truncated cabinet on the run and a currency of no value. Fortunes spent on human property were gone. Home to a majority of presidents before the war, Southern states would not provide another chief executive until Woodrow Wilson nearly a half century later. In four years the South lost a quarter of its men of military age, half of its wealth, and its position of political preeminence in the United States.

In contrast to the Confederacy, the North flourished. Washington, D.C., had grown from a sluggish burg of forty thousand to a papermill metropolis of well over one hundred thousand. Nearly invisible to most citizens before the war, the central government became the overriding power of the land, not yet a bureaucratic giant, but no longer a civic

331

afterthought. The triumph of the Union politically welded North with South, a transcontinental railroad would soon economically bind East with West, and a new monetary system forever altered the landscape of progress. Moreover, slavery was over in the United States. Whatever problems of emancipation that lay in wait, at least the country was finally ready to accept the awesome responsibility of its own Declaration that "all men are created equal."

Counting civilian and military deaths, the nation lost nearly seven hundred thousand souls. Domestic births and immigration replaced these numbers faster than they had occurred, and in fact the overall population increased by millions during the war. Yet the lives of fathers, brothers, friends, and sons lost could never be replaced.

Among the new graves, one contained a president. Mortally wounded at a public gathering while holding his wife's hand, Abraham Lincoln was but the first at the scene of the crime to receive a grim fate. His assassin died from a gunshot wound twelve days later, possibly self-inflicted. Maj. Henry R. Rathbone, the last-minute guest of the Lincolns, went on to marry his fellow witness and fiancée, the lovely Clara Harris. Years later, he progressively went insane and killed his wife, dying himself not long after in an asylum. Mary Todd Lincoln, having buried two sons and a husband by the end of the war, lived to bury yet another son. Her eldest and only surviving child, Robert, subsequently had her committed briefly to an asylum.

Falsely accused of being an accomplice in the Lincoln assassination, Jefferson Davis was captured while escaping southward from his fallen capital. Charged with treason, he was imprisoned for two years then released without trial. With financial backing from a handful of admirers, the continually ill and indebted former president wrote a legal and moral defense of the rebellion entitled *The Rise and Fall of the Confederate Government*. The two-volume work proved to be an argumentative and commercial failure, symbolic of Davis's final decades on earth. Among his setbacks, worst may have been his personal losses. Fathering four sons, Davis lost one before and one during his presidency. His remaining two sons died long before his own death in 1889.

Davis's most cherished general, the Virginia aristocrat Robert E. Lee, lived just five years after his surrender at Appomattox Court House. Accepting the presidency at Washington College in Lexington, Virginia,

Lee survived long enough to witness fame and recognition on a national level. Resisting such accolades, the former general solidified his image as an incorruptible gentleman. In honor of the idolized Rebel, his last post was renamed Washington and Lee College after his death in 1870.

Commanding general of all Union forces during the final year of the war, Ulysses S. Grant went on to become the eighteenth president of the United States. Serving two terms, his administration proved to be one of the most corrupt and ineffective in national history. Nearly bankrupt after several poor business decisions, Grant saved his family from abject poverty by completing his memoirs just before his death of throat cancer in 1885. It became a bestseller.

The nation as a whole recovered from the war very slowly. For Confederate soldiers, there was the long walk back from the battlefields. Defeated, penniless, stripped of their flag and cause, thousands discovered they had also lost their homes. After four years of warfare, whole counties of Georgia, Mississippi, Missouri, Virginia, and elsewhere lay in ruins. Adding to the misery, Federal military occupation continued into the 1870s. Economically, the cotton market rallied quickly, which merely benefited those with sufficient capital. Many of the fortunate few were the same families who owned considerable land and property before the war. Otherwise, livestock and industrial production took years to return to their prewar levels, which were modest to begin with. By the 1880s and 1890s most former Confederate states had recovered enough to provide pensions to impoverished veterans and widows, consisting of monthly or yearly payments of a few dollars. Some states managed to provide artificial limbs to qualifying applicants.

The Union soldier's outlook was naturally brighter by comparison. For the most part, however, the vast majority were not unlike my ancestor, Pvt. Andrew Cook. He returned to a life of subsistence farming, quietly living out his remaining years in the state that he represented on the field of battle. He was an unheralded man, yet lucky. Although more than two million veterans from both sides managed to survive the war, hundreds of thousands suffered from mental and physical wounds ever after. Burden of care for these veterans fell mostly upon their families.

Many soldiers never made it back home. Accidents and illness continued to claim lives with the same ease as during the war. Men died in military hospitals, in camp awaiting discharge, and en route to their loved ones. One incident cost more lives than the first day of the battle of Gettysburg. On April 27, 1865, a Federal transport steamer exploded while transporting more than two thousand passengers, many of whom were recently released from Confederate prison camps. The majority on board perished, equaling the number of deaths from the sinking of the luxury liner *Titanic* forty-seven years later.

In the wake of such national sacrifices, citizens hesitated to recollect the war, let alone venerate it. Most of the memorializing was left to the soldiers. In 1868 Union veterans promoted the start of an annual tradition, "for the purpose of strewing with flowers . . . the graves of comrades who died in defense of their country during the late rebellion." Aptly referred to as Decoration Day, the event eventually became Memorial Day, intended to honor all veterans of all American wars. Despite its altered title and purpose, Memorial Day testified to the lasting anguish of the defeated. The holiday was not celebrated in areas of the South until the late twentieth century.

By the 1880s, veterans on both sides began to form regimental reunions. In some cases, joint Union and Confederate reunions gathered to commemorate battle anniversaries, yet for the most part there pervaded a mutual respect and distance.

Gradually the war transferred from a possession of veterans to a ward of the nation. In the 1890s the federal government embarked on a plan to protect major battle sites. Descendants of veterans formed ancestral societies as their soldier relatives faded one by one. After the turn of the century, novels, histories, and the new medium of film presented the war to generations of Americans born well after the fighting. Emerging from these creations was the prominent theme of reconciliation, which evolved into a mainstay of American thinking. By 1920 grandchildren and great-grandchildren of veterans North and South commenced each school day with an increasingly popular verse, pledging allegiance to "one nation indivisible."

Generations later, the Civil War still echoes. Strangely, it is restless. From classrooms to Congress, the Union still fights to define itself, to balance state and national interests, and to address racial disharmony. A common casualty of this lingering unrest is the war itself. For many, there is an incentive to make the Civil War into something it was not, altering history to serve contemporary wants and needs. Heroes and villains are exaggerated, institutions take on characteristics they never possessed, battles are magnified as the greatest and the worst. It may be impossible to fully separate emotion from examination, but it is critical to view the past with some objectivity. Continual diligence and discretion are required, lest we attempt to build a stable present upon the brittle foundations of myth and misunderstanding.

In searching for truth, Americans in the 1800s paid great attention to a person's last words, as if parting utterances were the most pure and deliberate reflections of an entire being. Legend has it that Lincoln told his wife not to worry about appearing too possessive of him, Lee supposedly whispered battle commands and ended with "Strike the tent," and Davis uttered, "Pray excuse me, I cannot take it."

Appropriately, there has been no last word on the Civil War, no peace treaty, no final declaration, no irrefutable endpoint, because the past cannot truly be disconnected from the present. To this day, the historic struggle colors our current perceptions, and we are compelled to constantly examine and evaluate the issues left settled and unsettled by that uniquely American war.

Time Line

1860

November 6	Abraham Lincoln elected U.S. president
December 20	South Carolina becomes the first state to secede from the Union

1861

February 18	Jefferson Davis inaugurated as provisional president of the Confederacy
March 4	Lincoln inaugurated
March 21	Confederate capital transferred from Montgomery, Ala., to Richmond, Va.
April 12	South Carolina shells Fort Sumter in Charleston Harbor
April 15	Lincoln calls for 75,000 volunteer troops
April 19	Blockade of Confederacy begins
April 27	Lincoln suspends writ of habeas corpus
July 21	Battle of First Manassas (Bull Run), Manassas, Va. (C.S. victory)
August 5	Union enacts first national income tax
August 6	Union passes the Confiscation Act
August 10	Battle of Wilson's Creek, Mo. (C.S. victory)
November 8	Beginning of *Trent* Affair

1862

February 6	Battle of Fort Henry, Tenn. (U.S. victory)
February 14–16	Battle of Fort Donelson, Tenn. (U.S. victory)
February 25	U.S. Congress makes greenbacks legal tender
March 5–8	Battle of Pea Ridge, Ark. (U.S. victory)
March 9	Ironclads CSS *Virginia* and USS *Monitor* fight to a draw, Hampton Roads, Va.
March 23	At Kernstown, Va., Stonewall Jackson experiences his only defeat
April 5–May 4	George B. McClellan takes a month to siege and take Yorktown, Va.
April 6–7	Battle of Shiloh, Tenn. (U.S. victory)

April 16	Confederate Congress enacts first national Conscription Act
April 25	New Orleans, La., falls (U.S. victory)
May 8, 23–25	Jackson chases Nathaniel Banks out of Shenandoah Valley, Va.
May 20	U.S. Congress passes Homestead Act
July 1	U.S. Congress passes Pacific Railway Act
July 2	U.S. Congress passes Land-Grant Act
August 30	Battle of Second Manassas (Bull Run), Manassas, Va. (C.S. victory)
June 25–July 1	Seven Days' battles on Virginia Peninsula (U.S. wins five of six battles but retreats)
September 17	Battle of Antietam, Sharpsburg, Md. (U.S. victory)
September 22	Lincoln announces his Emancipation Proclamation
October 8	Battle of Perryville, Ky. (U.S. victory)
December 13	Battle of Fredericksburg, Va. (C.S. victory)
December 30	Beginning of battle of Stones River, Murfreesboro, Tenn.

1863

January 1	Emancipation Proclamation goes into effect
January 2	Conclusion of battle of Stones River, Murfreesboro, Tenn. (U.S. victory)
March 3	Union has its first wave of conscription
April 24	Confederate Congress passes Tax-in-Kind Measure
May 1–4	Battle of Chancellorsville, Va. (C.S. victory)
May 10	Stonewall Jackson dies
May 18	Union siege of Vicksburg, Miss., begins
June 9	Battle of Brandy Station, Va. (stalemate)
July 1–3	Battle of Gettysburg, Pa. (U.S. victory)
July 4	Besieged Vicksburg falls to Union
July 10,18	Union assaults repelled at Battery Wagner, S.C.
July 13	Draft riots break out in New York City
September 19–20	Battle of Chickamauga, Ga. (C.S. victory)
November 23–25	Battle of Chattanooga, Tenn. (U.S. victory)

1864

February 17	Submarine CSS *H. L. Hunley* sinks USS *Housatonic* outside Charleston Harbor
February 20	Battle of Olustee, Fla. (C.S. victory)
March 6	Grant becomes general in chief of Union army
April 12	Massacre of Union troops at Fort Pillow, Tenn.

May 5–7	Battle of the Wilderness, Va. (C.S. victory)
May 8–21	Battle of Spotsylvania, Va.
May 11	Jeb Stuart mortally wounded at Yellow Tavern, Va.
May 31–June 12	Battle of Cold Harbor, Va.; Union siege begins at Petersburg, Va.
June 10	Battle of Brice's Crossroads, Miss. (C.S. victory)
June 27	Battle of Kennesaw Mountain, Ga. (C.S. victory)
September 1	Atlanta, Ga., falls to Union army
November 8	Lincoln reelected
November 30	Battle of Franklin, Tenn. (U.S. victory)
December 15–16	Battle of Nashville, Tenn. (U.S. victory)

1865

January 31	U.S. Congress sends Thirteenth Amendment to the states for ratification
April 1	Richmond, Va., falls
April 9	Lee surrenders at Appomattox Court House, Va.
April 26	Joseph E. Johnston surrenders near Durham, N.C.
April 14	Lincoln assassinated by John Wilkes Booth
April 15	Lincoln dies
May 10	Jefferson Davis captured near Irwinville, Ga.

Notes

CHAPTER 1: ANTEBELLUM

1. For a synopsis of the major schools of thought on Civil War causation, see: David Donald, "American Historians and the Causes of the Civil War," *South Atlantic Quarterly* 59 (1960); Eric Foner, "The Causes of the American Civil War: Recent Interpretations and New Directions," *CWH* 20 (1974); Edwin C. Rozwenc, ed., *The Causes of the American Civil War* (Lexington, Mass.: Heath, 1972).

2. John Keegan, *A History of Warfare* (New York: Knopf, 1993) 305–6; J. G. Randall and David H. Donald, *The Civil War and Reconstruction* (Lexington, Ky.: Heath, 1969), 8. See also J. Matthew Gallman, *The North Fights the Civil War: The Home Front* (Chicago: Ivan R. Dee, 1994).

3. Mills Lane, ed., *Neither More nor Less Than Men: Slavery in Georgia* (Savannah, Ga.: Beehive Press, 1993), xxxv.

4. Population based on the U.S. National Census.

5. John Niven, *John C. Calhoun and the Price of Union* (Baton Rouge: Louisiana State University Press, 1988), 183; Stephen B. Oates, *The Fires of Jubilee: Nat Turner's Fierce Rebellion* (New York: Harper Perennial, 1990), 98–99, 121–23.

6. John Patrick Daly, *When Slavery Was Called Freedom* (Lexington: University Press of Kentucky, 2002), 47.

7. Kent Blaser, "North Carolina and John Brown's Raid," *CWH* 24 (1878): 199–201. For a review of topics on religion and the coming of the Civil War, see Randall M. Miller, Harry S. Stout, and Charles Reagan Wilson, *Religion and the American Civil War* (New York: Oxford University Press, 1998).

8. James M. McPherson, *Battle Cry of Freedom* (New York: Oxford University Press, 1988), 438.

9. For an overview of states' rights as part of Southern politics in the antebellum period, see Lewis O. Saum, "Schlesinger and 'The States Rights Fetish': A Note," *CWH* 24 (1978).

10. Lincoln quoted in David H. Donald, *Lincoln* (New York: Simon & Schuster, 1995), 206.

11. Merton Dillon, *The Abolitionists: The Growth of a Dissenting Minority* (DeKalb: Northern Illinois University Press, 1975), 175–76; McPherson, *Battle Cry of Freedom*, 80–81.

12. Herbert Aptheker, *Abolitionism: A Revolutionary Movement* (Boston: Twayne, 1989), 30. For details on the actual case and Taney's position, see Benjamin C.

Howard, *Report of the Decision of the Supreme Court of the United States and the Opinions of the Judges Thereof in the Case of Dred Scott versus John F. A. Sandford* (Washington, D.C.: Cornelius Wendell, 1857).

13. Bruce Collins, *The Origins of the American Civil War* (New York: Holmes & Meier, 1981), 109–10.

14. An excellent synopsis of the role of territorial expansionism in the Civil War can be found in McPherson, *Battle Cry of Freedom*, 47–77.

15. Gerald W. Wolff, "Party and Section: The Senate and the Kansas-Nebraska Bill," in *Beyond the Civil War Synthesis: Political Essays of the Civil War Era*, ed. Robert P. Swierenga (Westport, Conn.: Greenwood, 1975), 179–83.

16. Wolff, "Party and Section," 169.

17. Some of the more prominent historians who regard the Civil War as a result of poor leadership and unwarranted extremism include Allan Nevins, Charles W. Ramsdell, Avery O. Craven, and James G. Randall.

18. See also Michael F. Holt, *The Political Crisis of the 1850's* (New York: Norton, 1978), 183–85.

19. Robert A. Rutland, *The Newsmongers: Journalism in the Life of the Nation, 1690–1972* (New York: Dial Press, 1973), 178.

20. Johnson quoted in Carl N. Degler, *The Other South: Southern Dissenters in the Nineteenth Century* (New York: Harper & Row, 1974), 148; London *News*, March 12, 1861, quoted in Philip Van Doren Stern, *Secret Missions of the Civil War* (New York: Random House, 1987), 20.

21. Rutland, *Newsmongers*, 188.

22. For an examination of the reconciliation theme in post–Civil War America, see Alan T. Nolan, *Lee Considered: General Robert E. Lee and Civil War History* (Chapel Hill: University of North Carolina Press, 1991), 25–26; and Bruce Chadwick, *The Reel Civil War: Mythmaking in American Film* (New York: Knopf, 2001).

23. Nolan, *Lee Considered*, 27–28. Stephens and Smith quoted in Charles R. Lee Jr., *The Confederate Constitutions* (Chapel Hill: University of North Carolina Press, 1963), 110.

24. Historian Steven Mintz estimates more than 23 million Africans were exported for slavery, with 11.7 million sold to South and North America and 2 million of the latter dying during the Atlantic voyage; see Mintz, ed., *African American Voices: The Life Cycle of Slavery* (St. James, N.Y.: Brandywine Press, 1993), 2–10.

25. John B. Boles, *Black Southerners, 1619–1869* (Lexington: University Press of Kentucky, 1984), 41–42, 68–70.

26. Ibid., 53, 61–62. See also Edward E. Baptist, "The Migration of Planters to Antebellum Florida: Kinship and Power," *Journal of Southern History* 62 (1996): 533–34.

27. James L. Abrahamson, *The Men of Secession and the Civil War, 1859–1861* (Wilmington, Del.: SR Books, 2000), 84–86; Randall M. Miller and John David Smith, *Dictionary of Afro-American Slavery* (New York: Greenwood, 1988), 699–701.

28. William W. Freehling, *The Road to Disunion* (New York: Oxford University Press, 1990), 135–36; Miller and Smith, *Dictionary of Afro-American Slavery*, 699.

29. Charles S. Sydnor, *Slavery in Mississippi* (Gloucester, Mass.: Peter Smith, 1965), 245.

30. Larry E. Rivers, *Slavery in Florida: Territorial Days to Emancipation* (Gainesville: University of Florida Press, 2000), 2; Miller and Smith, *Dictionary of Afro-American Slavery,* 487–91.

31. Lane, *Neither More nor Less Than Men,* vii–viii.

32. Ibid., xxiii; McPherson, *Battle Cry of Freedom,* 6–7, 39; see also Clarence L. Mohr, *On the Threshold of Freedom: Masters and Slaves in Civil War Georgia* (Athens: University of Georgia Press, 1986).

33. Joseph K, Menn, *The Large Slaveholders of Louisiana—1860* (New Orleans: Pelican, 1964), 2–3. Following description of Jim Bowie's slave activities in Miller and Smith, *Dictionary of Afro-American Slavery,* 413.

34. Menn, *Slaveholders of Louisiana,* 1, 5, 9.

35. James B, Sellers, *Slavery in Alabama* (Birmingham: University of Alabama Press, 1950), 42.

36. Rivers, *Slavery in Florida,* 252–54; Julia Floyd Smith, *Slavery and Plantation Growth in Antebellum Florida, 1821–1860* (Gainesville: University of Florida Press, 1973), 10.

37. Rivers, *Slavery in Florida,* 253–54; David M. Kennedy and Thomas A. Bailey, *The American Pageant,* 2 vols. (Lexington, Mass.: Heath, 1986), 1:139.

38. Accounts of slaveholder migrations south and west in Baptist, "The Migration of Planters to Antebellum Florida," 533–34, and David S. Cecelski, *The Waterman's Story: Slavery and Freedom in Maritime North Carolina* (Chapel Hill: University of North Carolina Press, 2001), 105–6, 117. Account of poisonings and executions in North Carolina in Miller, 543.

39. Frederic Bancroft, *Slave-Traders in the Old South* (Baltimore: J. H. Furst Co., 1931), 237, 384–86.

40. Randolph B. Cambell, *The Peculiar Institution in Texas, 1821–1865* (Baton Rouge: Louisiana State University Press, 1989), 252.

41. Campbell, 56, 252. Following prices on slaves and acreage from Miller and Smith, *Dictionary of Afro-American Slavery,* 727.

42. For an excellent series of narratives from former slaves discussing their perspectives and experiences, see George P. Rawick, ed., *The American Slave: A Composite Autobiography* (Westport, Conn.: Greenwood, 1972).

43. Boles, *Black Southerners,* 101.

44. Mintz, *African American Voices,* 11.

45. Peter Kolchin, *American Slavery, 1619–1877* (New York: Hill and Wang, 1993), 138–39.

46. Ibid., 141.

47. Ibid., 142.

48. Mintz, *African American Voices,* 13–14.

49. John H. Franklin, *From Slavery to Freedom* (New York: Vintage Books, 1967), 202–3.

50. Eugene D. Genovese, *Roll, Jordan, Roll: The World the Slaves Made* (New York: Pantheon Books, 1974), 32. Account of slave school in Kentucky from Franklin, *From Slavery to Freedom,* 202.

51. Letter from R. W. Gibbes to South Carolina Gov. Allston on March 6, 1858, "Southern Slave Life," *De Bow's Review,* 25 (1858): 323; "Dr. Cartwright on the Caucasians and the Africans," *De Bow's Review,* 25 (1858): 46.

52. Miller and Smith, *Dictionary of Afro-American Slavery,* 283, 715.

53. Boles, *Black Southerners,* 155–57.

54. Kenneth M. Stampp, *The Peculiar Institution: Slavery in the Ante-bellum South* (New York: Vintage Books, 1956), 156–62.

55. Genovese, *Roll, Jordan, Roll,* 281–84; Boles, *Black Southerners,* 157–68; Kolchin, *American Slavery,* 143–44.

56. Stampp, *Peculiar Institution,* 198, 341.

57. Kolchin, *American Slavery,* 142–43; Mintz, *African American Voices,* 14–15.

58. Stampp, *Peculiar Institution,* 283–94.

59. Boles, *Black Southerners,* 96–97; Stampp, *Peculiar Institution,* 295–99.

60. Boles, *Black Southerners,* 99–100. Description of "miasmata" in Stampp, *Peculiar Institution,* 308.

61. Boles, *Black Southerners,* 65–69; Stampp, *Peculiar Institution,* 237–65.

62. Frederic Bancroft, *Slave Trading in the Old South* (1931; reprint, Columbia: University of South Carolina Press, 1996), 109–15.

63. Boles, *Black Southerners,* 65–69.

64. Genovese, *Roll, Jordan, Roll,* 648–49.

65. Franklin, *From Slavery to Freedom,* 259–60; McPherson, *Battle Cry of Freedom,* 79–80.

66. Boles, *Black Southerners,* 170; Stampp, *Peculiar Institution,* 120.

67. Boles, *Black Southerners,* 100–105.

68. John W. Blassingame, *The Slave Community: Plantation Life in the Ante-bellum South* (New York: Oxford University Press, 1972), 33–34. Slave life expectancy documented in Mintz, *African American Voices,* 12.

69. Thomas Goodrich, *War to the Knife: Bleeding Kansas, 1854–1861* (Mechanicsburg, Pa.: Stackpole, 1998), 124–27.

70. Mason Lowance, ed., *Against Slavery: An Abolitionist Reader* (New York: Penguin, 2000), 241.

71. Phillips quoted in ibid., 88; James B. Stewart, *Wendell Phillips: Liberty's Hero* (Baton Rouge: Louisiana State University Press, 1986), 172; and Irving H. Bartlett, *Wendell and Ann Phillips: The Community of Reform, 1840–1880* (New York: Norton, 1979), 53.

72. Herbert Aptheker, *Abolitionism: A Revolutionary Movement* (Boston: Twayne, 1989), 88; Stewart, *Wendell Phillips,* 100–101; Stewart, "Heroes, Villains, Liberty, and License: The Abolitionist Vision of Wendell Phillips," in *Antislavery Reconsidered: New Perspectives on the Abolitionists,* ed. Lewis Perry and Michael Fellman (Baton Rouge: Louisiana State University Press, 1979), 168–69.

73. Lowance, *Against Slavery*, 92.

74. David B. Chesebrough, *Frederick Douglass: Oratory from Slavery* (Westport, Conn.: Greenwood, 1998), 16. Garrison quoted in Avery Craven, *An Historian and the Civil War* (Chicago: University of Chicago Press, 1964), 37.

75. Lowance, *Against Slavery*, 92; Bertram Wyatt-Brown, "William Lloyd Garrison and the Antislavery Unity," in *The Abolitionists*, ed. Richard O. Curry (Hindsdale, Ill.: Dryden Press, 1973), 90–92.

76. Stanley Harrold, *The Abolitionists and the South, 1831–1861* (Lexington: University Press of Kentucky, 1995), 6; Wyatt-Brown, "William Lloyd Garrison and the Antislavery Unity," 93–95.

77. David W. Blight, *Frederick Douglass' Civil War: Keeping Faith in Jubilee* (Baton Rouge: Louisiana State University Press, 1989), 2.

78. Ibid., 26.

79. Douglass quoted in Chesebrough, *Frederick Douglass*, 55–56.

80. Blight, *Frederick Douglass' Civil War*, 2, 16–17, 148–49; Chesebrough, *Frederick Douglass*, xvi; John Stauffer, *The Black Hearts of Men: Radical Abolitionists and the Transformation of Race* (Cambridge, Mass.: Harvard University Press, 2002), 161.

81. The following account of Douglass's trip to England in Stauffer, *The Black Hearts of Men*, 158–61; Geoffrey C. Ward, *The Civil War: An Illustrated History* (New York: Knopf, 1990), 16.

82. Gerald Sorin, *The New York Abolitionists: A Case Study of Political Radicalism* (Westport: Greenwood, 1971), 27–30; Stauffer, *The Black Hearts of Men*, 120.

83. Sorin, *The New York Abolitionists*, 35; Stauffer, *The Black Hearts of Men*, 135, 157; Lowance, *Against Slavery*, 192.

84. Otto J. Scott, *The Secret Six: John Brown and the Abolitionist Movement* (New York: Times Books, 1979), 70–71; Wyatt-Brown, 94; Sorin, *The New York Abolitionists*, 36; Stauffer, *The Black Hearts of Men*, 240–45, 267.

85. Smith quoted in Stauffer, *The Black Hearts of Men*, 266.

86. Lowance, *Against Slavery*, 292.

87. Dillon, *The Abolitionists*, 191–92; Lowance, *Against Slavery*, 292.

88. Patricia R. Hill, "Writing Out the War: Harriet Beecher Stowe's Averted Gaze," in *Divided Houses: Gender and the Civil War*, ed. Catherine Clinton and Nina Silber (New York: Oxford University Press, 1992), 247–53.

89. Phillips quoted in Stauffer, *The Black Hearts of Men*, 118.

90. Robert H. Abzug, *Passionate Liberator: Theodore Dwight Weld and the Dilemma of Reform* (New York: Oxford University Press, 1980), 4–5.

91. Lowance, *Against Slavery*, 53; Benjamin P. Thomas, *Theodore Weld: Crusader for Freedom* (New Brunswick, N.J.: Rutgers University Press, 1950), 168–72.

92. Abzug, *Passionate Liberator*, 219, 246, 259.

93. Charles L. Blockson, *Hippocrene Guide to the Underground Railroad* (New York: Hippocrene Books, 1994), 24; Louis Filler, *The Crusade Against Slavery, 1830–1860* (New York: Harper & Brothers, 1960), 163.

94. Blockson, *Hippocrene Guide to the Underground Railroad*, 24.

95. Filler, *The Crusade Against Slavery*, 163; Stewart Sifakis, *Who Was Who in the Civil War* (New York: Facts on File, 1988), 240.

96. Charles E. Heller, *Portrait of an Abolitionist: A Biography of George Luther Stearns* (Westport, Conn.: Greenwood, 1996), 84; Scott, *The Secret Six*, 245; Frank P. Stearns, *The Life and Public Services of George Luther Stearns* (Philadelphia: Lippincott, 1907), 105, 118–19.

97. Sifakis, *Who Was Who*, 618.

98. Rhett quoted in *Democracy on Trial: A Documentary History of American Life, 1845–1877*, ed. Robert W. Johannsen (Urbana: University of Illinois Press, 1988), 144.

99. David M. Potter, *The Impending Crisis, 1848–1861* (New York: Harper & Row, 1976), 105. *Charleston Mercury* quoted in Michael F. Holt, *The Political Crisis of the 1850's* (New York: Norton, 1978), 223.

100. James L. Abrahamson, *The Men of Secession and the Civil War: 1859–1861* (Wilmington, Del.: Scholarly Resources, 2000), 33–36; William C. Davis, *"A Government of Our Own": The Making of the Confederacy* (New York: Free Press, 1994), 12.

101. Davis, *"A Government of Our Own,"* 92, 111, 204.

102. Eric H. Walther, *The Fire-Eaters* (Baton Rouge: Louisiana State University Press, 1992), 54.

103. Ibid., 55.

104. Potter, *Impending Crisis*, 408.

105. Emory M. Thomas, *The Confederate Nation, 1861–1865* (New York: Harper & Row, 1979), 172–73. Yancey's departure from the 1848 Democratic Party National Convention documented in William W. Freehling, *The Road to Disunion* (New York: Oxford University Press, 1990), 534–35.

106. John Niven, *John C. Calhoun and the Price of Union* (Baton Rouge: Louisiana State University Press, 1988), 184.

107. Freehling, *Road to Disunion*, 257–59.

108. Calhoun quoted in ibid., 282.

109. John C. Calhoun and Daniel Webster, *Speeches of Hon. John C. Calhoun and Hon. Daniel Webster* (New York: Stringer & Townsend, 1850), 7, 12.

110. Niven, *Calhoun and the Price of Union*, 184.

111. Abrahamson, *Men of Secession*, 42–43.

112. Ibid., 43–44.

113. Thomas, *Confederate Nation*, 92–93.

114. Walther, *Fire-Eaters*, 229–30.

115. Abrahamson, *Men of Secession*, 37.

116. Keitt quoted in Holt, *The Political Crisis of the 1850's*, 242.

117. Keitt quoted in Davis, *"A Government of Our Own,"* 125. Keitt's poor memory described in ibid., 47.

118. Abrahamson, *Men of Secession*, 39.

119. Davis, *"A Government of Our Own,"* 412.

120. Walther, *Fire-Eaters*, 202.

121. Ibid., 215.

122. De Bow quoted in Abrahamson, *Men of Secession*, 40. "Inferior" comment from *De Bow's Review* 27 (1859): 267. Nonslaveholder article quoted from Johannsen, *Democracy on Trial*, 52.

123. Walther, *Fire-Eaters*, 270–78.

124. Miles quoted in ibid., 287.

125. Nolan, *Lee Considered*, 20–21.

126. Cobb's excerpt from his *Law of Negro Slavery* quoted in Bancroft, *Slave Trading in the Old South*, 344.

127. Davis, *"A Government of Our Own,"* 121.

128. Ibid., 233–50.

129. Preston quoted in Charles B. Dew, *Apostles of Disunion: Southern Secession Commissioners and the Causes of the Civil War* (Charlottesville: University Press of Virginia, 2001), 75.

130. Ibid., 74–75.

CHAPTER 2: POLITICS

1. Felicity Allen, *Jefferson Davis, Unconquerable Heart* (Columbia: University of Missouri Press, 1999), 20, 114–16, 448–52; Bruce Chadwick, *The Two American Presidents* (Secaucus, N.J.: Carol, 1999), 5–7, 27–33; Clement Eaton, *Jefferson Davis* (New York: Free Press, 1977), 44; Douglas Wilson, *Honor's Voice: The Transformation of Abraham Lincoln* (New York: Knopf, 1998), 76–85.

2. Chadwick, *Two American Presidents*, 4–5, 25–29; William J. Cooper Jr., *Jefferson Davis, American* (New York: Knopf, 2000), 8.

3. Eaton, *Jefferson Davis*, 17.

4. Chadwick, *Two American Presidents*, 34–35; Wilson, *Honor's Voice*, 89–90.

5. Stephen B. Oates, *Abraham Lincoln: The Man Behind the Myth* (New York: New American Library, 1984), 6, 21, 40–41, 89–90; Wilson, *Honor's Voice*, 4–6.

6. Allen, *Jefferson Davis*, 9, 25, 68–69, 93, 197–98, 251, 348, 434–35; Mark Grimsley. "'We Will Vindicate the Right': An Account of the Life of Jefferson Davis," *Civil War Times Illustrated* (July–August 1991): 30–35.

7. Chadwick, *Two American Presidents*, 254–55.

8. Ibid., 238–39.

9. Allen, *Jefferson Davis*, 121–23, 213–15; Chadwick, *Two American Presidents*, 51–52, 66–67.

10. James M. McPherson, *Battle Cry of Freedom* (New York: Oxford University Press, 1988), 48.

11. Chadwick, *Two American Presidents*, 13–14, 46–47; McPherson, *Battle Cry of Freedom*, 104.

12. William E. Gienapp, *Abraham Lincoln and Civil War America* (Oxford: Oxford University Press, 2002), 51, 111–12; Oates, *Lincoln*, 101.

13. David H. Donald, *Lincoln* (New York: Simon & Schuster, 1995), 235–36.

14. McPherson, *Battle Cry of Freedom,* 216–21; Benjamin P. Thomas, *Abraham Lincoln* (New York: Modern Library, 1968), 208–14.

15. William C. Davis, *"A Government of Our Own": The Making of the Southern Confederacy* (New York: Free Press, 1994), 120, 127–28, 131–32.

16. Jefferson Davis quote from Cooper, *Jefferson Davis,* 301; James L. Abrahamson, *The Men of Secession* (Wilmington, Del.: Scholarly Resources, 2000), 7.

17. Oates, *Lincoln,* 77–78; Lincoln quoted in McPherson, *Battle Cry of Freedom,* 212.

18. Eaton, *Jefferson Davis,* 117.

19. Abrahamson, *Men of Secession,* 109–11; Allen, *Jefferson Davis,* 185, 189; Davis, "A Government of Our Own," 154.

20. Davis, "A Government of Our Own," 241.

21. McPherson, *Battle Cry of Freedom,* 259–61, 353–56, 700-702; John C. Waugh, *Reelecting Lincoln* (New York: Crown, 1997), 6, 53–57.

22. Donald, *Lincoln,* 277–78.

23. Chadwick, *Two American Presidents,* 135–37; Robert Dardenne, "Devil to Clown: News Coverage of the Capture of Jefferson Davis"; David B. Sachsman, S. Kittrell Rushing, and Debra Reddin van Tuyll, eds., *The Civil War and the Press* (New Brunswick, Conn.: Transaction, 2000), 389–406.

24. For a synopsis of the members of the Confederate Convention, see Charles R. Lee Jr., *The Confederate Constitutions* (Chapel Hill: University of North Carolina Press, 1963), 153–58.

25. Davis, "A Government of Our Own," 224–29. For further comments and details on the Provisional Confederate Constitution, see Lee, *Confederate Constitutions,* 60–81; Jefferson Davis, *A Short History of the Confederate States of America* (New York: Belford, 1890), 67. Historian Emory M. Thomas makes the intriguing observation that the Articles of Confederation were not considered as a viable alternative: Thomas, *The Confederate Nation, 1861–1865* (New York: Harper & Row, 1979), 63.

26. Thomas, *Confederate Nation,* 63.

27. The original Permanent Constitution of the Confederate States of America now resides at the University of Georgia. The Provisional Constitution is on display at the Confederate Museum in Richmond. For text of the Permanent Confederate Constitution, see Henry S. Commager, *The Civil War Archive: The History of the Civil War in Documents* (New York: Black Dog & Leventhal, 2000), 56–57; Lee, *Confederate Constitutions,* appendices; Thomas, *Confederate Nation,* 307–22.

28. Davis, "A Government of Our Own," 227, 246–47; Thomas, *Confederate Nation,* 63.

29. Davis, "A Government of Our Own," 228, 249, 252–53; Clement Eaton, *A History of the Southern Confederacy* (New York: Free Press, 1965), 50; Thomas, *Confederate Nation,* 65.

30. James G. Randall, *Lincoln: The President Midstream* (New York: Dodd, Mead, & Co., 1953), 66.

31. Davis, "A Government of Our Own," 226, 237.

32. Ibid., 245; Eaton, *History of the Southern Confederacy,* 52.

33. James G. Randall and David H. Donald, *The Civil War and Reconstruction* (Boston: Heath, 1961), 256–64.

34. Davis, *"A Government of Our Own,"* 227.

35. For an intriguing collection of letters and dissertations from several prominent political figures in early national politics, see Norma Cousins, ed., *"In God We Trust": The Religious Beliefs and Ideas of the American Founding Fathers* (New York: Harper & Brothers, 1958).

36. Harry S. Stout and Christopher Grasso, "Civil War, Religion, and Communications: The Case of Richmond," in *Religion and the American Civil War,* ed. Randall M. Miller, Harry S. Stout, and Charles Reagan Wilson (New York: Oxford University Press, 1998), 321–22; Eaton, *History of the Southern Confederacy,* 71–72.

37. Thomas, *Confederate Nation,* 32–33.

38. Davis, *"A Government of Our Own,"* 248, 250.

39. Alternative names contemplated for the Confederacy are noted by ibid., 103, and Lee, *Confederate Constitutions,* 67.

40. Benjamin P. Thomas, *Abraham Lincoln: A Biography* (New York: Modern Library, 1968), 377–78; Thomas, *Confederate Nation,* 150–52; Eaton, *History of the Southern Confederacy,* 66.

41. Russell F. Weigley, *A Great Civil War: A Military and Political History, 1861–1865* (Bloomington: Indiana University Press, 2000), 180–82.

42. Eaton, *History of the Southern Confederacy,* 222–23; Weigley, *Great Civil War,* 184–85.

43. McPherson, *Battle Cry of Freedom,* 354–56.

44. Oates, *Lincoln,* 105–6; Phillip S. Paludan, *The Presidency of Abraham Lincoln* (Lawrence: University of Kansas Press, 1994), 145–46.

45. Synopsis of Homestead Act in Commager, *Civil War Archive,* 813–14.

46. Notes and text of the Pacific Railway Act available in ibid., 814–16.

47. See C. F. Cross, *Justin Smith Morrill: Father of the Land-Grant Colleges* (East Lansing: Michigan State University, 1999).

48. Philip Van Doren Stern, *When the Guns Roared: World Aspects of the American Civil War* (Garden City, N.Y.: Doubleday, 1965), 156.

49. Davis quoted in McPherson, *Battle Cry of Freedom,* 566. London *Times,* October 21, 1862, quoted in Belle B. Sideman and Lillian Friedman, eds., *Europe Looks at the Civil War* (New York: Orion, 1960), 192.

50. James M. McPherson, *For Cause and Comrades: Why Men Fought in the Civil War* (New York: Oxford University Press, 1997), 124–25; Larry E. Nelson, *Bullets, Ballots, and Rhetoric: Confederate Policy for the United States Presidential Contest of 1864* (University: University of Alabama Press, 1980), 170.

51. For a condensed version of the Emancipation Proclamation and reactions from outside parties, see Commager, *Civil War Archive,* 577–81. For the gradual transformation of the proclamation from first draft to final signature, see Thomas, *Lincoln,* 333–64.

52. Eaton, *History of the Southern Confederacy,* 227.

53. McPherson, *Battle Cry of Freedom*, 616; Thomas, *Confederate Nation*, 198.

54. Thomas, *Lincoln*, 493–94.

55. Oates, *Lincoln*, 116–17.

56. Van Doren Stern, *When the Guns Roared*, 18.

57. Nelson, *Bullets, Ballots, and Rhetoric*, 167; Thomas, *Confederate Nation*, 290–91.

58. Michael Fellman, *The Making of Robert E. Lee* (New York: Random House, 2000), 213–17; McPherson, *Battle Cry of Freedom*, 831–37.

59. Synopsis of amnesty text in Commager, *Civil War Archive*, 802.

60. Michael Les Benedict, *The Impeachment and Trial of Andrew Johnson* (New York: Norton, 1973), 43.

61. Charles M. Hubbard, *The Burden of Confederate Diplomacy* (Knoxville: University of Tennessee Press, 1998), 23; Robert E. May, ed., *The Union, the Confederacy, and the Atlantic Rim* (West Lafayette, Ind.: Purdue University Press, 1995), 4–5.

62. Yancey letter dated July 3, 1861, quoted in Doren Stern, *When the Guns Roared*, 19.

63. Hubbard, *Burden of Confederate Diplomacy*, 18; Brian Jenkins, *Britain and the War for the Union* (Montreal: McGill-Queen's University Press, 1974), 79; Howard Jones, *Abraham Lincoln and a New Birth of Freedom: The Union and Slavery in the Diplomacy of the Civil War* (Lincoln: University of Nebraska Press, 1999), 9–10.

64. May, *The Union, the Confederacy, and the Atlantic Rim*, 11.

65. Van Doren Stern, *When the Guns Roared*, 63. For definitions in international law during the Civil War, see *Black's Law Dictionary*, 4th ed. (St. Paul, Minn.: West, 1951).

66. May, *The Union, the Confederacy, and the Atlantic Rim*, 10. See also Mark E. Neely Jr, "The Perils of Running the Blockade: The Influence of International Law in an Era of Total War," *CWH* 32 (1986).

67. Van Doren Stern, *When the Guns Roared*, 180.

68. McPherson, *Battle Cry of Freedom*, 380.

69. Van Doren Stern, *When the Guns Roared*, 143–49.

70. May, *The Union, the Confederacy, and the Atlantic Rim*, 11.

71. Ibid., 4–5. See also Gavin Wright, "Slavery and the Cotton Boom," *Explorations in Economic History* 12 (October 1975).

72. Jenkins, *Britain and the War*, 79; Van Doren Stern, *When the Guns Roared*, 64; Hubbard, *Burden of Confederate Diplomacy*, 21. For a more detailed perspective on the relationship between the free labor Union and free labor Britain, see Philip S. Foner, *British Labor and the American Civil War* (New York: Holmes & Meier, 1981).

73. Hubbard, *Burden of Confederate Diplomacy*, 27.

74. Dean B. Mahin, *One War at a Time: The International Dimensions of the American Civil War* (Washington, D.C.: Brassey's, 1999), 58–59.

75. Ibid., 61–63.

76. Gordon H. Warren, *Fountain of Discontent: The Trent Affair and Freedom of the Seas* (Boston: Northeastern University Press, 1981), 206.

77. Ibid., 205–12.

78. May, *The Union, the Confederacy, and the Atlantic Rim,* 8; Warren, *Fountain of Discontent,* 212. See also Norman Ferris, *The Trent Affair: A Diplomatic Crisis* (Knoxville: University of Tennessee Press, 1977).

79. Frank L. Owsley, *King Cotton Diplomacy: Foreign Relations of the Confederate States of America* (Chicago: University of Chicago Press, 1959), 88.

80. Thomas Schoonover, "Napoleon Is Coming! Maximillian Is Coming? The International History of the Civil War in the Caribbean Basin," in May, *The Union, the Confederacy, and the Atlantic Rim,* 101–2.

81. Jones, *Lincoln and a New Birth of Freedom,* 182–83; Schoonover, "Napoleon Is Coming!" 105, 121.

82. Jones, *Lincoln and a New Birth of Freedom,* 184–85. See also Colin M. MacLachlan and William H. Beezley, *El Gran Pueblo: A History of Greater Mexico* (Englewood Cliffs, N.J.: Prentice-Hall, 1994).

83. Jenkins, *Britain and the War,* 81.

84. Lincoln quoted in Donald, *Lincoln,* 189.

85. Albert A. Woldman, *Lincoln and the Russians* (Cleveland: World, 1952), 141.

86. Welles quoted in Van Doren Stern, *When the Guns Roared,* 233. An account of Lincoln's ambassadors to Russia is in Donald, *Lincoln,* 412–13.

87. Owsley, *King Cotton Diplomacy,* 498–99.

88. Van Doren Stern, *When the Guns Roared,* 235–36. Letter from Davis to Pope Pius IX quoted in Owsley, *King Cotton Diplomacy,* 501.

89. Owsley, *King Cotton Diplomacy,* 502–6.

90. Robin W. Winks, *Canada and the United States: The Civil War Years* (Baltimore: Johns Hopkins University Press, 1960), 3.

91. Ibid., 265.

92. Hubbard, *Burden of Confederate Diplomacy,* 166; Winks, *Canada and the United States,* 272–77, 285, 291, 297.

93. Winks, *Canada and the United States,* 298–301, 334. On ex-slaves in Canada in 1860, see ibid., 7–8.

94. Hubbard, *Burden of Confederate Diplomacy,* 171; McPherson, *Battle Cry of Freedom,* 837–38.

CHAPTER 3: MILITARY LIFE

1. For another story on sticks and stones breaking Federal bones, see Stephen D. Lutz, "Stick Charge at Stone's River," *CWTI* (December 2002): 60–72.

2. Gregory A. Coco, *The Civil War Infantryman* (Gettysburg, Pa.: Thomas, 1996), 65–66.

3. Bell I. Wiley, *The Life of Johnny Reb* (Baton Rouge: Louisiana State University, 1999), 288, 289.

4. Ibid., 55–56.

5. Detailed descriptions of the Springfield and Enfield appear in Philip Katcher, *The Civil War Source Book* (New York: Facts on File, 1995), 55–59; and Jack Coggins, *Arms and Equipment of the Civil War* (Wilmington, N.C.: Broadfoot, 1990), 31–32.

6. Mark M. Boatner III, *The Civil War Dictionary* (New York: Vintage Books, 1991), 52, 260; Coggins, *Arms and Equipment,* 29.

7. On the battle of Corinth, see Peter Cozzens, *The Darkest Days of the War: The Battles of Iuka and Corinth* (Chapel Hill: University of North Carolina Press, 1997) 183; William F. Fox, *Regimental Losses in the Civil War* (Albany: Albany Publishing Co., 1898), 77; James M. McPherson, *Battle Cry of Freedom* (New York: Oxford University Press, 1988), 659. "Bayonets" and other nicknames for the common soldier can be found in Webb Garrison, *The Encyclopedia of Civil War Usage* (Nashville, Tenn.: Cumberland House, 2001).

8. Katcher, *Civil War Source Book,* 60–61; Wiley, *Life of Johnny Reb,* 296–97. The story of Richard Brooke Garnett can be found in Ezra J. Warner, *Generals in Gray* (Baton Rouge: Louisiana State University Press, 1959), 99.

9. Boatner, *Civil War Dictionary,* 167; William A. Albaugh III and Edward N. Simmons, *Confederate Arms* (Harrisburg, Pa.: Stackpole, 1957), 9.

10. Bell I. Wiley, *The Life of Billy Yank* (Baton Rouge: Louisiana State University, 1978), 64; Wiley, *Life of Johnny Reb,* 294; Bruce Catton, *Glory Road* (New York: Doubleday, 1952) 245–46.

11. William Tecumseh Sherman, *Memoirs of General W. T. Sherman* (New York: Literary Classics, 1990), 219; Wiley, *Life of Johnny Reb,* 286.

12. Coco, *The Civil War Infantryman,* 67.

13. Coggins, *Arms and Equipment,* 58–59; Wiley, *Life of Billy Yank,* 63. For Lincoln and his fondness for testing weapons, see David H. Donald, *Lincoln* (New York: Simon & Schuster, 1995), 431–32; Robert V. Bruce, *Lincoln and the Tools of War* (Indianapolis: Bobbs-Merrill, 1956).

14. Coggins, *Arms and Equipment,* 97–98.

15. Jeffry D. Wert, *General James Longstreet: The Confederacy's Most Controversial Soldier, A Biography* (New York: Simon & Schuster, 1993), 352.

16. Boatner, *Civil War Dictionary,* 168.

17. Ibid., 119.

18. Wiley, *Life of Johnny Reb,* 298.

19. Ibid., 295–96.

20. The battle of Valverde is described in Boatner, *Civil War Dictionary,* 865.

21. Ibid., 68

22. Milton F. Perry, *Infernal Machines: The Story of Confederate Submarine and Mine Warfare* (Baton Rouge: Louisiana State University, 1965), 199–201.

23. Letter from Lt. John Burnham, Sixteenth Connecticut, to his family, October 4, 1862, from Annette Tapert, ed., *The Brothers' War* (New York: Time Books, 1988), 92.

24. John Keegan, *A History of Warfare* (New York: Knopf, 1993), 305–6; Robert C. Black III, *The Railroads of the Confederacy* (Chapel Hill: University of North Carolina Press, 1998), 198; Catton, *Glory Road,* 109.

25. George W. Adams, *Doctors in Blue* (Baton Rouge: Louisiana State University, 1996), 205.

26. Tapert, *Brothers' War*, 92.

27. Description of the role of water in the battle of Perryville in McPherson, *Battle Cry of Freedom*, 519–20.

28. John D. Billings, *Hardtack and Coffee* (Chicago: Donnelly & Sons, 1960), 122.

29. Ibid., 110, 119.

30. Ibid., 114–15; Robert Paul Jordan, *The Civil War* (Washington, D.C.: National Geographic Society, 1969), 92, 96.

31. Battle of Allatoona, Ga., October 5, 1864. See Boatner, *Civil War Dictionary*, 8.

32. Billings, *Hardtack and Coffee*, 109; Hans Halberstadt, *The Soldier's Story* (Washington, D.C.: Brassey's, 2001), 112.

33. Bruce Catton, *Mr. Lincoln's Army* (New York: Doubleday, 1962), 181; Michael J. Varhola, *Everyday Life in the Civil War* (Cincinnati: Writer's Digest Books, 1999), 89–95.

34. An enlightening example of Confederate ingenuity with salt pork and other meats can be found in Jefferson D. Freeman, *Reprint of Rare Confederate Cookbook* (Union City, Tenn.: Pioneer Press, 2000).

35. Billings, *Hardtack and Coffee*, 125.

36. Dorothy D. Volo and James M. Volo, *Daily Life in Civil War America* (Westport, Conn.: Greenwood, 1998), 122. Craig L. Symonds, *Stonewall of the West* (Lawrence: University of Kansas Press, 1997), 89; Wiley, *Life of Johnny Reb*, 92–93; Sam R. Watkins, *"Co. Aytch": A Side Show of the Big Show* (New York: Macmillan, 1962), 81, 92.

36. Billings, *Hardtack and Coffee*, 112, 138; Catton, *Mr. Lincoln's Army*, 182.

38. David Madden, *Beyond the Battlefield* (New York: Simon & Schuster), 2000), 136.

39. Catton, *Mr. Lincoln's Army*, 182.

40. Wiley, *Life of Johnny Reb*, 94.

41. Ibid., 102–3.

42. Volo and Volo, *Daily Life in Civil War America*, 120; Wiley, *Life of Johnny Reb*, 95.

43. Coco, *The Civil War Infantryman*, 25. Term "goober grabbers" from Garrison, *Encyclopedia of Civil War Usage*, 96.

44. Wiley, *Life of Johnny Reb*, 91, 98; Catton, *Mr. Lincoln's Army*, 182; Ella Lonn, *Desertion During the Civil War* (Lincoln: University of Nebraska Press, 1998), 9–10. Term "eating salt" from Garrison, *Encyclopedia of Civil War Usage*, 219.

45. Quote of soldier's bout with bad fruit from John T. Greene, ed., *The Ewing Family Civil War Letters* (East Lansing: Michigan State University Press, 1994), 101.

46. Lost or inaccurate records, reenlistments, bounty jumping, desertions, and early discharges make a grand total of Civil War veterans difficult to ascertain, and historical estimations vary by hundreds of thousands. There is a general consensus that approximately one million served in the Confederate military and two million in the Union. The total number of regulars or professional soldiers remained near their prewar levels, but the rest of the ranks were volunteers, draftees, and militia, making the Civil War definitively a citizens' war.

47. Boatner, *Civil War Dictionary*, 605–6.

48. Ibid., 177–201; Varhola, *Everyday Life During the Civil War,* 131–32, 203–4.

49. Boatner, *Civil War Dictionary,* 177.

50. James I. Robertson Jr., *Soldiers Blue and Gray* (Columbia: University of South Carolina Press, 1988), 23–24.

51. Wiley, *Life of Billy Yank,* 320.

52. For the Union roughly 80 percent of those in the land forces served in the infantry, 14 percent in the cavalry, and 6 percent in the artillery. Confederates divided their ground forces into 75 percent infantry, 20 percent cavalry, and 5 percent artillery.

53. Boatner, *Civil War Dictionary,* 612; Coco, *The Civil War Infantryman,* 10; Halberstadt, *The Soldier's Story,* 26.

54. Robertson, *Soldiers Blue and Gray,* 21–22.

55. Halberstadt, *Soldier's Story,* 26.

56. Account of file-closers in Webb Garrison, *The Amazing Civil War* (New York: MJF Books, 1998), 155.

57. Catton, *Mr. Lincoln's Army,* 179; Wiley, *Life of Johnny Reb,* 106.

58. Cozzens, *Darkest Days,* 207, 305, 319, 326–27; Steve Meyer, *Iowa Valor* (Garrison, Iowa: Meyer, 1994), 123–25; Iowa Adjutant General's Office, *Roster and Record of Iowa Soldiers in the War of the Rebellion,* 6 vols. (Des Moines, Iowa: E. H. English, 1908–11), 1:199.

59. John Duffy, *The Healers: A History of American Medicine* (Urbana: University of Illinois Press, 1979), 171–72.

60. Ibid., 214–16. Daniel Kilbride notes that many Southern physicians had actually trained in the North: Kilbride, "Southern Medical Students in Philadelphia, 1800–1861: Science and Sociability in the 'Republic of Medicine,'" *Journal of Southern History* 65 (1999): 697–732. For glimpses into the harsh conditions of hospital life, see Louisa May Alcott, *Hospital Sketches* (1863; reprint, Cambridge, Mass.: Harvard University Press, 1960); Henry S. Commager, *The Civil War Archive* (New York: Black Dog & Leventhal, 2000), 521–38; and Glenna R. Schroeder-Lein, *Confederate Hospitals on the Move* (Columbia: University of South Carolina Press, 1994).

61. For an excellent assembly of primary and secondary sources on the subject of Civil War medicine, see Frank R. Freemon, *Microbes and Minie Balls: An Annotated Bibliography of Civil War Medicine* (Cranbury, N.J.: Associated University Presses, 1993).

62. John S. Haller Jr., *American Medicine in Transition* (Urbana: University of Illinois Press, 1981), 83, 88, 89; Stewart M. Brooks, *Civil War Medicine* (Springfield, Ill.: Charles C. Thomas, 1966), 64.

63. George W. Adams, *Doctors in Blue* (Baton Rouge: Louisiana State University, 1980), 123; Stephen B. Oates, *A Woman of Valor: Clara Barton and the Civil War* (New York: Free Press, 1994), 48; Charles Beneulyn Johnson, *Muskets and Medicine* (Philadelphia: F. A. Davis, 1917), 130.

64. Duffy, *The Healers,* 212–13; Haller, *American Medicine in Transition,* 86–87.

65. Johnson, *Muskets and Medicine,* 130.

66. Adams, *Doctors in Blue,* 140.

67. Brooks, *Civil War Medicine,* 70.

68. Frank R. Freemon, *Gangrene and Glory* (Madison: Fairleigh Dickinson University Press, 1988), 218.

69. Symonds, *Stonewall of the West*, 4. For the effects of opiates upon veterans, see David T. Courtwright, "Opiate Addictions as a Consequence of the Civil War," *CWH*, 24 (1978).

70. Adams, *Doctors in Blue*, 125–26.

71. Walter D. Farr, "Samuel Preston Moore: Confederate Surgeon General," *CWH*, 41 (1995), 50; Brooks, *Civil War Medicine*, 85.

72. Freemon, *Gangrene and Glory*, 48–49.

73. C. Keith Wilbur, *Civil War Medicine, 1861–1865* (Guilford, Conn.: Globe Pequot, 1998), 14–15.

74. Farr, "Samuel Preston Moore," 50. Account of POW amputating his own feet is in Johnson, *Muskets and Medicine*, 258, and Lonnie R. Speer, *Portals to Hell: Military Prisons of the Civil War* (Mechanicsburg, Pa.: Stackpole Books, 1997), 276.

75. Farr, "Samuel Preston Moore," 40, 50; Adams, *Doctors in Blue*, 123; Freemon, *Gangrene and Glory*, 48–49

76. Alexander quote from J. Cutler Andrews, *The South Reports the Civil War* (Princeton, N.J.: Princeton University Press, 1970), 39. Descriptions of horsehair sutures are in Brooks, *Civil War Medicine*, 86–87, and Farr, "Samuel Preston Moore," 50.

77. Alcott, *Hospital Sketches*, 87–88.

78. Adams, *Doctors in Blue*, 122–24.

79. Freemon, *Gangrene and Glory*, 48.

80. Wilbur, *Civil War Medicine*, 52–55.

81. Adams, *Doctors in Blue*, 131, 133–34.

82. Freemon, *Gangrene and Glory*, 48; Brooks, *Civil War Medicine*, 65–66.

83. Freemon, *Gangrene and Glory*, 48.

84. Stonewall Jackson quote from John Bowers, *Stonewall Jackson: Portrait of a Soldier* (New York: Morrow, 1989) 423.

85. United States, Bureau of the Census, *Historical Statistics of the United States: Colonial Times to 1970*, 2 vols. (Washington D.C.: U.S. Government Printing Office, 1975), 1:365. In 1850, while approximately 85 percent of the U.S. free population was literate, much of the rest of the world lagged far behind. Comparatively, 67 percent in Britain and 25 percent in Eastern Europe could read and write. See McPherson, *Battle Cry of Freedom*, 19–21; Brayton Harris, *Blue and Gray in Black and White* (Washington, D.C.: Brassey's, 2000), 11.

86. Wiley, *Life of Billy Yank*, xxi.

87. David Madden, ed., *Beyond the Battlefield* (New York: Simon & Schuster, 2000), 83–85, 164–65.

88. Wiley, *Life of Johnny Reb*, 71.

89. Coggins, *Arms and Equipment*, 20; Halberstadt, *Soldier's Story*, 30–33.

90. E. J. Hobsbawm, *The Age of Capital: 1848–1875* (New York: New American Library, 1979), 59–61; Varhola, *Everyday Life During the Civil War*, 178.

91. Coggins, *Arms and Equipment*, 106–7.

92. Boatner, *Civil War Dictionary,* 792; Rod Gregg, *Civil War Quiz and Fact Book* (New York: Harper & Row, 1985), 146. On Lincoln and the War Department Telegraph Office, see Donald, *Lincoln,* 392; and David H. Bates, *Lincoln in the Telegraph Office* (New York: D. Appleton-Century Co., 1939).

93. Katcher, *Civil War Source Book,* 85.

94. Coggins, *Arms and Equipment,* 107.

95. United States, War Department, *The War of the Rebellion: A Compilation of the Official Records of the Union and Confederate Armies,* 128 vols. (Washington, D.C.: Government Printing Office, 1880–1901) (hereafter referred to as *OR*), ser. 1, vol. 27, pt. 1, 199–207; Coggins, *Arms and Equipment,* 107.

96. Boatner, *Civil War Dictionary,* 7, 576–77; Gerald S. Henig and Eric Niderost, *Civil War Firsts* (Mechanicsburg, Pa.: Stackpole, 2001), 91.

97. Madden, *Beyond the Battlefield,* 214–15.

98. Ibid., 217–18; Wiley, *Life of Johnny Reb,* 194.

99. Clifford Dowdey, *Lee's Last Campaign* (New York: Barnes & Noble Books, 1988), 298.

100. Boatner, *Civil War Dictionary,* 2. An account of the Union wounded at Fredericksburg shooting their rifles is in Commager, *Civil War Archive,* 192.

101. Wiley, *Life of Johnny Reb,* 81–82.

102. Herman Hattaway, *Shades of Blue and Gray* (Columbia: University of Missouri Press, 1997), 50.

103. Shelby Foote, *Fredericksburg to Meridian* (New York: Vintage Books, 1963), 459.

104. Andrews, *The South Reports the Civil War,* 515; William E. Huntzicker, *The Popular Press, 1833–1865* (Westport, Conn.: Greenwood, 1999), 138, 151.

105. Madden, *Beyond the Battlefield,* 165.

106. Ibid., 112; Wiley, *Life of Billy Yank,* 179–83.

107. Madden, *Beyond the Battlefield,* 113; Wiley, *Life of Billy Yank,* 25.

108. Madden, *Beyond the Battlefield,* 11; Bob Zeller, *The Civil War in Depth* (San Francisco: Chronicle Books, 1997), 13–17.

109. Henig and Niderost, *Civil War Firsts,* 251–52.

110. Ibid., 250–52.

111. Number of dead are rounded estimates from *OR;* Thomas L. Livermore, *Numbers and Losses in the Civil War in America: 1861–1865* (Bloomington: Indiana University Press, 1957); Frederick Phisterer, *Record of the Armies of the United States* (New York: Scribner's and Sons, 1893); and Paul E. Steiner, *Disease in the Civil War* (Springfield, Ill.: Charles C. Thomas, 1968).

112. E. B. Long and Barbara Long, *The Civil War Day by Day: An Almanac, 1861–1865* (Garden City, N.Y.: Da Capo Press, 1985), 713.

113. Johnson, *Muskets and Medicine,* 131–32; Adams, *Doctors in Blue,* 114.

114. Adams, *Doctors in Blue,* 17–20.

115. Ibid., 199–200.

116. Ibid., 225.

117. Watkins, *"Co. Aytch,"* 79.

118. Adams, *Doctors in Blue*, 135–36.

119. Johnson, *Muskets and Medicine,* 131.

120. Wiley, *Life of Johnny Reb*, 253. The *OR* estimates the number of Union typhoid deaths to be nearer twenty-seven thousand.

121. William A. R. Thompson, *Black's Medical Dictionary*, 29th ed. (New York: Barnes & Noble Books, 1972), 318–19.

122. Adams, *Doctors in Blue*, 227.

123. Freemon, *Gangrene and Glory,* 206.

124. For life and death in Civil War prisons, consult William B. Hesseltine, *Civil War Prisons* (Columbus: Ohio State University Press, 1930) and Speer, *Portals to Hell.*

125. Thompson, *Black's Medical Dictionary,* 708.

126. Brooks, *Civil War Medicine,* 77.

127. Freemon, *Gangrene and Glory,* 217.

128. Ibid., 209.

129. Benton McAdams. *Rebels at Rock Island: The Story of a Civil War Prison* (DeKalb: Northern Illinois University Press, 2000), 49.

130. Adams, *Doctors in Blue*, 219–20.

131. Thompson, *Black's Medical Dictionary,* 914–15.

132. Freemon, *Gangrene and Glory,* 210; Wiley, *Life of Johnny Reb,* 251; Wiley, *Life of Billy Yank,* 133.

CHAPTER 4: THE HOME FRONT

1. Phillip S. Paludan, *"A People's Contest": The Union and the Civil War, 1861–1865* (New York: Harper & Row, 1988), 174.

2. J. Matthew Gallman, *The North Fights the Civil War: The Home Front* (Chicago: Ivan R. Dee, 1994), 74–75.

3. Paludan, *"A People's Contest,"* 186; Amy E. Holmes, "'Such Is the Price We Pay': American Widows and the Civil War Pension System" in *Toward a Social History of the American Civil War,* ed. Maris A. Vinovskis (New York: Cambridge University Press, 1990), 174.

4. Gallman, *The North Fights the Civil War,* 76.

5. Hogs reportedly consumed unburied dead after the first day of Shiloh. In many instances elsewhere, hogs routinely dug up shallow graves.

6. Douglas Fermer, *James Gordon Bennett and the New York Herald: A Study of Editorial Opinion in the Civil War Era, 1854–1867* (New York: St. Martin's, 1986), 279; E. B. Long and Barbara Long, *The Civil War Day by Day, 1861–1865* (New York: Doubleday, 1971), 710–11.

7. Gerald S. Henig and Eric Niderost, *Civil War Firsts: The Legacies of America's Bloodiest Conflict* (Mechanicsburg, Pa.: Stackpole, 2001), 333.

8. Jeanue Attie, *Patriotic Toil: Northern Women and the American Civil War* (Ithaca, N.Y.: Cornell University Press, 1998), 244–45, 272–74; David T. Courtwright, "Opiate Addictions As a Consequence of the Civil War," *CWH,* 24 (1978): 101.

Statistic on artificial limbs from Shelby Foote, *Red River to Appomattox* (New York: Vintage Books, 1974), 1040.

9. Eric T. Dean, "'We Will All Be Lost and Destroyed': Post-Traumatic Stress Disorder and the Civil War," *CWH* 37 (1991): 138–40, 148; James Marten, "Exempt from the Ordinary Rules of Life: Researching Postwar Adjustment Problems of Union Veterans," *CWH* 47 (2001): 57, 62–64.

10. Dean, "'We Will All Be Lost and Destroyed,'" 140–42.

11. Ibid., 146. See also Gerald F. Linderman, *Embattled Courage: The Experience of Combat in the American Civil War* (New York: Free Press, 1987); James M. McPherson, *For Cause and Comrades: Why Men Fought in the Civil War* (New York: Oxford University Press, 1997), 43–45, 163–67. National divorce rate noted in Albert A. Nofi, *Civil War Journal* (New York: Promontory Press, 1993), 145.

12. James M. McPherson, *Battle Cry of Freedom* (New York: Oxford University Press, 1988), 384.

13. Ibid., 440. Young Confederate quoted in Marilyn Mayer Culpepper, *Trials and Triumphs: The Women of the American Civil War* (East Lansing: Michigan State University Press, 1991), 219.

14. Dorothy D. Volo and James M. Volo, *Daily Life in the Civil War* (Westport, Conn.: Greenwood, 1998), 230–34.

15. Michael Fellman, Lesley J. Gordon, and Daniel E. Sutherland, *This Terrible War: The Civil War and Its Aftermath* (New York: Longman, 2003), 197.

16. For an account of the partisan Confederate attack on St. Albans, Vermont, see Philip Van Doren Stern, *Secret Missions of the Civil War* (New York: Random House, 1987), 242–46. See also Donald S. Frazier, "'Out of Stinking Distance': The Guerrilla War in Louisiana" in *Guerrillas, Unionists, and Violence on the Confederate Home Front,* ed. Daniel E. Sutherland (Fayetteville: University of Arkansas Press, 1999), 152; Michael Fellman, "Inside Wars: The Cultural Crisis of Warfare and the Values of Ordinary People" in *Guerrillas, Unionists, and Violence on the Confederate Home Front,* ed. Daniel E. Sutherland (Fayetteville: University of Arkansas Press, 1999), 188–94.

17. Stephen V. Ash, *When the Yankees Came: Conflict and Chaos in the Occupied South, 1861–1865* (Chapel Hill: University of North Carolina Press, 1995), 23; David E. Sutherland, "Guerrilla Warfare, Democracy, and the Fate of the Confederacy," *Journal of Southern History* 68 (2002): 260–61.

18. Long and Long, *The Civil War Day by Day,* 719.

19. James Marten, *The Children's Civil War* (Chapel Hill, University of North Carolina Press, 1998), 8; James Lee McDonough and Thomas L. Connelly, *Five Tragic Hours: The Battle of Franklin* (Knoxville: University of Tennessee Press, 1983), 166–67.

20. Ernest B. Furgurson, *Ashes of Glory: Richmond at War* (New York: Knopf, 1996), 106–7; Allan Nevins, *The Organized War, 1863–1864* (New York: Scribner's, 1971), 354, 426.

21. Ash, *When the Yankees Came,* 166.

22. Mary E. Massey, *Refugee Life in the Confederacy* (Baton Rouge: Louisiana State University Press, 1964), 3–4.

23. Gallman, *The North Fights the Civil War*, 83.

24. Ibid., 66–67. Woman quoted in Bell I. Wiley, *The Plain People of the Confederacy* (Chicago: Quadrangle Books, 1963), 68.

25. Wiley, *Plain People of the Confederacy*, 39.

26. Culpepper, *Trials and Triumphs*, 112–13; Catherine Cooper's account can be found in ibid., 91.

27. Paludan, "*A People's Contest*," 180.

28. McPherson, *Battle Cry of Freedom*, 438–39.

29. Richard C. Burdekin and Farrokh K Langdana, "War Finance in the Southern Confederacy, 1861–1865," *Explorations in Economic History* 30 (1993): 353; Culpepper, *Trials and Triumphs*, 210; Jean V. Berlin, "Did Confederate Women Lose the War? Deprivation, Destruction, and Despair on the Home Front" in *The Collapse of the Confederacy*, ed. Mark Grimsley and Brooks D. Simpson (Lincoln: University of Nebraska Press, 2001), 173. Cost of Confederate dollar in Michael J. Varhola, *Everyday Life During the Civil War* (Cincinnati: Writer's Digest Books, 1999), 44.

30. Paludan, "*A People's Contest*," 181–86.

31. Jack D. Coombe, *Gunsmoke over the Atlantic: First Naval Actions of the Civil War* (New York: Bantam Books, 2002), 94; Gallman, *The North Fights the Civil War*, 104.

32. Mark M. Boatner III, *The Civil War Dictionary* (New York: Vintage Books, 1991), 74.

33. Carl N. Degler, *The Other South: Southern Dissenters in the Nineteenth Century* (New York: Harper & Row, 1974), 179–80.

34. John B. Boles, *Black Southerners, 1619–1869* (Lexington: University Press of Kentucky, 1984), 183–84; Emory M. Thomas, *The Confederate Nation, 1861–1865* (New York: Harper & Row, 1979), 236–37.

35. Boles, *Black Southerners*, 183–84.

36. Clement Eaton, *A History of the Southern Confederacy* (New York: Free Press, 1954), 235–36. Account of the Confederate White House fire in Thomas, *Confederate Nation*, 241–42.

37. McPherson, *For Cause and Comrades*, 124.

38. Degler, *Other South*, 171–73.

39. Nevins, *Organized War*, 162–65.

40. Wisconsin soldier quoted from McPherson, *For Cause and Comrades*, 145. On Joseph E. Brown and peace considerations with the Union, see J. G. Randall and David H. Donald, *The Civil War and Reconstruction* (Lexington, Mass.: Heath, 1969), 266–68. See also Frank L. Klement, *Dark Lanterns: Secret Political Societies, Conspiracies, and Treason Trials in the Civil War* (Baton Rouge: Louisiana State University Press, 1984).

41. Gary W. Gallagher, *The Confederate War* (Cambridge, Mass.: Harvard University Press, 1997), 30–31; Alan T. Nolan, *Lee Considered* (Chapel Hill: University of North Carolina Press, 1991), 81–83.

42. Joan E. Cashin, "Deserters, Civilians, and Draft Resistance in the North" in *The War Was You and Me: Civilians in the American Civil War,* ed. Joan E. Cashin (Princeton, N.J.: Princeton University Press, 2002), 165, 266; Gallagher, *Confederate War,* 32–33; James Marten, *Texas Divided: Loyalty and Dissent in the Lone Star State, 1856–1874* (Knoxville: University Press of Kentucky, 1990), 94.

43. Cashin, "Deserters, Civilians, and Draft Resistance," 270; Gallagher, *Confederate War,* 31; McPherson, *For Cause and Comrades,* 156; Nevins, *Organized War,* 120.

44. Nevins, *Organized War,* 128–29.

45. Marten, *Texas Divided,* 96; Cashin, "Deserters, Civilians, and Draft Resistance," 275.

46. Marten, *Texas Divided,* 95; Nevins, *Organized War,* 129. See also Albert B. Moore, *Conscription and Conflict in the Confederacy* (New York: Macmillan, 1924).

47. Cashin, "Deserters, Civilians, and Draft Resistance," 273–76.

48. McPherson, *Battle Cry of Freedom,* 609–11; Marten, *Texas Divided,* 88; Nevins, *Organized War,* 120–24.

49. Thomas F. Curran, "'Resist Not Evil': The Ideological Roots of Civil War Pacifism," *CWH* 36 (1990): 207.

50. Ibid., 197–203; Eaton, *History of the Confederacy,* 91.

51. See also Peter Brock, ed., *Liberty and Conscience: A Documentary History of the Experiences of Conscientious Objectors in America Through the Civil War* (New York: Oxford University Press, 2002).

52. Degler, *Other South,* 175.

53. Ibid., 174–75.

54. Boles, *Black Southerners,* 183; Webb Garrison, *The Encyclopedia of Civil War Usage* (Nashville: Cumberland House, 2001), 90.

55. Allan Nevins, *The Improvised War, 1861–1862* (New York: Scribner's, 1959), 139–40.

56. Edward Conrad Smith, *The Borderland in the Civil War* (New York: Macmillan, 1928), 358–60.

57. Eugene C. Murdock, *One Million Men: The Civil War Draft in the North* (Madison: State Historical Society of Wisconsin, 1971), 218–26.

58. Account of bounty jumper's demise near Indianapolis in ibid., 219–20. Use of photography to prevent desertion in ibid., 228.

59. Eaton, *History of the Confederacy,* 234–35.

60. Accounts of bread riots in ibid., 234–35; Thomas, *Confederate Nation,* 203–5.

61. Marten, *Texas Divided,* 86.

62. Nevins, *Organized War,* 354–61. Grant quoted in McPherson, *Battle Cry of Freedom,* 623.

63. Brayton Harris, *Blue and Gray in Black and White* (Washington, D.C.: Brassey's, 2000), 9.

64. Richard B. Kiebowicz, "The Telegraph, Censorship, and Politics at the Outset of the Civil War," *CWH* 40 (1994): 95–118; Louis M. Starr, *Bohemian Brigade: Newsmen in Action* (New York: Knopf, 1854), 258–59.

65. J. Cutler Andrews, *The South Reports the Civil War* (Princeton, N.J.: Princeton University Press, 1970), 514, 534–35.

66. Ibid., 513; William E. Huntzicker, *The Popular Press, 1833–1865* (Westport, Conn.: Greenwood, 1999), 132, 140; Donald E. Reynolds, *Editors Make War: Southern Newspapers in the Secession Crisis* (Nashville: Vanderbilt University Press, 1970), 3.

67. Andrews, *The South Reports the Civil War,* 508.

68. Robert A. Rutland, *The Newsmongers: Journalism in the Life of the Nation, 1690–1972* (New York: Dial Press, 1973), 163, 189, 193.

69. J. Cutler Andrews, *The North Reports the Civil War* (Pittsburgh: University of Pittsburgh Press, 1955), 19–21.

70. Alfred Grant, *The American Civil War and the British Press* (Jefferson, N.C.: McFarland, 2000) 122; Harris, *Blue and Gray in Black and White,* 21, 145, 167; account of First Manassas from *New York Herald,* July 24, 1861.

71. Harris, *Blue and Gray in Black and White,* 315.

72. Rutland, *The Newsmongers,* 168–69.

73. Harris, *Blue and Gray in Black and White,* 162–63; Andrews, *The North Reports the Civil War,* 368–69.

74. Report on Antietam in *New York Times,* September 20, 1862; Confederate troop count estimation quoted by Harris, *Blue and Gray in Black and White,* 277. Gatling gun story in Harris, *Blue and Gray in Black and White,* 280.

75. Greeley quoted in Harris, *Blue and Gray in Black and White,* 5.

76. *Tribune* headlines on Douglas quoted in Rutland, *The Newsmongers,* 188. *Tribune* quotation on McClellan in Harris, *Blue and Gray in Black and White,* 145.

77. Harris, *Blue and Gray in Black and White,* 56–60.

78. Meyer Berger, *The Story of the New York Times, 1851–1951* (New York: Simon & Schuster, 1951), 23. *Harper's Weekly* editorial on Fredericksburg quoted in Harris, *Blue and Gray in Black and White,* 238.

79. Andrews, *The South Reports the Civil War,* 32–33.

80. Ibid., 319. *Daily Dispatch* comment on Bragg quoted in Harris, *Blue and Gray in Black and White,* 169. *Daily Dispatch* account of Winchester quoted in Harris, *Blue and Gray in Black and White,* 293.

81. *Daily Dispatch* quoted in William J. Kimball, ed., *Richmond in Time of War* (Boston: Houghton Mifflin, 1960), 134.

82. Andrews, *The North Reports the Civil War,* 32.

83. John Tebbel and Mary Ellen Zuckerman, *The Magazine in America, 1741–1990* (New York: Oxford University Press, 1991), 23. Account of the Peninsula campaign in *Harper's Weekly,* April 19, 1862. Account of Second Manassas in *Harper's Weekly,* November 8, 1862.

84. Andrews, *The South Reports the Civil War,* 36–37.

85. *Charleston Mercury* quoted in William J. Cooper Jr., *Jefferson Davis, American* (New York: Knopf, 2000), 361.

86. On Rhett's aspirations for the Confederate presidency, see William C. Davis, *"A Government of Our Own": The Making of the Confederacy* (New York: Free Press,

1994), 32, 90, 111. On Lincoln subscribing to the *Mercury:* technically the Spring-field, Illinois, law office of Lincoln and Herndon subscribed to the *Richmond Enquirer* and the *Charleston Mercury.* See David H. Donald, *Lincoln* (New York: Simon & Schuster, 1995), 187.

87. Huntzicker, *The Popular Press,* 142–43; Starr, *Bohemian Brigade,* 241.

88. Starr, *Bohemian Brigade,* 240.

89. *Chicago Times* Gettysburg Address comments quoted in Huntzicker, *The Popular Press,* 154, and Donald, *Lincoln,* 466. Second Inaugural comments quoted in Donald, *Lincoln,* 568.

90. For an in-depth examination of Burnside's temporary closure of the paper, see Craig D. Tenny, "To Suppress or Not to Suppress: Abraham Lincoln and the Chicago *Times,"* *CWH* 27 (1981): 251.

91. *Enquirer* account of Peninsula campaign from Stephen W. Sears, *To the Gates of Richmond: The Peninsula Campaign* (New York: Ticknor & Fields, 1992), 343. *Enquirer* report on Antietam quoted in Harris, *Blue and Gray in Black and White,* 183.

92. Ernest B. Furguson, *Ashes of Glory: Richmond at War* (New York: Knopf, 1996), 165.

93. Quotes from *Richmond Enquirer,* June 2, 1864. *Enquirer* support of arming slaves described in Harris, *Blue and Gray in Black and White,* 304.

94. Andrews, *The South Reports the Civil War,* 29–32.

95. *Examiner* account of Bragg quoted in Harris, *Blue and Gray in Black and White,* 175. *Examiner* account of slaves quoted in William Barney, *The Road to Secession: A New Perspective on the Old South* (New York: Praeger, 1972), 3.

96. *Richmond Examiner* quoted in Foote, *Red River to Appomattox,* 95. *Examiner* call for Davis's overthrow in Foote, *Red River to Appomattox,* 768. *Examiner* comment on Union army quoted in Harris, *Blue and Gray in Black and White,* 55–56. *Examiner* comment on Lincoln quoted in Herbert Mitgang, *Abraham Lincoln: A Press Portrait* (Chicago: Quadrangle Books, 1971), 364. Daniels's comment on Lincoln's appearance quoted in Furguson, *Ashes of Glory,* 27.

97. Arguably the leading anti-administration newspapers in the South were the *Richmond Examiner, Raleigh Standard, Richmond Whig,* and *Charleston Mercury.* Clement Eaton, *Jefferson Davis* (New York: Free Press, 1977), 222. Account of Daniel's run-in with Edgar Allan Poe in Furguson, *Ashes of Glory,* 27.

98. Lincoln quoted in Rutland, *The Newsmongers,* 194.

99. Grant, *The American Civil War and the British Press,* 30, 121; London *Times,* July 20, 1863.

100. London *Times* depiction of Sherman's March to the Sea in Grant, *The American Civil War and the British Press,* 131–32. *Times* quotes from January 6, 1865, quoted from Grant, *The American Civil War and the British Press,* 131–32.

101. See also Grant, *The American Civil War and the British Press,* 122–24; Brian Jenkins, "Frank Lawley and the Confederacy," *CWH* 23 (1977): 144–60.

102. *Richmond Daily Dispatch,* May 12, 1862, quoted in Bell I. Wiley, *The Life of Johnny Reb* (Baton Rouge: Louisiana State University, 1978), frontispiece.

103. Roger L. Ransom, "Fact and Counterfact: The 'Second American Revolution' Revisited," *CWH* 45 (1999): 29.

104. For an analysis of the Civil War and how participants associated with the American Revolution, see James M. McPherson, *Abraham Lincoln and the Second American Revolution* (New York: Oxford University Press, 1991); George C. Rable, *The Confederate Republic: A Revolution Against Politics* (Chapel Hill: University of North Carolina Press, 1994), 123; and Ransom, "Fact and Counterfact: The 'Second American Revolution' Revisited."

105. William C. Davis, *The Lost Cause: Myths and Realities of the Confederacy* (Lawrence: University of Kansas Press, 1996), 178.

106. Mark W. Kruman, "Dissent in the Confederacy: The North Carolina Experience," *CWH* 27 (1981): 294. See also Lewis O. Saum, "Schlesinger and 'The States Rights Fetish': A Note," *CWH* 24 (1978).

107. For a synopsis of Lincoln's major speeches, see Henry S. Commager, ed., *The Civil War Archive: The History of the Civil War in Documents* (New York: Black Dog & Leventhal, 2000).

108. See Amy E. Murrell, "Union Father, Rebel Son: Families and the Question of Civil War Loyalty" in *The War Was You and Me: Civilians in the American Civil War*, ed. Joan E. Cashin (Princeton, N.J.: Princeton University Press, 2002), 358–91.

109. Details on Helm are in Boatner, *Civil War Dictionary*, 393; Benjamin P. Thomas, *Abraham Lincoln: A Biography* (New York: Modern Library, 1968), 480.

110. Thomas, *Lincoln*, 275–79.

111. For Lincoln's stance on compensated emancipation, see ibid., 311–14.

112. Hans Halberstadt, *The Soldier's Story: The American Civil War* (Washington, D.C.: Brassey's, 2001), 13–18.

113. Wiley, *Life of Johnny Reb*, 111.

CHAPTER 5: IN RETROSPECT

1. Jack D. Coombe, *Gunsmoke over the Atlantic: First Naval Actions of the Civil War* (New York: Bantam Books, 2002), 90–93; Herman Hattaway, *Shades of Blue and Gray: An Introductory Military History of the Civil War* (Columbia: University of Missouri Press, 1997), 17; Charles D. Ross, *Trial by Fire: Science, Technology, and the Civil War* (Shippensburg, Pa.: White Mane, 2000), 173.

2. James M. McPherson, *Battle Cry of Freedom* (New York: Oxford University Press, 1988), 438.

3. Ibid., 443–48.

4. Richard C. K. Burdekin and Farokh K. Langdana, "War Finance in the Southern Confederacy," *Explorations in Economic History* 30, no. 1 (1993): 357.

5. McPherson, *Battle Cry of Freedom*, 447.

6. J. Matthew Gallman, *The North Fights the Civil War: The Home Front* (Chicago: Ivan R. Dee, 1994), 47; James A. Rawley, *The Politics of Union* (Hinsdale, Ill.: Dryden Press, 1974), 49.

7. Gallman, *The North Fights the Civil War*, 96.

8. Ibid., 98; Rawley, *The Politics of Union*, 50.

9. Coombe, *Gunsmoke over the Atlantic,* 90–93; William H. Roberts, *Civil War Ironclads* (Baltimore: Johns Hopkins University Press, 2002), 9.

10. Coombe, *Gunsmoke over the Atlantic,* 106; McPherson, *Battle Cry of Freedom,* 376–77.

11. Coombe, *Gunsmoke over the Atlantic,* 114.

12. For the fiscal costs of ironclad production, see ibid., 92, 97.

13. Shelby Foote, *Fort Sumter to Perryville* (New York: Vintage Press, 1958), 394.

14. An account of Lincoln's honorary substitute is in Webb Garrison, *The Amazing Civil War* (New York: MJF Books, 1998), 92–93; Geoffrey C. Ward, *The Civil War* (New York: Knopf, 1990), 242.

15. Robert V. Bruce, *Lincoln and the Tools of War* (Indianapolis: Bobbs-Merrill, 1956), 68.

16. Ibid., 73–76.

17. Allan Nevins, *War Becomes Revolution, 1862–1863* (New York: Scribner's, 1960), 493–94.

18. Ibid., 494.

19. George Lang, Raymond L. Collins, and Gerard F. White, comps., *Medal of Honor Recipients, 1863–1994,* 2 vols. (New York: Facts on File, 1995), 1:xiii–xvii.

20. Gerald S. Henig and Eric Niderost, *Civil War Firsts: The Legacies of America's Bloodiest Conflict* (Mechanicsburg, Pa.: Stackpole, 2001), 326.

21. Frank Foster and Lawrence Borts, *U.S. Military Medals 1939 to Present,* 5th ed. (Greenville, S.C.: Medals of America Press, 2000), 851.

22. Foote, *Fort Sumter to Perryville,* 376. See also Foster and Borts, *U.S. Military Medals,* 54; Henig and Niderost, *Civil War Firsts,* 326.

23. Mary E. Massey, *Bonnet Brigades* (New York: Knopf, 1966), 9–10.

24. Stewart Brooks, *Civil War Medicine* (Springfield, Ill.: Charles C. Thomas, 1966), 28.

25. Mary E. Massey, *Women in the Civil War* (Lincoln: University of Nebraska Press, 1966), 62–63.

26. Elizabeth D. Leonard, *Yankee Women: Gender Battles in the Civil War* (New York: Norton, 1994), 136–37; Massey, *Women in the Civil War,* 62–63.

27. Ross, *Trial by Fire,* 175.

28. Brian Hicks and Schuyler Kropf, *Raising the Hunley* (New York: Ballantine Books, 2002), 29–39; Ross, *Trial by Fire,* 85, 87, 93.

29. Ross, *Trial by Fire,* 100–103.

30. Hicks and Kropf, *Raising the Hunley,* 64–71.

31. Ibid., 109; Ross, *Trial by Fire,* 100–103.

32. One of the best and most vivid accounts of the Lincoln assassination is in Shelby Foote, *Red River to Appomattox* (New York: Vintage Books, 1974), 974–88. See also David H. Donald, *Lincoln* (New York: Simon & Schuster, 1995), 585–99.

33. James L. Swanson and Daniel R. Weinberg, *Lincoln's Assassins* (Chicago: Arena Editions, 2001), 14.

34. Guy W. Moore, *The Case of Mrs. Surratt* (Norman: University of Oklahoma Press, 1954), 96–97; Elizabeth Steger Trindal, *Mary Surratt: An American Tragedy* (Gretna, La.: Pelican, 1996), 117.

35. Confederate soldier quoted in Geoffrey C. Ward, *The Civil War: An Illustrated History* (New York: Knopf, 1990), 112.

36. Herman Hattaway, *Shades of Blue and Gray* (Columbia: University of Missouri Press, 1997), 50–51.

37. Stephen R. Wise, *Lifeline of the Confederacy: Blockade Running During the Civil War* (Columbia: University of South Carolina Press, 1988), 74.

38. George C. Rable, *The Confederate Republic: A Revolution Against Politics* (Chapel Hill: University of North Carolina Press, 1994), 137.

39. Casualty numbers from Mark M. Boatner III, *The Civil War Dictionary* (New York: Vintage Books, 1991), 592.

40. Stephen W. Sears, *To the Gates of Richmond: The Peninsula Campaign* (New York: Ticknor & Fields, 1992) 337.

41. Casualty figures for the Seven Days' battles and other engagements from Thomas L. Livermore, *Numbers and Losses in the Civil War in America: 1861–1865* (Bloomington: Indiana University Press, 1957).

42. Russell quoted in Belle Becker Sideman and Lillian Friedman, eds., *Europe Looks at the Civil War* (New York: Orion Press, 1960), 174–75.

43. One historian suggests Antietam increased rather than decreased the likelihood of British diplomatic recognition of the Confederacy. Although intriguing, Howard Jones's arguments are not wholly convincing; see Howard Jones, *Union in Peril: The Crisis over British Intervention in the Civil War* (Chapel Hill: University of North Carolina Press, 1992).

44. Alan T. Nolan, *Lee Considered: General Robert E. Lee and Civil War History* (Chapel Hill: University of North Carolina Press, 1991), 83l. See also James M. McPherson, *Antietam: Crossroads of Freedom* (New York: Oxford University Press, 2002); Stephen W. Sears, *Landscape Turned Red: The Battle of Antietam* (New York: Ticknor & Fields, 1983).

45. J. Cutler Andrews, *The North Reports the Civil War* (Pittsburgh: University of Pittsburgh Press, 1955), 369.

46. Stephen B. Oates, *Abraham Lincoln: The Man Behind the Myths* (New York: Meridian Books, 1984), 133. Sumner quoted in Ernest B. Furgurson, *Chancellorsville, 1863* (New York: Knopf, 1992), 331.

47. The following example of government contractor fraud at Chancellorsville in Webb Garrison, *The Amazing Civil War* (New York: MJF Books, 1998), 81.

48. The leading what-if with Gettysburg considers the effects of a Confederate victory there. A popular conclusion surmises that Lee would have marched on Washington and won the war. Such a deduction ignores the Confederate precedent. The South scored convincing victories in the East before Gettysburg—First Manassas, Fredericksburg, Second Manassas, and Chancellorsville—and none inspired a move on the most fortified city in the Western world.

49. McPherson, *For Cause and Comrades,* 157. Lincoln quoted in Benjamin P. Thomas, *Abraham Lincoln: A Biography* (New York: Modern Library, 1968), 389.

50. See also Gary W. Gallagher, "'Lee's Army Has Not Lost Any of Its Prestige': The Impact of Gettysburg on the Army of Northern Virginia and the Confederate Home Front" in *The Third Day at Gettysburg and Beyond*, ed. Gary W. Gallagher (Chapel Hill: University of North Carolina Press, 1994).

51. Account of Lincoln's hearing the news of Union victory at Vicksburg in Thomas, *Lincoln*, 387.

52. Ibid., 387–88.

53. Robert E. May, ed., *The Union, the Confederacy, and the Atlantic Rim* (West Lafayette, Ind.: Purdue University Press, 1995), 10; Philip Van Doren Stern, *When the Guns Roared: World Aspects of the American Civil War* (Garden City, N.Y.: Doubleday, 1965), 208.

54. Casualty totals of Wilderness from Russell Weigley, *A Great Civil War: A Military and Political History, 1861–1865* (Bloomington: Indiana University Press, 2000), 330.

55. Union soldier quoted in Hattaway, *Shades of Blue and Gray*, 209.

56. Lincoln quoted in Thomas, *Lincoln*, 443.

57. Emory M. Thomas, *The Confederate Nation: 1861–1865* (New York: Harper & Row, 1979), 271.

58. John C. Waugh, *Reelecting Lincoln* (New York: Crown, 1997), 296–97.

59. Rudolph Von Abele, *Alexander A. Stephens* (New York: Knopf, 1946), 227–29.

60. For a well-respected and impressive compendium of short biographies on practically every general of the war, consult Ezra J. Warner, *Generals in Gray* (Baton Rouge: Louisiana State University Press, 1959); idem, *Generals in Blue* (Baton Rouge: Louisiana State University Press, 1964).

61. Authors Lenoir Chambers and Andrew C. Holman make convincing cases for the commonality of health misconceptions in nineteenth-century United States. See Lenoir Chambers, *Stonewall Jackson*, 2 vols. (New York: Morrow, 1959), and Andrew C. Holman, "Thomas J. Jackson and the Idea of Health: A New Approach to the Social History of Medicine," *CWH* 38 (1992): 131–55. On Jackson and his personal traits, see Joseph B. Mitchell, *Military Leaders of the Civil War* (New York: Putnam, 1972), 37–38.

62. Mitchell, *Military Leaders of the Civil War*, 48, 56.

63. McPherson, *Battle Cry of Freedom*, 526–28.

64. Lee quote from Chambers, *Jackson*, 2:428. Jackson's early recognition of Stuart's abilities is noted in Robert J. Trout, *They Followed the Plume: The Story of J. E. B. Stuart and His Staff* (Mechanicsburg, Pa.: Stackpole, 1993), 2.

65. For an in-depth look at Sherman's personality and its relation to his war record, see John F. Marszalek, *Sherman: A Soldier's Passion for Order* (New York: Vintage Books, 1994).

66. Mitchell, *Military Leaders of the Civil War*, 155. For Sherman's accounts of the events involving his request for two hundred thousand troops and the subsequent rumors that he had gone insane, see William T. Sherman, *Memoirs of W. T. Sherman* (1886; reprint, New York: Literary Classics, 1990), 218–32.

67. Mitchell, *Military Leaders of the Civil War,* 153. Comparisons of Sherman and Grant in John D. McKenzie, *Uncertain Glory: Lee's Generalship Re-Examined* (New York: Hippocrene Books, 1997), 344–45; Charles E. Vetter, *Sherman: Merchant of Terror, Advocate of Peace* (Gretna, La.: Pelican, 1992), 296. Casualty numbers at battle of Kennesaw Mountain from Boatner, *Civil War Dictionary,* 252–53. Among Sherman's larger defeats in battle are Chickasaw Bluffs during the Vicksburg campaign, Missionary Ridge at Chattanooga, and Dalton and Kennesaw Mountain outside of Atlanta; Stanley P. Hirshson, *The White Tecumseh: A Biography of General William T. Sherman* (New York: Wiley, 1997), 391.

68. John F. Marszalek, *Sherman's Other War: The General and the Civil War Press* (Memphis: Memphis State University Press, 1981), 192.

69. Thomas L. Connelly and Archer Jones, *The Politics of Command: Factions and Ideas in Confederate Strategy* (Baton Rouge: Louisiana State University Press, 1973), 32–33; H. J. Eckenrode and Bryan Conrad, *James Longstreet: Lee's War Horse* (Chapel Hill: University of North Carolina Press, 1986), foreword; Nolan, *Lee Considered,* 66–67, 84–85.

70. Mitchell, *Military Leaders of the Civil War,* 64–65; Connelly and Jones, *Politics of Command,* 37–38; Steve H. Newton, *Joseph E. Johnston and the Defense of Richmond* (Lawrence: University of Kansas Press, 1998), 209.

71. Connelly and Jones, *Politics of Command,* 32–33; Eckenrode and Conrad, *Longstreet,* foreword; McKenzie, *Uncertain Glory,* 349; Nolan, *Lee Considered,* 66–67.

72. For a biography on Grant, there are few that can match the appeal and honesty of Grant's own memoirs; see Ulysses S. Grant, *Personal Memoirs of U. S. Grant* (1885; reprint, New York: Literary Classics, 1990).

73. Bruce Catton, *Grant Moves South* (Boston: Little, Brown, 1960), 164–72, 225–33; see also Edwin C. Bearss, "Unconditional Surrender: The Fall of Fort Donelson," *Tennessee Historical Quarterly* 21 (1962).

74. Jeffry D. Wert, *General James Longstreet: The Confederacy's Most Controversial Soldier—A Biography* (New York: Simon & Schuster, 1993), 84–85; John J. Hennessey, *Return to Bull Run* (New York: Simon & Schuster, 1993), 206.

75. Wert, *Longstreet,* 459.

76. Ibid., 205.

77. Warner, *Generals in Gray,* 192–93; Wert, *Longstreet,* 114–15, 405.

78. Longstreet's criticism of Lee at Gettysburg was actually a repeat of his official report of July 27, 1863, in which he stated: "The order for this attack, which I could not favor under better auspices, would have been revoked had I felt that I had that privilege." See United States, War Department, *The War of the Rebellion: A Compilation of the Official Records of the Union and Confederate Armies,* 128 vols. (Washington, D.C.: Government Printing Office, 1880–1901) (hereafter referred to as *OR*), ser. 1, vol. 27, pt. 2, 357–63 (Longstreet to Col. R. H. Chilton, assistant adjutant general and inspector general). See also Thomas L. Connelly and Barbara L. Bellows, *God and General Longstreet: The Lost Cause and the Southern Mind* (Baton Rouge: Louisiana State University Press 1982); James Longstreet,

From Manassas to Appomattox (1895; reprint, Bloomington: Indiana University Press, 1960).

79. Trout, *They Followed the Plume,* 28–29.

80. Boatner, *Civil War Dictionary,* 815–16.

81. Warner, *Generals in Gray,* 296–97.

82. Foote, *Fort Sumter to Perryville,* 749–50.

83. Trout, *They Followed the Plume,* 16; Allan Nevins, *The War for the Union: The Organized War, 1863–1864* (New York: Scribner's, 1971), 448–49.

84. Those who blame Lee for Stuart's poorly timed ride include Allan Nevins and Ezra Warner. Those more critical of Stuart include Shelby Foote, Philip Katcher, Clement Eaton, and Bruce Catton. Lee rarely complained about Stuart's other raids but was incensed at Gettysburg. In his report on the battle, Lee wrote, "The movements of the army preceding the battle of Gettysburg had been much embarrassed by the absence of the cavalry" (*OR,* ser. 1, vol. 27, pt. 2, 321; Lee to Adj. Gen. Samuel Cooper, January 20, 1864).

85. Thomas B. Buell, *The Warrior Generals: Combat Leadership on the Civil War* (New York: Crown, 1997), 276. See also Francis MacDonnell, "The Confederate Spin on Winfield Scott and George Thomas," *CWH* 44 (1998): 255–66.

86. Buell, *Warrior Generals,* 275. Thomas quoted in Shelby Foote, *Fredericksburg to Meridian* (New York: Vintage Books, 1963), 94.

87. James M. McPherson, *Ordeal by Fire: The Civil War and Reconstruction* (New York: Knopf, 1982), 336; See *OR,* ser. 1, vol. 30, pt, 1, 140. Lincoln quote from Foote, *Fredericksburg to Meridian,* 768.

88. Herman Hattaway and Archer Jones, *How the North Won: A Military History of the Civil War* (Urbana: University of Illinois Press, 1983), 653–54.

89. Foote, *Red River to Appomattox,* 686–706.

90. McKenzie, *Uncertain Glory,* 345; Roy Morris Jr., *Sheridan: The Life and Wars of General Phil Sheridan* (New York: Crown, 1992), 220; Warner, *Generals in Blue,* 438.

91. Morris, *Sheridan,* 2; McKenzie, *Uncertain Glory,* 346–47.

92. McPherson, *Battle Cry of Freedom,* 580–83; Morris, *Sheridan,* 107–8, 111.

93. Boatner, *Civil War Dictionary,* 133–34; Paul A. Hutton, *Phil Sheridan and His Army* (Lincoln: University of Nebraska Press, 1973), 17; Morris, *Sheridan,* 230. For a detailed account of Sheridan's 1864 Shenandoah campaign, see John L. Heatwole, *The Burning: Sheridan in the Shenandoah Valley* (Charlottesville, Va.: Rockbridge, 1998).

94. Cleburne as celebrated by historians recognized in Christopher Losson, *Tennessee's Forgotten Warriors: Frank Cheatham and His Confederate Division* (Knoxville: University of Tennessee Press, 1981), 197.

95. Craig L. Symonds, *Stonewall of the West: Patrick Cleburne and the Civil War* (Lawrence: University of Kansas Press, 1997), 73–77.

96. Ibid., 81–82, 92.

97. Ibid., 98.

98. Boatner, *Civil War Dictionary*, 141–47, 803–8.

99. Howell Purdue and Elizabeth Purdue, *Pat Cleburne: Confederate General* (Hillsboro, Tex.: Hill Junior College Press, 1973), 267–78; Symonds, *Stonewall of the West*, 113, 158. Lee quote from Warner, *Confederates in Gray*, 53–54.

100. Cleburne's wounding in the mouth is described in Symonds, *Stonewall of the West*, 91.

101. Robert S. Henry, *Nathan Bedford Forrest: "First with the Most"* (New York: Smithmark, 1991), 13; Warner, *Generals in Gray*, 92–93.

102. Boatner, *Civil War Dictionary*, 85.

103. Ibid., 295–96; John Cimprich and Robert C. Mainfort Jr., "Fort Pillow Revisited: New Evidence About an Old Controversy," *CWH* 28 (1982): 293–306. Historians who have downplayed the massacre include Clement Eaton, *A History of the Southern Confederacy* (New York: Free Press, 1954), 263, 277; Jack Hurst, *Nathan Bedford Forrest: A Biography* (New York: Knopf, 1993), 384; James G. Randall and David H. Donald, *The Civil War and Reconstruction* (Boston: Heath, 1961), 394.

104. For records of attrition for commissioned generals, consult Warner, *Generals in Gray*, xix, and idem, *Generals in Blue*, xxi.

105. Grady McWhiney, *Braxton Bragg and Confederate Defeat: Field Command* (New York: Columbia University Press, 1969), 237.

106. Boatner, *Civil War Dictionary*, 644; McWhiney, *Bragg*, 323.

107. McWhiney, *Bragg*, 319–20.

108. Buell, *Warrior Generals*, 273. Longstreet quote is to Confederate Secretary of War James A. Seddon, September 26, 1863. See *OR*, ser. 1, vol. 30, pt. 4, 706.

109. Grant, *Memoirs*, 449; Foote, *Fredericksburg to Meridian*, 692–94.

110. Two Federal soldiers found the famous lost orders of Lee at an abandoned Confederate campsite near Frederick, Maryland, on September 13, 1862. Wrapped around three cigars, a copy of Special Orders No. 191 described how Lee had divided his army into four small parts, with miles and rivers separating them, what their targets were, and which routes and crossings were to be used. Much blame for overestimations of enemy strength has been placed on McClellan's chief of secret service, Allan Pinkerton, but McClellan often took Pinkerton's already exorbitant guesses and inflated them further. See Stephen W. Sears, *Controversies and Commanders: Dispatches from the Army of the Potomac* (Boston: Houghtlin Mifflin, 1999), 16. See also Edwin C. Fishel, "Pinkerton and McClellan: Who Deceived Whom?" *CWH* 34 (1998); and Mitchell, *Military Leaders in the Civil War*.

111. Mitchell, *Military Leaders of the Civil War*, 16–17, 34.

112. Telegraph dispatch from McClellan to Lincoln on June 27, 1862. See David H. Bates, *Lincoln in the Telegraph Office* (New York: D. Appleton-Century Co., 1939), 109–10.

113. William Marvel, *Burnside* (Chapel Hill: University of North Carolina Press, 1991), 346; McPherson, *Battle Cry of Freedom*, 803, 806. There are theories aplenty as to the cause of McClellan's tragic lethargy in battle: contempt for Lincoln, inept informants, a tolerance for slavery. The most convincing are a simple hatred of warfare

and an overwhelming fear of failure. See McPherson, *Battle Cry of Freedom*, 359–60; Mitchell, *Military Leaders of the Civil War*, 35.

114. Hattaway, *Shades of Blue and Gray*, 107; Marvel, *Burnside*, 39–40, 52-61; McPherson, *Battle Cry of Freedom*, 372–73.

115. Marvel, *Burnside*, 99–100, 110–11, 156–58.

116. Hattaway, *Shades of Blue and Gray*, 112.

117. Burnside's prewar career is summarized in Bruce Catton, *Glory Road* (Garden City, N.Y.: Doubleday, 1952), 19–20.

118. Steven E. Woodworth, *Jefferson Davis and His Generals* (Lawrence: University of Kansas Press, 1990), 29–30.

119. Ibid., 279. See also Joseph H. Parks, *General Leonidas Polk, CSA: The Fighting Bishop* (Baton Rouge: Louisiana State University, 1962).

120. Peter Cozzens, *The Darkest Days of the War: The Battles of Iuka and Corinth* (Chapel Hill: University of North Carolina Press, 1997), 6–7; Boatner, *Civil War Dictionary*, 867.

121. Eaton, *History of the Southern Confederacy*, 155; Warner, *Generals in Gray*, 325–26; McPherson, *Battle Cry of Freedom*, 405.

122. Woodworth, *Davis and His Generals*, 155.

123. Cozzens, *Darkest Days*, 277–78, 306.

124. Robert K. Krick, *Conquering the Valley* (New York: Morrow, 1996), 236, 238.

125. Frémont's Missouri bodyguards are described in Webb Garrison, *The Amazing Civil War* (New York: MJF Books, 1998), 229.

126. Bruce Catton, *Mr. Lincoln's Army* (Garden City, N.Y.: Doubleday, 1951), 29.

127. Boatner, *Civil War Dictionary*, 689. Grant quote from *OR*, ser. 1, vol. 36, pt. 3, 524.

128. Woodworth, *Davis and His Generals*, 119–20.

129. Richard M. McMurry, *John Bell Hood and the War for Southern Independence* (Knoxville: University of Kentucky Press, 1982), 167, 190; Symonds, *Stonewall of the West*, 243; Woodworth, *Davis and His Generals*, 124, 270–71.

130. Geoffrey C. Ward, *The Civil War* (New York: Knopf, 1990), 344.

131. See also John Dyer, *The Gallant Hood* (Indianapolis: Bobbs-Merrill, 1950).

132. Robert S. Holzman, *Stormy Ben Butler* (New York: Macmillan, 1954), 46.

133. Hans L. Trefousse, *Ben Butler: The South Called Him Beast!* (New York: Twayne, 1957), 122–23.

134. Ibid., 175.

135. Craig L. Symonds, *Joseph E. Johnston* (New York: Norton, 1992), 383–84; Sam R. Watkins, *"Co. Aytch": A Side Show of the Big Show* (New York: Macmillan, 1962), 125–29.

136. See also Steven H. Newton, *Joseph E. Johnston and the Defense of Richmond* (Lawrence: University of Kansas Press, 1998).

137. Watkins, *"Co. Aytch,"* 171.

138. Casualty statistics are derived from Boatner, *Civil War Dictionary*; Livermore, *Numbers and Losses*; Frederick Phisterer, *Statistical Record of the Armies of the United States* (New York: Scribner, 1893); and the *OR*.

139. Peter Cozzens, *This Terrible Sound: The Battle of Chickamauga* (Urbana: University of Illinois Press, 1992), 368.

140. For William S. Rosecrans's official report on the battle, see *OR*, ser. 1, vol. 30, pt. 1, 59–64. For an illuminating exchange of accusations and counteraccusations involving the gap created in the Union lines at Chickamauga, see *OR*, ser. 1, vol. 20, pt. 1, 101–5.

141. For detail on the fighting at the sunken road, see Sears, *Landscape Turned Red*, 236–47; B. Keith Toney, "Horrors of the Bloody Lane," *America's Civil War* (September 1997): 62–69, 88.

142. Before the battle, the bridge was known as Rohrbach's Bridge. See Sears, *Landscape Turned Red*, 169. See also McPherson, *Crossroads of Freedom*.

143. Gary W. Gallagher, ed., *The Wilderness Campaign* (Chapel Hill: University of North Carolina Press, 1997), 106–30; Gordon C. Rhea, *The Battle of the Wilderness, May 5–6, 1864* (Baton Rouge: Louisiana State University Press, 1994), 22–29.

144. Grant, *Memoirs*, 2:534.

145. Stephen W. Sears, *Chancellorsville* (Boston: Houghton Mifflin, 1996), 504–5.

146. Historian Stephen W. Sears, by way of unit-by-unit casualty analysis, gives the total dead and wounded from Chancellorsville to be 22,323, which would place Chancellorsville above the Wilderness on this list. See Sears, *Chancellorsville*, 475–501.

147. Sherman's quote to Grant is in the *OR*, ser. 1, vol. 10, pt. 1, 93–94.

148. McPherson, *Battle Cry of Freedom*, 571–74.

149. Hennessy, *Return to Bull Run*, 222–23.

150. Ibid., 361–65.

151. Gordon C. Rhea, *The Battles for Spotsylvania Court House* (Baton Rouge: Louisiana State University Press, 1997).

152. Randall and Donald, *Civil War and Reconstruction*, 333–39.

153. Camp capacities and death rates are from Robert E. Denney, *Civil War Prisons and Escapes* (New York: Sterling, 1993); Lonnie R. Speer, *Portals to Hell: Military Prisons of the Civil War* (Mechanicsburg, Pa.: Stackpole, 1997). Historians vary greatly in their estimation of Civil War captures. National Park Service historian Ed Bearss quotes a 1903 U.S. Army adjutant general report that states there were 211,411 Union soldiers captured and 462,634 Confederates captured. The latter number assuredly includes the number of soldiers who capitulated at war's end. An 1866 War Department report claimed there were 126,000 Union and 220,000 Confederate soldiers captured and imprisoned. In 1906 James Ford Rhodes calculated 194,000 Federals and 215,000 Confederates were captured; see Denney, *Civil War Prisons and Escapes*, 7, 12.

154. Andersonville was originally sixteen acres but was expanded in June 1864 to twenty-six acres; per Speer, *Portals to Hell*, 261–62.

155. Speer, *Portals to Hell*, 261–62.

156. William B. Hesseltine, *Civil War Prisons: A Study in War Psychology* (Columbus: Ohio State University Press, 1930), 137; William Marvel, *Andersonville: The Last Depot* (Chapel Hill: University of North Carolina Press, 1994), 39–41, 97–100.

157. Hesseltine, *Civil War Prisons*, 41–42.

158. Ibid., 181.

159. Ibid., 203. For a detailed account of the prison see George Levy, *To Die in Chicago: Confederate Prisoners at Camp Douglas, 1862–1865* (Evanston, Ill.: Evanston Publishing, 1994).

160. Hesseltine, *Civil War Prisons*, 189.

161. Speer, *Portals to Hell*, 151–54, 187–88.

162. Hesseltine, *Civil War Prisons*, 182.

163. Speer, *Portals to Hell*, 31–32.

164. Hesseltine, *Civil War Prisons*, 159.

165. Speer, *Portals to Hell*, 210–13.

166. Ibid., 242.

167. Ibid., 244.

168. Michael P. Gray, *The Business of Captivity: Elmira and Its Civil War Prison* (Kent, Ohio: Kent State University Press, 2001), 142–44.

169. Speer, *Portals to Hell*, 276–77.

170. Ibid., 273–75.

171. Ibid., 45–46, 143–47.

172. Hesseltine, *Civil War Prisons*, 184; Speer, *Portals to Hell*, 144, 163–64.

173. Hesseltine, *Civil War Prisons*, 48, 178–79.

174. Speer, *Portals to Hell*, 81–82, 137–38.

175. Ibid., 182–83.

176. Benton McAdams, *Rebels at Rock Island: The Story of a Civil War Prison* (DeKalb: Northern Illinois University Press, 2000), 45–47, 49; Hesseltine, *Civil War Prisons*, 182.

177. McAdams, *Rebels at Rock Island*, 113, xi.

178. Speer, *Portals to Hell*, 75–76.

179. Hesseltine, *Civil War Prisons*, 202; Speer, *Portals to Hell*, 75–76, 140–41.

180. Herman Hattaway and Richard E. Beringer, *Jefferson Davis, Confederate President* (Lawrence: University of Kansas Press, 2002), 191–92. See also Gregory J. W. Urwin, "'We Cannot Treat Negroes . . . as prisoners of war': Racial Atrocities and Reprisals in Civil War Arkansas," *CWH* 42 (1996).

181. McPherson, *Battle Cry of Freedom*, 566–67, 791–96; Urwin, "'We Cannot Treat Negroes,'" 42.

182. James Lee McDonough and Thomas L. Connelly, *Five Tragic Hours* (Knoxville: University of Tennessee Press, 1983), 3–4.

183. McPherson, *Battle Cry of Freedom*, 812–13.

184. McDonough and Connelly, *Five Tragic Hours*, 61–65, 157–58.

185. Numbers of Confederate captured are based on Boatner, *Civil War Dictionary*, 397, and Grant, *Memoirs*, 212.

186. Bruce Catton, *Terrible Swift Sword* (New York: Doubleday, 1963), 156.

187. Grant, *Memoirs*, 208. Historians who believe Pillow was inspired by the ease of his escape and wanted to save the fort include Boatner, *Civil War Dictionary*, 396–97, and Catton, *Terrible Swift Sword*, 157–58. Those who suggest Pillow halted the retreat for fear of Federal reinforcements include Thomas L. Connelly, *Army of the Heartland* (Baton Rouge: Louisiana State University, 1967), 121–22; Eaton, *History of the Southern Confederacy*, 158–59; and McPherson, *Battle Cry of Freedom*, 400–401. Foote contends that Pillow claimed to send the men back to retrieve their equipment; Shelby Foote, *Fort Sumter to Perryville* (New York: Vintage Books, 1986), 210.

188. Foote, *Fort Sumter to Perryville*, 213; Grant, *Memoirs*, 212.

189. *OR*, ser. 1, vol. 27, pt. 2, 320; McPherson, *Battle Cry of Freedom*, 665.

190. Pickett quoted in Foote, *Fredericksburg to Merdian*, 568. Contrary to Shelby Foote and others, historian Michael Fellman contends that Lee did not apologize to the enlisted men; Michael Fellman, *The Making of Robert E. Lee* (New York: Random House, 2000), 143.

191. See also Carol Reardon, *Pickett's Charge in History and Memory* (Chapel Hill: University of North Carolina Press, 1997). For Longstreet's official report on the battle, see *OR*, ser. 1, vol. 27, pt. 2, 357–63, submitted to Col. R. H. Chilton, assistant adjutant and inspector general, July 27, 1863. For Lee's official report to Adj. Gen. Sam Cooper on the battle of Gettysburg, see *OR*, ser. 1, vol. 27, pt 2, 313–25. Noteworthy is the date of submittal: Lee dated the report January 20, 1864, six months after the campaign.

192. Foote, *Fort Sumter to Perryville*, 86; Steven E. Woodworth, *No Band of Brothers: Problems in the Rebel High Command* (Columbia: University of Missouri Press, 1999), 16.

193. Foote, *Fort Sumter to Perryville*, 88.

194. Woodworth, *No Band of Brothers*, 38–40.

195. Foote, *Fort Sumter to Perryville*, 88; Emory M. Thomas, *The Confederate Nation: 1861–1865* (New York: Harper & Row, 1979), 124.

196. Lincoln quoted in Ward, *The Civil War*, 174.

197. Bryce A. Suderow, "The Battle of the Crater: The Civil War's Worst Massacre," *CWH* 43 (1997): 224.

198. Clifford Dowdey, *Lee's Last Campaign* (New York: Barnes & Noble Books, 1988), 296–97; *OR*, ser. 1, vol. 36, pt. 3, 526; Grant quoted in McPherson, *Battle Cry of Freedom*, 734.

199. Sears, *Chancellorsville*, 262.

200. Hattaway, *Shades of Blue and Gray*, 116.

201. Ibid., 118.

202. McPherson, *Battle Cry of Freedom*, 543–44.

203. Foote, *Fort Sumter to Perryville*, 696–700; McPherson, *Battle Cry of Freedom*, 543–44.

204. Drew G. Faust, *Mothers of Invention: Women of the Slaveholding South in the American Civil War* (Chapel Hill: University of North Carolina Press, 1996), 88; Gallman, *The North Fights the Civil War*, 105.

205. Mary E. Massey offers the compelling hypothesis that lower wages played the major role in expanding female employment opportunities, gains that were not readily given up once the war ended. See Massey, *Women in the Civil War*. See also Jeanie Attie, *Patriotic Toil: Northern Women and the American Civil War* (Ithaca, N.Y.: Cornell University Press, 1998), 272–74.

206. Francis B. Simkins and James W. Patton, *The Women of the Confederacy* (Richmond: Garrett and Massie, 1936), 89–94.

207. Massey, *Women in the Civil War*, 148.

208. Attie, *Patriotic Toil*, 268; Faust, *Mothers of Invention*, 89–90.

209. Faust, *Mothers of Invention*, 96.

210. Stephen B. Oates, *A Woman of Valor: Clara Barton and the Civil War* (New York: Free Press, 1994), 3–4, 21–22.

211. Marilyn M. Culpepper, *Trials and Triumphs: Women of the American Civil War* (East Lansing: Michigan State University, 1991), 321; Oates, *Woman of Valor*, ix, 85.

212. Henig and Niderost, *Civil War Firsts*, 336.

213. Massey, *Women in the Civil War*, 331–32.

214. Barton quoted in Oates, *Woman of Valor*, 382.

215. For prominent families who named their daughters after Barton and for details on her postwar career, see ibid., 370–82.

216. Faust, *Mothers of Invention*, 96–97.

217. Bickerdyke quoted in Nina B. Baker, *Cyclone in Calico: The Story of Mary Ann Bickerdyke* (Boston: Little Brown, 1952), 52.

218. Grant quoted in Massey, *Women in the Civil War*, 49.

219. Ibid., 55.

220. Account of Bickerdyke's postwar career in ibid., 300–303.

221. Simkins and Patton, *Women of the Confederacy*, 94.

222. Mary Denis Maher, *To Bind Up the Wounds: Catholic Sister Nurses in the United States Civil War* (New York: Greenwood Press, 1989), 2, 27–29; Oates, *Woman of Valor*, 377.

223. Maher, *To Bind Up the Wounds*, 101.

224. Ibid., 1, 13–14, 27–29. Davis and Lincoln quoted in Ignatius Sumner, *Angels of Mercy* (Baltimore: Cathedral Foundation Press, 1998), xii–xiii.

225. Lyde Cullen Sizer, "Acting Her Part: Narratives of Union Women Spies" in *Divided Houses: Gender and the Civil War*, ed. Catherine Clinton and Nina Silber (New York: Oxford University Press, 1992), 118.

226. Charles L. Blockson, *Hippocrene Guide to the Underground Railroad* (New York: Hippocrene Books, 1994), 78–79; Elizabeth Leonard, *All the Daring of the Soldier: Women of the Civil War Armies* (New York: Norton, 1999), 71; Massey, *Women in the Civil War*, 269–70.

227. For details on the Underground Railroad and the locations of homes and routes used, see Blockson, *Guide to the Underground Railroad*.

228. Eaton, *History of the Southern Confederacy*, 103.

229. Culpepper, *Trials and Triumphs,* 249–51; William Q. Maxwell, *Lincoln's Fifth Wheel: The Political History of the United States Sanitary Commission* (New York: Longmans, 1956), 224. See also Mary A. Livermore, *My Story of the War* (Hartford, Conn.: A. D. Worthington and Co., 1889).

230. Faust, *Mothers of Invention,* 112.

231. Massey, *Women in the Civil War,* 47–48.

232. Ward, *The Civil War* 149.

233. Dix quoted in Culpepper, *Trials and Triumphs,* 323.

234. Oates, *Woman of Valor,* 376.

235. Massey, *Women in the Civil War,* 330.

236. Elizabeth Cady Stanton, *Eighty Years and More: Reminiscences, 1815–1897* (1898; reprint, Boston: Northeastern University Press, 1993), ix; Wendy Venet, *Neither Ballots nor Bullets: Women Abolitionists and the Civil War* (Charlottesville: University Press of Virginia, 1991), 17.

237. Venet, *Neither Ballots nor Bullets,* 17–18; Lois W. Banner, *Elizabeth Cady Stanton: A Radical for Women's Rights* (Boston: Little, Brown, 1980), 61–62. Anthony quoted in Lynn Sherr, *Failure Is Impossible: Susan B. Anthony in Her Own Words* (New York: Random House, 1995), 51. Some of Stanton's most tangible successes were in terms of property rights for women. Her antebellum efforts in her native New York helped pass two reform bills allowing married women to own and control their own property. See Kathryn Cullen-Du Pont, *Elizabeth Cady Stanton and Women's Liberty* (New York: Facts on File, 1992), 74–75.

238. Massey, *Women in the Civil War,* 165.

239. Culpepper, *Trials and Triumphs,* 351–52; Leonard, *All the Daring of the Soldier,* 107–9.

240. Ibid., 111.

241. Richard B. Harwell, ed., *Kate: The Journal of a Confederate Nurse* (Baton Rouge: Louisiana State University Press, 1959), xii.

242. Kate Cumming quoted in Culpepper, *Trials and Triumphs,* 318; and Simkins and Patton, *Women of the Confederacy,* 90. The Southern condition of higher-status women in the Confederacy is examined with particular insight in Faust, *Mothers of Invention;* George Rable, "'Missing in Action': Women of the Confederacy," in Catherine Clinton, *Tara Revisited* (New York: Abbeville Press, 1995).

243. George C. Rable, *Civil Wars: Women and the Crisis of Southern Nationalism* (Urbana: University of Illinois Press, 1989), 123.

CHAPTER 6: PURSUING THE WAR

1. According to Bruce Chadwick, the reconciliation theme was an extenuation of popular novels and preceded the film era. See Bruce Chadwick, *The Reel Civil War: Mythmaking in American Film* (New York: Knopf, 2001), 23–29.

2. See also Frank J. Wetta and Stephen J. Curley, *Celluloid Wars: A Guide to Film and the American Experience of War* (New York: Greenwood, 1992).

3. James M. McPherson, "Glory" in *Past Imperfect: History According to the Movies,* ed. Mark C. Carnes (New York: Henry Holt, 1995), 128–31.

4. See also Martin H. Blatt, Thomas J. Brown, and Donald Yacovone, eds., *Hope and Glory: Essays on the Legacy of the 54th Massachusetts Regiment* (Amherst: University of Massachusetts Press, 2001); Russell Duncan, ed., *Blue-Eyed Child of Fortune: The Civil War Letters of Colonel Robert Gould Shaw* (Athens: University of Georgia Press, 1992); Douglas Brode, *Denzel Washington: His Films and His Career* (Secaucus, N.J.: Carol, 1997), 74–89. On the issue of unequal pay, see Herman Belz, "Law, Politics, and Race in the Struggle for Equal Pay During the Civil War," *CWH* 22 (1976): 197–13.

5. Chadwick, *Reel Civil War,* 276–79, 285–87.

6. Brock Garland, *War Movies* (New York: Facts on File, 1987), 169; John McCarty, *The Films of John Huston* (Secaucus, N.J.: Citadel Press, 1987); Jack Spears, *The Civil War on the Screen and Other Essays* (New York: A. S. Barnes and Co., 1977), 102–5.

7. Chadwick, *Reel Civil War,* 256–57.

8. Spears, *Civil War on the Screen,* 34–35.

9. Chadwick, *Reel Civil War,* 121–29.

10. Leon F. Litwack, "The Birth of a Nation," in *Past Imperfect: History According to the Movies,* ed. Mark C. Carnes (New York: Henry Holt, 1995), 136. See also Richard Schickel, *D. W. Griffith: An American Life* (New York: Simon & Schuster, 1984); Valerie Smith, ed., *Representing Blackness: Issues in Film and Video* (New Brunswick, N.J.: Rutgers University Press, 1997).

11. Garland, *War Movies,* 106.

12. See also Richard Harwell, ed., *Gone with the Wind as Book and Film* (Columbia: University of South Carolina Press, 1983).

13. For an especially critical view of the production, see William Marvel, "Andersonville: The Myth Endures," *Civil War Times Illustrated* 35 (1996).

14. Chadwick, *Reel Civil War,* 139–40; George Amberg, *The New York Times Film Reviews: 1913–1970* (New York: Arno Press, 1971), 64. See also Joe Franklin, *Classics of the Silent Screen* (Secaucus, N.J.: Citadel, 1983).

15. Chadwick, *Reel Civil War,* 232–33, 291.

16. For contemporary biographies on Stonewall Jackson, consider James I. Robertson Jr., *Stonewall Jackson: The Man, the Soldier, the Legend* (New York: Macmillan, 1997); Byron Farwell, *Stonewall: A Biography of General Thomas J. Jackson* (New York: Norton, 1992), and John Bowers, *Stonewall Jackson: Portrait of a Soldier* (New York: Morrow, 1989).

17. Philip Katcher, *The Civil War Source Book* (New York: Facts on File, 1995), 305.

18. For "housewife" and other slang, consult Webb Garrison, *The Encyclopedia of Civil War Usage* (Nashville, Tenn.: Cumberland House, 2001).

19. George W. Adams, *Doctors in Blue* (Baton Rouge: Louisiana State University Press, 1980), 226–27; Bell I. Wiley, *The Life of Johnny Reb: The Common Soldier of the Confederacy* (Baton Rouge: Louisiana State University Press, 1978), 256–58.

20. Henry S. Commager, ed., *The Civil War Archive: The History of the Civil War in Documents* (New York: Black Dog & Leventhal, 2000), 216–17.

21. For a review of skin-care issues among Union soldiers, see Adams, *Doctors in Blue,* 226.

22. Eric T. Dean, "'We Will All Be Lost and Destroyed': Post-Traumatic Stress Disorder and the Civil War," *CWH* 37 (1991): 146–47. For one of the best works on the effects of combat on infantry soldiers, see Denis Winter, *Death's Men* (New York: Penguin Books, 1978). For a light read on the sensations of reenacting, see Kent Courtney, *Returning to the Civil War* (Salt Lake City: Gibbs Smith, 1997). *Medical and Surgical History of the Rebellion* quote on depression from C. Keith Wilbur, *Civil War Medicine, 1861–1865* (Guilford, Conn.: Globe Pequot, 1998), 88.

23. Slang terms from Garrison, *Encyclopedia of Civil War Usage*, 162, 230.

24. David W. Blight, "Healing and History: Battlefields and the Problem of Civil War Memory" in *Rally on the High Ground: The National Park Service Symposium on the Civil War*, ed. Robert K. Sutton (Washington, D.C.: Eastern National, 2001), 28. Lee quote from Michael Fellman, *The Making of Robert E. Lee* (New York: Random House, 2000), 299.

25. Georgie Boge and Margie Holder Boge, *Paving Over the Past: A History and Guide to Civil War Battlefield Preservation* (Washington, D.C.: Island Press, 1993), 16.

26. Blight, "Healing and History," 25.

27. For a detailed state-by-state anthology of places of Civil War interest, see Alice Cromie, *A Tour Guide to the Civil War* (Nashville, Tenn.: Rutledge Hill, 2002). See also Joseph E. Stevens, *America's National Battlefield Parks* (Norman: University of Oklahoma Press, 1990).

28. Boge and Boge, *Paving Over the Past*, 47.

29. Progress and details of park improvements are available via the Web (www.nps. gov/gett).

30. Reservations for the Piper House Bed and Breakfast can be made by phone: (301) 797-1862.

31. Boge and Boge, *Paving Over the Past*, 16–17.

32. Richard J Lenz, *The Civil War in Georgia* (Watkinsville, Ga.: Infinity Press, 1995), 10–17.

33. Boge and Boge, *Paving Over the Past*, 21–22.

34. For statistics on the budgets and visitation of Petersburg, go to the Web site of the National Park Service (www.nps.gov). For an account of Lincoln's stay at City Point during the final weeks of the siege, see Benjamin P. Thomas, *Abraham Lincoln* (New York: Modern Library, 1968), 507–14.

35. For a comparison of Wilson's Creek casualty rates compared to other battles, see Thomas L. Livermore, *Numbers and Losses in the Civil War in America: 1861–1865* (Bloomington: Indiana University Press, 1957).

36. For an extensive history on the land and its trials, see Joan M. Zenzen, *Battling for Manassas: The Fifty-Year Preservation Struggle at Manassas National Battlefield Park* (State College: Pennsylvania State University Press, 1998).

37. Stevens, *America's National Battlefield Parks*, 115–18.

38. The Manassas Battlefield Park includes the Henry Hill Visitors Center, which is fully accessible. There is a bookstore, museum, and film entitled *Manassas: End of Innocence*. The park receives more than 830,000 visitors per year. New to the park

and made possible by the stoppage of mall construction is the Stuart's Hill Center and Museum, open during summer weekends.

39. Margaret E. Wagner, Gary W. Gallagher, and Paul Finkelman, eds., *The Library of Congress Civil War Desk Reference* (New York: Simon & Schuster, 2002), 905.

40. Ibid., 904.

41. For a brief overview of the reenacting experience, see Kent Courtney, *Returning to the Civil War* (Salt Lake City: Gibbs Smith, 1997).

42. The fate of the site of Big Bethel is described in Robert L. Holzman, *Stormy Ben Butler* (New York: Macmillan, 1954), 227. For a personal account of living on the battlefield of Cross Keys, Virginia, see Peter Svenson, *Battlefield: Farming a Civil War Battleground* (New York: Ballantine Books, 1992).

Bibliography

PERIODICALS

America's Civil War

Blue & Gray

Civil War History

Civil War Times Illustrated

De Bow's Review

Explorations in Economic History

Hallowed Ground

Journal of Southern History

South Atlantic Quarterly

Tennessee Historical Quarterly

NEWSPAPERS

Charleston Mercury

Chicago Times

Chicago Tribune

Cincinnati Commercial

Dubuque Herald

Harper's Weekly Journal of Civilization

Punch (Britain)

London News

London Times

Mobile Register

New Orleans Picayune

New York Herald

New York Times

New York Tribune

Philadelphia Enquirer

Richmond Daily Dispatch

Richmond Enquirer

Richmond Examiner

Richmond Whig

BOOKS

Abdill, George B. *Civil War Railroads.* Seattle: Superior Publishing Co., 1961.

Abrahamson, James L. *The Men of Secession and the Civil War: 1859–1861.* Wilmington, Del.: Scholarly Resources, 2000.

Abzug, Robert H. *Passionate Liberator: Theodore Dwight Weld and the Dilemma of Reform.* New York: Oxford University Press, 1980.

Adams, George W. *Doctors in Blue: The Medical History of the Union Army in the Civil War.* Baton Rouge: Louisiana State University, 1952.

Albaugh, William A., III, and Edward N. Simmons. *Confederate Arms.* Harrisburg, Pa.: Stackpole, 1957.

Alcott, Louisa May. *Hospital Sketches.* Cambridge, Mass.: Harvard University Press, 1960.

Allen, Felicity. *Jefferson Davis, Unconquerable Heart.* Columbia: University of Missouri Press, 1999.

Amberg, George. *The New York Times Film Reviews: 1913–1970.* New York: Arno, 1971.

Anderson, Bern. *By Sea and River: The Naval History of the Civil War.* New York: Da Capo, 1962.

Andrews, J. Cutler. *The North Reports the Civil War.* Pittsburgh: University of Pittsburgh Press, 1955.

———. *The South Reports the Civil War.* Princeton, N.J.: Princeton University Press, 1970.

Aptheker, Herbert. *Abolitionism: A Revolutionary Movement.* Boston: Twayne, 1989.

Ash, Stephen V. *When the Yankees Came: Conflict and Chaos in the Occupied South, 1861–1865.* Chapel Hill: University of North Carolina Press, 1995.

Attie, Jeanie. *Patriotic Toil: Northern Women and the America Civil War.* Ithaca, N.Y.: Cornell University Press, 1998.

Baker, Nina B. *Cyclone in Calico: The Story of Mary Ann Bickerdyke.* Boston: Little, Brown, 1952.

Bancroft, Frederic. *Slave Trading in the Old South.* 1931. Reprint, Columbia: University of South Carolina Press, 1996.

Banner, Lois W. *Elizabeth Cady Stanton: A Radical for Women's Rights.* Boston: Little, Brown, 1980.

Barney, William. *The Road to Secession: A New Perspective on the Old South.* New York: Praeger, 1972.

Bartlett, Irving H. *Wendell and Ann Phillips: The Community of Reform, 1840–1880.* New York: Norton, 1979.

Bass, Harold F., Jr. *Historical Dictionary of United States Parties.* Lanham, Md.: Scarecrow, 2000.

Bates, David H. *Lincoln in the Telegraph Office: Recollections of the United States Military Telegraph Corps During the Civil War.* New York: D. Appleton-Century Co., 1939.

Berger, Meyer. *The Story of the New York Times, 1851–1951.* New York: Simon & Schuster, 1951.

Berry, Mary F. *Military Necessity and Civil Rights Policy: Black Citizenship and the Constitution, 1861–1868.* Port Washington, N.Y.: Kennikat, 1977.

Billings, John D. *Hardtack and Coffee.* Williamstown, Mass.: Corner House, 1973.

Black, Robert C., III. *The Railroads of the Confederacy.* Chapel Hill: University of North Carolina Press, 1998.

Blassingame, John W. *The Slave Community: Plantation Life in the Ante-bellum South.* New York: Oxford University Press, 1972.

Blatt, Martin H., Thomas J. Brown, and Donald Yacovone, eds. *Hope and Glory: Essays on the Legacy of the 54th Massachusetts Regiment.* Amherst: University of Massachusetts Press, 2001.

Blight, David W. *Frederick Douglass' Civil War: Keeping Faith in Jubilee.* Baton Rouge: Louisiana State University Press, 1989.

Blockson, Charles L. *Hippocrene Guide to the Underground Railroad.* New York: Hippocrene Books, 1994.

Boatner, Mark M., III. *The Civil War Dictionary.* New York: Vintage Books, 1988.

Boge, Georgie, and Margie Holder Boge. *Paving Over the Past: A History and Guide to Civil War Battlefield Preservation*. Washington, D.C.: Island Press, 1993.

Bogue, Allan G. *The Earnest Men: Republicans of the Civil War Senate*. Ithaca, N.Y.: Cornell University Press, 1981.

Boles, John B. *Black Southerners: 1619–1869*. Lexington: University Press of Kentucky, 1984.

Bowers, John. *Stonewall Jackson: Portrait of a Soldier*. New York: Morrow, 1989.

Bowman, John S., ed. *The Civil War: Day by Day*. New York: Barnes & Noble Books, 1995.

Brock, Peter, ed. *Liberty and Conscience: A Documentary History of the Experiences of Conscientious Objectors in America Through the Civil War*. New York: Oxford University Press, 2002.

Brode, Douglas. *Denzel Washington: His Films and His Career*. Secaucus, N.J.: Carol, 1997.

Brooks, Stewart M. *Civil War Medicine*. Springfield, Ill.: Charles C. Thomas, 1966.

Bruce, Robert V. *Lincoln and the Tools of War*. Indianapolis: Bobbs-Merrill, 1956.

Bruun, Erik, and Jay Crosby, eds. *Our Nation's Archive: The History of the United States in Documents*. New York: Black Dog & Leventhal, 1999.

Buell, Thomas B. *The Warrior Generals: Combat Leadership on the Civil War*. New York: Crown, 1997.

Cambell, Randolph B. *The Peculiar Institution in Texas, 1821–1865*. Baton Rouge: Louisiana State University Press, 1989.

Carnes, Mark C., ed. *Past Imperfect: History According to the Movies*. New York: Henry Holt, 1995.

Cashin, Joan E., ed. *The War Was You and Me: Civilians in the American Civil War*. Princeton, N.J.: Princeton University Press, 2002.

Catton, Bruce. *The Centennial History of the Civil War: Terrible Swift Sword*. Garden City, N.Y.: Doubleday, 1963.

———. *Glory Road*. Garden City, N.Y.: Doubleday, 1952.

———. *Grant Moves South*. Boston: Little, Brown, 1960.

———. *Mr. Lincoln's Army*. Garden City, N.Y.: Doubleday, 1951.

Cecelski, David S. *The Waterman's Story: Slavery and Freedom in Maritime North Carolina*. Chapel Hill: University of North Carolina Press, 2001.

Chadwick, Bruce. *The Reel Civil War: Mythmaking in American Film*. New York: Knopf, 2001.

———. *The Two American Presidents*. Secaucus, N.J.: Carol, 1999.

Chambers, Lenoir. *Stonewall Jackson*. New York: Morrow, 1959.

Chesebrough, David B. *Frederick Douglass: Oratory from Slavery*. Westport, Conn.: Greenwood, 1998.

Clinton, Catherine. *Tara Revisited*. New York: Abbeville, 1995.

———, and Nina Silber, eds. *Divided Houses: Gender and the Civil War*. New York: Oxford University Press, 1992.

Coco, Gregory A. *The Civil War Infantryman: In Camp, on the March, and in Battle.* Gettysburg, Pa.: Thomas, 1996.

Coggins, Jack. *Arms and Equipment of the Civil War.* Wilmington, N.C.: Broadfoot, 1962.

Collins, Bruce. *The Origins of the American Civil War.* New York: Holmes & Meier, 1981.

Commager, Henry S., ed. *The Civil War Archive: The History of the Civil War in Documents.* New York: Black Dog & Leventhal, 2000.

Connelly, Thomas L. *Army of the Heartland.* Baton Rouge: Louisiana State University, 1967.

———, and Barbara L. Bellows. *God and General Longstreet: The Lost Cause and the Southern Mind.* Baton Rouge: Louisiana State University Press, 1982.

———, and Archer Jones. *The Politics of Command: Factions and Ideas in Confederate Strategy.* Baton Rouge: Louisiana State University Press, 1973.

Cooper, William J., Jr. *Jefferson Davis, American.* New York: Knopf, 2000.

Coombe, Jack D. *Gunsmoke over the Atlantic: First Naval Actions of the Civil War.* New York: Bantam Books, 2002.

Courtney, Kent. *Returning to the Civil War: Grand Reenactments of an Anguished Time.* Salt Lake City: Gibbs Smith, 1997.

Cousins, Norma, ed. *"In God We Trust": The Religious Beliefs and Ideas of the American Founding Fathers.* New York: Harper and Brothers, 1958.

Cozzens, Peter. *The Darkest Days of the War: The Battles of Iuka and Corinth.* Chapel Hill: University of North Carolina Press, 1997.

———. *This Terrible Sound: The Battle of Chickamauga.* Urbana: University of Illinois Press, 1992.

Craven, Avery. *An Historian and the Civil War.* Chicago: University of Chicago Press, 1964.

Cromie, Alice. *A Tour Guide to the Civil War.* Nashville, Tenn.: Rutledge Hill, 2002.

Cross, C. F. *Justin Smith Morrill: Father of the Land-Grant Colleges.* East Lansing: Michigan State University, 1999.

Cullen-Du Pont, Kathryn. *Elizabeth Cady Stanton and Women's Liberty.* New York: Facts on File, 1992.

Culpepper, Marilyn M. *Trials and Triumphs: Women of the American Civil War.* East Lansing: Michigan State University, 1991.

Curry, Richard O., ed. *The Abolitionists.* Hinsdale, Ill.: Dryden Press, 1973.

Daly, John Patrick. *When Slavery Was Called Freedom.* Lexington: University Press of Kentucky, 2002.

Davis, Burke. *To Appomattox: Nine April Days, 1865.* New York: Eastern Acorn Press, 1981.

Davis, Jefferson. *A Short History of the Confederate States of America.* New York: Belford, 1890.

Davis, William C. *"A Government of Our Own": The Making of the Confederacy.* New York: Free Press, 1994.

———. *The Lost Cause: Myths and Realities of the Confederacy.* Lawrence: University of Kansas Press, 1996.

Degler, Carl N. *The Other South: Southern Dissenters in the Nineteenth Century.* New York: Harper & Row, 1974.

Denney, Robert E. *Civil War Medicine.* New York: Sterling, 1994.

———. *Civil War Prisons and Escapes.* New York: Sterling, 1993.

Dew, Charles B. *Apostles of Disunion: Southern Secession Commissioners and the Causes of the Civil War.* Charlottesville: University Press of Virginia, 2001.

Dillon, Merton. *The Abolitionists: The Growth of a Dissenting Minority.* DeKalb: Northern Illinois University Press, 1975.

Donald, David H. *Lincoln.* New York: Simon & Schuster, 1995.

Dowdey, Clifford. *Lee's Last Campaign: The Story of Lee and His Men Against Grant— 1864.* New York: Barnes & Noble Books, 1988.

Duffy, John. *The Healers: A History of American Medicine.* Urbana: University of Illinois Press, 1979.

Duncan, Russell, ed. *Blue-Eyed Child of Fortune: The Civil War Letters of Colonel Robert Gould Shaw.* Athens: University of Georgia Press, 1992.

Dyer, John P. *The Gallant Hood.* Indianapolis: Bobbs-Merrill, 1950.

Eaton, Clement. *A History of the Southern Confederacy.* New York: MacMillan, 1954.

———. *Jefferson Davis.* New York: Free Press, 1977.

Eckenrode, H. J., and Bryan Conrad. *James Longstreet: Lee's War Horse.* Chapel Hill: University of North Carolina Press, 1986.

Eicher, David J. *The Civil War in Books: An Analytical Bibliography.* Urbana: University of Illinois Press, 1997.

Elder, Donald C. *A Damned Iowa Greyhound: The Civil War Letters of William Henry Harrison Clayton.* Iowa City: University of Iowa Press, 1998.

Farwell, Byron. *Stonewall: A Biography of General Thomas J. Jackson.* New York: Norton, 1992.

Faust, Drew G. *Mothers of Invention: Women of the Slaveholding South in the American Civil War.* Chapel Hill: University of North Carolina Press, 1996.

Fellman, Michael. *The Making of Robert E. Lee.* New York: Random House, 2000.

———, Lesley J. Gordon, and Daniel E. Sutherland. *This Terrible War: The Civil War and Its Aftermath.* New York: Longman, 2003.

Fermer, Douglas. *James Gordon Bennett and the New York Herald: A Study of Editorial Opinion in the Civil War Era, 1854–1867.* New York: St. Martin's, 1986.

Ferris, Norman. *The Trent Affair: A Diplomatic Crisis.* Knoxville: University of Tennessee Press, 1977.

Filler, Louis. *The Crusade Against Slavery, 1830–1860.* New York: Harper and Brothers, 1960.

Foner, Philip S. *British Labor and the American Civil War.* New York: Holmes & Meier, 1981.

Foote, Shelby. *A Civil War Narrative: Fort Sumter to Perryville.* New York: Vintage Books, 1958.

———. *A Civil War Narrative: Fredericksburg to Meridian.* New York: Vintage Books, 1963.

———. *A Civil War Narrative: Red River to Appomattox.* New York: Vintage Books, 1974.

Fowler, William M., Jr. *Under Two Flags: The American Navy in the Civil War.* New York: Norton, 1990.

Fox, William F. *Regimental Losses in the Civil War.* Albany, N.Y.: Albany Publishing Co., 1898.

Franklin, Joe. *Classics of the Silent Screen.* Secaucus, N.J.: Citadel, 1983.

Franklin, John H. *From Slavery to Freedom: A History of African Americans.* New York: Vintage Books, 1967.

Freehling, William W. *The Road to Disunion: Secessionists at Bay, 1776–1854.* Oxford: Oxford University Press, 1990.

Freeman, Jefferson D. *Reprint of Rare Confederate Cookbook.* Union City, Tenn.: Pioneer Press, 2000.

Freemon, Frank R. *Gangrene and Glory: Medical Care During the American Civil War.* London: Associated University Presses, 1998.

———. *Microbes and Minie Balls: An Annotated Bibliography of Civil War Medicine.* Cranbury, N.J.: Associated University Presses, 1993.

Furguson, Ernest B. *Ashes of Glory: Richmond at War.* New York: Knopf, 1996.

Gallagher, Gary W. *The Confederate War.* Cambridge, Mass.: Harvard University Press, 1997.

———, ed. *The Third Day at Gettysburg and Beyond.* Chapel Hill: University of North Carolina Press, 1994.

———, ed. *The Wilderness Campaign.* Chapel Hill: University of North Carolina Press, 1997.

Gallman, J. Matthew. *The North Fights the Civil War: The Home Front.* Chicago: Ivan R. Dee, 1994.

Garland, Brock. *War Movies.* New York: Facts on File Publications, 1987.

Garrison, Webb. *The Amazing Civil War.* New York: MJF Books, 1998.

———. *The Encyclopedia of Civil War Usage.* Nashville, Tenn.: Cumberland House. 2001.

Genovese, Eugene D. *Roll, Jordan, Roll: The World the Slaves Made.* New York: Pantheon, 1974.

Gienapp, William E. *Abraham Lincoln and Civil War America.* Oxford, England: Oxford University Press, 2002.

Goodrich, Thomas. *War to the Knife: Bleeding Kansas, 1854–1861.* Mechanicsburg, Pa.: Stackpole, 1998.

Grant, Alfred. *The American Civil War and the British Press.* Jefferson, N.C.: McFarland and Co., 2000.

Grant, Ulysses S. *Personal Memoirs of U. S. Grant.* 1885. Reprint, New York: Literary Classics, 1990.

Gray, Michael P. *The Business of Captivity: Elmira and Its Civil War Prison.* Kent, Ohio: Kent State University Press, 2001.

Gregg, Rod. *Civil War Quiz and Fact Book.* New York: Harper & Row, 1985.

Grimsley, Mark, and Brooks D. Simpson, eds. *The Collapse of the Confederacy.* Lincoln: University of Nebraska Press, 2001.

Halberstadt, Hans. *The Soldier's Story.* Washington, D.C.: Brassey's, 2001.

Haller, John S., Jr. *American Medicine in Transition, 1840–1910.* Urbana: University of Illinois Press, 1981.

Harris, Brayton. *Blue and Gray in Black and White: Newspapers in the Civil War.* Washington, D.C.: Brassey's, 1999.

Harrison, Lowell H. *Lincoln of Kentucky.* Lexington: University of Kentucky Press, 2000.

Harrold, Stanley. *The Abolitionists and the South, 1831–1861.* Lexington: University Press of Kentucky, 1995.

Harwell, Richard B., ed. *Kate: The Journal of a Confederate Nurse.* Baton Rouge: Louisiana State University Press, 1959.

———, ed. *Gone with the Wind as Book and Film.* Columbia: University of South Carolina Press, 1983.

Hattaway, Herman. *Shades of Blue and Gray: An Introductory Military History of the Civil War.* Columbia: University of Missouri Press, 1997.

———, and Archer Jones. *How the North Won: A Military History of the Civil War.* Urbana: University of Illinois Press, 1983.

———, and Richard E. Beringer. *Jefferson Davis, Confederate President* Lawrence: University of Kansas Press, 2002.

Hearn, Chester G. *When the Devil Came Down to Dixie: Ben Butler in New Orleans.* Baton Rouge: Louisiana State University Press, 1997.

Heatwole, John L. *The Burning: Sheridan in the Shenandoah Valley.* Charlottesville, Va.: Rockbridge, 1998.

Heidler, David S., and Jeanne T. Heidler, eds. *Encyclopedia of the American Civil War: A Political, Social, and Military History.* Santa Barbara, Calif.: ABC-CLIO, 2000.

Heller, Charles E. *Portrait of an Abolitionist: A Biography of George Luther Stearns.* Westport, Conn.: Greenwood, 1996.

Henig, Gerald S., and Eric Niderost. *Civil War Firsts: The Legacies of America's Bloodiest Conflict.* Mechanicsburg, Pa.: Stackpole, 2001.

Hennessy, John J. *Return to Bull Run: The Campaign and Battle of 2nd Manassas.* New York: Simon & Schuster, 1993.

Henry, Robert S. *Nathan Bedford Forrest: "The First with the Most."* New York: Smithmark Publishing, 1991.

Hesseltine, William B. *Civil War Prisons: A Study in War Psychology.* Columbus: Ohio State University Press, 1930.

Hicks, Brian, and Schuyler Kropf. *Raising the Hunley.* New York: Ballantine Books, 2002.

Hirshson, Stanley P. *The White Tecumseh: A Biography of General William T. Sherman.* New York: Wiley, 1997.

Hobsbawm, E. J. *The Age of Capital: 1848–1875.* New York: New American Library, 1979.

Holt, Michael F. *The Political Crisis of the 1850's.* New York: Norton, 1983.

Holzer, Harold. *Dear Mr. Lincoln: Letters to the President.* Reading, Mass.: Addison Wesley, 1995.

Holzman, Robert S. *Stormy Ben Butler.* New York: Macmillan, 1954.

Howard, Benjamin C. *Report of the Decision of the Supreme Court of the United States and the Opinions of the Judges Thereof in the Case of Dred Scott Versus John F. A. Sandford.* Washington, D.C.: Cornelius Wendell, Printer, 1857.

Hudson, J. Blaine Hudson. *Fugitive Slaves and the Underground Railroad in the Kentucky Borderland.* Jefferson, N.C.: McFarland, 2002.

Huntzicker, William E. *The Popular Press, 1833–1865.* Westport, Conn.: Greenwood, 1999.

Hurst, Jack. *Nathan Bedford Forrest: A Biography.* New York: Knopf, 1993.

Hutton, Paul A. *Phil Sheridan and His Army.* Lincoln: University of Nebraska Press, 1973.

Irvine, Dallas D. *Military Operations of the Civil War: A Guide-Index to the Official Records of the Union and Confederate Armies, 1861–1865.* Washington, D.C.: National Archives, 1968–80.

Jenkins, Brian. *Britain and the War for the Union.* Montreal: McGill-Queen's University Press, 1974.

Johannsen, Robert W., ed. *Democracy on Trial: A Documentary History of American Life, 1845–1877.* 2d ed. Urbana: University of Illinois Press, 1988.

Johnson, Charles B. *Muskets and Medicine: Army Life in the Sixties.* Philadelphia: F. A. Davis Co., 1917.

Johnson, Clint. *Civil War Blunders.* Winston-Salem, N.C.: John F. Blair, 1997.

Jones, Howard. *Abraham Lincoln and a New Birth of Freedom: The Union and Slavery in the Diplomacy of the Civil War.* Lincoln: University of Nebraska Press, 1999.

Jordan, Robert Paul. *The Civil War.* Washington D.C.: National Geographic Society, 1969.

Katcher, Philip. *The Civil War Source Book.* New York: Facts on File, 1995.

Keegan, John. *A History of Warfare.* New York: Knopf, 1993.

Kennedy, David M., and Thomas A. Bailey. *The American Pageant.* 2 vols. Lexington, Mass.: Heath, 1986.

Kennedy, Frances H., ed. *The Civil War Battlefield Guide.* Boston: Houghton Mifflin, 1998.

———, and Douglas R. Porter. *Dollar$ and Sense of Battlefield Preservation: The Economic Benefits of Protecting Civil War Battlefield.* Washington, D.C., Preservation Press, 1994.

Kimball, William J., ed. *Richmond in Time of War.* Boston: Houghton Mifflin, 1960.

King, Wilma. *Stolen Childhood: Slave Youth in Nineteenth-Century America.* Bloomington: Indiana University Press, 1995.

Kinnard, Roy. *The Blue and the Gray on the Silver Screen.* Secaucus, N.J.: Carol, 1996.

Klein, Maury. *Days of Defiance: Sumter, Secession, and the Coming of the Civil War.* New York: Knopf, 1997.

Klein, Philip S. *President James Buchanan: A Biography.* University Park: Pennsylvania State University Press, 1962.

Klement, Frank L. *Dark Lanterns: Secret Political Societies, Conspiracies, and Treason Trials in the Civil War.* Baton Rouge: Louisiana State University Press, 1984.

Kolchin, Peter. *American Slavery, 1619–1877.* New York: Hill and Wang, 1993.

Krick, Robert. *Conquering the Valley: Stonewall Jackson at Port Republic.* New York: Morrow, 1996.

Lane, Mills, ed. *Neither More nor Less Than Men: Slavery in Georgia.* Savannah, S.C.: Beehive Press, 1993.

Lang, George, Raymond L. Collins, and Gerard F. White. *Medal of Honor Recipients, 1863–1994.* New York: Facts on File, 1995.

Lee, Charles R., Jr. *The Confederate Constitutions.* Chapel Hill: University of North Carolina Press, 1963.

Lenz, Richard J. *The Civil War in Georgia.* Watkinsville, Ga.: Infinity Press, 1995.

Leonard, Elizabeth. *All the Daring of the Soldier: Women of the Civil War Armies.* New York: Norton, 1999.

———. *Yankee Women: Gender Battles in the Civil War.* New York: Norton, 1994.

Les Benedict, Michael. *The Impeachment and Trial of Andrew Johnson.* New York: Norton, 1973.

Levine, Bruce. *Half Slave and Half Free: The Roots of the Civil War.* New York: Noonday Press, 1992.

Levy, George. *To Die in Chicago: Confederate Prisoners at Camp Douglas, 1862–1865.* Evanston, Ill.: Evanston Publishing, 1994.

Linderman, Gerald F. *Embattled Courage: The Experience of Combat in the American Civil War.* New York: Free Press, 1987.

Livermore, Mary A. *My Story of the War.* Hartford, Conn.: A. D. Worthington and Co., 1889.

Livermore, Thomas L. *Numbers and Losses in the Civil War in America: 1861–1865.* Bloomington: Indiana University Press, 1957.

Long, E. B., and Barbara Long. *The Civil War Day by Day: An Almanac, 1861–1865.* New York: Da Capo, 1985.

Longstreet, James. *From Manassas to Appomattox.* 1895. Reprint, Bloomington: Indiana University Press, 1960.

Lord, Francis A. *Civil War Collectors Encyclopedia.* Harrisburg, Pa.: Stackpole, 1963.

Losson, Christopher. *Tennessee's Forgotten Warriors: Frank Cheatham and His Confederate Division.* Knoxville: University of Tennessee Press, 1981.

Lowance, Mason, ed. *Against Slavery: An Abolitionist Reader.* New York: Penguin Books, 2000.

McAdams, Benton. *Rebels at Rock Island: The Story of a Civil War Prison.* DeKalb: Northern Illinois University Press, 2000.

MacLachlan, Colin M., and William H. Beezley. *El Gran Pueblo: A History of Greater Mexico.* Englewood Cliffs, N.J.: Prentice-Hall, 1994.

McCarty, John. *The Films of John Huston.* Secaucus, N.J.: Citadel, 1987.

McClellan, George B. *McClellan's Own Story.* New York: C. L. Webster, 1887.

McDonough, James Lee, and Thomas L. Connelly. *Five Tragic Hours: The Battle of Franklin.* Knoxville: University of Tennessee Press, 1983.

McKenzie, John D. *Uncertain Glory: Lee's Generalship Re-Examined.* New York: Hippocrene Books, 1997.

McMurry, Richard M. *John Bell Hood and the War for Southern Independence.* Knoxville: University of Kentucky Press, 1982.

McPherson, James M. *Battle Cry of Freedom: The Civil War Era.* New York: Oxford University Press, 1988.

———. *Crossroads of Freedom: Antietam.* New York: Oxford University Press, 2002.

———. *For Cause and Comrades: Why Men Fought in the Civil War.* New York: Oxford University Press, 1997.

———. *Ordeal by Fire: The Civil War and Reconstruction.* New York: Knopf, 1982.

McWhiney, Grady. *Braxton Bragg and Confederate Defeat: Field Command.* New York: Columbia University Press, 1969.

Madden, David, ed. *Beyond the Battlefield.* New York: Simon & Schuster, 2000.

Maher, Mary Denis. *To Bind Up the Wounds: Catholic Sister Nurses in the United States Civil War.* New York: Greenwood, 1989.

Mahin, Dean B. *One War at a Time: The International Dimensions of the American Civil War.* Washington, D.C.: Brassey's, 1999.

Marten, James. *The Children's Civil War.* Chapel Hill: University of North Carolina Press, 1998.

———. *Texas Divided: Loyalty and Dissent in the Lone Start State, 1856–1874.* Knoxville: University Press of Kentucky, 1990.

Marvel, William. *Andersonville: The Last Depot.* Chapel Hill: University of North Carolina Press, 1994.

———. *Burnside.* Chapel Hill: University of North Carolina Press, 1991.

Marszalek, John F. *Sherman: A Soldier's Passion for Order.* New York: Vintage Books, 1994.

Massey, Mary E. *Ersatz in the Confederacy.* Columbia: University of South Carolina Press, 1952.

———. *Refugee Life in the Confederacy.* Baton Rouge: Louisiana State University Press, 1964.

———. *Women in the Civil War.* Lincoln: University of Nebraska Press, 1994.

Maxwell, William Quentin. *Lincoln's Fifth Wheel: The Political History of the United States Sanitary Commission.* New York: Longmans, 1956.

May, Robert E., ed. *The Union, the Confederacy, and the Atlantic Rim.* West Lafayette, Ind.: Purdue University Press, 1995.

Meyer, Steve. *Iowa Valor.* Garrison, Iowa: Meyer, 1994.

Miller, Randall M., and John David Smith. *Dictionary of Afro-American Slavery.* New York: Greenwood, 1988.

———, Harry S. Stout, and Charles Reagan Wilson. *Religion and the American Civil War.* New York: Oxford University Press, 1998.

Mintz, Steven, ed. *African American Voices: The Life Cycle of Slavery.* St. James, N.Y.: Brandywine, 1993.

Mitchell, Joseph B. *Military Leaders in the Civil War.* New York: Putnam, 1972.

Mitgang, Herbert. *Abraham Lincoln: A Press Portrait.* Chicago: Quadrangle Books, 1971.

Mohr, Clarence L. *On the Threshold of Freedom: Masters and Slaves in Civil War Georgia*. Athens: University of Georgia Press, 1986.

Moore, Albert B. *Conscription and Conflict in the Confederacy*. New York: Macmillan, 1924.

Moore, Guy W. *The Case of Mrs. Surratt*. Norman: University of Oklahoma Press, 1954.

Morris, Roy, Jr. *Sheridan: The Life and Wars of General Phil Sheridan*. New York: Crown, 1992.

Murdock, Eugene C. *One Million Men: The Civil War Draft in the North*. Madison: State Historical Society of Wisconsin, 1971.

Nelson, Larry E. *Bullets, Ballots, and Rhetoric: Confederate Policy for the United States Presidential Contest of 1864*. University: University of Alabama Press, 1980.

Nevins, Allan. *The War for the Union: The Organized War, 1863–1864*. New York: Scribner, 1971.

———. *The War for the Union: War Becomes Revolution, 1862–1863*. New York: Scribner, 1960.

———, ed. *Polk: The Diary of a President: 1845–1849*. London: Longmans, 1929.

Newton, Steven H. *Joseph E. Johnston and the Defense of Richmond*. Lawrence: University of Kansas Press, 1998.

Niven, John. *John C. Calhoun and the Price of Union*. Baton Rouge: Louisiana State University Press, 1988.

Nofi, Albert A., ed. *A Civil War Journal*. New York: Galahad Books, 1993.

Nolan, Alan T., *Lee Considered: General Robert E. Lee and Civil War History*. Chapel Hill: University of North Carolina Press, 1991.

Oates, Stephen B. *Abraham Lincoln: The Man Behind the Myths*. New York: Meridian, 1984.

———. *The Fires of Jubilee: Nat Turner's Fierce Rebellion*. New York: Harper Perennial, 1990.

———. *A Woman of Valor: Clara Barton and the Civil War*. New York: Free Press, 1994.

Owsley, Frank L. *King Cotton Diplomacy: Foreign Relations of the Confederate States of America*. Chicago: University of Chicago Press, 1959.

Paludan, Phillip S. *"A People's Contest": The Union and the Civil War, 1861–1865*. New York: Harper & Row, 1988.

———. *The Presidency of Abraham Lincoln*. Lawrence: University of Kansas Press, 1994.

Parish, Peter J. *The American Civil War*. New York: Holmes & Meier, 1981.

Parks, Joseph H. *General Leonidas Polk, CSA: The Fighting Bishop*. Baton Rouge: Louisiana State University Press, 1962.

Perry, Lewis, and Michael Fellman, eds. *Antislavery Reconsidered: New Perspectives on the Abolitionists*. Baton Rouge: Louisiana State University Press, 1979.

Perry, Milton F. *Infernal Machines: The Story of Confederate Submarine and Mine Warfare*. Baton Rouge: Louisiana State University, 1965.

Phisterer, Frederick. *Statistical Record of the Armies of the United States*. New York: Scribner, 1893.

Potter, David M. *The Impending Crisis, 1848–1861*. New York: Harper & Row, 1976.

Purdue, Howell, and Elizabeth Purdue. *Pat Cleburne: Confederate General.* Hillsboro, Tex.: Hill Junior College Press, 1973.

Rable, George C. *Civil Wars: Women and the Crisis of Southern Nationalism.* Urbana: University of Illinois Press, 1989.

————. *The Confederate Republic: A Revolution Against Politics.* Chapel Hill: University of North Carolina Press, 1994.

Randall, James G. *Lincoln: The President Midstream.* New York: Dodd, Mead, & Co., 1953.

————, and David H. Donald. *The Civil War and Reconstruction.* Boston: Heath, 1961.

Rawick, George P. *The American Slave: A Composite Autobiography.* Westport, Conn.: Greenwood, 1972.

Rawley, James A. *The Politics of Union.* Hinsdale, Ill.: Dryden Press, 1974.

Reardon, Carol. *Pickett's Charge in History and Memory.* Chapel Hill: University of North Carolina Press, 1997.

Reynolds, Donald E. *Editors Make War: Southern Newspapers in the Secession Crisis.* Nashville: Vanderbilt University Press, 1970.

Rhea, Gordon C. *The Battles for Spotsylvania Court House and the Road to Yellow Tavern, May 7–12, 1864.* Baton Rouge: Louisiana State University Press, 1997.

————. *The Battle of the Wilderness, May 5–6, 1864.* Baton Rouge: Louisiana State University Press, 1994.

Rivers, Larry E. *Slavery in Florida: Territorial Days to Emancipation.* Gainesville: University of Florida Press, 2000.

Roberts, William H. *Civil War Ironclads.* Baltimore: Johns Hopkins University Press, 2002.

Robertson, James I., Jr. *Soldiers Blue and Gray.* Columbia: University of South Carolina Press, 1988.

Ross, Charles D. *Trial by Fire: Science, Technology, and the Civil War.* Shippensburg, Pa.: White Mane, 2000.

Rozwenc, Edwin C., ed. *The Causes of the American Civil War.* Lexington, Mass.: Heath, 1972.

Rutland, Robert A. *The Newsmongers: Journalism in the Life of the Nation, 1690–1972.* New York: Dial Press, 1973.

Sachsman, David B., S. Kittrell Rushing, and Debra Reddin van Tuyll, eds. *The Civil War and the Press.* New Brunswick, Conn.: Transaction, 2000.

Schickel, Richard. *D. W. Griffith: An American Life.* New York: Simon & Schuster, 1984.

Schroeder-Lein, Glenna R. *Confederate Hospitals on the Move: Samuel H. Stout and the Army of Tennessee.* Columbia: University of South Carolina Press, 1994.

Scott, Otto J. *The Secret Six: John Brown and the Abolitionist Movement.* New York: Times Books, 1979.

Sears, Stephen W. *Chancellorsville.* Boston: Houghton Mifflin, 1996.

————. *Controversies and Commanders: Dispatches from the Army of the Potomac.* Boston: Houghton Mifflin, 1999.

————. *Landscape Turned Red: The Battle of Antietam.* New Haven, Conn.: Ticknor & Fields, 1983.

————. *To the Gates of Richmond: The Peninsula Campaign.* New York: Ticknor & Fields, 1992.

Sellers, James B. *Slavery in Alabama.* Birmingham: University of Alabama Press, 1964.

Severance, Frank H., ed. *Millard Fillmore Papers.* 2 vols. Buffalo, N.Y.: Buffalo Historical Society, 1907.

Sherman, William Tecumseh. *Memoirs of W. T. Sherman.* 1886. Reprint, New York: Literary Classics, 1990.

Sherr, Lynn. *Failure Is Impossible: Susan B. Anthony in Her Own Words.* New York: Random House, 1995.

Sideman, Belle B., and Lillian Friedman, eds. *Europe Looks at the Civil War.* New York: Orion Press, 1960.

Sifakis, Stewart. *Who Was Who in the Civil War.* New York: Facts on File, 1988.

Simkins, Francis B., and James W. Patton. *The Women of the Confederacy.* Richmond: Garrett and Massie, 1936.

Smith, Edward Conrad. *The Borderland and the Civil War.* New York: Macmillan, 1927.

Smith, Valerie, ed. *Representing Blackness: Issues in Film and Video.* New Brunswick, N.J.: Rutgers University Press, 1997.

Sommerville, George W. *Immortal Blue: Co. "H" 19th Iowa Volunteer Infantry, 1862–1865.* Bonaparte, Iowa: Record Republican, 1966.

Sorin, Gerald. *The New York Abolitionists: A Case Study of Political Radicalism.* Westport, Conn.: Greenwood, 1971.

Spears, Jack. *The Civil War on the Silver Screen and Other Essays.* New York: A. S. Barnes and Co., 1977.

Speer, Lonnie R. *Portals to Hell: Military Prisons of the Civil War.* Mechanicsburg, Pa.: Stackpole, 1997.

Stampp, Kenneth M. *The Peculiar Institution: Slavery in the Antebellum South.* New York: Vintage Books, 1956.

Stanton, Elizabeth Cady. *Eighty Years and More: Reminiscences, 1815–1897.* 1898. Reprint, Boston: Northeastern University Press, 1993.

Starr, Louis M. *Bohemian Brigade: Newsmen in Action.* New York: Knopf, 1854.

Stauffer, John. *The Black Hearts of Men: Radical Abolitionists and the Transformation of Race.* Cambridge: Harvard University Press, 2002.

Stearns, Frank P. *The Life and Public Services of George Luther Stearns.* Philadelphia: Lippincott, 1907.

Steiner, Paul E. *Disease in the Civil War.* Springfield, Ill.: Charles C. Thomas, 1968.

Stevens, Joseph E. *America's National Battlefield Parks.* Norman: University of Oklahoma Press, 1990.

Stewart, James B. *Wendell Phillips: Liberty's Hero.* Baton Rouge: Louisiana State University Press, 1986.

Sumner, Charles. *The Selected Letters of Charles Sumner.* Boston: Northeastern University Press, 1990.

Sumner, Ignatius. *Angels of Mercy.* Baltimore: Cathedral Foundation Press, 1998.

Sutherland, Daniel E. *Fredericksburg and Chancellorsville: The Dare Mark Campaign.* Lincoln: University of Nebraska Press, 1998.

———, ed. *Guerrillas, Unionists, and Violence on the Confederate Home Front.* Fayetteville: University of Arkansas Press, 1999.

Sutton, Robert K., ed. *Rally on the High Ground: The National Park Service Symposium on the Civil War.* Washington, D.C.: Eastern National, 2001.

Svenson, Peter. *Battlefield: Farming a Civil War Battleground.* New York: Ballantine Books, 1992.

Swanson, James L., and Daniel R. Weinberg. *Lincoln's Assassins.* Chicago: Arena Editions, 2001.

Swierenga, Robert P., ed. *Beyond the Civil War Synthesis: Political Essays of the Civil War Era.* Westport, Conn.: Greenwood, 1975.

Sword, Wiley. *Southern Invincibility: A History of the Confederate Heart.* New York: St. Martin's, 1999.

Sydnor, Charles S. *Slavery in Mississippi.* Gloucester, Mass.: Peter Smith, 1965.

Symonds, Craig L. *Joseph E. Johnston.* New York: Norton, 1992.

———. *Stonewall of the West: Patrick Cleburne and the Civil War.* Lawrence: University of Kansas Press, 1997.

Tanner, Robert G. *Stonewall in the Valley.* Mechanicsburg, Pa.: Stackpole Books, 1996.

Tapert, Annette, ed. *The Brothers' War: Civil War Letters to Their Loved Ones from the Blue and the Gray.* New York: Time Books, 1988.

Tatum, Georgia Lee. *Disloyalty in the Confederacy.* New York: AMS Press, 1934.

Tebbel, John, and Mary Ellen Zuckerman. *The Magazine in America, 1741–1990.* New York: Oxford University Press, 1991.

Thomas, Benjamin P. *Abraham Lincoln.* New York: Modern Library, 1968.

———. *Lincoln: A Biography.* New York: Knopf, 1952.

———. *Theodore Weld: Crusader for Freedom.* New Brunswick, N.J.: Rutgers University Press, 1950.

Thomas, Emery M. *The Confederate Nation: 1861–1865.* New York: Harper & Row, 1979.

Thompson, William A. R. *Black's Medical Dictionary,* 29th ed. New York: Barnes & Noble Books, 1972.

Trefousse, Hans L. *Ben Butler: The South Called Him Beast!* New York: Twayne, 1957.

Trindal, Elizabeth Steger. *Mary Surratt: An American Tragedy.* Gretna, La.: Pelican, 1996.

Trout, Robert J. *They Followed the Plume: The Story of J. E. B. Stuart and His Staff.* Mechanicsburg, Pa.: Stackpole, 1993.

U.S. Surgeon General. *Medical and Surgical History of the War of the Rebellion (1861–1865).* 6 vols. Washington, D.C.: Government Printing Office, 1870–88.

Vandiver, Frank E. *Civil War Battlefields and Landmarks.* New York: Random House, 1996.

Van Doren Stern, Philip. *Secret Missions of the Civil War.* New York: Random House, 1987.

———. *When the Guns Roared: World Aspects of the American Civil War.* Garden City, N.Y.: Doubleday, 1965.

Varhola, Michael J. *Everyday Life During the Civil War.* Cincinnati, Ohio: Writer's Digest Books, 1999.

Venet, Wendy. *Neither Ballots nor Bullets: Women Abolitionists and the Civil War.* Charlottesville: University Press of Virginia, 1991.

Vetter, Charles E. *Sherman: Merchant of Terror, Advocate of Peace.* Gretna, La.: Pelican, 1992.

Vinovskis, Maris A., ed. *Toward a Social History of the American Civil War.* New York: Cambridge University Press, 1990.

Volo, Dorothy D., and James M. Volo. *Daily Life in the Civil War.* Westport, Conn.: Greenwood, 1998.

Von Abele, Rudolph. *Alexander A. Stephens: A Biography.* New York: Knopf, 1946.

Wagner, Margaret E., Gary W. Gallagher, and Paul Finkelman, eds. *The Library of Congress Civil War Desk Reference.* New York: Simon & Schuster, 2002.

Wakelyn, Jon L. *Biographical Dictionary of the Confederacy.* Westport, Conn.: Greenwood, 1977.

Walther, Eric H. *The Fire Eaters.* Baton Rouge: Louisiana State University Press, 1992.

Ward, Geoffrey C. *The Civil War: An Illustrated History.* New York: Knopf, 1990.

Warner, Ezra J. *Generals in Blue: Lives of the Union Commanders.* Baton Rouge: Louisiana State University Press, 1978.

———. *Generals in Gray: Lives of the Confederate Commanders.* Baton Rouge: Louisiana State University Press, 1978.

Warren, Gordon H. *Fountain of Discontent: The Trent Affair and Freedom of the Seas.* Boston: Northeastern University Press, 1981.

Watkins, Sam R. *"Co. Aytch": A Side Show of the Big Show.* New York: MacMillan, 1962.

Waugh, John C. *Reelecting Lincoln: The Battle for the 1864 Presidency.* New York: Crown, 1997.

Weigley, Russell F. *A Great Civil War: A Military and Political History, 1861–1865.* Bloomington: Indiana University Press, 2000.

Wert, Jeffry D. *General James Longstreet: The Confederacy's Most Controversial Soldier, A Biography.* New York: Simon & Schuster, 1993.

Wetta, Frank J., and Stephen J. Curley. *Celluloid Wars: A Guide to Film and the American Experience of War.* New York: Greenwood, 1992.

Wilbur, C. Keith. *Civil War Medicine, 1861–1865.* Guilford, Conn.: Globe Pequot, 1998.

Wiley, Bell Irvin. *The Life of Billy Yank: The Common Soldier of the Union.* Baton Rouge: Louisiana State University Press, 1978.

———. *The Life of Johnny Reb: The Common Soldier of the Confederacy.* Baton Rouge: Louisiana State University Press, 1978.

———. *The Plain People of the Confederacy.* Chicago: Quadrangle Books, 1963.

Wilson, Charles Reagan. *Religion and the American Civil War.* New York: Oxford University Press, 1998.

Wilson, Douglas. *Honor's Voice: The Transformation of Abraham Lincoln*. New York: Knopf, 1998.

Winks, Robin W. *Canada and the United States: The Civil War Years*. Baltimore: Johns Hopkins University Press, 1960.

Winter, Denis. *Death's Men: Soldiers of the Great War*. New York: Penguin, 1978.

Wise, Stephen R. *Lifeline of the Confederacy: Blockade Running During the Civil War*. Columbia: University of South Carolina Press, 1988.

Woldman, Albert A. *Lincoln and the Russians*. Cleveland: World, 1952.

Woodworth, Steven E. *Jefferson Davis and His Generals: The Failure of Confederate Command in the West*. Lawrence: University of Kansas Press, 1990.

———. *No Band of Brothers: Problems in the Rebel High Command*. Columbia: University of Missouri Press, 1999.

———, ed. *The American Civil War: A Handbook of Literature and Research*. Westport, Conn.: Greenwood, 1996.

Wooster, Ralph. *The Secession Conventions of the South*. Princeton, N.J.: Princeton University Press, 1962.

Yearns, Wilfred B. *The Confederate Congress*. Athens: University of Athens Press, 1960.

Zeller, Bob. *The Civil War in Depth*. San Francisco: Chronicle Books, 1997.

Zenzen, Joan M. *Battling for Manassas: The Fifty-Year Preservation Struggle at Manassas National Battlefield Park*. State College: Pennsylvania State University Press, 1998.

Index